Cold War Liberalism

In the mid twentieth century, Cold War liberalism exerted a profound influence on the US state, US foreign policy, and liberal thought across the North Atlantic world. The essays in this volume examine the history of this important ideology from a variety of perspectives. Whereas most prior works that analyze Cold War liberalism have focused on small groupings of canonical intellectuals, this book explores how the ideology transformed politics, society, and culture writ large. From impacting US foreign policy in the Middle East, to influencing the ideological contours of industrial society, to shaping the urban landscape of Los Angeles, Cold War liberalism left an indelible mark on modern history. This collection also illuminates the degree to which Cold War liberalism continues to shape how intellectuals and policymakers understand and approach the world.

Daniel Bessner is the Anne H. H. and Kenneth B. Pyle Associate Professor in American Foreign Policy in the Henry M. Jackson School of International Studies, University of Washington. He is the author of *Democracy in Exile: Hans Speier and the Rise of the Defense Intellectual*; the coeditor, with Michael Brenes, of *Rethinking US World Power: Domestic Histories of US Foreign Relations*; and the coeditor, with Nicolas Guilhot, of *The Decisionist Imagination: Sovereignty, Social Science, and Democracy in the 20th Century*.

Michael Brenes is the codirector of the Brady-Johnson Program in Grand Strategy and Lecturer in History at Yale University. He has authored and edited several books, including *For Might and Right: Cold War Defense Spending and the Remaking of American Democracy* and, with Daniel Bessner, *Rethinking US World Power: Domestic Histories of US Foreign Relations*.

Military, War, and Society in Modern American History

Series Editors
Beth Bailey, University of Kansas
Andrew Preston, University of Virginia
Kara Dixon Vuic, Texas Christian University

Military, War, and Society in Modern American History is a new series that showcases original scholarship on the military, war, and society in modern US history. The series builds on recent innovations in the fields of military and diplomatic history and includes historical works on a broad range of topics, including civil-military relations and the militarization of culture and society; the military's influence on policy, power, politics, and political economy; the military as a key institution in managing and shaping social change, both within the military and in broader American society; the effect the military has had on American political and economic development, whether in wartime or peacetime; and the military as a leading edge of American engagement with the wider world, including forms of soft power as well as the use of force.

Cold War Liberalism
Power in a Time of Emergency

Edited by
Daniel Bessner
University of Washington

Michael Brenes
Yale University

Shaftesbury Road, Cambridge CB2 8EA, United Kingdom

One Liberty Plaza, 20th Floor, New York, NY 10006, USA

477 Williamstown Road, Port Melbourne, VIC 3207, Australia

314–321, 3rd Floor, Plot 3, Splendor Forum, Jasola District Centre, New Delhi – 110025, India

103 Penang Road, #05–06/07, Visioncrest Commercial, Singapore 238467

Cambridge University Press is part of Cambridge University Press & Assessment, a department of the University of Cambridge.

We share the University's mission to contribute to society through the pursuit of education, learning and research at the highest international levels of excellence.

www.cambridge.org
Information on this title: www.cambridge.org/9781009448734

DOI: 10.1017/9781009448703

© Cambridge University Press & Assessment 2026

This publication is in copyright. Subject to statutory exception and to the provisions of relevant collective licensing agreements, no reproduction of any part may take place without the written permission of Cambridge University Press & Assessment.

When citing this work, please include a reference to the
DOI 10.1017/9781009448703

First published 2026

Cover image: Two Worlds by Robert M. Chapin, 6 January 1950. From TIME. © 1950 TIME USA LLC. All rights reserved. Used under license.

A catalogue record for this publication is available from the British Library

A Cataloging-in-Publication data record for this book is available from the Library of Congress

ISBN 978-1-009-44868-0 Hardback
ISBN 978-1-009-44873-4 Paperback

Cambridge University Press & Assessment has no responsibility for the persistence or accuracy of URLs for external or third-party internet websites referred to in this publication and does not guarantee that any content on such websites is, or will remain, accurate or appropriate.

For EU product safety concerns, contact us at Calle de José Abascal, 56, 1°, 28003 Madrid, Spain, or email eugpsr@cambridge.org

For Courtney and Leo Bessner
and
Michelle and Nathan Brenes

Contents

List of Figures		*page* ix
List of Contributors		x
Acknowledgments		xii

1. Introduction: Cold War Liberalism in Historical Perspective   1
   DANIEL BESSNER

2. Free World Leadership and the Limits of Liberalism   33
   PETER SLEZKINE

3. Precursors, Practitioners, and Legacies of Cold War Liberalism in the Middle East   60
   JOSHUA DONOVAN

4. Walter Lippmann: The Cold War Liberal as Conservative Isolationist   88
   MARK EDWARDS

5. Catholic Internationalism and American Empire: The Cold War Liberalism of William Pfaff   104
   CHRISTOPHER SCHAEFER

6. The Productive Character: Cold War Liberal Social Psychology from Totalitarianism to Entrepreneurship   128
   ERIK BAKER

7. Cold War Liberalism or Socialist Revisionism? Transatlantic Sociology, "Industrial Society," and the Anti-totalitarian Style between France and America   147
   DAVID SESSIONS

8. "Slavery Old and New": Cold War Liberals in the Global Forced Labor Debate, 1947–1953   166
   EMMA KUBY

viii   Contents

9 The City That Could Have Been: Planning Los Angeles
   for the Postwar Era   184
   COURTNEY RAWLINGS

10 Richard Hofstadter and the Demonology of the
   Cold War Right   203
   DANIEL SMITH AND ANTON JÄGER

11 Conservatives in a "Liberal Age": Rethinking the
   Neoconservative Turn in the 1960s   224
   MICHAEL BRENES AND MICHAEL FRANCZAK

12 The Noncommunist Boom: The Transformation of
   Carlos Fuentes and the Democratic Left in Latin America,
   1959–1990   246
   ANDRÉS SÁNCHEZ-PADILLA

13 Afterword   272
   SAMUEL MOYN

Index   276

Figures

9.1 Maynard Parker, photographer, "Projects by Paul R. Williams: Photomontage: Hacienda and Pueblo del Rio Housing Projects, Airport, Zangston Terrace, Arrowhead Springs Hotel," 1940. *page* 186
9.2 Julius Shulman, photographer, "Job 6464: Pueblo del Rio (Los Angeles, California)," 1940–1941. 191
9.3 Baldwin Hills Village (or The Village Green), Clarence Stein, Reginald Johnson, Robert Alexander, Fred Barlow, Jr., Lewis E. Wilson, architects, 1942. 193
9.4 Leonard Nadel, photographer, "Children Playing on Front Lawn," 1942. 195
9.5 "Exterior of Finished Buildings at Project's 'Point #3,'" 1942. 195
9.6 Julius Shulman, photographer, "Job 056: Pueblo del Rio (Los Angeles, California)," 1942. 197
9.7 "Before and After" of Pueblo del Rio, Los Angeles, California, Paul R. Williams, main architect, 1942. 198
9.8 Louis Clyde Stoumen, photographer, "Project's 'Garden of the Month' Contest Winner," c. 1942. 200

Contributors

ERIK BAKER is Lecturer in the History of Science at Harvard University.

DANIEL BESSNER is the Anne H. H. and Kenneth B. Pyle Associate Professor in American Foreign Policy in the Henry M. Jackson School of International Studies at the University of Washington.

MICHAEL BRENES is the codirector of the Brady-Johnson Program in Grand Strategy and Lecturer in History at Yale University.

JOSHUA DONOVAN is History and Social Studies Instructor at Phillips Andover Academy.

MARK EDWARDS is Professor of U.S. History at Spring Arbor University.

MICHAEL FRANCZAK is Senior Researcher in Multilateralism and Global Governance at the United Nations University's Centre for Policy Research.

ANTON JÄGER is Lecturer in the History of Political Thought at the University of Oxford.

EMMA KUBY is Associate Professor of History at the University of Wisconsin-Madison.

SAMUEL MOYN is the Kent Professor of Law and History at Yale University.

COURTNEY RAWLINGS is an architectural historian and critic working at the Quincy Institute for Responsible Statecraft.

ANDRÉS SÁNCHEZ-PADILLA is Assistant Professor of History at the Carlos III University of Madrid.

CHRISTOPHER SCHAEFER is Visiting Assistant Professor of History at Mount St. Mary's University.

DAVID SESSIONS is an intellectual historian and journalist working at The CNET Group.

PETER SLEZKINE is Senior Fellow and Director of the Russia Program at the Stimson Center.

DANIEL SMITH is American Australian Association Postdoctoral Fellow at the United States Studies Centre at the University of Sydney.

Acknowledgments

This project is many years in the making. It began as a virtual workshop in 2020, during the height of the COVID-19 pandemic, and was designed to create a community of scholars in a time of immense loss and confusion. Daniel Steinmetz-Jenkins was part of that effort; he was, as they say, present at the creation. We would thus like to thank Danny for the work he put into preparing and running the virtual workshop that led to this volume. We would also like to thank those who participated in the workshop for spending a difficult period meeting to discuss Cold War liberalism in its various facets and forms. Furthermore, we extend our gratitude to Sam Moyn, a scholar and friend, who graciously agreed to write the afterword to this volume.

Thanks also go to Andrew Preston and Beth Bailey, who envisioned this project as part of their "Military, War, and Society in Modern American History" series with Cambridge University Press. Andrew was a particular champion of this project and having him in our corner was an enormous blessing. Our editor at Cambridge, Cecelia Cancellaro, also supported the project from its inception, and we thank her for doing so.

We'd also like to give our thanks to the scholars who inspired our work on Cold War liberalism in the first place: Malachi Hacohen, Alex Roland, Jonathan Rosenberg, and the late Judith Stein. Even if they might not agree with everything contained in this volume, it couldn't have been written without their inspiration.

Finally, we could not do any of this without our families. Thanks to Courtney Bessner, Leo Bessner, Michelle Brenes, and Nathan Brenes. We love you. Here's another one to add to our already crowded bookshelves.

1 Introduction
Cold War Liberalism in Historical Perspective

Daniel Bessner

On January 20, 1961, President John F. Kennedy assumed the podium stationed at the East Portico of the U.S. Capitol to deliver his inaugural address. In his speech, the young president – only forty-three years old – provided a mission statement to the United States, and the world, about how he and his administration intended to govern. Though remembered as a sterling example of American oratory, the speech was most important for embodying the "Cold War liberalism" that by the early 1960s had come to define American politics, society, economy, and culture.[1] Above all, when it came to domestic and geopolitics, Cold War liberals such as Kennedy believed two things: that elites, not the mass public, must make most policy decisions of consequence and that the United States needed to dominate the world.[2]

Both ideas found expression in Kennedy's inaugural address. In fact, the speech's most resonant line – "ask not what your country can do for you – ask what you can do for your country" – implied a reversal in the American political contract, a reversal that expressed how Cold War liberals had transformed the *demos* from the subject into the object of politics. With this single line, Kennedy revealed that he intended to tell Americans what to do instead of having them do the telling. Kennedy's address also emphasized the importance of U.S. global hegemony. As

---

[1] According to the historian Ari N. Cushner, "the phrase 'cold war liberal' was not used with great frequency until the 1960s, arising among activists and historians connected to the New Left." Specifically, it was used by the New Left to lambast liberal Democrats for supporting the Vietnam War. Against this, the class of intellectuals identified as Cold War liberals, at least those in the United States, called themselves "liberal anti-communists." Ari N. Cushner, "Cold War Comrades: Left-Liberal Anticommunism and American Empire, 1941–1968" (PhD diss., University of California at Santa Cruz, 2017), 5–6. Also, see Samuel Moyn, *Liberalism against Itself: Cold War Intellectuals and the Making of Our Times* (New Haven, CT: Yale University Press, 2023), 1.
[2] This essay focuses primarily, if not totally, on the political, institutional, and policy history of Cold War liberalism. There are other core features of the Cold War liberal tradition, including its valorization of private property, individual rights, capitalist development, and religious liberty, that lie mostly outside this essay's scope.

the president's insistence that the United States "shall pay any price, bear any burden, meet any hardship, support any friend, [and] oppose any foe to assure the survival and the success of liberty" makes plain, Kennedy was devoted to an imperialist politics that considered the parts of the world not under Soviet domination to be within the United States' potential sphere of influence.[3] These two beliefs – that elites should make policy and that the United States must govern and direct international affairs – were the defining political features of Cold War liberalism.

In two distinct ways, Cold War liberals such as Kennedy departed from long-standing American traditions. First, their cordoning off the public from policymaking rejected and abandoned democratizing impulses that had been evident in the Republic since the Revolutionary Era. If the story of American history from 1776 until the middle of the twentieth century is, at least in part, a story of the gradual and forced expansion of a racialized, gendered, and classed democracy to include previously excluded groups, the story from World War II down into the present is a story of how elites limited the political influence of the growing *demos* even as bottom-up activism ensured the franchise slowly continued to expand. Second, from George Washington's "Farewell Address" of 1796, in which the first president warned against Americans "interweaving our destiny with that of any part of Europe," until the 1940s, manifold U.S. elites were skeptical about becoming too formally intertwined in extra-hemispheric political and military affairs (with the U.S. domination of the Philippines, Guam, Hawaii, and part of the Samoan Islands being notable exceptions).[4] Cold War liberals, for their part, cast off these anxieties to claim that U.S. security and prosperity depended on precisely the foreign entanglements Washington warned against.

How were Cold War liberals able to impel such profound transformations in U.S. history? The answer is simple: the advent of the Soviet Union as a global superpower, the Soviet acquisition of nuclear weapons, and the emergence of a global communist movement that appeared to threaten the present and future of liberal capitalist democracy – that is, the beginning of the Cold War – compelled many Cold War liberals to diagnose a world-historical existential crisis, which, in turn, led them to appeal to an emergency politics that justified radical, and oftentimes

---

[3] John F. Kennedy, "Inaugural Address" (speech, January 20, 1961), John F. Kennedy Presidential Library and Museum, www.jfklibrary.org/learn/about-jfk/historic-speeches/inaugural-address.
[4] George Washington, "Washington's Farewell Address to the People of the United States," Senate Document No. 106-21 (Washington, DC: U.S. Government Printing Office, 2000 [September 19, 1796]), 27.

identifiably illiberal, actions that in "ordinary" times they considered anathema. The appeal to "emergency" and "crisis," in effect, served as the means through which Cold War liberals constructed era-defining ideological, and, more important, institutional, edifices that reshaped U.S. domestic and geopolitics. And while the first Cold War liberals frequently avowed that when the Cold War concluded, the state of exception could end and things could return to normal, in point of fact this did not happen; the institutionalization of Cold War liberal beliefs in specific organizations such as the National Security Council (NSC) and Central Intelligence Agency (CIA) ensured that the ideology's distinguishing features remained core elements of the U.S. elite's approach to politics long after the Soviet Union collapsed.[5]

Despite its significant influence on U.S. and world history, Cold War liberalism remains understudied. And when Cold War liberalism has been studied, it has primarily been approached as a transatlantic intellectual phenomenon to which some of the major and minor figures of midcentury intellectual history adhered. In particular, scholars have identified Hannah Arendt, Raymond Aron, Daniel Bell, Bernard Berelson, Isaiah Berlin, Norberto Bobbio, Ernst Fraenkel, John Kenneth Galbraith, Michael Harrington, Louis Hartz, Richard Hofstadter, Sidney Hook, Irving Howe, Herman Kahn, Eugen Kogon, Irving Kristol, Melvin Lasky, Seymour Martin Lipset, Karl Loewenstein, Reinhold Niebuhr, Michael Polanyi, Karl Popper, Walt Whitman Rostow, Arthur M. Schlesinger, Jr., Edward Shils, Judith N. Shklar, Hans Speier, Manès Sperber, George D. Stoddard, Samuel Stouffer, Jacob Talmon, Lionel Trilling, and James Wechsler as Cold War liberals.[6]

---

[5] On the notion of things returning to normal after the end of the Cold War, see Daniel Bessner, *Democracy in Exile: Hans Speier and the Rise of the Defense Intellectual* (Ithaca, NY: Cornell University Press, 2018), 127–128.

[6] Several scholars have extended the label of Cold War liberal to include some intellectuals traditionally identified with the conservative tradition, including James Burnham, Whittaker Chambers, Friedrich Hayek, George Kennan, and Michael Oakeshott. For Burnham, see James Chappel, "The God That Won: Eugen Kogon and the Origins of Cold War Liberalism," *Journal of Contemporary History* 55, no. 2 (April 2020), 352. For Chambers, see Johannes Voelz, "Cold War Liberalism and the Problem of Security," *Post-Exceptionalist American Studies: REAL-Yearbook of Research in English and American Literature* 30 (December 2014), 261–267. For Hayek, see Terry Nardin, "Introduction: Michael Oakeshott's Cold War Liberalism," in *Michael Oakeshott's Cold War Liberalism*, ed. Terry Nardin (New York: Palgrave Macmillan, 2015), 2. For Kennan, see Jacob Heilbrunn, *They Knew They Were Right: The Rise of the Neocons* (New York: Doubleday, 2008), 49; Jason K. Duncan, *John F. Kennedy: The Spirit of Cold War Liberalism* (New York: Routledge, 2014), 4. For Oakeshott, see Nardin, "Introduction"; Jan-Werner Müller, "Introduction: Concepts, Character, and the Specter of New Cold Wars," in *Isaiah Berlin's Cold War Liberalism*, ed. Jan-Werner Müller (Singapore: Palgrave Macmillan, 2019), 7.

Though these intellectuals obviously disagreed with one another about various issues, they nevertheless comprised a "thought collective" that, scholars have shown, was defined by several shared beliefs.[7] In addition to their core skepticism of mass politics and faith in U.S. empire, most of the aforementioned Cold War liberals argued that evil was ineradicable; politics was a tragic sphere of life defined by conflict; utopian thinking must be rejected; extreme forms of instrumental reason were dangerous; intellectuals should strive to protect negative liberty; the welfare state and Keynesian fiscal stimulus were necessary features of modern economic governance; central planning must be avoided; psychology was a crucial means to understand human behavior; and that the struggle between the working classes and capitalists had been displaced by the struggle between liberal capitalist democracy and communist authoritarianism.[8] As this suggests, Cold War liberalism

---

[7] For a discussion of the term "thought collective," see Dieter Plehwe, "Introduction," in *The Road from Mont Pèlerin: The Making of the Neoliberal Thought Collective*, ed. Philip Mirowski and Dieter Plehwe (Cambridge, MA: Harvard University Press, 2009), 35. Plehwe defines the neoliberal thought collective as follows: "The members of the neoliberal thought collective ... disagree on specific issues, and they try hard, and certainly not without success, to convince both intellectuals and the general public of the merits of neoliberal reasoning. Their capacity to jointly develop and widely distribute neoliberal knowledge is due to a set of shared values and principled beliefs, which allow community members to effectively communicate across disciplines and audiences in the pursuit of hegemonic strategies." Replace "neoliberal" and "neoliberalism" with "Cold War liberal" and "Cold War liberalism" where appropriate, and this stands as a good definition of the Cold War liberal thought collective.

[8] The major works on Cold War liberalism, which focus primarily on the United States, but also on Western Europe, include Philip Green, "'Cold War Liberalism,' Review of *Believing Skeptics: American Political Intellectuals, 1945–1964*, by Robert Booth Fowler," *Reviews in American History* 7, no. 4 (December 1979), 591–596; Richard H. Pells, *The Liberal Mind in a Conservative Age: American Intellectuals in the 1940s and 1950s* (New York: Harper & Row, 1985); John Ehrman, *The Rise of Neoconservatism: Intellectuals and Foreign Affairs, 1945–1994* (New Haven, CT: Yale University Press, 1995), chapter 1; Kenneth R. Janken, "From Colonial Liberation to Cold War Liberalism: Walter White, the NAACP, and Foreign Affairs, 1941–1955," *Ethnic and Racial Studies* 21, no. 6 (November 1998), 1074–1095; Mark L. Kleinman, *A World of Hope, A World of Fear: Henry A. Wallace, Reinhold Niebuhr, and American Liberalism* (Columbus: Ohio State University Press, 2000); Uta G. Poiger, "American Music, Cold War Liberalism, and German Identities," in *Transactions, Transgressions, Transformations: American Culture in Western Europe and Japan*, ed. Heide Fehrenbach and Uta G. Poiger (New York: Berghahn, 2000), 127–147; Jonathan Bell, *The Liberal State on Trial: The Cold War and American Politics in the Truman Years* (New York: Columbia University Press, 2004); Nicholas Wisseman, "Falsely Accused: Cold War Liberalism Reassessed," *The Historian* 66, no. 2 (Summer 2004), 320–334; Jan-Werner Müller, "Free and Freedom: On 'Cold War Liberalism,'" *European Journal of Political Theory* 7, no. 1 (January 2008), 45–64; Malachi H. Hacohen, "Jacob Talmon between Zionism and Cold War Liberalism," *History of European Ideas* 34, no. 2 (June 2008), 146–157; Malachi Haim Hacohen, "'The Strange Fact That the State of Israel Exists': The Cold War Liberals between Cosmopolitanism and Nationalism," *Jewish Social Studies: History, Culture, Society*

was, *pace* the philosopher Judith N. Shklar, a pessimistic "liberalism of fear" whose advocates shared a tragic sensibility that emphasized preventing the worst instead of achieving the best.[9]

However much they agreed with each other, though, Cold War liberal intellectuals never developed a coherent system of thought. Rather, as the historian James Chappel has highlighted, these intellectuals offered "a constellation of concepts and keywords" that provided a "new language of 'moral anti-totalitarianism'" that defined elite and popular discourses in the 1940s, 1950s, and 1960s.[10] In works like Reinhold Niebuhr's *The Children of Light and the Children of Darkness* (1944), Karl Popper's *The Open Society and Its Enemies* (1945), Arthur

15, no. 2 (Winter 2009), 37–81; Justin Vaïsse, *Neoconservatism: The Biography of a Movement*, trans. Arthur Goldhammer (Cambridge, MA: Harvard University Press, 2010), chapter 1; Arie M. Dubnov, "Anti-Cosmopolitan Liberalism: Isaiah Berlin, Jacob Talmon, and the Dilemma of National Identity," *Nations and Nationalism* 16, no. 4 (October 2010), 559–578; Amanda Anderson, "Character and Ideology: The Case of Cold War Liberalism," *New Literary History* 42, no. 2 (Spring 2011), 209–229; Jennifer A. Delton, *Rethinking the 1950s: How Anticommunism and the Cold War Made America Liberal* (New York: Cambridge University Press, 2013); Landon R. Y. Storrs, *The Second Red Scare and the Unmaking of the New Deal Left* (Princeton, NJ: Princeton University Press, 2013), chapter 5; Voelz, "Cold War Liberalism and the Problem of Security"; Nardin, "Michael Oakeshott's Cold War Liberalism"; Aurelian Craiutu, *Faces of Moderation: The Art of Balance in an Age of Extremes* (Philadelphia: University of Pennsylvania Press, 2017), chapter 3; Cushner, "Cold War Comrades"; Bessner, *Democracy in Exile*; Jan-Werner Müller, "What Cold War Liberalism Can Teach Us Today," *New York Review of Books* (November 26, 2018), www nybooks .com/online/2018/11/26/what-cold-war-liberalism-can-teach-us-today/; Samuel Moyn, "Before – and Beyond – the Liberalism of Fear," in *Between Utopia and Realism: The Political Thought of Judith N. Shklar*, ed. Samantha Ashenden and Andreas Hess (Philadelphia: University of Pennsylvania Press, 2019), 24–46; Jan-Werner Müller, "Calming the Ideological Storms? Reflections on Cold War Liberalism," in *Ideological Storms: Intellectuals, Dictators, and the Totalitarian Temptation*, ed. Vladimir Tismaneanu and Bogdan C. Iacob (Hungary: Central European University Press, 2019), 465–485; Malachi Haim Hacohen, "The Jewishness of Cold War Liberalism," in *Jews, Liberalism, Antisemitism: A Global History*, ed. Abigail Green and Simon Levis Sullam (Switzerland: Palgrave Macmillan, 2020), 387–410; Pankaj Mishra, "Grand Illusions," *New York Review of Books* LXVII, no. 18 (November 19, 2020), 31–32; Dillon Stone Tatum, *Liberalism and Transformation: The Global Politics of Violence and Intervention* (Ann Arbor: University of Michigan Press, 2021), chapter 5; Michael Brenes and Daniel Steinmetz-Jenkins, "Legacies of Cold War Liberalism," *Dissent* 68, no. 1 (Winter 2021), 116–124; Moyn, *Liberalism against Itself*; Daniel Bessner, Michael Brenes, and Michael Franczak, "A Brief History of Cold War Liberalism," *Cold War History* 24, no. 2 (April 2024), 299–308.

[9] On the liberalism of fear, see Judith N. Shklar, "The Liberalism of Fear," in *Liberalism and the Moral Life*, ed. Nancy L. Rosenblum (Cambridge, MA: Harvard University Press, 1989), 21–38. On Cold War liberal pessimism, see Dillon Stone Tatum, "Liberal Pessimism: An Intellectual History of Suspicion in the Cold War," in *Pessimism in International Relations: Provocations, Possibilities, Politics*, ed. Tim Stevens and Nicholas Michelsen (Switzerland: Palgrave Macmillan, 2020), 67–81.

[10] Chappel, "The God That Won," 342, 341.

M. Schlesinger, Jr.'s *The Vital Center* (1949), Lionel Trilling's *The Liberal Imagination* (1950), Jacob Talmon's *The Origins of Totalitarian Democracy* (1952), Raymond Aron's *L'Opium des intellectuels* (1955, translated into English in 1957), and Isaiah Berlin's "Two Concepts of Liberty" (1958), Cold War liberal intellectuals transformed their convictions into the common sense of an era. They were aided in this effort by prominent cultural organizations, above all the CIA-funded American Committee for Cultural Freedom and Congress for Cultural Freedom, as well as political advocacy groups such as the Americans for Democratic Action and magazines such as *The New Leader* and *Partisan Review*.[11] For the first two decades of U.S. global hegemony, Cold War liberal ideas permeated the American, and Western European, imaginations.

The scholarship on Cold War liberal intellectuals has been very useful in highlighting how a coherent, transnational group of thinkers understood liberalism's relationship to politics, society, economy, and culture in the middle of the twentieth century. This volume aims to augment this literature in three ways. First, it builds on the historiography by expanding the group of intellectuals considered to be Cold War liberals to include individuals like the author Carlos Fuentes, the journalist Walter Lippmann, the politician Daniel Patrick Moynihan, the writer William Pfaff, and the architect Paul R. Williams, among others, demonstrating how Cold War liberalism's impact was even wider than previously delineated. Second, it examines Cold War liberalism in practice, focusing on how the ideology shaped – and continues to shape – politics, policy, economics, and culture in the United States, Western Europe, and beyond. Finally, this introduction provides a genealogy of Cold War liberalism that connects it to earlier instantiations of liberalism. In so doing, it complicates the claim, recently proffered by the historian Samuel Moyn, that "Cold War liberalism was a betrayal of liberalism itself" because it departed from the "emancipatory and futuristic" liberalism that, Moyn argues, reigned before the Cold War.[12] Against this

---

[11] For these as the major institutions of Cold War liberalism, see Cushner, "Cold War Comrades," 7. The Congress for Cultural Freedom (CCF) in particular has been the subject of a significant literature. A good summary of the CCF and its historiography may be found in Patrick Iber, "The Spy Who Funded Me: Revisiting the Congress for Cultural Freedom," review of *Campaigning Culture and the Global Cold War: The Journals of the Congress for Cultural Freedom*, by Giles Scott-Smith and Charlotte A. Lerg, *Los Angeles Review of Books* (June 11, 2017), https://lareviewofbooks.org/article/the-spy-who-funded-me-revisiting-the-congress-for-cultural-freedom/.

[12] Moyn, *Liberalism against Itself*, 2, 7. Scholars have been lobbying this criticism at Cold War liberals for decades. See, for example, Green, "Cold War Liberalism," 594; Kevin Mattson, *When America Was Great: The Fighting Faith of Postwar Liberalism*

assertion, I argue that Cold War liberalism is best understood not as a departure from liberal precepts but as the apotheosis of certain anti-democratic, imperialist, anxious, and pessimistic strands of liberalism that had been core parts of the ideology since its beginnings.

It is to this genealogy that I now turn.

Liberalism before Cold War Liberalism

Few questions have bedeviled historians more than "What is liberalism?"[13] Liberalism's origins, in fact, remain widely disputed. One scholar traces the ideology's beginnings to Saint Paul, whose universalistic argument that Christ saved particular humans, he claims, paved the way for the individualism upon which modern liberalism rests.[14] Some have argued that liberalism's origins are best found in the writings of early modern thinkers like the French philosopher Michel de Montaigne or the English philosopher John Locke.[15] The philosopher Judith N. Shklar, for her part, connected the advent of modern liberalism to a radical eighteenth-century Enlightenment project of human emancipation from external authority. "The essence of [this] radicalism," Shklar argued, "is the idea that man can do with himself and with his society whatever he wishes."[16]

From my perspective, liberalism first truly emerged as an identifiable ideological and political project during the revolutionary period in France, when many intellectuals began to view radical, Enlightenment-inspired emancipation – and the "mass" politics it threatened – with

---

(New York: Routledge, 2004), 24–25; Delton, *Rethinking the 1950s*, 2, 8; Tatum, "Liberal Pessimism," 68, 77; Tatum, *Liberalism and Transformation*, 87–91; Brenes and Steinmetz-Jenkins, "Legacies of Cold War Liberalism," 117.

[13] Gary Gerstle, "The Protean Character of American Liberalism,' *American Historical Review* 99, no. 4 (October 1994): 1043–1073; Edmund Fawcett, *Liberalism: The Life of an Idea* (Princeton, NJ: Princeton University Press, 2014), introduction; Duncan Bell, *Reordering the World: Essays on Liberalism and Empire* (Princeton, NJ: Princeton University Press, 2016), 2, 5–6, 19, 104; Helena Rosenblatt, *The Lost History of Liberalism: From Ancient Rome to the Twenty-First Century* (Princeton, NJ: Princeton University Press, 2018), 178; James Traub, *What Was Liberalism? The Past, Present, and Promise of a Noble Idea* (New York: Basic Books, 2019), 5; Joshua L. Cherniss, *Liberalism in Dark Times: The Liberal Ethos in the Twentieth Century* (Princeton, NJ: Princeton University Press, 2021), 3.

[14] Larry Siedentop, *Inventing the Individual: The Origins of Western Liberalism* (Cambridge, MA: Harvard University Press, 2014), 60.

[15] Patrick J. Deneen, *Why Liberalism Failed* (New Haven, CT: Yale University Press, 2018), 32, 136; Adam Gopnik, *A Thousand Small Sanities: The Moral Adventure of Liberalism* (New York: Basic Books, 2019), 27.

[16] Judith N. Shklar, *After Utopia: The Decline of Political Faith* (Princeton, NJ: Princeton University Press, 1957), 5.

suspicion. In particular, the violent excesses of the Reign of Terror, during which hundreds of thousands of people were imprisoned and 17,000 sentenced to death, led thinkers such as Benjamin Constant and Madame Germaine de Staël, two of the first genuine "liberals," to attempt to chart a middle path between revolutionary terror and counterrevolutionary reaction by promoting an elite-driven, rationalist, and reformist politics that was skeptical of mass publics but nonetheless dedicated to emancipating ordinary people.[17] Intellectuals such as Constant and de Staël, in effect, hoped to embrace the novel realities of political modernity while avoiding, or at least taming, its extremes. As the tensions inherent in the Constant-de Staël project suggest, from its inception liberalism has been defined, as the historian Malachi Hacohen aptly puts it, by its "constant negotiation of conflicting aims, volatile management of democracy, [and] inability to commit to democracy or deny it." Liberals have always lived "an in-between existence" in which lack of commitment is constitutive of their ideology.[18]

As industrial democracy started to percolate throughout Western and Central Europe over the course of the nineteenth century, liberals became ever more concerned with the "masses," whom they continuously derided as irrational, irresponsible, foolish, and dangerous. Against the masses, liberal thinkers extolled an "elite" that, they avowed, was able to govern wisely and justly.[19] While the exact composition of this

[17] For the numbers of those imprisoned and sentenced to death during the Reign of Terror, see Ronen Steinberg, "Trauma and the Effects of Mass Violence in Revolutionary France: A Critical Inquiry," *Historical Reflections/Réflexions Historiques* 41, no. 3 (Winter 2015), 29. On Constant, de Staël, and the origins of liberalism, see Rosenblatt, *The Lost History of Liberalism*, chapter 2. Rosenblatt identifies Constant's *Principles of Politics Applicable to All Governments* (1815) as one of liberalism's key founding texts (65).

[18] Hacohen, "Jacob Talmon between Zionism and Cold War Liberalism," 153. Hacohen goes so far as to claim that the best way to define "liberalism" is not to try to identify a "liberal core," but instead "to look for historical patterns of liberal dilemmas" over time. Specifically, Hacohen affirms that "volatile management of democracy and nationalism, and an inability to commit to or deny either, are liberalism's historical trademarks." Hacohen, "The Jewishness of Cold War Liberalism," 388. Amanda Anderson similarly argues that "liberalism's own character can only be discerned ... if one sees liberalism not only as a philosophy aiming to set out fundamental principles of political life, but also, and almost from the start, as a situated response to historical challenges." Anderson, "Character and Ideology," 212.

[19] On liberalism and the skepticism of mass and democratic politics, see Pells, *The Liberal Mind in a Conservative Age*, 19–20; Gerstle, "Protean Character," *passim*; Brett Gary, *The Nervous Liberals: Propaganda Anxieties from World War I to the Cold War* (New York: Columbia University Press, 1999), *passim*; Ira Katznelson, *Fear Itself: The New Deal and the Origins of Our Time* (New York: Liveright, 2013), 5, 12, 19; Udi Greenberg, *The Weimar Century: German Émigrés and the Ideological Foundations of the Cold War* (Princeton, NJ: Princeton University Press, 2015), chapter 4; Jan-Werner Müller, *What Is Populism?* (Philadelphia: University of Pennsylvania Press, 2016), *passim*; Bessner, *Democracy in Exile*, *passim*; Deneen, *Why Liberalism Failed*, *passim*; Rosenblatt, *The Lost*

elite changed over time – for example, from white, Christian, and male landowners in the nineteenth century to a multiracial, multigender, and multiethnic group of meritocrats in the twentieth and twenty-first centuries – the general ontological division between "mass" and "elite" has remained remarkably stable in the liberal political imagination. Indeed, and despite liberalism's infamously protean character, the fear of the masses and the valorization of elites have united liberals across time and space. Nevertheless, one must be careful not to overstate the importance of elitist thinking on liberal practice. In actual historical time, the impact of anxieties about mass politics on liberal thought and policy has ebbed and flowed; sometimes this angst was more important, sometimes it was less. Cold War liberalism is best thought of as a liberalism in which various events, phenomena, and processes that defined the twentieth century's middle third – above all, the "irrational" public response to the Great Depression; the failure of democracy in Germany; the emergence of "totalitarianism" in Germany and the Soviet Union; the latter's affirming dictatorial control of its Eastern European satellites and its acquisition of nuclear weapons; and the rise of a global communist movement that appeared to threaten capitalist democracy – led these anxieties to be placed front and center.

Liberalism, in other words, was never *tout court* indifferent to ordinary people. For the entirety of the ideology's existence, liberals have embraced projects of social uplift that sought to "civilize" and reform the masses, helping them achieve what liberals considered to be the best life. In the *fin de siècle*, for example, a transatlantic cohort of European liberals and American Progressives – the latter being the closest U.S. analogue to the former between 1890 and 1920 – focused on improving urban infrastructure, ending corporate monopolies, and establishing social democratic welfare programs. Before World War I, in fact, liberals and Progressives on both sides of the Atlantic instituted urban housing reforms, unemployment insurance policies, and public works projects that enhanced the lives of innumerable people.[20] In these and other ways, liberals sought to reconcile their elitism with their genuine desire for social transformation.

But liberals and Progressives began to alter their outlook toward politics and policy in the 1910s, as various "emergencies," above all World War I, compelled them to act illiberally, in violation of their own stated

History of Liberalism, passim; Traub, *What Was Liberalism?*, 5–6; Cherniss, *Liberalism in Dark Times*, 24.

[20] On Progressive Era reform in the United States and Western Europe, see Daniel T. Rodgers, *Atlantic Crossings: Social Politics in a Progressive Age* (Cambridge, MA: Harvard University Press, 1998).

principles. And it is here that the story of liberalism becomes primarily an American one, as it was during the 1910s and 1920s that the United States emerged as a genuine global power – and the bastion of international liberalism.[21] In effect, after the United States entered World War I in April 1917, Progressive President Woodrow Wilson, a southern Democrat, used the opportunity of war to pass the Espionage Act of 1917. Then, after the Bolsheviks seized power in Russia in the autumn of 1917, anxieties about domestic communist insurgency led Wilson to bolster the Espionage Act with the Sedition Act of 1918 and the Immigration Act of 1918. Taken together, these acts allowed the government to arrest or deport political radicals, ethnic and racial minorities, and antiwar activists.[22] Wilson's appeal to geopolitical and domestic crises to justify illiberal behavior, in fact, established a pattern that persists to this day.

The next signal moment in the history of modern American liberalism came in 1929, with the onset of the Great Depression. International credit markets and banks collapsed, unemployment soared, and homelessness became endemic. In the United States, Republican President Herbert Hoover's attempts at staving off the Depression's worst effects through new tariffs, the encouragement of public works programs, and other initiatives were piecemeal efforts unable to halt or reverse the collapse. Crucially, though Hoover's efforts failed, they did not attenuate liberals' interest in reshaping society but rather heightened their desire to use the federal government for the public good; Hoover, they insisted, simply had not gone far enough. In the coming years, liberals would use the opportunity provided by the Depression to build upon their Progressive forbears and expand the purview of the federal state into novel arenas of social and political life.

In 1933, the Democrat Franklin Delano Roosevelt ascended to the American presidency. Promising Americans a "New Deal," Roosevelt's election made the Democratic Party liberals' primary political home (though liberalism remained a meaningful force in the Republican Party until the late 1960s, when liberal Governor Nelson Rockefeller (R-NY) lost his final bid for the Republican presidential nomination).[23] Aided by his "Brain Trust," a cadre of educated elites that

---

[21] According to a Google Ngram analysis of American English, the term "liberalism" only began to be widely used in the 1920s. See https://books.google.com/ngrams/graph?content=liberalism&year_start=1800&year_end=2022&corpus=en-US&smoothing=3.

[22] Wilson's illiberalism was on display from the beginning of his presidency; in 1913, shortly after taking office, he resegregated the federal workforce.

[23] On Roosevelt deploying the term "liberalism" to describe his political project and the term "liberal" to describe himself, see Kevin M. Schultz, *Why Everyone Hates White Liberals (Including White Liberals): A History* (Chicago: University of Chicago Press,

included the lawyer Adolf Berle, the administrator Harry Hopkins, and the economist Rexford Tugwell, Roosevelt argued that the only way to save liberal democratic capitalism was to provide the masses with assistance and employment that, in turn, would ensure they did not pursue a political revolution.[24] The president thus instituted public works initiatives, jobs programs, development and modernization projects, unemployment insurance, and labor reforms that, for the first time, established a type of widespread social democracy in the United States. Nevertheless, the New Deal was decidedly an expert-led initiative; it was designed *for* the masses, but it was not *of* them.

Thus, while Roosevelt curtailed corporate power, strengthened labor unions, brought jobs and economic development to the people, and instituted novel schemes such as social security, the fundamental skepticism of mass politics continued unabated among the liberal political elite. The question is why, and the answer is two-fold. On the one hand, the Great Depression had engendered bank runs and militant communist-organized labor activity that seemed to illustrate ordinary people's irrationality and the ease with which they could succumb to anti-systemic mob psychology. On the other hand, and more important, disorder on the global stage compounded liberal anxieties about the fate of democracy at home. In fact, it was events abroad, more than domestic affairs, that inspired the development of the unique form of liberalism that eventually coalesced into a proper Cold War liberalism in the late 1940s. Namely, the collapse of the Weimar Republic in 1930, the rise of Adolf Hitler to the German chancellorship in 1933, and the outbreak of World War II in 1939 indicated to American liberals that unbridled mass politics were a significant threat to liberal democracy's future both at home and abroad.[25]

2025), 11–15. With regards the decline of liberal Republicans, the political scientists Sarah E. Kreps and Douglas L. Kriner report that "beginning in the 1970s, the median Republican steadily became considerably more conservative" than the median Republican had been previously. Sarah E. Kreps and Douglas L. Kriner, "Unfettered Foreign Policy? Domestic Checks on Presidential Powers after 9/11," in *Checking the Costs of War: Sources of Accountability in Post-9/11 U.S. Foreign Policy*, ed. Sarah E. Kreps and Douglas L. Kriner (Chicago: University of Chicago Press, 2025), 3.

[24] On the New Deal as an effort to prevent political revolution, see Eric Rauchway, *Why the New Deal Matters* (New Haven, CT: Yale University Press, 2021), 32.

[25] The year 1930 is chosen as the end date for the Weimar Republic because that was the year that German Chancellor Heinrich Brüning, a politician from the Centre Party, began governing by emergency decree, thereby acting as a dictator. On liberals and mass politics during this period, see Gary, *The Nervous Liberals*, chapters 1–2; Bessner, *Democracy in Exile*, chapter 3; Daniel Bessner and Nicolas Guilhot, "Introduction: Who Decides?" in *The Decisionist Imagination: Sovereignty, Social Science, and Democracy in the 20th Century*, ed. Daniel Bessner and Nicolas Guilhot (New York: Berghahn, 2019), 7–10.

American liberals believed events in Europe suggested three things. First, that liberal democracy was inherently fragile. Second, that preventive, even illiberal, measures were sometimes required to save democracy from the masses. And third, that a powerful military was necessary to survive in a hostile world. If American liberals failed to heed these lessons, many thought, the United States would fall prey either to fascist threats on the right or, as they had been worried about since 1917, communist threats on the left.[26] As a result of these anxieties, Roosevelt enhanced the power of the Federal Bureau of Investigation to pursue counterespionage activities; initiated a peacetime draft; and endorsed the Alien Registration Act of 1940, which prohibited revolutionary language and activity in peacetime and compelled non-U.S. citizens to register with the federal government.[27] Similar to Woodrow Wilson, Roosevelt was willing to act illiberally for the sake of liberalism.

Indeed, throughout his time in office, Roosevelt bucked liberal norms when doing so helped him address a political or economic emergency. The president thus enacted a bank moratorium; established the National Recovery Administration in clear violation of the Constitution; issued manifold executive orders (eventually reaching 3,721, by far the highest of any president); and, after winning the 1932 election in a landslide, ran for, and won, the presidency three additional times (more than any previous executive).[28] While Roosevelt undertook these actions because he considered them essential to aiding ordinary Americans, in pursuing them he legitimized an emergency politics that justified illiberal behavior. This politics soon became a defining feature of Cold War liberalism.

The Politics of Emergency and the Advent of Cold War Liberalism

It was during World War II that the crisis-infused version of American liberalism that had coalesced in the 1910s, 1920s, and 1930s became

---

[26] Intriguingly, the historian Bruce Kuklick has suggested that it was the liberal encounter with fascism that helped give rise to the modern political spectrum used in the United States, in which liberalism is understood to be in the "center" and fascism and communism is understood to be on the "right" and "left," respectively. Kuklick, however, dates the embrace of this political spectrum to World War II. Bruce Kuklick, *Fascism Comes to America: A Century of Obsession in Politics and Culture* (Chicago: University of Chicago Press, 2022), 94–97.

[27] Donna T. Haverty-Stacke, *Trotskyists on Trial: Free Speech and Political Persecution since the Age of FDR* (New York: New York University Press, 2015), 2–3; Beverly Gage, *G-Man: J. Edgar Hoover and the Making of the American Century* (New York: Viking, 2022), 215–216.

[28] Gerhard Peters and John T. Woolley, "Executive Orders," in John T. Woolley and Gerhard Peters, ed., *The American Presidency Project* (Santa Barbara, CA, 1999–2025), www.presidency.ucsb.edu/statistics/data/executive-orders; Bessner, *Democracy in Exile*, 5.

fused with a wartime, and later national security, state. The war's outbreak in September 1939 forced Roosevelt to begin transforming himself from "Dr. New Deal" into "Dr. Win-the-War."[29] The president rapidly embraced military Keynesianism, constructing an "arsenal of democracy" that not only served the United States and its Allies well against the Axis but also helped lift the country, finally, out of the Depression.[30] By August 1941, production for war had brought unemployment to under 10 percent; by August 1945, the month the war ended, that number had dropped to 1.5 percent.[31] War, it appeared to many liberals, had allowed them to achieve their long-standing goal of low unemployment.

Despite this domestic achievement, the war years solidified liberals' pessimistic understanding of geopolitics. Of particular importance was the Japanese attack on Pearl Harbor, Guam, and the Philippines of December 7/8, 1941, which became a signal moment in the history of Cold War liberalism. The logistically challenging assault shocked both elite and ordinary Americans. After it, "Pearl Harbor" assumed a prime place in U.S. political, foreign policy, and cultural discourse as a metaphor for what could go wrong when the United States refused to invest in its military.[32] Combined with the earlier fall of France to Hitler's armies in June 1940, Pearl Harbor demonstrated to New Deal *cum* wartime liberals that military mobilization was the only means to

---

[29] On these sobriquets, see Franklin Delano Roosevelt, "Excerpts from the Press Conference" (press conference, December 28, 1943), in John T. Woolley and Gerhard Peters, ed., *The American Presidency Project* (Santa Barbara, CA, 1999–2025), www.presidency.ucsb.edu/documents/excerpts-from-the-press-conference-8.

[30] Franklin Delano Roosevelt, "Fireside Chat" (speech, December 29, 1940), in John T. Woolley and Gerhard Peters, ed., *The American Presidency Project* (Santa Barbara, CA, 1999–2025), www.presidency.ucsb.edu/documents/fireside-chat-9; Paul A. C. Koistinen, *Arsenal of World War II: The Political Economy of American Warfare, 1940–1945* (Lawrence: University Press of Kansas, 2004), 419; Jeffrey A. Engel, "Not Yet a Garrison State: Reconsidering Eisenhower's Military-Industrial Complex," *Enterprise & Society* 12, no. 1 (March 2011), 185; Michael Brenes, *For Might and Right: Cold War Defense Spending and the Remaking of American Democracy* (Amherst: University of Massachusetts Press, 2020), 26; Timothy Barker, "'Don't Discuss Jobs Outside the Room': Reconsidering Military Keynesianism in the 1970s," in *The Military and the Market*, ed. Jennifer Mittelstadt and Mark R. Wilson (Philadelphia: University of Pennsylvania Press, 2022), 135.

[31] Bureau of Labor Statistics, "Graph of U.S. Unemployment Rate, 1930–1945," *SHEC: Resources for Teachers*, https://shec.ashp.cuny.edu/items/show/1510; Bureau of Labor Statistics, "Unemployment Rate and Timing of Changes to Current Population Survey Measurement, 1940–2017," www.bls.gov/opub/mlr/2018/images/data/haugen-figure1.stm.

[32] On Pearl Harbor as metaphor, see Emily S. Rosenberg, *A Date Which Will Live: Pearl Harbor in American Memory* (Durham, NC: Duke University Press, 2005); John Dower, *Cultures of War: Pearl Harbor/Hiroshima/9-11/Iraq* (New York: W.W. Norton, 2010), Part I.

ensure domestic security and the future of western "civilization" writ large.[33] Furthermore, Pearl Harbor also helped persuade liberals that they needed to move beyond traditional notions of "national defense," which emphasized the defense of U.S. territory, and endorse a novel paradigm of "national security," which, the historian Andrew Preston explains, was premised on the notion "that distant threats could eventually harm the basic safety of the United States in a variety of ways, ideologically and economically as well as physically."[34] From late 1941 onward, many liberals started to insist that a broadly defined U.S. security depended on global hegemony.

In 1945, the United States, with the aid of Great Britain and especially the Soviet Union, defeated the Axis and emerged as the most powerful nation on Earth. The previous sixteen years of U.S. and global history had been defined by two major emergencies: the Great Depression and World War II. Soon, another emergency – the Cold War – would become the structuring condition of international and domestic politics. But the Cold War differed from the Depression and the war. Above all, the state of emergency that prevailed during the Cold War was unlike these earlier states of emergency because it did not have a perceived end. Specifically, the fact that American and Soviet leaders would reveal that they were unwilling to fight a direct war with one another – a war that could be world-ending, particularly once the Soviets acquired nuclear weapons, which they did in 1949 – led elites to conclude that the Cold War state of emergency was unresolvable. At the same time, for two reasons liberals were unwilling to hand the reins of policymaking to the public. First, they were worried that if foreign policy was left to ordinary Americans, the latter might not commit to fighting the Cold War so soon after World War II.[35] Second, revelations about the Holocaust ratified liberals' – especially Jewish liberals' – anxieties about the masses.[36] For all of these reasons, in the late 1940s liberal elites began institutionalizing emergency measures, making them permanent features of the U.S. state and society. During the Cold War, the extraordinary became ordinary.

---

[33] Michael J. Hogan, *A Cross of Iron: Harry S. Truman and the Origins of the National Security State, 1945–1954* (New York: Cambridge University Press, 1998), 2–3; Douglas Stuart, *Creating the National Security State: A History of the Law That Transformed America* (Princeton, NJ: Princeton University Press, 2008), 2–9; Stephen Wertheim, *Tomorrow, the World: The Birth of U.S. Global Supremacy* (Cambridge, MA: Harvard University Press, 2020), 48–49.

[34] Andrew Preston, *Total Defense: The New Deal and the Invention of National Security* (Cambridge, MA: Harvard University Press, 2025), 1.

[35] Bessner, *Democracy in Exile*, 127–128.

[36] On the importance of the Holocaust to Jewish Cold War liberals' thinking, see Hacohen, "The Strange Fact That the State of Israel Exists."

In 1947, for example, the Harry S. Truman Administration referred to the developing Cold War to justify what might be thought of as a "Second New Deal."[37] Where the "First New Deal" of the 1930s focused on welfare and social security, the Second New Deal of the late 1940s focused on warfare and national security. Namely, Truman and Congress worked together to increase the war and intelligence powers of the executive branch by establishing highly secretive alphabet-soup agencies such as the NSC, CIA, Department of Defense (DoD), and National Security Agency (NSA), which together formed a novel "national security state."[38] Beyond these specific groups, the government also fostered the creation of "military–industrial" and "military–intellectual" complexes that were comprised of state bodies, industrial organizations, and parastatal institutions such as academic centers and think tanks that were mostly free from public and congressional interference.[39] These agencies and complexes were intended to achieve liberal ends, even as they were designed to escape the purview of the *demos*.

---

[37] In the historiography, the "Second New Deal" typically refers to a second period of reform inaugurated by the Roosevelt Administration in the mid-1930s. As the historian Morton Keller explains, "the major conceptual framework of the literature is the distinction between a recovery-minded First New Deal rooted in the past, and a reform-minded Second New Deal that under the political, intellectual, and demographic pressures of change unfolded into something broader and more original." Morton Keller, "The New Deal: A New Look," *Polity* 31, no. 4 (Summer 1999), 657. The Second New Deal was defined by, as the historian Steve Fraser elucidates, "the Wagner Act, the Social Security Act, the second banking act, the public utility holding company act, [and] the wealth tax act." Steve Fraser, "The 'Labor Question,'" in *The Rise and Fall of the New Deal Order, 1930–1980*, ed. Steve Fraser and Gary Gerstle (Princeton, NJ: Princeton University Press, 1989), 68. However, both the traditional "first" and "second" New Deals focused on domestic reform and may therefore be situated as part of the same process. The Second New Deal referred to in this essay departed from the First New Deal in that it emphasized foreign policy and national security and was thus a meaningful extension and expansion into new issue areas of the New Deal of the 1930s. Indeed, there is some precedent in the literature for understanding the institutional innovations of the late 1940s as augmentations of the New Deal. In his *In Spies We Trust*, for example, the historian Rhodri Jeffreys-Jones remarks that "the CIA was, amongst other things, the New Deal's last great agency." Rhodri Jeffreys-Jones, *In Spies We Trust: The Story of Western Intelligence* (Oxford: Oxford University Press, 2013), 101.
[38] On the establishment of the national security state, see Hogan, *A Cross of Iron*, and Stuart, *Creating the National Security State*.
[39] On these complexes, see Stuart W. Leslie, *The Cold War and American Science: The Military-Industrial-Academic Complex at MIT and Stanford* (New York: Columbia University Press, 1993); Ron Theodore Robin, *The Making of the Cold War Enemy: Culture and Politics in the Military-Intellectual Complex* (Princeton, NJ: Princeton University Press, 2001); Bessner, *Democracy in Exile*; Alex Roland, *Delta of Power: The Military-Industrial Complex* (Baltimore: Johns Hopkins University Press, 2021); Jennifer Mittelstadt and Mark R. Wilson, "The Politics of U.S. Military Privatization, 1945–2000," in *The Military and the Market*, ed. Jennifer Mittelstadt and Mark R. Wilson (Philadelphia: University of Pennsylvania Press, 2022), 11–30.

First, the founding of the NSC, CIA, DoD, and NSA fulfilled liberals' desire to create a rationalized state able to manage not only domestic, but also international, affairs. Second, the military–industrial complex institutionalized a military Keynesianism that provided thousands of jobs all over the country.[40] Finally, the military–intellectual complex formally brought civilian foreign policy, defense, and area experts into the halls of power.[41] Again, emergency – in this instance, the Cold War – impelled a type of liberal progress, though it came at significant cost. Most important, the culture of secrecy that surrounded these agencies and complexes, and which was bolstered by Truman's Executive Order 9835 of 1947, which instituted a "loyalty program" for executive branch employees, and his Executive Order 10290 of 1951, which established the modern classification system, engendered a paranoid environment of which right-wing demagogues such as Senator Joseph R. McCarthy (R-WI) easily took advantage.[42]

McCarthy himself and McCarthyism as a phenomenon, however, were mostly spent by the mid-1950s; it was Cold War liberalism that was the status quo ideology in the United States between the end of World War II and the late 1960s.[43] Nonetheless, there is no exact moment when New Deal *cum* wartime liberalism transformed into an identifiable Cold War liberalism. Similar to the Cold War itself, which became the defining logic of geopolitics for different people at different times, different thinkers, activists, and politicians became Cold War liberals at different times.[44] Suffice to say that by 1949 – the year the Soviet Union detonated its first atomic weapon, China "fell" to the communists, and

---

[40] Brenes, *For Might and Right*.
[41] Bessner, *Democracy in Exile*; Bessner, "The Progressive Origins of Project RAND," in *Ideology in U.S. Foreign Relations: New Histories*, ed. Christopher McKnight Nichols and David Milne (New York: Columbia University Press, 2022), 385–411.
[42] Harry S. Truman, "Executive Order 9835," March 21, 1947, Harry S. Truman Library and Museum, www.trumanlibrary.gov/library/executive-orders/9835/executive-order-9835; Harry S. Truman, "Executive Order 10290," September 24, 1951, Harry S. Truman Library and Museum, www.trumanlibrary.gov/library/executive-orders/10290/executive-order-10290. On secrecy in the Cold War, see Janet Farrell Brodie, "Learning Secrecy in the Early Cold War: The RAND Corporation," *Diplomatic History* 35, no. 4 (September 2011), 643–670, and Sam Lebovic, *State of Silence: The Espionage Act and the Rise of America's Secrecy Regime* (New York: Basic Books, 2023), chapter 6. On McCarthyism and the Red and Lavender Scares that emerged during the Cold War, see Ellen Schrecker, *Many Are the Crimes: McCarthyism in America* (Boston: Little, Brown, 1998); David K. Johnson, *The Lavender Scare: The Cold War Persecution of Gays and Lesbians in the Federal Government* (Chicago: University of Chicago Press, 2004); Storrs, *The Second Red Scare and the Unmaking of the New Deal Left*.
[43] Delton, *Rethinking the 1950s*, 8.
[44] On the Cold War having different starting points for different people, see Bessner, *Democracy in Exile*, 127.

Arthur M. Schlesinger, Jr., published *The Vital Center* – a Cold War liberal sensibility had been embraced by enough people to become the dominant tendency within both the American liberal tradition and U.S. politics writ large.

As its name indicates, Cold War liberalism was an ideology primarily oriented toward national security, foreign affairs, and international relations. Nevertheless, in several ways, Cold War liberals used the perceived existential struggle between the United States and Soviet Union to promote progressive social causes. One of the most crucial areas that Cold War liberals emphasized was U.S. race relations. In effect, Cold War liberals were worried that Soviet propaganda, which frequently lambasted American racism, would prevent the United States from promoting its system of liberal democratic capitalism throughout the emergent Third World. For this reason, between the mid-1940s and mid-1960s, Cold War liberals aided in enacting a domestic anti-racist program that was intended to counter Soviet propaganda by bringing Black Americans fully into the U.S. political community.[45] In 1946, Cold War liberals established the President's Committee on Civil Rights; in 1948, they added a civil rights plank to the Democratic Party platform, began the desegregation of the United States military, and created the Civil Service Commission's Fair Employment Board; in 1954, they lobbied the Supreme Court to end segregation with its *Brown v. Board of Education* decision; in 1964, they helped pass the Civil Rights Act; and in 1965, they helped pass the Voting Rights Act.[46] In so doing, Cold War liberals used the Cold War to pursue reforms that reshaped American race relations, even though racism remained a key feature of U.S. society.

Cold War liberals also utilized the Cold War to reformulate the United States' political economy. In particular, after the Korean War broke

---

[45] As the historian Ruth Feldstein succinctly puts it, "by the late 1940s, many liberals who considered race relations through the prism of the Cold War concluded that overt prejudice was antithetical to the democratic ethos that the United States had to promote nationally and internationally." In particular, these liberals worried that "excessive or violent prejudice ... was a propaganda tool with which the Soviet Union discredited American democracy." Ruth Feldstein, *Motherhood in Black and White: Race and Sex in American Liberalism, 1930–1965* (Ithaca, NY: Cornell University Press, 2000), 73.

[46] Cold War liberals, of course, were pressured to enact these programs, policies, and laws by on-the-ground activists, and were rarely, if ever, the sole instigators of these efforts. There is a rich literature on the relationship between the Cold War and the Black freedom movement, broadly understood. Representative works include Penny M. Von Eschen, *Race against Empire: Black Americans and Anticolonialism, 1937–1957* (Ithaca, NY: Cornell University Press, 1997); Mary Dudziak, *Cold War Civil Rights: Race and the Image of American Democracy* (Princeton, NJ: Princeton University Press, 2000); Nikhil Pal Singh, *Black Is a Country: Race and the Unfinished Struggle for Democracy* (Cambridge, MA: Harvard University Press, 2004).

out in June 1950 Truman enacted a form of military Keynesianism that through rearmament helped encourage economic growth and decrease unemployment.[47] Military Keynesianism, in fact, became a defining feature of the "golden age" of capitalism and the concurrent "golden age" of liberalism, both of which lasted from roughly the late 1940s to the early 1970s.[48] During this period, military spending was a very significant part of the U.S. economy – between 1950 and 1970, it never fell below a 9 percent share of gross domestic product – and it aided in spurring material prosperity in specific regions, most notably the American Sunbelt.[49] Military Keynesianism, in short, allowed Cold War liberals to simultaneously mobilize U.S. society, invigorate American capitalism, and aid certain workers. Americans, Cold War liberals demonstrated, could have both "guns" and "butter."

Still, in various ways the Cold War emergency precluded more radical social and economic reforms. First, in the late 1940s and early 1950s, Cold War liberals embraced a hardline anti-communist program and kicked leftists out of the liberal-left coalition that had gained prominence in the 1930s and 1940s.[50] In early 1947, as mentioned earlier, Truman issued an executive order that instituted a loyalty program in the executive branch; later that year, Truman's Attorney General Thomas C. Clark published a list of "subversive organizations" that included the Communist Party of the United States of America, the Civil Rights Congress, and the Hollywood Writers Mobilization for Defense, among other groups.[51] Furthermore, throughout the early Cold War communists were arrested, and sometimes deported, under the authority of the Alien Registration Act of 1940, the Internal Security Act of 1950, and the Immigration and Nationality Act of 1952.[52] Predictably, labor, already weakened by the passage of the Labor Management Relations Act of 1947, which placed significant restrictions on union activity,

---

[47] Brenes, *For Might and Right*, 52–54; Tim Barker, "Cold War Capitalism: The Political Economy of American Military Spending, 1947–1990" (PhD diss., Harvard University, 2022), chapter 3.

[48] Barker, "Cold War Capitalism," chapters 3–5.

[49] Brenes, *For Might and Right*, 55; Barker, "Cold War Capitalism," 4.

[50] Bell, *The Liberal State on Trial*; Storrs, *The Second Red Scare and the Unmaking of the New Deal Left*.

[51] Harry S. Truman, "Executive Order 9835"; "Groups Called Disloyal," *The New York Times* (December 5, 1947), 18.

[52] Ellen Schrecker, "Immigration and Internal Security: Political Deportations during the McCarthy Era," *Science & Society* 60, no. 4 (Winter 1996/1997), 393–426; Von Eschen, *Race against Empire*, 115; Adam Goodman, *The Deportation Machine: America's Long History of Expelling Immigrants* (Princeton, NJ: Princeton University Press, 2020), 52.

was especially affected by Cold War liberals' anti-communist program.[53] Most important, communists and communist-affiliated unions were forced out of the organized labor movement, with the Congress of Industrial Organizations expelling eleven unions that communists had supposedly infiltrated.[54] This all ensured that the Cold War liberalism that dominated in the Truman years and beyond was decidedly reformist, focused on attenuating social ills as opposed to engaging in the root-and-branch reform necessary to transform social structures.

Second, and similarly, the early Cold War witnessed liberals' embrace of a meliorist approach to civil rights.[55] Like their counterparts in the labor movement, Black liberals forced leftists out of their coalition and pursued a strategy whereby they endorsed the federal government's Cold War programs in exchange for a seat at the proverbial policymaking table. In so doing, as the historian Kenneth R. Janken has argued, Black liberal groups like the National Association for the Advancement of Colored People "abdicated [their] duty to press for wide-ranging change in the way the government operated."[56] Moreover, Black liberals' embrace of the Cold War and Cold War liberalism attenuated international solidarities that they had developed with anti-colonial movements during, and in the period immediately following, World War II.[57] When it came to race, from the late 1940s onward, reform, not revolution, was the name of the game.

The politics of emergency engendered by the geopolitical struggle between the United States and Soviet Union enabled Cold War liberals to achieve several important goals, from the creation of a rationalized state and parastatal apparatus designed to manage foreign affairs to high levels of employment to the further incorporation of Black Americans into the U.S. political community. But, because these achievements occurred under the shadow of the Cold War crisis, they were tempered: the rationalized state and parastatal apparatus had little democratic accountability; many Americans worked in defense industries whose very existence encouraged war and militarism; and Black

---

[53] Eva Bertram, "Whose Work Counts? Congressional Republicans and the Battle over Employment Status, 1947–48," *Studies in American Political Development* 37, no. 2 (October 2023), 170.
[54] Feldstein, *Motherhood in Black and White*, 83; Ellen Schrecker, "Labor and the Cold War: The Legacy of McCarthyism," in *American Labor and the Cold War: Grassroots Politics and Postwar Political Culture*, ed. Robert W. Cherny, William Issel, and Kieran Walsh Taylor (New Brunswick, NJ: Rutgers University Press, 2004), 10–11.
[55] Feldstein, *Motherhood in Black and White*, 83–84.
[56] Janken, "From Colonial Liberation to Cold War Liberalism," 1091.
[57] Von Eschen, *Race against Empire*, chapter 5; Janken, "From Colonial Liberation to Cold War Liberalism."

Americans were allowed to join white society only if they abandoned the left. The central tension of Cold War liberals' domestic project was that progress came at the cost of liberalism.

Nowhere was this seen more than on the world stage. After World War II, the Truman Administration began building a globe-spanning empire the likes of which had never been seen in history. And, as they had with their domestic state-building efforts, administration officials used the battle against Soviet communism to justify the United States' rise to global hegemony. According to Truman and his advisors, the only way liberal capitalist democracy could be made safe was for the United States to do what it had refused to do in the 1920s and 1930s: accept the mantle of global leadership and confront communism head on.[58] American liberals thus accepted, and indeed embraced, a form of world empire that many of their forebears would have found anathema.[59] It is this empire that remains Cold War liberals' most lasting contribution to U.S. and international history, and it is this empire to which I now turn.

Cold War Liberalism and Empire

Cold War liberalism was the founding ideology of the global American empire, the most powerful empire that has ever existed. Since liberalism's beginnings, many of its advocates conceived of themselves as engaging in an international, imperial project.[60] From John Stuart Mill to Giuseppe Mazzini to Woodrow Wilson to Samantha Power, liberals have long considered it their right and duty to spread their beliefs abroad, sometimes at the barrel of a gun.[61] (Tellingly, the very

---

[58] On the Truman Administration and the U.S. rise to global hegemony, see Melvyn P. Leffler, *A Preponderance of Power: National Security, the Truman Administration, and the Cold War* (Stanford, CA: Stanford University Press, 1992); John Lewis Gaddis, *Strategies of Containment: A Critical Appraisal of American National Security Policy during the Cold War*, rev. ed. (New York: Oxford University Press, 2005), chapters 3–4.

[59] On this transition among the liberal elite during World War II, see Wertheim, *Tomorrow, the World*.

[60] As the political scientist Jennifer Pitts has argued, "many of the staple concepts of liberal political thought have ... been mobilized in favor of the European imperial enterprise, and ... European liberalism was forged alongside, and deeply affected by, imperial expansion." Jennifer Pitts, *A Turn to Empire: The Rise of Imperial Liberalism in Britain and France* (Princeton, NJ: Princeton University Press, 2005), 4.

[61] On Mill, see Pitts, *A Turn to Empire*, chapter 5. On Mazzini, see Rosenblatt, *The Lost History of Liberalism*, 96–97. On Wilson, see George C. Herring, *From Colony to Superpower: U.S. Foreign Relations since 1776* (New York: Oxford University Press, 2008), chapter 10. On Power, see Daniel Bessner, "The Fog of Intervention," review of *The Education of an Idealist: A Memoir*, by Samantha Power, *The New Republic* 250, no. 9, iss. 5032 (September 2019), 53–57.

term "liberal" was itself disseminated across Europe by the armies of Napoleon Bonaparte.)[62] For British and French liberals in particular, empire was a means to promote human progress. Thus, in the nineteenth century, these liberals claimed that seizing colonies not only benefitted metropoles, but "barbarian" subject peoples as well, and for this reason was legitimate.[63] West European liberals went so far as to argue that, even if violence was sometimes needed to subdue colonies, such violence was acceptable in the service of the greater good.[64] American Cold War liberalism was part and parcel of this tradition. American Cold War liberals, like their European predecessors, considered liberal values universal, exportable, and, when necessary, worth promoting with illiberal and often violent means.[65] For Cold War liberals, the struggle against the Soviet Union, as the political scientist Dillon Stone Tatum put it, was "an exciting opportunity to expand their vision, integrate it into a global context, and .. spread a liberal messianism beyond the boundaries of Western developed nations."[66]

Nevertheless, the form the Cold War liberal empire assumed differed from earlier liberal empires. Unlike the British and French empires (and, one might add, the post-Cold War U.S. empire), Cold War liberals rarely promoted so-called humanitarian interventions, instead stressing the importance of "modernization" projects and other forms of economic, political, and cultural development aid.[67] They also emphasized the importance of local "self-determination" and deemphasized the need to directly govern large spaces, like the British and French

---

[62] Rosenblatt, *The Lost History of Liberalism*, 57.
[63] Pitts, *A Turn to Empire*, passim; Bell, *Reordering the World*, passim; Rosenblatt, *The Lost History of Liberalism*, 116–118, 250–252.
[64] Pitts, *A Turn to Empire*, 21.
[65] These trends in Cold War liberal thought may also be connected to trends in American thought more broadly. As the historian Walter LaFeber has put it, U.S. foreign policy has from its outset been defined by "the continuing contradiction ... between the principle of self-determination, whose value has been self-evident to the U.S. mind, and the expansion of [U.S.] power, whose value has also been self-evident." Walter LaFeber, *Inevitable Revolutions: The United States in Central America*, 2nd ed. (New York: W.W. Norton, 1993), 22.
[66] Tatum, *Liberalism and Transformation*, 87.
[67] On modernization and development, see Michael E. Latham, *Modernization as Ideology: American Social Science and "Nation Building" in the Kennedy Era* (Chapel Hill: University of North Carolina Press, 2000); Nils Gilman, *Mandarins of the Future: Modernization Theory in Cold War America* (Baltimore: Johns Hopkins University Press, 2003); David Ekbladh, *The Great American Mission: Modernization and the Construction of an American World Order* (Princeton, NJ: Princeton University Press, 2010); Michael E. Latham, *The Right Kind of Revolution: Modernization, Development, and U.S. Foreign Policy from the Cold War to the Present* (Ithaca, NY: Cornell University Press, 2011); Daniel Immerwahr, *Thinking Small: The United States and the Lure of Community Development* (Cambridge, MA: Harvard University Press, 2015).

overseas, and the American continental, empires had before them.[68] Indeed, Cold War liberals helped construct what the political scientist Chalmers Johnson has referred to as an "empire of bases," or what the historian Daniel Immerwahr has termed a "pointillist empire," premised far more on power projection, economic domination, the covert activities of intelligence agencies, and the assistance of allies and client states than the formal governance of territories.[69] In so doing, Cold War liberals attempted to build a more humane type of empire that would allow them to govern the world in ways that were distinctly less violent than the brutalities of European and American empires past.[70]

Cold War liberals further rejected the explicitly religious and racialized approach to empire that had defined earlier British, French, and American imperialisms. From the French Revolution onward, liberal imperialists have identified "others" against which they juxtaposed and defined themselves. In the pre-World War II period, these identifications usually assumed religious and racialized forms, as liberals affirmed Christian and white "civilization" over Black, brown, and non-Christian "barbarism."[71] For two reasons, however, Cold War liberals did not embrace the unambiguously Christian and racist discourses of their

[68] On the United States fighting for the principle of "self-determination" during the Cold War, in this case on behalf of the Republic of Vietnam (South Vietnam), see Lyndon B. Johnson, "Annual Message to the Congress on the State of the Union" (speech, January 12, 1966), in John T. Woolley and Gerhard Peters, ed., *The American Presidency Project* (Santa Barbara, CA, 1999–2025), www.presidency.ucsb.edu/documents/annual-message-the-congress-the-state-the-union-27 and Lyndon B. Johnson, "Remarks at a Luncheon Honoring the Foreign Ministers Attending a Meeting of the Organization of American States" (speech, September 22, 1967), in John T. Woolley and Gerhard Peters, ed., *The American Presidency Project* (Santa Barbara, CA, 1999–2025), www.presidency.ucsb.edu/documents/remarks-luncheon-honoring-the-foreign-ministers-attending-meeting-the-organization.
[69] On the United States' overseas basing network, see David Vine, *Base Nation: How U.S. Military Bases Abroad Harm America and the World* (New York: Skyhorse Publishing, 2017). On the notion of the United States as an "empire of bases," see Chalmers Johnson, "America's Empire of Bases," *TomDispatch*, January 15, 2004, https://tomdispatch.com/best-of-tomdispatch-chalmers-johnson-on-garrisoning-the-planet/. On the notion of the United States as a "pointillist empire," see Daniel Immerwahr, *How to Hide an Empire: A History of the Greater United States* (New York: Farrar, Straus and Giroux, 2019), Part II.
[70] This was long a feature of U.S. international thought. See Richard W. Maass, *The Picky Eagle: How Democracy and Xenophobia Limited U.S. Territorial Expansion* (Ithaca, NY: Cornell University Press, 2020), 7. On the pursuit of "humane" forms of imperial governance, see Samuel Moyn, *Humane: How the United States Abandoned Peace and Reinvented War* (New York: Farrar, Strauss, and Giroux, 2021).
[71] As the political scientist Jennifer Pitts highlights, "the liberal turn to empire [in the nineteenth century] was … accompanied by the eclipse of nuanced and pluralist theories of progress [that] gave way to more contemptuous notions of 'backwardness' and a cruder dichotomy between barbarity and civilization." Pitts, *A Turn to Empire*, 2.

forebears. First, many Cold War liberals hailed from minority communities that were themselves religiously and racially suspect, above all Jews and Catholics.[72] Second, and as mentioned earlier, during the Cold War liberals committed themselves to an anti-communist crusade that depended on winning the "hearts and minds" of Third World populations.[73] Cold War liberals therefore could not point explicitly to religion or race to justify their civilizational superiority, and ultimately, their imperialism, without attenuating their own global project.

This is not to say, of course, that Cold War liberals evacuated religion and race from their imperial practice; far from it. Both the Korean War (1950–1953) and Vietnam War (1954–1975) were in significant respects wars fought against religious and, especially, racialized others. Still, Cold War liberals differed from earlier generations of liberal imperialists by not (usually) deploying religion and race as the explicit rationalization for foreign intervention. Instead, they embraced a universalist discourse that insisted the United States intended to lead a "free world" (which they identified as the entire "non-communist world") whose benefits were available to all, regardless of religion or race.[74] In this way, Cold War liberals created a liberal imperialist rhetoric that blended anti-communism, religious pluralism, and anti-racism (or at least race neutralism) and which attempted to reconcile their search for military and economic primacy with their claims to universalism.

As the earlier references to the Korean and Vietnam Wars suggest, the problems and prospects of the Cold War liberal empire were felt most acutely in Asia, which after the "fall" of China in 1949 became of especial interest to Cold War liberals who feared that the communist victory would inspire anti-colonial and anti-Western revolts throughout the region.[75] Cold War liberals thus attempted to walk a fine line: on one hand, they claimed that American rule was democratic, anti-racist,

---

[72] Bessner, *Democracy in Exile*, 129; Christopher Schaefer, "Catholic Internationalism and American Empire: The Cold War Liberalism of William Pfaff," this volume. For reasons of length, this essay could not discuss how Cold War liberals helped the United States become a more religiously pluralistic nation, though there is significant work to be done on this topic.

[73] On the importance of the Third World to the Cold War, see Odd Arne Westad, *The Global Cold War: Third World Interventions and the Making of Our Times* (Cambridge: Cambridge University Press, 2005).

[74] Peter Slezkine, "Free World Leadership and the Limits of Liberalism," this volume.

[75] On the centrality of Asia to the Cold War, see Paul Thomas Chamberlin, *The Cold War's Killing Fields: Rethinking the Long Peace* (New York: HarperCollins, 2018), Parts I and II. As Chamberlin notes, "more than 70 percent of the people killed during the Cold War died along the eastern, southern, and western periphery of the Asian landmass." Chamberlin, *The Cold War's Killing Fields*, 6.

and focused on improving the lives of local peoples; on the other hand, they did all they could to preserve the highly unequal relationships between Asian countries and the west that had defined the region's history for decades. Predictably, Cold War liberal governance in Asia manifested in deeply contradictory ways. In Japan, the U.S. military government initiated radical land, education, and social reforms as it simultaneously suppressed the labor movement and left-wing groups.[76] In the Philippines, the United States surrendered formal control of the country as it continued to collaborate with local elites to shape the islands' politics.[77] In Indonesia, the United States supported a coup and the mass slaughter of civilians, many of whom were deemed communist sympathizers, in the name of aiding groups believed to be friendly to American interests.[78] And in South Korea and South Vietnam, the United States prosecuted near-genocidal anti-communist wars as it sought to stabilize and modernize these countries through economic development projects that, Americans hoped, would demonstrate the superiority of U.S.-style development to the world.[79] As in domestic affairs, when it came to managing the world, Cold War liberals were usually willing to put liberalism aside.

U.S. imperial rule throughout the Cold War, in fact, was brutal. The political scientists Monica Duffy Toft and Sidita Kushi have discovered that during the Cold War era (1946–89), the United States militarily intervened with "the threat, display, or direct usage of force" in foreign societies 104 times, at the rate of 2.42 interventions per year.[80] Between 1947 and 1989, Americans also attempted to covertly overthrow foreign regimes sixty-five times; in twenty-five of those instances, U.S.-supported forces assumed power.[81] Finally, more than 20 million people

---

[76] Jennifer M. Miller, *Cold War Democracy: The United States and Japan* (Cambridge, MA: Harvard University Press, 2019).

[77] Colleen Woods, *Freedom Incorporated: Anticommunism and Philippine Independence in the Age of Decolonization* (Ithaca, NY: Cornell University Press, 2020).

[78] Bradley R. Simpson, *Economists with Guns: Authoritarian Development and U.S.-Indonesian Relations, 1960–1968* (Stanford, CA: Stanford University Press, 2008).

[79] Ekbladh, *The Great American Mission*, chapter 4; Edward Miller, *Misalliance: Ngo Dinh Diem, the United States, and the Fate of South Vietnam* (Cambridge, MA: Harvard University Press, 2013); Andrew J. Gawthorpe, *To Build as Well as Destroy: American Nation Building in South Vietnam* (Ithaca, NY: Cornell University Press, 2018).

[80] Monica Duffy Toft and Sidita Kushi, *Dying by the Sword: The Militarization of U.S. Foreign Policy* (New York: Oxford University Press, 2023), 14, 19–26; Sidita Kushi and Monica Duffy Toft, "Introducing the Military Intervention Project: A New Dataset on U.S. Military Interventions, 1776–2019," *Journal of Conflict Resolution* 67, no. 4 (April 2023), 767.

[81] Lindsey A. O'Rourke, *Covert Regime Change: America's Secret Cold War* (Ithaca, NY: Cornell University Press, 2018), 3.

died in Cold War–era conflicts.[82] Despite what the Cold War liberals had hoped, governing the world turned out to be an inherently violent, illiberal project that relied on the inhumane use of force to "succeed."[83]

Still, one cannot overlook the fact that many people who became Cold War liberals also helped establish institutions of global governance that, in theory at least, paved the way for the eventual creation of a genuinely international society. Organizations such as the International Bank for Reconstruction and Development/World Bank (1944), the International Monetary Fund (1944), the United Nations (1945), and the General Agreement on Tariffs and Trade (1947) were all designed in part to help liberals manage global affairs in a rational, humane, and progressive manner.[84] While in practice these institutions were often utilized as tools through which Cold War liberals forced their own views of politics, society, economy, and culture onto the world, their very creation did reflect an honest attempt to move beyond the aggressive power politics that had defined the history of international relations. Perhaps these groups would have had a more peaceable effect on world affairs if the Cold War had never broken out.

Over the course of the late 1940s, 1950s, and 1960s, Cold War liberals created a global empire; according to a Senate subcommittee report from 1970, "by the mid-60s, the United States was firmly committed to more than 43 nations by treaty and agreement and had some 375 major foreign military bases and 3,000 minor military facilities spread all over the world, virtually surrounding both the Soviet Union and Communist China."[85] This empire regularly acted violently, especially in the Third World, and was directly responsible for the death and deracination of millions of innocent people. In championing the cause of American hegemony, Cold War liberals demonstrated that, for many of them, winning the Cold War and governing the world was more important than acting according to liberal precepts. Eventually, Cold War liberals' commitment to empire, most notably in Vietnam, wound up undermining the Cold War liberal project itself. Nevertheless, though after the late 1960s Cold War liberalism was weakened, it never fully went away; rather, it transformed, moving in new and unexpected directions.

---

[82] Chamberlin, *The Cold War's Killing Fields*, 19.
[83] On the inherent violence and illiberalism of global hegemony, see Patrick Porter, *The False Promise of Liberal Order: Nostalgia, Delusion, and the Rise of Trump* (Cambridge: Polity, 2020).
[84] G. John Ikenberry, *A World Safe for Democracy: Liberal Internationalism and the Crises of Global Order* (New Haven, CT: Yale University Press, 2020), 178–179.
[85] *United States Security Agreements and Commitments Abroad: Hearings before the Subcommittee on United States Security Agreements and Commitments Abroad of the Committee on Foreign Relations*, 91st Cong. 2417 (1971).

The Afterlives of Cold War Liberalism

Cold War liberalism was the dominant strain of liberalism among American elites from the late 1940s to the late 1960s. Though at times the Harry S. Truman, Dwight D. Eisenhower, John F. Kennedy, and Lyndon B. Johnson Administrations enacted different policies, at their core each of these administrations embraced the two primary elements of the Cold War liberal project: skepticism of the masses and a commitment to global U.S. empire. And while Cold War liberals were criticized by the emergent Buckleyite right and the old socialist left, neither was able to seriously challenge Cold War liberalism's ideological hegemony. For the first twenty or so years of the Cold War, Cold War liberalism reigned.

But over the course of the mid to late 1960s, Cold War liberalism's authority started to wither as various events and phenomena – above all, the failures of the Vietnam War, but also the successes of political movements that stressed the importance of novel types of racial, gender, and sexual identities, as well as the decolonization of the Third World – made it seem less vital and viable. Of special importance was the rise of a "New Left" that rejected many of the Cold War liberals' assumptions and approaches to domestic and world politics. Where Cold War liberals centered anti-communism, the New Left was more sympathetic to this ideology (even as New Left activists criticized the Soviet Union); where Cold War liberals emphasized piecemeal reform, including when it came to the economy and civil rights, the New Left promoted revolutionary transformation; where Cold War liberals embraced traditional notions of sex, gender, and sexuality, the New Left wanted to fundamentally alter how Americans approached these spheres of life; where Cold War liberals fetishized experts, the New Left returned to the Deweyan idea that democracy required an educated and enlightened public; where Cold War liberals were skeptical or ambivalent about decolonization, the New Left endorsed it; and where Cold War liberals considered U.S. hegemony a guarantor of global peace, the New Left considered it imperialism.

For a brief moment in the late 1960s and early 1970s, the New Left reaction to Cold War liberalism seemed like it might impel a change in U.S. political culture. But by the mid-1970s, a novel form of liberal politics, which historians now term "neoliberalism," began to emerge.[86]

---

[86] The theory and practice of neoliberalism has engendered a large literature. Representative works include David Harvey, *A Brief History of Neoliberalism* (New York: Oxford University Press, 2005); Melinda Cooper, *Family Values: Between Neoliberalism and the New Social Conservatism* (New York: Zone Books, 2017); Quinn Slobodian,

Neoliberals combined a desire to use the state to defend and protect the "free" market with an imperialist mindset that insisted the future of the United States, and the world, depended on the nation defending and promoting capitalism and American hegemony. As neoliberalism became dominant in the late 1970s and early 1980s, the New Left, partially due to government repression by the same forces that helped usher in Cold War liberalism, faded from the scene. The same was true for many of the social democratic accomplishments of the Cold War liberals. In particular, the latter's social welfare programs were attenuated or eliminated by a bipartisan group of politicians, intellectuals, and administrators that supported austerity measures and anti-union policies designed to confront the "stagflation" that hit the U.S. economy in the 1970s. Military spending, however, remained high; in 1980, the United States expended $146.7 billion in the category "defense and international" (5.3 percent of GDP); in 1985, it spent $268.9 billion (6.3 percent of GDP); and in 1990, it spent $313.1 billion (5.3 percent of GDP).[87] Cold War liberals had insisted that social democracy and empire went together; what the neoliberals demonstrated was that you could have "guns" without "butter."

Indeed, it was in the realm of foreign affairs that Cold War liberalism continued to exert a profound influence on U.S. and global history, primarily through the "neoconservative" movement that was spun off from it.[88] Neoconservatives such as Midge Decter, Irving Kristol,

Globalists: The End of Empire and the Birth of Neoliberalism (Cambridge, MA: Harvard University Press, 2018); Kim Phillips-Fein, "The History of Neoliberalism," in *Shaped by the State: Toward a New Political History of the Twentieth Century*, ed. Brent Cebul, Lily Geismer, and Mason B. Williams (Chicago: University of Chicago Press, 2019), 347–362; Fritz Bartel, *The Triumph of Broken Promises: The End of the Cold War and the Rise of Neoliberalism* (Cambridge, MA: Harvard University Press, 2022); Gary Gerstle, *The Rise and Fall of the Neoliberal Order: America and the World in the Free Market Era* (New York: Oxford University Press, 2022).

[87] U.S. Office of Management and Budget, *Budget FY 2025 – Historical Tables, Budget of the United States Government, Fiscal Year 2025*, "Table 14.4 – Total Government Expenditures by Major Category of Expenditure: 1948–2023" (2024), www.govinfo.gov/content/pkg/BUDGET-2025-TAB/xls/BUDGET-2025-TAB-15-4.xlsx; U.S. Office of Management and Budget, *Budget FY 2025 – Historical Tables, Budget of the United States Government, Fiscal Year 2025*, "Table 14.5 – Total Government Expenditures by Major Category of Expenditure as Percentages of GDP: 1948–2023" (2024), www.govinfo.gov/content/pkg/BUDGET-2025-TAB/xls/BUDGET-2025-TAB-15-5.xlsx.

[88] On neoconservatism, see Ehrman, *The Rise of Neoconservatism*; Jim Mann, *Rise of the Vulcans: The History of Bush's War Cabinet* (New York: Viking, 2004); Heilbrunn, *They Knew They Were Right*; Vaïsse, *Neoconservatism*; Alan M. Wald, *The New York Intellectuals: The Rise and Decline of the Anti-Stalinist Left from the 1930s to the 1980s*, Thirtieth Anniversary Edition (Chapel Hill: University of North Carolina Press, 2017), chapter 11; Daniel Steinmetz-Jenkins and Michael Franczak, "Cold War Liberals, Neoconservatives, and the Rediscovery of Ideology," in *Ideology in U.S.*

Richard Perle, Norman Podhoretz, and Paul Wolfowitz, among others, were former Cold War liberals who had left the Democratic Party due to their disaffection with what they considered to be the party's embrace of the New Left, the antiwar movement, and the more militant phase of the civil rights movement. Similar to the Cold War liberals, neoconservatives insisted that the future of liberalism depended on U.S. military and economic primacy. From the 1970s onward, when Perle and Wolfowitz worked under the arch Cold War liberal Senator Henry M. "Scoop" Jackson (D-WA), neoconservatives have advocated a very hawkish approach to international relations, reaching the apotheosis of their influence in the run-up to the Iraq War of 2003.

In several other ways, the impact of Cold War liberalism endures. Most important, Cold War liberals' skepticism of democracy has colonized the American state. Power has been centralized in the executive branch (and, increasingly, in the White House itself); the government surveils American citizens without their informed consent; information and government activities remain classified whether or not they imperil national security; and an unelected and unaccountable elite, within both state and parastatal institutions, plays a crucial role in determining U.S. foreign, security, and macroeconomic policy. Furthermore, the crisis rhetoric of Cold War liberalism persists in the work of intellectuals such as Anne Applebaum, Mark Lilla, Yascha Mounk, George Packer, and Timothy Snyder, all of whom embrace various elements of the Cold War liberal program, from the idea that international politics is often a struggle between Manichean enemies to the notion that subversive antidemocratic agents threaten liberal democracy from within.[89] In fact, in the last several decades, a diversity of supposedly existential enemies – al-Qaeda, Iraq, Iran, North Korea, postmodernism, Donald Trump, identity politics, fascism, populism, China, Vladimir Putin – have arisen to occupy the liberal imagination.[90] And, similar to their forebears, many, if not all, of the children of Cold War liberalism argue

---

Foreign Relations: New Histories, ed. Christopher McKnight Nichols and David Milne (New York: Columbia University Press, 2022), 412–434; Michael Brenes and Michael Franczak, "Conservatives in a 'Liberal Age': Rethinking the Neoconservative Turn in the 1960s," this volume.

[89] Brenes and Steinmetz-Jenkins, "Legacies of Cold War Liberalism"; Daniel Steinmetz-Jenkins, "Yesterday's Men," review of *Liberalism in Dark Times: The Liberal Ethos in the Twentieth Century,* by Joshua L. Cherniss, and *Hannah Arendt and Isaiah Berlin: Freedom, Politics, and Humanity,* by Kei Hiruta, *The Baffler,* December 16, 2021, https://thebaffler.com/latest/yesterdays-men-steinmetz-jenkins.

[90] On the importance of existential threats to U.S. imperial governance, see Daniel Bessner, "The American Empire and Existential Enemies," *Foreign Exchanges,* September 7, 2020, https://fx.substack.com/p/the-american-empire-and-existential.

that the existential nature of political conflict sometimes justifies illiberal behavior. Cold War liberalism is thus not only one of the most influential ideologies in modern history; it remains with us today.

Summary of Volume

Each of the chapters in *Cold War Liberalism* explores how this ideology shaped a given idea, person, event, movement, or phenomenon. In the volume's first chapter, Peter Slezkine examines the ideological origins and political impact of the American concept of the "free world." From the late 1940s to the early 1960s, "free world leadership" served as the organizing principle of U.S. foreign policy. Though American officials imagined the "free world" as the self-evident expression of international liberalism, they defined it negatively as equivalent to the entire "non-communist world." Cold War liberals' persistent failure to fill the "free world" concept with positive content, Slezkine shows, forced them to maintain a series of inflexible and ultimately counterproductive positions, including a commitment to global containment, an intolerance of nonalignment, and an axiomatic insistence on the enduring and existential nature of the Soviet threat. While the "free world" concept mostly fell out of circulation after the 1960s, Slezkine suggests that its logic has continued to underpin an American project of global "leadership" that derives its purpose from the prior identification of a single extraordinary threat.

Joshua Donovan's chapter uses Secretary of State John Foster Dulles as an archetype to explore the role Cold War liberalism played in influencing U.S. foreign policy in the Middle East. Donovan argues that Cold War liberals like Dulles sought to build and defend a world order premised on a preponderance of American power rather than on more traditionally liberal projects like binding international laws and enforceable human rights norms. Though Dulles, like many in his cohort of U.S. foreign policymakers, opposed "formal" imperialism, he wound up repeating the mistakes of empires past. Donovan demonstrates that Dulles's emphasis on shaping the Middle East through regional alliances and covert interventions ultimately undermined the democratic norms and human rights he considered essential to liberalism itself.

Mark Edwards's chapter explores the career and thought of Walter Lippmann, one of the most influential journalists in twentieth-century U.S. history. Despite popularizing the term "Cold War," Lippmann is generally not ranked among the Cold War liberals, mostly due to the fact that over the course of the 1950s and 1960s he transformed into a self-identified conservative. Yet Edwards demonstrates that Lippmann is one of the foundational theorists of Cold War liberalism who provided powerful justifications for liberal empire abroad and emergency politics at home. Indeed, Edwards's analysis of Lippmann's career highlights the difficulties of talking about "Cold War liberalism" – a multivariate, diverse, and complex ideological formation – in the singular.

While there has recently been a renaissance in the literature exploring the impact of Catholic thinking on political realism and international thought, few scholars have explored how Catholics shaped Cold War liberalism. In his chapter, Christopher Schaefer redresses this gap by examining the career of the Catholic intellectual William Pfaff. By analyzing Pfaff's writing and work for *The Commonweal*, a liberal Catholic journal of ideas, Schaefer shows that the midcentury convergence of American liberalism and liberal Catholicism enabled thinkers like Pfaff to integrate into elite structures from which they had been excluded. Nevertheless, though Pfaff endorsed U.S. foreign policy in the 1950s, liberals' prosecution of the Vietnam War undermined his faith in U.S. empire, highlighting the contingency of Catholic support for liberal imperialism.

Erik Baker's chapter argues that one of the paradigmatic intellectual innovations of Cold War liberal psychologists was to pursue a renovation of classical liberal theory by embracing the concept of totalitarianism and drawing on the intellectual resources of contemporary personality studies and social psychology. Totalitarianism, according to Cold War liberals, was not merely an unjust or illiberal form of government, but a type of psychopathology rooted in the inadequate development of individual psyches in a particular society. As such, they argued, the ideal liberal society must become a site of psychological health and personal growth. Such a society would allow individuals to develop a "productive character" that was characterized by a stable sense of self-expression and was achieved through participation in meaningful work. In this way, Cold War liberal psychologists combined a novel anti-totalitarianism with a traditional liberal commitment to productive labor.

Anti-totalitarianism shaped the discipline of sociology as well. In his chapter, David Sessions uses the sociological paradigm of "industrial society" to compare the politics of social democrats and Cold War liberals, concluding that the distinctive features of Cold War liberalism lie less in its substantive political ideas than its temperamental reactions to political events. Sessions argues that American and European sociologists' fear that too much democracy would lead to totalitarianism compelled them to embrace an "anti-totalitarian style" defined by an alarmist, paranoid reaction to popular movements on the left. This style,

Sessions demonstrates, was a remarkably stable feature of Cold War liberal thought both within and beyond the social sciences.

Emma Kuby's chapter explores Cold War liberals' involvement in an international propaganda campaign against Soviet "slavery" that occurred in the late 1940s and early 1950s. By contrasting Cold War liberals' legalistic and economistic case against Joseph Stalin's use of forced labor with the more robustly moral critique offered by non-liberal opponents of the Soviet Union, especially French anti-totalitarians, Kuby shows that Cold War liberalism was less focused on cruelty, and less philosophically coherent, than many scholars have claimed. Kuby also demonstrates that American Cold Warriors abandoned specifically liberal terms of censure when such language started to become politically inconvenient, which suggests that "liberalism" itself might be best understood not as a governing Cold War principle but as one strategic Cold War rhetoric among multiple others.

In her chapter, Courtney Rawlings examines the low-cost housing projects envisioned by the Los Angeles–based Black architect Paul R. Williams to explore why centralized planning and affordable housing, which were both embraced by liberals during the New Deal, became anathema to Cold War liberals. Rawlings shows that, before the 1950s, what is today known as midcentury modern architecture gave physical form to the liberal belief that democracies ought to provide their citizens with low-cost, amenity-rich communities. But in the era of McCarthyism, this conviction came under severe assault, ultimately leading architects like Williams to evacuate midcentury modern architecture of its once progressive political valence.

Daniel Smith's and Anton Jäger's chapter analyzes the work of the historian Richard Hofstadter, whose scholarship and public writings on populism and the radical right made concepts such as "status anxiety" and "the paranoid style" into anchors of Cold War liberalism's anti-populist ethos. Hofstadter, Smith and Jäger argue, helped establish a "demonology" of the New Right that shaped Cold War liberals' psychosocial diagnosis of populism. Unfortunately, the authors show, this diagnosis misunderstood both the rise and appeal of the New Right. Indeed, Smith and Jäger demonstrate that Hofstadterian language continues to influence how intellectuals study populism and warn that focusing too much on social psychology blinds contemporary thinkers to the reasons why the American radical right has proved so powerful and long-lasting.

As Smith's and Jäger's essay highlights, many of the ideas put forth by Cold War liberals long outlasted their heyday, a fact underlined in Michael Brenes's and Michael Franczak's chapter. Brenes and Franczak argue that Cold War liberalism, which went into abeyance in the late 1960s, experienced resurgent strength in the 1970s due to the intellectual and political networks formed by Daniel Bell, Hubert Humphrey, Irving Kristol, Daniel Patrick Moynihan, and other Cold War liberals. In effect, these networks helped Cold War liberals – many of whom rebranded themselves as "neoconservatives" – regain their strength and transform American foreign policy in the 1970s and 1980s. Brenes and Franczak thus reveal that the "neoconservative" turn in American politics is overstated; neoconservatism, it turns out, shared significant features with Cold War liberalism.

Finally, Andrés Sánchez-Padilla's chapter expands beyond the United States to examine how Cold War liberalism influenced Carlos Fuentes, one of the most prominent Mexican writers of the twentieth century. Sánchez-Padilla traces Fuentes's ideological trajectory from social democrat to neoliberal, arguing that the author's transformation was the result of internal divisions within the Latin American left over how to respond to the Cuban Revolution, the "dirty wars," and the general economic problems experienced by the region in the 1970s and 1980s. Sánchez-Padilla shows that Fuentes's Cold War liberal fear of the masses merged with a novel anxiety about the role of the state in politics, ultimately leading the writer to champion a neoliberal agenda that earlier in his career he would have found anathema.

Taken together, the chapters in this volume demonstrate that Cold War liberalism shaped diverse historical phenomena in the United States and abroad. Nevertheless, there remains much work to be done on the complex historical trajectories of Cold War liberalism, especially when considering the ideology's relationship to race, gender, sexuality, and class. Furthermore, the degree to which Cold War liberalism interacted with other liberalisms that were less dominant during the period of its hegemony remains an open question for future historians to explore. In the final analysis, I hope this volume encourages scholars to take Cold War liberalism more seriously than they have. If they do, our understanding of liberalism, modern governance, and the United States itself will be enlarged and improved.

2 Free World Leadership and the Limits of Liberalism

Peter Slezkine

Over the course of a decade and a half, from the late 1940s through the early 1960s, the United States massively and enduringly expanded its presence in the world. Many of the "emergency" measures improvised by American officials during the war were elaborated and institutionalized during this period of relative great-power peace. According to the editors of this volume, the result was "a globe-spanning empire the likes of which had never before been seen in history." To better understand this profound transformation, they suggest that scholars focus more on the American empire's "founding ideology" – Cold War liberalism.

The difficulty is in defining the object of investigation. Both the noun and its modifier are equally tough to pin down. Liberalism is a "protean" concept with a long history and many parents. The "cold war," meanwhile, entered the American vocabulary as an awkward label for an unprecedented and uncategorizable condition. It may be simpler to identify what Cold War liberals opposed (totalitarianism, the masses) than what they espoused; and to pick out particular Cold War liberals (by their proximity to the mid twentieth-century establishment) than to define a consistent and coherent Cold War liberalism. Even the chronology of the ideology appears uncertain. Although the "cold war" may serve to characterize a particular brand of liberalism that reached its apogee in the 1950s, many of its principal components were already contained in the crusading spirit of Wilsonianism, the anxious response to the economic and political travails of the 1930s, and the official justifications for American entry into World War II. At the other end of the time span, Cold War liberalism survived both détente and the collapse of the Soviet Union, enjoying "afterlives" in a renewed confrontation with the "evil empire," a global "war on terror," and a universal contest between "democracies" and "autocracies."

One way to gain a clearer picture of the target, at least in the realm of foreign policy, is to determine how American officials themselves characterized the United States' global role. What purpose were they pursuing, how far did their interests extend, and what constituency did they claim to represent? The answer to these questions is as evident as it is historiographically invisible. The midcentury American officials who committed the United States to a globe-spanning role did so explicitly in the name of leading the "free world." As President Truman declared in 1950: "all our international policies, taken together, form a program designed to strengthen and unite the free world."[1] Such statements were not political hyperbole. From the late 1940s through the 1960s, the "free world" functioned as the prime category in public speeches, government memoranda, and top-secret strategy documents. American policymakers' efforts to lead, unite and strengthen a spatially defined "free world" fundamentally transformed the United States' global role.

Like Cold War liberalism more broadly, the concept of the "free world" derived much of its content from ideological developments in the first half of the twentieth century. Yet the phrase "the free world" did not enter the American vocabulary until 1949–50 and is thus anchored directly to the Cold War. The sudden centrality of the "free world" in American foreign policy was both a product of the United States' deepening divide with the Soviet Union and a key factor in determining its conduct in the conflict. In fact, the concept of the "free world" proved considerably more impactful than the very idea of the "cold war" – a term that American policymakers used relatively sparingly and whose meaning they never quite figured out.

The "free world" also reflected Cold War liberalism in that it lacked much independent content and derived its meaning and mission from what it opposed. American officials imagined the "free world" as the natural endpoint of human history, a truly global community of sovereign states patterned after liberal societies made up of autonomous individuals. Yet the "free world" they sought to lead came into being precisely because it fell short of this ideal. The self-confident leadership of the self-evident "free world" relied on the prior recognition of an evil Other. According to American officials, the contours of the "free world" coincided exactly with those of the "noncommunist world." Nevertheless, this negative definition did not make the "free world" an empty signifier. The borders of the free world circumscribed a measurable territory and a distinct group of peoples, and the American claim to lead the entire noncommunist portion of the globe forced policymakers to maintain a series of awkward and inflexible positions that would not have been necessary otherwise: a commitment to global anti-communist containment, an intolerance of Cold War nonalignment, and an insistence on the enduring and existential nature of the Soviet threat.

---

[1] Harry S. Truman, "Address in Laramie, Wyoming," May 9, 1950. Retrieved from www.presidency.ucsb.edu/documents/address-laramie-wyoming.

An investigation of the peculiar logic of "free world leadership" also reveals the distinctiveness of the United States relative to other "liberal" or "informal" empires – notably Great Britain. American officials understood "free world leadership" as an essentially defensive enterprise with existential stakes, requiring constant vigilance across the entire globe. As Allen Dulles, the director of the CIA and brother of John Foster, explained in a top-secret memorandum in 1956: "Unlike Britain in the 19th century ... the US today must take seriously, as a potential threat to the cohesion and determination of the Free World, every situation of weakness that develops anywhere in the non-communist world from Chile to Vietnam."[2]

Over the course of the 1960s, the "free world" slowly fractured along three separate axes. The routinization of the Cold War and the Sino-Soviet split reduced official insistence on an existentially menacing and monolithic "communist world"; the increased importance of the "underdeveloped countries of the free world" resulted in the recognition of a separate Third World; and the growing countercultural movement within the West challenged the meaning of freedom within the "free world." Nevertheless, the legacy of the "free world" lived on in the country's commitment to global "leadership," which no longer needed to be *of* anything in particular, and in the maintenance of the United States' military alliances, which eventually became an end in itself. The concept has also remained available for redeployment. In 2004, at the height of the War on Terror, George W. Bush used the phrase more often than any president in any year since 1964.[3] More recently, President Biden proposed to renew "the spirit and shared purpose of the nations of the Free World" as part of a struggle against global "autocracy," a category identified primarily with the United States' Cold War adversaries: Russia and China.[4]

***

The phrase "free world" first entered the American vocabulary in the early 1940s and only gained widespread circulation at the end of the decade.[5] Yet hardly anyone at the time noticed the novelty of

---

[2] "Paper Prepared by the Director of Central Intelligence," November 18, 1954. https://history.state.gov/historicaldocuments/frus1952-54v02p1/d132.

[3] Based on a search of presidential speeches in the American Presidency Project – at www.presidency.ucsb.edu.

[4] Joseph R. Biden, Jr., "Why America Must Lead Again: Rescuing U.S. Foreign Policy after Trump," Foreign Affairs (March/April 2020), www.foreignaffairs.com/articles/united-states/2020-01-23/why-america-must-lead-again.

[5] See Google Ngram Viewer: https://books.google.com/ngrams/graph?content=the+free+world&year_start=1900&year_end=2019&case_insensitive=on&corpus=28&smoothing=0.

the concept. While other neologisms from around the same period, such as "totalitarianism" and "cold war," served as labels for apparently new and strange phenomena, the "free world" seemed a natural description of a self-evident reality.[6] The concept proved productive precisely because it felt familiar. The "free world" of the 1950s was indeed new – as a common phrase, an imagined space, and an object of policy. At the same time, many of the assumptions embedded in the concept had long held sway over the American imagination. As a result, the vast and transformative commitments entailed by "free world leadership" could appear as the necessary product of a long legacy of American liberalism.

The notion of a single globe divided into two "worlds" emerged as soon as Europeans started settling the American continent. For the Puritan inhabitants of New England and the American revolutionaries thereafter, the New World represented a land of liberty in contrast to an Old World of tyranny.[7] Yet the relationship between these "worlds" was not zero sum. The distance between the two hemispheres permitted peaceful coexistence. This principle became national policy in 1796, when President Washington warned Americans against political entanglement with the "foreign world."[8] In 1823, President Monroe issued the same message to an Old-World audience, warning Europeans against any further encroachment into the New World.[9]

---

[6] On the concept of the "cold war," see Anders Stephanson, "Cold War Degree Zero," in *Uncertain Empire: American History and the Idea of the Cold War*, ed. Duncan Bell and Joel Isaac (New York: Oxford University Press, 2012), 19–50; Nils Gilman, "The Cold War as an Intellectual Force Field," *Modern Intellectual History* 13, no. 2 (2016), 507–523. On totalitarianism, see Benjamin Alpers, *Dictators, Democracy, and American Public Culture: Envisioning the Totalitarian Enemy, 1920s–1950s* (Chapel Hill: University of North Carolina Press, 2003); Abbott Gleason, *Totalitarianism: The Inner History of the Cold War* (New York: Oxford University Press, 1995); Les K. Adler and Thomas G. Paterson, "Red Fascism: The Merger of Nazi Germany and Soviet Russia in the American Image of Totalitarianism, 1930's–1950's," *American Historical Review* 75, no. 4 (April 1970), 1046–1064; Thomas R. Maddux, "Red Fascism, Brown Bolshevism: The American Image of Totalitarianism in the 1930s," *The Historian* 40, no. 1 (November 1977), 85–103.

[7] Anders Stephanson, *Manifest Destiny: American Expansionism and the Empire of Right* (New York: Hill and Wang, 1996); Eric Foner, *The Story of American Freedom* (New York: Picador, 1999).

[8] George Washington, "Farewell Address," September 19, 1796. Retrieved from www.ourdocuments.gov/doc.php?flash=false&doc=15&page=transcript. Also, see Felix Gilbert, *To the Farewell Address: Ideas of Early American Foreign Policy* (Princeton: Princeton University Press, 1961).

[9] James Monroe, "Seventh Annual Message to Congress," December 2, 1823. Retrieved from www.presidency.ucsb.edu/documents/seventh-annual-message-1. Also, see Ernest May, *The Making of the Monroe Doctrine* (Cambridge, MA: Harvard University Press, 1975); Gale McGee, "The Monroe Doctrine – A Stopgap Measure," *Mississippi Valley Historical Review* 38, no. 2 (September 1951), 233–250; Jay Sexton, *The Monroe Doctrine: Empire and Nation in Nineteenth-Century America* (New York: Hill & Wang, 2011).

As Thomas Jefferson wrote in a letter to Monroe in advance of his doctrine's adoption: "While [Europe] is laboring to become the domicile of despotism our endeavor should surely be to make our hemisphere that of freedom."[10]

While New World republicanism might coexist with Old World despotism, friction between the Union's free and slave states threatened all-consuming conflict. During his unsuccessful run for Senate in 1858, Abraham Lincoln described the United States as a "house divided." The country, he declared, could not endure "permanently half *slave* and half *free*." It would have to become "*all* one thing or *all* the other."[11] Whereas the American revolutionaries had deemed separation sufficient to secure their freedom from a tyranny originating across the Atlantic (and the Southern Confederates continued to regard secession as a legitimate defense of state liberty), Lincoln insisted on the indivisibility of the Union and the incompatibility of freedom and slavery within its bounds. Lincoln's election to the Presidency and the outbreak of civil war ultimately resulted in the defeat of American slavery and a "new birth of freedom" for the nation. The United States, at last, had become "*all* one thing."[12]

The victory of the North and the settlement of the West consolidated the American nation and turned the United States into an aspiring great power with an active interest in global affairs. As the nineteenth century came to a close, American officials increasingly prioritized world civilization over New World separation. After the Spanish-American War of 1898, the United States acquired a substantial colony in the Philippines and committed to a "civilizing mission" far beyond the Western Hemisphere. Meanwhile, the United States became a leading champion of international law as a means of rationalizing relations among the "advanced" peoples of the world. Civilization remained an ongoing project, but its reach was now global and its impact ever-growing. As Theodore Roosevelt announced in a speech in 1910: "the whole world" was "bound together like never before" and the "world movement of civilization" was "felt throbbing in every corner of the globe."[13]

---

[10] Thomas Jefferson, "To the President of the United States," October 24, 1823. Retrieved from www.mtholyoke.edu/acad/intrel/thomas.htm.

[11] Abraham Lincoln, "House Divided," June 16, 1858. Retrieved from www.abrahamlincolnonline.org/lincoln/speeches/house.htm.

[12] Abraham Lincoln, "Gettysburg Address," November 19, 1863. Retrieved from www.abrahamlincolnonline.org/lincoln/speeches/gettysburg.htm. Also, see Eric Foner, *Politics and Ideology in the Age of the Civil War* (Oxford: Oxford University Press, 1981).

[13] Paul Kramer, *The Blood of Government: Race, Empire, the United States, and the Philippines* (Chapel Hill: University of North Carolina Press, 2005); Benjamin Coates, *Legalist Empire: International Law and American Foreign Relations in the Early Twentieth*

The outbreak of world war in the Civilized World's European core disrupted this story of steady global progress. Although Woodrow Wilson initially sought to insulate the United States from an apparent revival of Old-World anarchy, he eventually deemed neutrality unsustainable and brought the United States into the conflict on the side of the Allied Powers. In so doing, Wilson pitted German "autocracy" against "free peoples" everywhere, effectively adapting Lincoln's zero-sum logic to the global arena and remapping America's traditional division between the New and Old Worlds onto the two sides of the ongoing war. According to Wilson, the very "existence of autocratic governments" constituted a "menace ... to peace and freedom" and only their elimination could make "the world ... safe for democracy." Wilson promised that the United States, having entered the war, would establish a new global order based on popular government, sovereign equality, and international cooperation, finally completing History's forward march: "we shall fight for ... a universal dominion of right by such a concert of free peoples as shall bring peace and safety to all nations and make the world itself at last free."[14]

The Allied Powers won the war, but the United States refused to join Wilson's concert of free peoples. Internal divisions among liberal internationalists and an enduring distrust of extra-hemispheric entanglement combined to keep the United States out of the League of Nations. After Wilson's defeat, three successive Republican administrations attempted to straddle a two-part foreign policy, maintaining an axiomatic commitment to New World nonentanglement alongside a liberal pursuit of international harmony in an interdependent world. As Warren Harding declared in his 1921 inaugural address, the United States would "seek no part in directing the destinies of the Old World" and did "not mean to be entangled." Yet Americans remained "ready

---

Century (New York: Oxford University Press, 2016); Theodore Roosevelt, "The World Movement," *Outlook* 95, no. 2 (May 12, 1910), 18, 40. For more on Roosevelt's address, see Frank Ninkovich, "Theodore Roosevelt: Civilization as Ideology," *Diplomatic History* 10, no. 3 (1986), 221–245.

[14] Woodrow Wilson, "Address to a Joint Session of Congress Requesting a Declaration of War against Germany," April 2, 1917. Retrieved from www.presidency.ucsb.edu/documents/address-joint-session-congress-requesting-declaration-war-against-germany. Also, see Thomas J. Knock, *To End All Wars: Woodrow Wilson and the Quest for a New World Order* (Princeton: Princeton University Press, 1995); Lloyd Ambrosius, *Woodrow Wilson and the American Diplomatic Tradition: The Treaty Fight in Perspective* (Cambridge: Cambridge University Press, 1987); Trygve Throntveit, *Power without Victory: Woodrow Wilson and the American Internationalist Experiment* (Chicago: University of Chicago Press, 2017); Frank A. Ninkovich, *Modernity and Power: A History of the Domino Theory in the Twentieth Century* (Chicago: University of Chicago Press, 1994).

to encourage, eager to initiate, anxious to participate in any seemly program likely to lessen the probability of war" and promote the "brotherhood of mankind."[15] At decade's end, Herbert Hoover promised adherence to the same two principles: "Fortunately the New World is largely free from the inheritances of fear and distrust which have so troubled the Old World. We should keep it so." At the same time, "the United States fully accepts the profound truth that our own progress, prosperity, and peace are interlocked with the progress, prosperity, and peace of all humanity."[16]

By the mid-1930s, this precarious balance had begun to break down. The ongoing crisis of the Great Depression and the rapid rise of revisionist regimes had rendered liberal progress an uncertain prospect in America and across the globe. Over the second half of the 1930s, Congress sought safety in New World retrenchment, passing a series of Neutrality Acts that sacrificed international intercourse in the name of avoiding foreign entanglement. Meanwhile, a growing chorus of liberal internationalists argued that global interdependence had made isolationism impossible. They claimed that peaceful coexistence between geographically distant New and Old Worlds had given way to immediate and existential conflict between the worlds of democracy and dictatorship. Hamilton Fish Armstrong, the editor-in-chief of *Foreign Affairs*, described the stakes of this struggle in his 1935 volume *"We or They": Two Worlds in Conflict*: "Lenin was right. Mussolini and Hitler are right: between the two doctrines there is no compromise. Our society or theirs. We or they."[17]

Whereas Wilson had expected to make "the world itself at last free" by defeating the last vestiges of Old-World autocracy, liberal internationalists in the 1930s sought to mount a defense against an apparently more energetic enemy. In the face of such a challenge, liberalism could only prevail if it ceased to take progress for granted. As Thomas Mann declared in a lecture delivered in the United States in early 1938:

---

[15] Warren Harding, "Inaugural Address," March 4, 1921. Retrieved from www.presidency.ucsb.edu/documents/inaugural-address-49.
[16] Herbert Hoover, "Inaugural Address," March 4, 1929. Retrieved from www.presidency.ucsb.edu/documents/inaugural-address-9.
[17] Hamilton Fish Armstrong, *"We or They": Two Worlds in Conflict* (New York: MacMillan, 1936), 103; David Foglesong, *The American Mission and the "Evil Empire": The Crusade for a "Free Russia" since 1881* (New York: Cambridge University Press, 2007); Stephen Wertheim, *Tomorrow, the World: The Birth of U.S. Global Supremacy* (Cambridge, MA: Harvard University Press, 2020); Alpers, *Dictators, Democracy, and American Public Culture*; Gleason, *Totalitarianism*; Maddux, "Red Fascism, Brown Bolshevism"; Udi Greenberg, *The Weimar Century: German Émigrés and the Ideological Foundations of the Cold War* (Princeton: Princeton University Press, 2014).

"Freedom must discover its virility. It must learn to walk in armour and to defend itself against its deadly enemies."[18] Yet not all were convinced that liberalism was suited to ideological combat. In its yearly review of world affairs, published in the spring of 1938, the Council on Foreign Relations warned of a worrying asymmetry between liberal democracy and its rivals: "democracy is not an 'ideology' within the current meaning of that word. It lacks a complete and consistent set of interlocking dogmas. It is not a fighting creed."[19]

The sudden outbreak of World War II largely spared liberalism the test of direct ideological competition against more dogmatic alternatives. After all, Allied success relied substantially on the communist contribution and ultimately derived from material factors. The most significant American ideological offensive of the war occurred on the domestic front before the attack on Pearl Harbor, as liberal advocates of aid to the Allies sought to persuade the public of the impossibility of "isolationism."[20] Franklin Roosevelt's future Secretary of the Navy, Frank Knox, was one of many who invoked Lincoln's authority to illustrate the United States' existential stake in a distant conflict: "The world, now so closely knit together, cannot continue to be half slave, and half free. It will either become all slave, or all free."[21] Over the course of the war, this line of argument led to the first few appearances of the phrase "free world." Most prominently, a major wartime magazine took the term as its title, and the introductory film in the government series *Why We Fight* depicted a clash between a "free world" and a "slave world" (represented as white and black globes, respectively).[22] Yet the "free world" never caught on as a wartime concept. The movement of a dynamic front and the expectation of a decisive resolution made it difficult to imagine the two sides of the conflict as enduring ideological spaces. As a result, the focus soon shifted to the promise of One World, a phrase popularized by the former Republican presidential candidate, Wendell Willkie, in his

---

[18] Thomas Mann, *The Coming Victory of Democracy*, trans. Agnes Meyer (London: Martin Secker and Warburg, 1938), 72.
[19] Whitney Shepardson, *The United States in World Affairs: 1937* (New York: Harper and Brothers for the Council on Foreign Relations, April 1938).
[20] Wertheim, *Tomorrow the World*; Andrew Johnstone, *Against Immediate Evil: American Internationalists and the Four Freedoms on the Eve of World War II* (Ithaca, NY: Cornell University Press, 2014); Warren Kimball, *The Juggler: Franklin Roosevelt as Wartime Statesman* (Princeton: Princeton University Press, 1991).
[21] Frank Knox, "The Gravity of the World Situation," *Vital Speeches of the Day* VI, no. 14 (May 1, 1940), 419.
[22] *Prelude to War*, directed by Frank Capra (Office of War Information, 1942); John Fousek, *To Lead the Free World: American Nationalism and the Cultural Roots of the Cold War* (Chapel Hill: University of North Carolina Press, 2000).

1943 bestseller by the same name.[23] The term quickly became a shorthand for the desired postwar order, in which international cooperation would finally match the ever-growing interdependence of the globe.[24]

As the institutional realization of One World, the United Nations garnered overwhelming public support and bipartisan backing in Congress.[25] For many Americans, the signing of the UN Charter represented the first step on a path toward closer global union rather than the culmination of international institution building. A 1946 Gallup poll, for example, showed that 63 percent of Americans supported a world legislature with binding powers over all countries.[26] One World, in this context, stood for the liberal aspiration of international consolidation, eventually culminating in world government, perpetual peace, and the end of history. Of course, the actual structure of the new United Nations was pointedly realist, prioritizing great-power cooperation over universal legislation. The Truman administration, meanwhile, was far more interested in world leadership than world government. Yet the United States' postwar policy was nonetheless expressed in One World terms. The risk of another major war – and the novel threat of nuclear power – required that humanity hold together. As Secretary of State James Byrnes declared in late 1945: "There must be one world for all of us, or there will be no world for any of us."[27]

The United States' public espousal of a One World policy did little to prevent a growing divide with the Soviet Union. For American officials, this failure of international cooperation could only stem from the perversity of the communist faith. The canonical statement of this theory came in the form of a "long telegram" dictated from Moscow by the career diplomat George Kennan on February 22, 1946. In his message, Kennan argued that the Soviets remained committed to the communist postulate that "permanent peaceful coexistence" with the "capitalist world"

---

[23] Wendell Willkie, *One World* (New York: Simon and Schuster, 1943); Samuel Zipp, *The Idealist: Wendell Willkie's Wartime Quest to Build One World* (Cambridge: The Belknap Press of Harvard University Press, 2020).

[24] Or Rosenboim, *The Emergence of Globalism: Visions of World Order in Britain and the United States, 1939–1950* (Princeton: Princeton University Press, 2019).

[25] Mark Mazower, *No Enchanted Palace: The End of Empire and the Ideological Origins of the United Nations* (Princeton: Princeton University Press, 2009); Mark Mazower, *Governing the World: The History of an Idea* (New York: Penguin, 2012); Townsend Hoopes and Douglas Brinkley, *FDR and the Creation of the U.N.* (New Haven, CT: Yale University Press, 1997).

[26] Fritz Bartel, "Surviving the Years of Grace: The Atomic Bomb and the Specter of World Government, 1945–1950," *Diplomatic History* 39, no. 2 (2015), 275–302; Joseph Baratta, *The Politics of World Federation* (Westport, CT: Praeger, 2004).

[27] James Byrnes, "Neighboring Nations in One World," *Department of State Bulletin* XIII, no. 332 (November 4, 1945), 711.

was impossible. It did not matter, he added, that actual experience had proven this premise to be "simply not true." The "disrespect of Russians for objective truth – indeed their disbelief in its existence" guaranteed that they would continue to act on the assumption of a divided world, regardless of American action. There was little hope, therefore, that the United Nations could turn into a strong and productive international body: "Moscow has no abstract devotion to UNO ideals" and its "attitude to that organization will remain essentially pragmatic and tactical." According to Kennan, the liberal desire for mutually beneficial cooperation within One World would inevitably run up against the communists' dogmatic commitment to a divided globe.[28]

After a year of deepening conflict with the Soviet Union, the administration openly declared the existence of a global divide on March 12, 1947, in what came to be known as the Truman Doctrine. A few months earlier, British officials had informed their American counterparts that they could no longer afford to financially support the governments in Greece and Turkey. The White House decided that it would have to foot the bill in order to preserve influence in the Eastern Mediterranean and prevent a possible communist takeover in Greece. Yet the administration worried that the Republican-controlled Congress would oppose the expenditure. As a result, Truman deliberately formulated his request for funds in stark moral terms reminiscent of wartime anti-Axis rhetoric. In his speech to Congress, the President explained that "at the present moment in world history nearly every nation must choose between alternative ways of life" – one guaranteeing "individual liberty" and the other relying "upon terror and oppression." It should be the policy of the United States, he declared, to "help free peoples to maintain their free institutions and their national integrity against aggressive movements that seek to impose upon them totalitarian regimes."[29]

The invocation of a pervasive communist menace helped rally support for the administration's aid bill. At the same time, the apparently

---

[28] George Kennan, "Long Telegram," February 22, 1946. Retrieved from https://digitalarchive.wilsoncenter.org/document/116178.pdf; Anders Stephanson, *Kennan and the Art of Foreign Policy* (Cambridge, MA: Harvard University Press, 1989); John Lewis Gaddis, *George Kennan: An American Life* (New York : Penguin Press, 2011); John Lewis Gaddis, *Strategies of Containment: A Critical Reappraisal of Postwar American National Security Policy* (New York: Oxford University Press, 1982); Melvyn P. Leffler, *A Preponderance of Power: National Security, the Truman Administration, and the Cold War* (Stanford: Stanford University Press, 1992); Michael Hogan, *A Cross of Iron: Harry S. Truman and the Origins of the National Security State, 1945–1954* (New York: Cambridge University Press, 1998); Dean Acheson, *Present at the Creation: My Years in the State Department* (New York: Norton, 1969).

[29] Harry S. Truman, "Address before a Joint Session of Congress," March 12, 1947. Retrieved from www.presidency.ucsb.edu/documents/special-message-the-congress-greece-and-turkey-the-truman-doctrine.

universal formulation of the Truman Doctrine suggested enduring and global commitments that the White House did not mean to meet. In the weeks after Truman's speech, the bill's backers sought to set clear limits on the scope of American intervention, emphasizing that aid to Greece and Turkey would not automatically lead to equivalent support for other "free peoples" in the future. Senator Arthur Vandenberg of Michigan, the Republican chair of the Senate Committee on Foreign Relations and a key administration ally, made the point explicit: "I emphatically repeat that we do not here set a universal precedent."[30] Support for Greece and Turkey was local and ad hoc, and the "free peoples" did not yet constitute a bloc. When the administration announced the much more comprehensive Marshall Plan a few months later, it ostensibly promised to provide aid to any communist country willing to participate, including the Soviet Union.[31]

There were some in the administration who worried about this reticence to recognize a fully divided globe. In a memorandum dated August 30, 1947, Chip Bohlen, then serving as Counselor of the Department of State, insisted on recognizing the "disagreeable fact" that there were "two worlds instead of one." He argued that persistent attempts to make "policy based on the nonexistent thesis of one world" might lead the administration to "neglect to take such measures as would make the non-Soviet world possible of existence." Only by drawing "closer together politically, economically, financially, and, in the last analysis, militarily" could a "free and non-Soviet world hope to survive in the face of the centralized and ruthless direction of the Soviet world."[32] Not only did Bohlen insist on the immediate creation of a U.S.-led bloc, but he also identified the "free world" with the entire "non-Soviet world." A House subcommittee, established in May 1947, ultimately came to the same conclusion in its report on the "Strategy and Tactics of World Communism." In order to secure access to sufficient resources, the United States should aim to create an international system with an area "approximately the same as the present non-Communist world."[33]

Meanwhile, a group of influential Republicans criticized the administration, not for sticking to a "one world" premise, but for refusing to

---

[30] *Congressional Record, Proceedings and Debates of the 80th Congress First Session*, 93, Part 3 (Washington, DC: U.S. Government Printing Office, 1947), 3195.
[31] Michael Hogan, *The Marshall Plan: America, Britain, and the Reconstruction of Western Europe, 1947–1952* (Cambridge: Cambridge University Press, 1987); Benn Steil, *The Marshall Plan: Dawn of the Cold War* (New York: Simon and Schuster, 2018).
[32] "Memorandum by the Counselor of the Department of State (Bohlen) to the under Secretary of State (Lovett)," September 2, 1947. Retrieved from https://history.state.gov/historicaldocuments/frus1947v01/d391.
[33] House Subcommittee #5, "The Strategy and Tactics of World Communism" (Washington, DC: U.S. Government Printing Office, 1948), 58.

meet the universal challenge identified in the Truman Doctrine. They argued that American support for the "free peoples" of Europe should be matched by an equal anti-communist effort in Asia. In this context, New York's Republican Governor, Thomas Dewey, who had run against Roosevelt in the 1944 presidential election and would represent the Republican Party once again in 1948, became one of the first prominent postwar politicians to invoke "the free world" – complete with the definite article and an implied spatial referent – in several speeches in late 1947. On November 24, he declared that "the free world is now in the desperate position of a man who has gangrene in both legs – in Western Europe and in Asia. As a doctor, our government is telling the world we have a very good cure for gangrene but we will apply it to one leg only while the gangrene in the other leg destroys the patient."[34] The "free world," in Dewey's conception, had to be understood as an organic and indivisible whole.

The 1949 "loss of China," which Republicans laid at the feet of the Truman administration, greatly increased the political cost the White House would have had to face if any further "free peoples" fell to communism. Meanwhile, the Soviet explosion of a nuclear bomb and the signing of the North Atlantic Pact combined to make the communist menace appear more immediate and the division of Europe more permanent. By early 1950, the Truman administration had fully abandoned its postwar embrace of One World and progressed from a policy of ad hoc support for diffuse "free peoples" to an enduring commitment to an indivisible "free world." NSC-68, a top-secret strategy document submitted to the president on April 7, both reflected and cemented this outlook. The report, which would lay the foundation for official American Cold War policy, described a zero-sum conflict between a "free world" and a "Soviet world"; declared "a defeat of free institutions anywhere" to be "a defeat everywhere"; and concluded by calling on the United States to build up "the political, economic, and military strength of the free world."[35]

A May 8 memorandum from the Deputy Chief of the Division of Estimates conveyed a lonely critique against the "free world" framing of NSC-68:

---

[34] Thomas E. Dewey, "China Deserves Aid," *Vital Speeches of the Day* XIV, no. 5 (December 15, 1947), 135.
[35] "NSC 68: A Report to the National Security Council by the Executive Secretariat on United States Objectives and Programs for National Security," April 14, 1950. Retrieved from https://history.state.gov/historicaldocuments/frus1950v01/d85; Ernest May, *American Cold War Strategy: Interpreting NSC 68* (Boston: Bedford Books, 1993); Curt Cardwell, *NSC 68 and the Political Economy of the Early Cold War* (New York: Cambridge University Press, 2011).

While it is true that the USSR and its satellites constitute something properly called a slave world, it is not true that the U.S. and its friends constitute a free world. Are the Indo-Chinese free? Can the peoples of the Philippines be said to be free under the corrupt Quirino government? ... To classify as "free" all those peoples whose governments oppose Russia, or we seek to have oppose Russia, is a travesty on the word.[36]

Truman did not have such qualms. On May 9, a day after the deputy chief's expression of dissent, the President publicly declared that "all our international policies, taken together, form a program designed to strengthen and unite the free world in its resistance to the spread of communism." If Truman had previously been vague about the full roster of "free peoples," he now identified a group with clear borders, a definite population, and quantifiable resources. Such precision was made possible by equating freedom with the absence of communism: "The non-Communist nations together have two-thirds of the world's people and three-fourths of the world's productive power. And we have much more than mere quantity and mere strength. We have the greatest attraction of all – we have human freedom."[37]

The outbreak of the Korean War on June 25 and the Truman administration's decision to send American troops to the peninsula put theory into practice. Secretary of State Dean Acheson's exclusion of Korea from the United States' "defensive perimeter" in a speech earlier that year had drawn considerable attention as an indication of the United States' vital interests.[38] Yet John Foster Dulles's address to the Korean National Assembly just six days before the start of the war proved far more predictive of the United States' position. "The American people," Dulles told the South Koreans, "welcome you as an equal partner in the great company of those who comprise the free world." Specific considerations of strategic priorities would matter less than the United States' overarching commitment to "free world" defense. As Dulles explained, "the free world has no written charter, but it is no less real for that."[39] The U.S.-led forces in Korea would go on to fight under the banner of the United Nations (a move made possible by a Soviet boycott of

---

[36] "Memorandum by the Deputy Chief of the Division of Estimates, Bureau of the Budget (Schaub) to the Executive Secretary of the National Security Council (Lay)," May 8, 1950. Retrieved from https://history.state.gov/historicaldocuments/frus1950v01/d90.
[37] Harry S. Truman, "Address in Laramie, Wyoming," May 9, 1950. Retrieved from www.presidency.ucsb.edu/documents/address-laramie-wyoming.
[38] Dean Acheson, "Crisis in Asia – An Examination of U.S. Policy," *Department of State Bulletin* XX, no. 551 (January 23, 1950), 116.
[39] John Foster Dulles, "The Korean Experiment in Representative Democracy," *Department of State Bulletin* XXIII, no. 574 (July 3, 1950), 13.

the U.N. over its denial of representation to the People's Republic of China), but American officials repeatedly claimed that it was the "free world" that the conflict had galvanized into action. Truman stressed that "the significance of Korea" lay in the fact that "the free world [had] made it clear" that "lawless aggression would be met with force."[40] NSC-68 had posited a global zero-sum relationship between the free and Soviet "worlds." The American response in Korea transformed this stance into an actionable precedent and an enduring commitment. The United States would defend the "free world" along its entire perimeter.[41]

The passage of the 1951 Mutual Security Act formalized the adoption of a "free world" foreign policy, combining the country's disparate postwar aid efforts into a single program with the express purpose of building up the "defenses of the free world" as a whole and for the long haul.[42] As Truman explained to Congress in a speech supporting the bill, the "free world" focus of the Mutual Security Act would account for three major aspects of the communist menace: "First, the Soviet threat is world-wide. Second, the Soviet threat is total ... Third, the Soviet threat is of indefinite duration."[43] The scale and novelty of this commitment shocked even some of the most enthusiastic internationalists in Congress, but the incremental steps taken in preceding years made the logic of the Mutual Security Act seem almost unavoidable. This dynamic was evident in an exchange between the head of the Economic Cooperation Administration, William Foster, and the Chairman of the Senate Committee on Foreign Relations, Senator Tom Connally:

Mr. FOSTER. ... this is an economic assistance program not only to Western Europe, but an assistance program which also helps countries in the free world in south Asia, southeast Asia, the Far East, Latin America, the Near East and Middle East.
[...]

---

[40] Harry S. Truman, "Special Message to the Congress Reporting on the Situation in Korea," July 19, 1950. Retrieved from www.presidency.ucsb.edu/documents/special-message-the-congress-reporting-the-situation-korea.

[41] Steven Casey, *Selling the Korean War: Propaganda, Politics, and Public Opinion in the United States, 1950–1953* (New York: Oxford University Press, 2008); Hajimu Masuda, *Cold War Crucible: The Korean Conflict and the Postwar World* (Cambridge, MA: Harvard University Press, 2015).

[42] Chester Pach, *Arming the Free World: The Origins of the United States Military Assistance Program, 1945–1950* (Chapel Hill: The University of North Carolina Press, 2010); Michael Brenes, *For Might and Right: Cold War Defense Spending and the Remaking of American Democracy* (Amherst: University of Massachusetts Press, 2020).

[43] Harry S. Truman, "Special Message to the Congress on the Mutual Security Program," May 24, 1951. Retrieved from www.presidency.ucsb.edu/documents/special-message-the-congress-the-mutual-security-program-7.

The CHAIRMAN. You think that is our business, to maintain the whole free world?
Mr. FOSTER. I believe so.
[...]
The CHAIRMAN. Where are the instructions from Congress that you have to take care of the whole free world? That is what you said. Where is it? Where is the law?
Mr. FOSTER. Congress has passed the Foreign Assistance Act; it has passed an act in the general area of China. The Congress has passed the Mutual Defense Assistance Program. The Congress passed the Technical Cooperation Act. All of those cover the items which we are requesting from you, sir, in this bill.[44]

Congress soon passed the Mutual Security Act, institutionalizing a foreign policy based on the premise of an enduring global dichotomy. Although the U.S. government would continue to draw strategic distinctions within the "free world," sending more resources to some places than others, support for each part now required justification in terms of the whole. At first, much of the aid distributed through the Mutual Security Program was destined for Europe as a replacement for the funds provided by the Marshall Plan, but the balance began to even out over the next few years, with considerably larger sums directed to Asia and elsewhere.[45]

The final step necessary to consolidate the "free world" as an anti-communist coalition was to incorporate freedom's former enemies. On December 8, 1950, John Foster Dulles, whom Truman had put in charge of peace negotiations with Japan, told Acheson that there "should be a prompt effort definitely to commit Japan, spiritually and politically, to the cause of the free world."[46] On September 8, 1951, the United States and Japan signed a peace treaty in San Francisco, excluding the Soviet Union. Then, on May 26, 1952, the United States, Great Britain, and France issued a convention on relations with the Federal Republic of Germany, which included a West German commitment to contribute "to the common aims of the free world" and declared that "the mission of the armed forces stationed by the Three Powers in the Federal territory will be the defense of the free world, of which the Federal Republic and Berlin

---

[44] Senate Committee on Foreign Relations and Committee on Armed Services, *Hearings on S. 1762*, 82nd Cong., 1st sess., 1951, 74, 77–78.
[45] By 1954, only 50 percent of the funds distributed by the Mutual Security Program were earmarked for Europe. *Report to Congress on the Mutual Security Program: For the Six Months Ended June 30, 1953* (Washington, DC: U.S. Government Printing Office, 1953), 10.
[46] "Memorandum by the Consultant to the Secretary (Dulles) to the Secretary of State," December 8, 1950. Retrieved from https://history.state.gov/historicaldocuments/frus1950v06/d788.

form part."[47] The following year, Konrad Adenauer adopted a new slogan to boast of his success: "He tied the strings to the free world."[48]

By the end of Truman's second term, the United States had fully committed to its "new role" as leader of the entire noncommunist "free world." The 1954 edition of the Brookings Institution's yearly volume on foreign affairs described this development with the benefit of hindsight:

> By the end of 1952, there was little doubt that the basic purposes of the Truman Administration, as far as the foreign policy of the United States was concerned, were clearly defined and partially realized. The concept of a free world, organized to defend itself against the Soviet Union and the Communist bloc, and supplied and guided by the United States, was generally understood and in considerable part accepted.[49]

The defining feature of the "free world" was its negative construction. As Senator Richard Russell remarked at a 1951 executive session meeting of the Senate Committee on Foreign Relations: "I call everything outside of the Iron Curtain a free nation."[50] His colleague Senator J. William Fulbright concurred: "Free means 'free from the domination of Moscow.'"[51] On the rare occasions when government documents explicitly defined the "free world," they almost always did so indirectly, by listing the countries that it excluded. Cold War liberals believed that historical progress would eventually resume its natural course toward a fully free globe, but in the meantime, the extent of the existing "free world" could be found by subtracting the Communist bloc from the One World that should have been. The "free world," as an already existing liberal ideal, gained specific shape in response to Soviet action. It preceded the "communist world" – while at the same time being produced by it.

Since the communist and noncommunist "worlds" abutted each other at every point, American leadership of the indivisible "free world" necessarily required a commitment to global containment, despite consistent concern that such a policy might stretch American resources and cede initiative to the Kremlin. The well-known columnist Walter

---

[47] "Convention on Relations between the Three Powers and the FRG," May 26, 1952, *Handbook of German Affairs* (Press Office, German Diplomatic Mission: 1954), 154. Patrick Thaddeus Jackson, *Civilizing the Enemy: German Reconstruction and the Invention of the West* (Ann Arbor: University of Michigan Press, 2006).

[48] Konrad Adenauer Stiftung, Er knüpfte die Fäden zur freien Welt (Motiv Konrad Adenauer). Retrieved from www.kas.de/en/web/geschichte-der-cdu/wahlprogramme-und-slogans.

[49] Brookings Institution, *Major Problems in US Foreign Policy* (Washington, DC: Brookings, 1954).

[50] Senate Committee on Foreign Relations, *Executive Sessions of the Senate Foreign Relations Committee: Vol. 3, Part 1* (Washington, DC: U.S. Government Printing Office, 1976), 189.

[51] Ibid.

Lippmann made this critique in 1947, immediately after the publication of George Kennan's initial formulation of the "containment" idea in his anonymous "X Article" for *Foreign Affairs*.[52] In 1948, NSC 7 made the same point, arguing that "a defensive policy, by attempting to be strong everywhere, runs the risk of being weak everywhere" and "leaves the initiative to the Kremlin." Anxiety about strategic overreach persisted even after global anti-communist containment had been put into practice in Korea. A month into the war, Senator Henry Cabot Lodge Jr. asked Acheson whether universal opposition to communist expansion was strategically sustainable: "Aren't we ... going to have to cede some areas taken by the Soviets if we are not going to find ourselves hopelessly committed all over the world?" Acheson agreed.[53] Yet over the next two decades, the United States would continue to resist the advance of communism everywhere in the indivisible "free world."

Another consequence of a "free world" foreign policy was the American insistence on the impossibility of Cold War nonalignment. In a conflict between mutually exclusive opposites "neutralism [was] an unreal choice."[54] All noncommunist nations belonged to the "free world" by default. Rejections of "free world" membership caused puzzlement, but did not produce any attempt to revise the category. By contrast, any sign that a self-proclaimed neutral might have accepted the reality of the "free world" received special attention, as in a 7 November 1951 cable to Secretary Acheson from the American Ambassador to India reporting a conversation in which Jawaharlal Nehru had discussed: "best interests of India, US and entire free world (he used word 'free')."[55]

The United States did not always wait patiently for noncommunist countries to declare "free world" membership on their own initiative. In a July 26, 1950 cable to the Embassy in Indonesia, Acheson insisted that "however bemused it may be Indo Govt shld [sic] understand ... that in struggle between USSR and free world Indonesian choice is not only unavoidable but has been made."[56] In 1952, the United States put the

---

[52] George Kennan, "The Sources of Soviet Conduct," *Foreign Affairs* (July 1947), 566–582; Walter Lippmann, *The Cold War: A Study in US Foreign Policy* (New York: Harper, 1947).
[53] Senate Committee on Foreign Relations, *Reviews of the World Situation, 1949–1950* (Washington, DC: U.S. Government Printing Office, 1974), 327.
[54] "Study Prepared by the Department of State: NSC 114/2, Annex 5," October 12, 1951. Retrieved from https://history.state.gov/historicaldocuments/frus1951v01/d332.
[55] "The Ambassador in India (Bowles) to the Secretary of State," November 7, 1951. Retrieved from https://history.state.gov/historicaldocuments/frus1951v06p2/d488.
[56] "The Secretary of State to the Embassy in Indonesia," July 26, 1950. Retrieved from https://history.state.gov/historicaldocuments/frus1950v06/d646.

Indonesian government to the test. Under the Mutual Security Act, all countries that received military assistance from the United States had to pledge their contribution to the "defensive strength of the free world."[57] When the Indonesian foreign minister signed a statement to that effect, the domestic outcry brought down the entire cabinet.[58] That same year, the United States suspended military aid to Iran after Prime Minister Mosaddegh refused to make a public commitment to the "free world."[59]

On other occasions, foreign governments invoked the cause of the "free world" as a means of eliciting American support. The Nationalist Chinese and South Korean leaders, Chiang Kai-Shek and Syngman Rhee, regularly proclaimed themselves to be bulwarks along the border of the "free world" and requested the resources such a responsibility required. France, meanwhile, demanded acknowledgement for defending the interests of the "free world" in Indochina. In 1952, the North Atlantic Council officially recognized the French military effort as "an essential contribution to the common security of the free world."[60] That same year, the United States publicly acknowledged the United Kingdom's "struggle in Malaya as an integral part of the free world's common effort to halt Communist aggression."[61]

For the U.S. government, the greatest perceived challenge in fostering "free world" unity was the potential appeal of communist propaganda. As Truman explained in April 1950: "Propaganda is one of the most powerful weapons the Communists have" in what was "a struggle, above all else, for the minds of men." Although Truman declared Americans immune to communist "deceit, distortion, and lies," he warned that foreign peoples without "free access to accurate information" might well succumb to Soviet falsehood. It was therefore essential for the United States to engage in "a sustained, intensified program to promote the cause of freedom against the propaganda of slavery. We must make ourselves heard round the world in a great campaign of truth."[62]

---

[57] "Mutual Security Act of 1951," Public Law 165, 65 Stat. 373 (1951), 381.
[58] Richard P. Stebbins and the Research Staff of the Council on Foreign Relations, *The United States in World Affairs, 1952* (New York: Harper and Brothers for the Council on Foreign Relations, 1953), 196.
[59] Ibid.
[60] NATO Digital Archives, North Atlantic Council, "Resolution on Indochina," December 17, 1952. Retrieved from https://archives.nato.int/resolution-on-indochina.
[61] Dean Acheson, "British Policy on Malaya Welcomed," *Department of State Bulletin* XXVI, no. 664 (March 17, 1952), 427.
[62] Harry S. Truman, "Address on Foreign Policy at a Luncheon of the American Society of Newspaper Editors," April 20, 1950. Retrieved from www.presidency.ucsb.edu/documents/address-foreign-policy-luncheon-the-american-society-newspaper-editors. Daniel Bessner, *Democracy in Exile: Hans Spier and the Rise of the Defense Intellectual* (Ithaca: Cornell University Press, 2018); Laura Belmonte, *Selling the American Way:*

In public – and in the abstract – members of the Truman administration consistently expressed confidence in the superior attraction of liberal values. In a fair marketplace of ideas, communist propaganda was destined to lose. As Truman put it in a speech in the summer of 1949: "In the battle for men's minds our faith is more appealing, more dynamic, and stronger than any totalitarian force."[63] In private – and in practice – American policymakers continuously struggled to put together a positive message that could appeal to members of the "free world." As early as 1948, the House Subcommittee report on the "Strategy and Tactics of World Communism" stressed the need to counter Soviet propaganda with a clear alternative: "One factor in the weakness of morale in the non-Communist world, and in the strength of morale in the Communist world, is the clarity of their ideas and the vagueness of ours."[64] Three years later, a 1951 study by the Joint Chiefs of Staff was still searching for an "inspiring or animating principle which will pervade every thought, feeling, or action of people in the free world."[65] That same year, the Foreign Minister of Ireland, Sean MacBride, complained to Acheson that Americans had not "been able to state to the people of the free world in simple language what the whole conception of democracy meant."[66]

As perceptive observers understood, the failure of a "great campaign of truth" to convey a convincing "free world" faith derived from the very nature of liberalism. Acheson publicly acknowledged this difficulty in late 1950: "many in this country have been concerned about the problem of why communism has been able to set forth a neat package of its beliefs,

---

U.S. Propaganda and the Cold War (Philadelphia: University of Pennsylvania Press, 2010); Scott Lucas, *Freedom's War: America's Crusade Against the Soviet* Union (New York: New York University Press, 1999); Giles Scott-Smith, *Cultural Cold War in Western Europe, 1945-60* (London: Rank Cast, 2004); Walter Hixson, *Parting the Curtain: Propaganda, Culture, and the Cold War* (New York: St. Martin's Press, 1997); Frances Stonor Saunders, *The Cultural Cold War: The CIA and the World of Arts and Letters* (New York: New Press, 2000); Volker Berghahn, *America and the Intellectual Cold Wars in Europe: Shepard Stone between Philanthropy, Academy, and Diplomacy* (Princeton: Princeton UP, 2001); Greg Barnhisel, *Cold War Modernists: Art, Literature, and American Cultural Diplomacy* (New York: Columbia University Press, 2015); Louis Menand, *The Free World: Art and Thought in the Cold War* (New York: Farrar, Straus and Giroux, 2021).

[63] Harry S. Truman, "Address in Chicago before the Imperial Council Session of the Shrine of North America," July 19, 1949. Retrieved from www.presidency.ucsb.edu/documents/address-chicago-before-the-imperial-council-session-the-shrine-north-america.

[64] House Subcommittee #5, "The Strategy and Tactics of World Communism," 59–60.

[65] "Study by the Joint Chiefs of Staff," January 15, 1951. Retrieved from https://history.state.gov/historicaldocuments/frus1951v01/d17.

[66] "Memorandum of Conversation, by the Secretary of State," March 23, 1951. Retrieved from https://history.state.gov/historicaldocuments/frus1951v04p1/d227.

whereas democracy seems to have such a hard time explaining what it is about." According to Acheson, this concern could not be resolved. As it turned out, "the difficulty of finding an adequate democratic ideology" was "inherent in democracy itself." In contrast to communism, "democracy [had] no dogma, no orthodoxy."[67] American-style liberal democracy was not a faith and could not claim access to a single truth. Nevertheless, policymakers' emphasis on the "battle for men's minds" as part of an existential conflict between opposing "worlds" made this ideological asymmetry a continuous cause for concern.

American policymakers' failure to foster a positive faith in the "free world" forced them to base their claim to leadership on the negative invocation of a universal and existential communist threat. As a result, any softening of the Soviet stance posed a direct challenge to "free world" unity. In particular, the apparent success of the communist-directed peace campaign caused the American government a great deal of apprehension. Beginning in 1948, the Cominform organized a series of international peace conferences, which eventually resulted in the establishment of the World Peace Council in Warsaw in November 1950. The organization's members included many well-known American and European cultural figures, including Pablo Picasso, W. E. B. Du Bois, and Jean-Paul Sartre.[68] A July 1951 NSC report on the "specious peace campaign" raised the concern that "by such wiles the USSR may yet lull the free world into a false sense of security, with adverse effect upon both its military posture and its political cohesion."[69] American "free world leadership," framed as a response to the communist challenge, had come to rely on its persistence.

Despite these difficulties, the United States government continued to formulate foreign policy aims in terms of "free world" interests. The 1952 election of the Republican Dwight D. Eisenhower confirmed the bipartisan commitment to the basic objective of "free world leadership." According to Eisenhower and his advisors, any difficulty in defining a positive "free world" policy was a product of Democratic ineptitude. In an article published in *Life* before the election, Eisenhower's future

---

[67] Dean Acheson, "The Shield of Faith," *Department of State Bulletin* XXIII, no. 594 (November 20, 1950), 800.

[68] Petra Goedde, *The Politics of Peace: A Global Cold War History* (New York: Oxford University Press, 2019); Timothy Johnston, "Peace or Pacifism? The Soviet 'Struggle for Peace in All the World,' 1948–54," *The Slavonic and East European Review* 86, no. 2 (April 2008), 259–282; Vladimir Dobrenko, "Conspiracy of Peace: The Cold War, the International Peace Movement, and the Soviet Peace Campaign, 1946–1956" (PhD diss., London School of Economics, 2016).

[69] "Report to the President by the National Security Council: NSC 114/1," August 8, 1951. Retrieved from https://history.state.gov/historicaldocuments/frus1951v01/d38.

Secretary of State, John Foster Dulles, bemoaned "the negative policy of 'containment,'" proposing instead to work more actively toward the "liberation" of "captive peoples." He also advocated a "*dynamic*" foreign policy that would "use *ideas* as weapons" to redress the country's deficiency in "faith."[70] As Eisenhower put it in his first State of the Union address: "We have learned that the free world cannot indefinitely remain in a posture of paralyzed tension, leaving forever to the aggressor the choice of time and place and means to cause greatest hurt to us at least cost to himself." His administration, therefore, had "begun the definition of a new, positive foreign policy."[71]

Yet the new turned out to be much the same as the old, and the Eisenhower administration's efforts on behalf of the "free world" encountered many of the obstacles faced by the Truman administration. The difficulty in formulating a positive "free world" policy stemmed from the logic of the concept itself. The very fact of circumscribing a territorially defined "free world" had temporarily naturalized the extent of the "communist world." As a result, the goals of "liberation" and "rollback" could recede into the distant future, allowing the "negative" policy of containment to prevail once again in the present. Eisenhower's acceptance of the existing borders between the two "worlds" became clear after he decided against supporting the 1953 uprising in East Germany, a position he maintained during the Hungarian Revolution of 1956.[72] In a 1954 meeting of the National Security Council, Eisenhower himself concluded that "in many respects, despite the plea for a more dynamic U.S. policy, our policies were not dynamic, but negative."[73]

The new administration's attempt to deepen faith within the "free world" and weaponize ideas in the battle against communism also followed the pattern that had been set by the Truman administration. While Eisenhower greatly expanded the United States' psychological and information programs, the "free world" made no progress toward a positively constructed and universally applicable message. A mission report from 1955 made the familiar complaint that "one of the chief weaknesses of a negative definition of free world philosophy ... is that

---

[70] John Foster Dulles, "A Policy of Boldness," *Life* 32, no. 20 (May 19, 1952), 146–157.
[71] Dwight D. Eisenhower, "Annual Message to the Congress on the State of the Union," February 2, 1953. Retrieved from www.presidency.ucsb.edu/documents/annual-message-the-congress-the-state-the-union-16.
[72] Bessner, *Democracy in Exile*, chapter 6.
[73] "Memorandum of Discussion at the 225th Meeting of the National Security Council," November 24, 1954. Retrieved from https://history.state.gov/historicaldocuments/frus1952-54v02p1/d136; William Hitchcock, *The Age of Eisenhower: America and the World in the 1950s* (New York: Simon & Schuster, 2018); Gaddis, *Strategies of Containment*.

it offers nothing specific or concrete which can be conveyed to the targets. ... How can the United States translate freedom into terms which will be meaningful to the Indonesian?"[74] So long as American officials insisted on leading a "free world," which they ultimately identified with the "noncommunist world," then a positive policy and common philosophy would always remain out of reach.

In the absence of a new, positive formulation of "free world" principles, American policymakers continued to rely on repeated reiterations of the communist menace as the primary means of producing unity under U.S. leadership. As a result, the apparent abatement of the Soviet threat after Stalin's death in 1953 and Khrushchev's "Secret Speech" in 1956 struck the Eisenhower administration as a potential blow to "free world" cohesion. A 1956 National Security Council Report, for example, warned that "if the USSR succeeds in improving its reputation for peaceful intentions, such efforts will present the United States with a serious threat ... likely to lead to gradual erosion of free world positions."[75] A year earlier, a National Intelligence Estimate had voiced a similar concern: "One of the most dangerous political trends over the next several years will probably be a further blurring of the lines which have divided the Communist and non-Communist worlds ... if the Bloc persists in a convincing demonstration of peaceful intent," then the result might be "increasing neutralism and a trend toward a greater number of uncommitted states."[76] Rather than welcome the prospect of peace, American policymakers perceived it as a direct threat to the firmly established priority of "free world leadership."

In 1960, John F. Kennedy ran for the presidency on a familiar "free world" platform. In his televised debate against Richard Nixon, Kennedy paraphrased Abraham Lincoln to question whether the world could persist half slave and half free.[77] After Kennedy won the election, one of his principal advisors, Walt Whitman Rostow, began an effort to prepare a "basic national security policy" (BNSP), once again attempting to frame American objectives in positive terms. Although Rostow continued to invoke the "free world," he self-consciously centered a new category – "the community of free nations" – in order to draw attention to

---

[74] Quote from Barnhisel, *Cold War Modernists*, p. 267; Bessner, *Democracy in Exile*, chapter 6.
[75] "National Security Council Report: NSC 5602/1," March 15, 1956. Retrieved from https://history.state.gov/historicaldocuments/frus1955-57v19/d66.
[76] "National Intelligence Estimate: NIE 100–7–55," November 1, 1955. Retrieved from https://history.state.gov/historicaldocuments/frus1955-57v19/d39.
[77] A search in the American Presidency Project finds 29 such speeches between September and November 1960.

the United States' "constructive task." Rostow's BNSP laid the greatest priority on the establishment of positive relations between "developed nations at the 'core' of the community of free nations" and the "less developed nations."[78] As the free community cohered, Rostow hoped that its "attractive power" would eventually result in the adherence of peoples currently under Communist control. Ultimately, however, Rostow's attempts to devise a positive and multi-layered picture of an expanding "community of free nations" once again depended on a prior commitment to the immediate task of anti-communist containment and the fundamental axiom of a two-part globe. Against "the Communist thesis that the nations of the world now find themselves, and will continue to find themselves, in either one of three blocs – Communist, capitalist, and neutral," the United States should advance "the thesis that the nations are divided only between those that want to be free and those that would destroy that freedom."[79]

Unlike a decade earlier, the champions of the "free world" did not get the last word. Rostow's BNSP faced considerable internal criticism and, despite repeated revisions over the course of two years, never received official approval. Kennan, who was then serving as Ambassador to Yugoslavia, submitted a scathing critique of the report.[80] The President's Deputy Special Assistant for National Security Affairs, Carl Kaysen, derisively referred to Rostow's BNSP as "bean soup" and rejected the need for a universal statement on global policy.[81] Indeed, the coming of the Kennedy administration marked an abrupt decline in internal government references to the "free world," setting a trend that would continue until the near abandonment of the phrase by the end of the decade.[82] On the one hand, the American political establishment had already internalized many of the commitments that had come with "free world leadership," including an embrace of entangling alliances, a belief in the global extent of vital interests, and an enduring

---

[78] Nils Gilman, *Mandarins of the Future: Modernization Theory in Cold War America* (Baltimore: Johns Hopkins University Press, 2003); David Ekbladh, *The Great American Mission: Modernization and the Construction of American World Order* (Princeton: Princeton University Press, 2010); Michael Latham, *The Right Kind of Revolution: Modernization, Development, and U.S. Foreign Policy from the Cold War to the Present* (Ithaca, NY: Cornell University Press, 2010).

[79] "Memorandum from McGhee to under Secretary: Basic National Security Policy," December 5, 1961. Retrieved from https://history.state.gov/historicaldocuments/frus1961-63v07-09mSupp/d248.

[80] David Milne, *America's Rasputin: Walt Rostow and the Vietnam War* (New York: Hill and Wang, 2008), chapter 4.

[81] "Carl Kaysen Oral History Interview," July 11, 1966. Retrieved from www.jfklibrary.org/asset-viewer/archives/JFKOH/Kaysen%2C%20Carl/JFKOH-CK-01/JFKOH-CK-01.

[82] From author-generated n-gram of year-by-year mentions of "free world" in FRUS.

opposition to the Soviet Union. As a result, the concept was no longer as politically productive as it had originally been. On the other hand, the tensions that had characterized the concept from the start were becoming increasingly apparent. During the 1950s, policymakers consistently forced external realities into a "free world" mold. Over the course of the 1960s, they increasingly loosened the "free world" frame whenever the subject seemed not to fit.[83]

The strict two-part division of the globe, problematic to begin with, appeared particularly illusory at the start of the 1960s. The Non-Aligned Movement, officially inaugurated in Yugoslavia in 1961, combined with the economic and political importance of a proliferating group of postcolonial states, made an already unwieldy "free world" increasingly incoherent. In his critique of Rostow's BNSP, Kaysen emphasized this problem in particular: "The world as viewed in this document divides neatly into two parts – a free world and a Communist world." Yet the world was in fact "divided into at least three, rather than two, parts, the boundary lines of which are by no means well-defined or firm."[84] In his own critique, Thomas L. Hughes, the Director of the Bureau of Intelligence and Research, also emphasized the importance of what he called "the in-between world" or "the underdeveloped world."[85]

Meanwhile, the "communist world," which had provided the "free world" with its purpose and shape, had begun to lose its own coherence. After the successful avoidance of major catastrophes in Cuba and Berlin in the early 1960s, the Cold War became increasingly routinized, and the existential threat of Communist aggression appeared less immediate. Perhaps more important, the Sino-Soviet split created a deep crack in the communist "monolith."[86] The Tito-Stalin split in 1948 had appeared as an anomaly that had only confirmed the rule of Kremlin control, and Yugoslavia itself was marginal enough that its

---

[83] For an account of the shift to a new foreign policy paradigm after the 1960s, see Daniel J. Sargent, *A Superpower Transformed: The Remaking of American Foreign Relations in the 1970s* (New York: Oxford University Press, 2015).

[84] "Memorandum from the President's Deputy Special Assistant for National Security Affairs (Kaysen) to the Chairman of the Policy Planning Council and Counselor of the Department of State (Rostow)," April 16, 1962. Retrieved from https://history.state.gov/historicaldocuments/frus1961-63v08/d79; Jason C. Parker, *Hearts, Minds, Voices: US Cold War Public Diplomacy and the Formation of the Third World* (New York: Oxford University Press, 2016).

[85] "Memorandum from Hughes to Rostow: INR-62," March 6, 1962. Retrieved from https://history.state.gov/historicaldocuments/frus1961-63v07-09mSupp/d263.

[86] For more on the Communist bloc as a "monolith," see Marc Selverstone, *Constructing the Monolith: The United States, Great Britain, and International Communism, 1945–1950* (Cambridge, MA: Harvard University Press, 2009).

incorporation into the "free world" caused little consternation.[87] The Sino-Soviet split, on the other hand, destroyed Moscow's monopoly on international communism, and China was too big for the "free world" to swallow. By the second half of the 1960s, the "communist world" had become an awkward condominium, eventually opening the door for Nixon's visit to China. In the absence of a clear and consolidated opposite number, the "free world" lost much of its *raison d'être*.

Finally, a burgeoning countercultural movement in the West called into question many of the liberal notions of freedom, truth, and progress that had made the idea of the "free world" seem so natural in the first place. Popular novels such as Ken Kesey's *One Flew Over the Cuckoo's Nest* (1962) and Anthony Burgess's *A Clockwork Orange* (1962), as well as scholarly works such as Michel Foucault's *Madness and Civilization* (1961) and Erving Goffman's *Asylums* (1961), relocated the main threat to individual expression from communist totalitarianism to domestic institutions.[88] Kesey made this reversal explicit by having his hero, Randle McMurphy, successfully escape from a North Korean POW camp only to meet his demise in an American asylum. Big Nurse had become more fearsome than Big Brother, and the freedom of the "free world" could no longer be taken for granted.[89]

The Vietnam War, meanwhile, represented an anomaly and an anachronism. The Korean War, which represented a quagmire of a different kind, had been fought on "free world" premises at a time when the United States was energetically embracing the cause of "free world leadership." The Vietnam War, on the other hand, was waged on "free world" terms at a time when the assumption of a dichotomous globe was losing purchase among policymakers and the American public. This disconnect contributed greatly to the controversy surrounding the conflict. An NSC memo forwarded from Kissinger to Nixon in early 1969 addressed this issue explicitly: "America's assistance to South Vietnam against communist insurgency was initiated as a perfectly consistent application of the policy enunciated in the Truman Doctrine" and yet the "the costs

---

[87] As a country outside the Soviet bloc, Yugoslavia was mostly included in the "free world" by default. For an example of an explicit inclusion of Yugoslavia in the "free world," see The President's Committee to Study the United States Military Assistance Program, *Volume II: Supplement to the Composite Report of the President's Committee to Study the United States Military Assistance Program* (Washington, DC: U.S. Government Printing Office, 1959), 7.

[88] Michel Foucault's *Folie et Déraison.: Histoire de la folie à l'âge classique* was originally published in French in 1961. An English translation only came out in 1964.

[89] Menand, *Free World*; Daniel Rogers, *Age of Fracture* (Cambridge, MA: Harvard University Press, 2011); Jeremi Suri, *Power and Protest: Global Revolution and the Rise of Détente* (Cambridge, MA: Harvard University Press, 2003).

and frustrations that followed ... called that rationale into question. In contrast, the adversities of the Korean War led only to a more intensive application of containment to Asia."[90]

By the end of the 1960s, references to the "free world" had mostly disappeared from government documents and political discourse.[91] Nevertheless, the logic underpinning the "free world" remained readily deployable. In the 1970s and 1980s, the idea of a fundamental struggle between freedom and its opposite continued to structure U.S. relations with the Soviet Union. In the 1990s, after the sudden collapse of the Communist bloc, many American policymakers assumed that it might finally be possible to "make the world itself at last free." Yet the destruction of the Twin Towers on September 11, 2001, marked a return to a dichotomized world, with George W. Bush immediately proclaiming a global conflict between freedom and terrorism. In 2004, he appealed to the "free world" directly, using the phrase more often than any president in any year since 1964.[92] "Terror," however, proved too diffuse to serve as an effective opposite, and the revival of the "free world" was quickly cut short. Still, the concept did not remain off stage for long. President Biden entered office promising to renew "the spirit and shared purpose of the nations of the Free World" as part of a global struggle between democracy and autocracy.[93] At first, this framing echoed the liberal anxiety of the 1930s, with its focus on an eclectic and burgeoning list of bad actors at home and abroad. Before long, however, the "free world" regained its familiar Cold War shape, with Russia and China identified as exceptional autocracies and enduring adversaries.

★★★

The concept of the "free world" – anchored to a long liberal legacy, embraced as the keystone of Cold War policy, and repeatedly resurrected through the present day – possesses a number of peculiar qualities that serve to distinguish the American brand of postwar "leadership" from historical empires.[94] First, its scope is inherently global. Rather

---

[90] "Memorandum from the President's Assistant for National Security Affairs (Kissinger) to President Nixon," October 20, 1969. Retrieved from https://history.state.gov/historicaldocuments/frus1969-76v01/d41; Fredrik Logevall, *Embers of War: The Fall of an Empire and the Making of America's Vietnam* (New York: Random House, 2012).

[91] This decline is evident in author-generated n-grams of FRUS and in Google ngram viewer.

[92] Based on a search of the American Presidency Project.

[93] Biden, "Why America Must Lead Again."

[94] Daniel Immerwahr, *How to Hide an Empire* (New York: Farrar, Straus, and Giroux, 2019); Charles Maier, *Among Empires: American Ascendancy and Its Predecessors* (Cambridge, MA: Harvard University Press, 2006); Julian Go, *Patterns of Empire: The British and American Empires, 1688 to the Present* (New York: Cambridge University Press, 2011).

than proceed outward from an imperial center, "free world leadership" begins with the assumption of one free world as the natural and necessary political community. Second, the failure to attain a suitably liberal One World produces a rigid global dichotomy between undifferentiated zones of freedom and tyranny. In the resulting "free world," the periphery acquires central significance as the floodgate stemming the tide of tyranny's advance. Finally, in this two-part globe, the "free world" gains shape and substance as a function of its opposite. Essential liberal precepts – historical progress, the invisible hand, the golden mean, and the marketplace of ideas – work best when they are taken for granted. Challenged by a self-confident adversary, liberalism struggles to represent itself as a coherent ideology with access to a particular truth.

3 Precursors, Practitioners, and Legacies of Cold War Liberalism in the Middle East

Joshua Donovan

Despite charged political rhetoric that might suggest otherwise, U.S. foreign policymakers have adopted remarkably consistent approaches to the Middle East over the past several decades.[1] Indeed, even as apoplectic foreign policy observers warned that Donald Trump's election in 2016 portended an unprecedented, existential threat to the liberal world order,[2] Trump's approach to the Middle East was more similar to Obama's than members of either administration might care to admit.[3] Similarly, while Antony Blinken began his tenure as President Biden's Secretary of State by implicitly repudiating the previous administration's contempt for democracy and human rights,[4] the Biden administration's approach to the region remained largely consistent with past practice: Dictators were coddled, security alliances were prioritized over human rights, Palestinian concerns were routinely dismissed, and regional proxy wars continued apace. With few exceptions, differences have been more of style and degree than of substance. In this chapter, I attribute this remarkably consistent approach to U.S. foreign policymaking in the Middle East to the enduring legacies of Cold War liberalism.[5]

---

[1] On this point, see Andrew Bacevich, *American Empire: The Realities and Consequences of U.S. Diplomacy* (Cambridge, MA: Harvard University Press, 2004).

[2] Inter alia, G. John Ikenberry, "The Plot against American Foreign Policy: Can the Liberal Order Survive?" *Foreign Affairs* 96:3 (May/June 2017), 2–9; Martin Wolf, "Donald Trump's War on the Liberal World Order," *Financial Times*, July 3, 2018; Stewart M. Patrick, "Can Trump's Successor Save the Liberal International Order," *World Politics Review*, Feb. 10, 2020.

[3] The only major divergence was Trump's withdrawal from the Joint Comprehensive Plan of Action with Iran negotiated during the Obama Administration. However, it is worth noting that two of the most powerful Democratic Senators, Charles Schumer and then-Chairman of the Senate Foreign Relations Committee Robert Menendez, Jr., sided with Republicans in publicly opposing the deal, along with over two dozen Democratic members of the House of Representatives. Notably, the Biden Administration failed to negotiate a new nuclear deal with Iran.

[4] Antony J. Blinken, "Remarks to the 46th Session of the Human Rights Council," https://geneva.usmission.gov/2021/02/24/secretary-hrc/ (accessed Oct. 12, 2022).

[5] Michael Brenes and Daniel Steinmetz-Jenkins, "Legacies of Cold War Liberalism," *Dissent* 68:1 (Winter 2021), 116–124; Rashid Khalidi, *Sowing Crisis: The Cold War and American Dominance in the Middle East* (Boston: Beacon Press, 2009), 200–246.

If attention to Cold War liberalism as an ideology can explain continuities in U.S. foreign policymaking, it raises several questions. What, exactly, is Cold War liberalism? What are its origins and core tenets? Finally, how has it shaped U.S. foreign policy in the Middle East? To answer these questions, I focus primarily on the policies and positions of John Foster Dulles, who served as President Dwight Eisenhower's Secretary of State from 1953 until the former's death in 1959. I do so because Dulles was both archetypal and influential. His ideology and tenure illustrate what I call the "postcolonial paradox" of Cold War liberalism – that is, the glaring incongruence of the United States' liberal rhetoric of freedom, democracy, and self-determination, on the one hand, and its decidedly antidemocratic or even neo-imperialistic politics in the postcolonial world, on the other. Historian Richard Immerman called Dulles the "most notorious practitioner of the Cold War."[6] He also played an outsized role in the early years of the Cold War. In Dulles's obituary in *The New York Times*, Eisenhower was quoted as saying: "If anything should happen to Foster, where could I find a man able to replace him?"[7]

As a protégé of President Woodrow Wilson's, Dulles also helps situate Cold War liberalism within the broader American liberal tradition. Because his uncle, Robert Lansing, served as President Wilson's Secretary of State from 1915 to 1920, Dulles was afforded rare opportunities as a young lawyer to try his hand as a diplomat. One of his most formative experiences was serving as chief counsel for the American delegation on the Commission on Reparations at the Paris Peace Conference in 1919. Consistent with Wilson's position, Dulles fiercely (and unsuccessfully) opposed Allied efforts to foist steep financial burdens on Germany, fearing that doing so would jeopardize global stability.[8] Although the two Princetonian Presbyterians belonged to different political parties, they shared similar philosophical principles and proclivities regarding global order and, as we will see, the Middle East.

Finally, John Foster Dulles was a pivotal figure in the history of U.S.–Middle East relations. Whereas the United States had long-standing and extensive economic and military interests and engagements in the

---

[6] Richard H. Immerman, *John Foster Dulles: Piety, Pragmatism, and Power in U.S. Foreign Policy* (Wilmington, DE: Scholarly Resources Inc., 1999), 196.
[7] "Dulles Formulated and Conducted U.S. Foreign Policy for More than Six Years," *The New York Times*, May 25, 1959.
[8] John Robinson Beal, *John Foster Dulles: A Biography* (New York: Harper Brothers, 1957), 44–53, 61–69; Immerman, *John Foster Dulles*, 6–11. See also John Foster Dulles, "Statement on Behalf of the American Delegates," dated February 13, 1919, in John Foster Dulles Papers; MC016, Public Policy Papers, Department of Special Collections, Princeton University Library [hereafter *DP*], Box 2, Reel 1.

Pacific, East Asia, and the Western Hemisphere dating back to the nineteenth century, American involvement in the Middle East at that time had primarily taken the form of nongovernmental philanthropic, educational, religious, and cultural exchanges.[9] After World War I, Wilson expressed a fleeting interest in reimagining the region, and American oil barons began turning their gaze toward the Arabian Peninsula in the 1930s, but overt military action and covert intelligence operations began in earnest only after World War II.[10] Dulles dramatically accelerated the transition toward greater U.S. intervention in the region with help from his brother, Allen, who served as the director of the Central Intelligence Agency (CIA) from 1953 to 1961.

During his tenure, Dulles prioritized the Middle East in an unprecedented way. Less than four months into his tenure, he became the first U.S. Secretary of State to make a sweeping tour of the region, meeting with leaders in Egypt, Israel, Jordan, Syria, Lebanon, Iraq, Saudi Arabia, Turkey, Libya, and other neighboring countries over the course of two weeks.[11] According to Wilbur Eveland, a CIA operative who was close to both Dulles brothers and was deeply enmeshed in the agency's covert activities in the Levant during the Eisenhower administration, Secretary Dulles took "personal charge of the Middle East," particularly during the second half of his time at the State Department.[12] This included fostering personal relationships with Middle Eastern leaders and diplomats. By examining some of these relationships, this study shows how Cold War liberalism not only shaped American policymakers but also influenced actors from the Middle East who adopted and adapted some of its ideological elements as well.

I highlight three interrelated characteristics of Cold War liberalism that built upon Wilsonian liberalism and continue to shape American

---

[9] On this earlier history, see Karine V. Walther, *Sacred Interests: The United States and the Islamic World, 1821–1921* (Chapel Hill, NC: The University of North Carolina, 2015), 99–155, 241–318; and Ussama Makdisi, *Faith Misplaced: The Broken Promise of U.S.-Arab Relations: 1820–2001* (New York: Public Affairs, 2010), 19–146. (The only military conflicts of this era were the Barbary Wars fought against North African corsairs from 1801 to 1805 and 1815).

[10] Khalidi, *Sowing Crisis*, 7–11, 40–69, 82–90; Douglas Little, *American Orientalism: The United States and the Middle East since 1945*, 3rd ed. (Chapel Hill: The University of North Carolina Press, 2008), 43–58, 117–127.

[11] Secretaries of State Cordell Hull and Edward Stettinus, Jr., made short trips to Morocco, Algeria, Egypt, and Iran, but Dulles's trip was unprecedented in length and scope; it would not be surpassed until Henry Kissinger's tenure two decades later. "Travels Abroad of the Secretary of State," *US Department of State Office of the Historian*, https://history.state.gov/departmenthistory/travels/secretary (accessed Aug. 1, 2022).

[12] Wilbur Crane Eveland, *Ropes of Sand: America's Failure in the Middle East* (New York: W.W. Norton & Company, 1980), 195.

foreign policy in the Middle East. First, like Wilson at Versailles, Cold War liberals were preoccupied with creating a global order and resolutely believed that the United States must shape and lead it. Crucially, however, the order they envisioned was not "rules-based," as some claim. Quite the contrary. In fact, both Wilson and Cold War liberals explicitly opposed efforts to create a global system of binding international laws. Instead, Cold War liberalism was premised on the preponderance of unaccountable American power augmented by regional alliances.[13] Even before the United States had entered World War II, Dulles argued that "there can be no new world order without the active participation of the United States, which alone combines the resources, the intellectual capacity, and prestige to lead the way in a world which otherwise is distraught and largely ruined."[14] The United States, for Dulles, was "the indispensable nation" in global politics.[15]

Second, Cold War liberalism was rhetorically and, at least in some senses, sincerely anti-imperialist. Like Wilson, Dulles disdained the centuries-old practice of rapacious European empires carving up the world for their own benefit. However, by casting Soviet Communism as an omnipresent geopolitical threat, Cold War liberals – again, following Wilson – justified policies that were tantamount to an imperialism without colonies.[16] Anti-imperialist rhetoric provided the alibi necessary "to imagine a world of empires without imperialism," and to deflect criticism in the postcolonial age.[17] Rather than pursuing territorial acquisition and formal colonies as his grandfather and namesake, Secretary of State John Foster had done, Dulles and his colleagues exerted imperial influence through less formal means. This included exploitative global capitalism, regional security alliances, an infamous

---

[13] The lack of enforceable international laws has led to what Kenneth Waltz termed the "anarchy" of the international system in *Man, the State, and War* (New York: Columbia University Press, 1959). See also Brian Schmidt, *The Political Discourse of Anarchy: A Disciplinary History of International Relations* (Albany: State University of New York Press, 1998).

[14] John Foster Dulles, "The United States and the World of Nations" (National Study Conference on the Churches and the International Situation, Philadelphia, Pennsylvania, Feb. 27, 1940) in *DP*, Box 290, p. 8.

[15] An allusion to Madeleine Albright, interview on NBC-TV "The Today Show" with Matt Lauer, Columbia, OH, Feb. 19, 1998.

[16] Harry Magdoff, *Imperialism without Colonies* (New York: Monthly Review Press, 2003), 91–113. See also Douglas Little, "Impatient Crusaders: The Making of America's Informal Empire in the Middle East," in Frank Costigliola and Michael J. Hogan, eds., *American in the World: The Historiography of US Foreign Relations since 1941* (New York: Cambridge University Press, 2014), 212–235.

[17] Jeanne Morefield, *Empires without Imperialism: Anglo-American Decline and the Politics of Deflection* (Oxford: Oxford University Press, 2014), 4.

coup in Iran (1953), and less-famous episodes of ham-fisted meddling in Syria (1955–75) and election-rigging in Lebanon (1957–58).

Third, like Wilson before him, Dulles was skeptical of genuine expressions of democracy and mass politics – especially in the Global South. Although he divested himself of the blatantly racist language of earlier generations of western policymakers, Dulles largely operated on the paternalistic assumption that newly-independent peoples were incapable of self-governance, or at least that they were incapable of repelling Soviet influence without American guidance. He could seldom begin to contemplate, let alone understand, the richness and diversity of Arab political thought in the postcolonial period. Nor was he particularly interested in supporting fragile postcolonial democracies in the Middle East when authoritarian alternatives seemed more suitable to American interests. Despite stubbornly persistent claims to the contrary (including those made by well-meaning critics of American hubris), U.S. foreign policy in the Middle East has never seriously prioritized democracy promotion.[18]

Not Law, but Order

The brutality and scale of World War I left the world shellshocked. Even before its end, Wilson was preoccupied with devising a new basis for a global order aimed at reducing the likelihood of future wars.[19] As mentioned earlier, Dulles personally participated in Wilson's quixotic effort until the U.S. Senate Foreign Relations Committee adopted a resolution disapproving of continued American involvement in the reparations group that Dulles was part of.[20] Dulles returned to the United States, defeated. But decades later, he had another opportunity to reshape international affairs in the aftermath of a second world war. Scholars have contrasted the United States' ideological and political positions after each world war. Most important is the observation that Wilson's world order did not rest on U.S. global supremacy whereas the Cold

---

[18] For a longer historical discussion, see Khalidi, *Sowing Crisis*, 159–200.

[19] Erez Manela, *The Wilsonian Moment: Self-Determination and the International Origins of Anticolonial Nationalism* (New York: Oxford University Press, 2007). Arguably, the most thorough account of the "Wilsonian Moment" in the Levant is Elizabeth F. Thompson's *How the West Stole Democracy from the Arabs: The Syrian Arab Congress of 1920 and the Destruction of Its Historic Liberal-Islamic Alliance* (New York: Atlantic Monthly Press, 2020).

[20] Letter from Allen Dulles to John Foster Dulles, Aug. 29, 1919; and undated and unsigned letter [presumably written by JF Dulles in June or July 1919] both in *DP*, Box 2, Reel 1, pp. 173 and 317–322, respectively.

War liberal order did.[21] Even so, in both instances, American foreign policymakers discounted binding international laws in favor of largely toothless forums for international politics and sought to enforce global order by cultivating regional alliances.

World War I saw the proliferation of internationally-minded thinkers, activists, and politicians in the United States. One of the most prominent visions of American internationalism came from the League to Enforce Peace (LEP). The LEP was led by some of Wilson's most prominent political rivals, including former presidents Theodore Roosevelt and William Howard Taft, both of whom he had defeated in the 1912 presidential election. These conservative internationalists believed that war could be avoided by creating a system of arbitration between states guided by enforceable international laws.[22] Although interstate arbitration, in principle, was incorporated into the League of Nations Covenant, there were no explicit or automatic enforcement mechanisms.[23] As Stephen Wertheim explained, Wilson opposed the "legalist-sanctionist" approach because he believed that problems would be better solved through parliamentary politics and moral opprobrium.[24]

The other, albeit less-discussed, pillar of Wilson's world order was regional security alliances and, if those failed, military intervention in the Global South. The President first floated regional alliances at the Second Pan-American Scientific Conference in 1915–16 when he proposed the ultimately ill-fated Pan-American Pact designed to formalize the Monroe Doctrine and present American influence in the Western Hemisphere in a less imperialistic light. When the multinational pact failed, Wilson resorted to military force to impose his vision of order on the Western Hemisphere, including a "punitive expedition" in Mexico and a years-long occupation of the Dominican Republic.[25] Although

---

[21] Stephen Wertheim, *Tomorrow, The World: The Birth of U.S. Global Supremacy* (Cambridge, MA: Harvard University Press, 2020), 22–28.

[22] Thomas J. Knock, *Woodrow Wilson and the Quest for a New World Order* (Princeton, NJ: Princeton University Press, 1992), 50–58; Stephen Wertheim, "The League That Wasn't: American Designs for a Legalist-Sanctionist League of Nations and the Intellectual Origins of International Organization, 1914–1920," *Diplomatic History* 35:5 (Nov. 2011), 802–815.

[23] Articles 12–15 are vaguely worded. Even Article 16, which contains the Covenant's strongest language, avoids the kind of automatic sanctions or military action favored by the LEP. "The Covenant of the League of Nations," The United Nations Office at Geneva. www.ungeneva.org/en/library-archives/league-of-nations/covenant (accessed Oct. 24, 2022).

[24] Wertheim, "The League That Wasn't," 802, 816–820, 828–832.

[25] Knock, *To End All Wars*, 70–84; G. Pope Atkins and Larman C. Wilson, *The Dominican Republic and the United States: From Imperialism to Transnationalism* (Atlanta: University of Georgia Press, 1998), 1–5, 35–36, 43–58.

Wilson's intervention in Latin America did not match the scope and scale of British and French colonial rule in the Middle East under the League of Nations Mandates system, it was similarly premised on abrogating the national sovereignty of some countries in the name of regional or global security.

The end of World War II created a second opportunity to reshape a world in turmoil. Delegates from around the world – this time including several countries from the Global South – met to draft the UN Charter in 1945 and, later, the Universal Declaration of Human Rights (UDHR) in 1948. In doing so, world leaders established a new forum for global politics and promulgated an aspirational declaration of principles. However, as with the League of Nations, the UN lacked any meaningful enforcement mechanisms; it was ultimately a moral-political not a legalist-sanctionist approach to international affairs. Dulles approved, provided that the United States played a leading role this time. Others, however, were unsatisfied and began working to craft a legally binding human rights covenant.

These two competing views were on display at a New York City dinner sponsored by the World Council of Churches' Commission of Churches on International Affairs held on April 29, 1949, just ten days after workers broke ground on what would become the permanent UN Headquarters. Among the speakers were John Foster Dulles and Charles Malik. Both men were deeply engaged in foreign affairs. Dulles was then a prominent advisor for Republican officials, including Thomas Dewey who unsuccessfully ran for president in 1948. Malik was Lebanon's ambassador to the UN and played a leading role in drafting the UDHR. In their speeches, Dulles and Malik both focused on the role of religion in foreign policy, stressed the importance of human rights, and suggested that Soviet Communism was incompatible with their notions of world order. But they disagreed about how that order should be upheld.

Malik devoted his speech to defending his ongoing work to draft a binding human rights covenant at Lake Success, New York with the UN Economic and Social Council (UNESC). Deeply influenced by American missionaries in Lebanon and his former professor, Martin Heidegger, Malik believed that the postwar world order had to center the atomized individual above all else. Articulating human rights principles in the UDHR was an important first step, but the "real test" was whether all states would sign a legally binding pledge to respect and defend those principles. "Either there is a common morality about man which can be codified and not only respected but also actually observed under a rule of law, or we are on the verge of chaos," he warned. Acutely aware of his audience, Malik criticized the "hedging and hesitation" of American foreign policymakers who were unwilling to adopt a binding human rights covenant and help lead a genuinely rules-based world order.[26]

Dulles was the last speaker of the evening. Without referencing Malik or the work of the UNESC, he argued that the only real power the UN possessed (or should possess) was moral authority. The UN's effectiveness depended, he said, "on a public opinion that pays attention to its debates and comes to a verdict of 'right' or 'wrong.'" He dismissed proposals to amend or replace the UN Charter with something more forceful. International principles, norms, and laws would have to be "mostly self-enforcing," he claimed, so he implored churches around the world to help build a moral consensus on human rights and proper state behavior. He also teased a Manichean struggle by pitting his "religious view" of human nature against that of the atheistic Soviet Union.[27] That struggle, however, would unfold without any binding rules or laws.

Ultimately, the Human Rights Covenant languished and Dulles's Cold War liberal order prevailed. After unsuccessfully pressing his case to other influential Americans – including one of his counterparts on the UN Human Rights Commission, Eleanor Roosevelt – Malik eventually gave up on the prospects of a binding human rights covenant.[28] Instead, as we will see, he came to embrace western intervention in the Middle East as the only way to combat what he perceived to be the threats of Soviet Communism and Arab nationalism in the region.[29]

In the absence of binding international laws or covenants, Dulles inherited and relied on regional security pacts – a strategy some historians have dubbed "pactomania."[30] The most prominent Middle East alliance during the Eisenhower administration was the Baghdad Pact (1955–58),

---

[26] Charles Malik, "The Spiritual Implications of the Human Rights Covenant," Christian Responsibility in World Affairs: A Symposium, Apr. 29, 1949, New York, NY, in Charles Habib Malik Papers, Manuscript Division, Library of Congress, Washington, DC, box 193, folder 1.

[27] John Foster Dulles, "The Churches and the United Nations," Christian Responsibility in World Affairs: A Symposium, Apr. 29, 1949, New York, NY, in *DP* Box 297.

[28] "The Covenant: Its Scope and Ratification Strategy on Today with Mrs. Roosevelt, 14 May 1950," in Eleanor Roosevelt, *The Eleanor Roosevelt Papers, Vol. 2: The Human Rights Years, 1949–1952*, ed., Allida Black (Charlottesville: University of Virginia Press, 2012), document 104.

[29] Joshua Donovan, "Imagining Antioch: Sectarianism, Nationalism, and Migration in the Greek Orthodox Levant, 1860–1958," (PhD diss., Columbia University, 2022, 245–288); and Nathaniel George, "'Survival in an Age of Revolution'": Charles Malik, Philo-Colonialism, and Global Counterrevolution," *The American Historical Review* 130:2 (June 2025), 600–637.

[30] John Lewis Gaddis, "The Cold War: Some Lessons for Policymakers," *Naval War College Review* 27:3 (Nov.–Dec. 1974), 5.

which was comprised of the United Kingdom, Iraq, Pakistan, Iran, and Turkey.[31] The Pact owed its existence, in large part, to western-backed leaders such as Iraq's King Faysal II, effectively a vassal of the British Empire, and Iran's Shah Mohammad Reza Pahlavi, who exerted near complete control of his country after the Anglo-American coup orchestrated during Dulles's first year in office (with the Secretary's enthusiastic support).[32] Most Arab states, including some with pro-western monarchs such as Jordan's King Hussein, declined to join because the arrangements were deeply unpopular in the region. In these cases, the U.S. pursued informal security arrangements.[33]

Western-led security pacts did not aim to promote human rights or enforce international laws. They were merely a way for western governments to project their vision of order and stability onto the region. Such arrangements imposed a bipolar understanding of the world onto the Middle East that operated both on a global level (the United States versus the Soviet Union) and a regional level (pro-western monarchies versus revolutionary nationalist movements).[34] Ironically, the repressive, antidemocratic politics required to sustain the pacts provoked convulsive explosions of popular protest that damaged western interests in the region. For example, the Baghdad Pact crumbled in 1958 after leftist army officer 'Abd al-Karim Qasim violently deposed King Faysal II; its successor, the Central Treaty Organization (CENTO), met a similarly ignominious end after Iran's Shah was overthrown in 1979.

While formal regional security alliances were important to Dulles, he sensed that they might have their limitations early on in his tenure. During his May 1953 tour of the region, for example, he came to feel that Egypt as a whole was too unstable to rely on as a security partner. Thus, when he returned to Washington, Dulles persuaded Eisenhower to scrap plans for a Truman-era defense pact called the Middle East

---

[31] Behcet Kemal Yesilbursa, *The Baghdad Pact: Anglo-American Defense Policies in the Middle East, 1950–59* (London: Routledge, 2004); Kevin Ruane, "Seato, Medo, and the Baghdad Pact: Anthony Eden, British Foreign Policy and the Collective Defense of Southeast Asia and the Middle East, 1952–1955," *Diplomacy and Statecraft* 16:1 (Mar. 2005), 169–199.

[32] See Ervand Abrahamian, *The Coup: 1953, the CIA, and the Roots of Modern U.S. Iranian Relations* (New York: The New Press, 2013); and David S. Painter and Gregory Brew, The *Struggle for Iran: Oil, Autocracy, and the Cold War, 1951–1954* (Chapel Hill: The University of North Carolina Press, 2022).

[33] Joseph A. Massad, *Colonial Effects: The Making of National Identity in Jordan* (New York: Columbia University Press, 2001), 184–185; Betty S. Anderson, *Nationalist Voices in Jordan: The Street and the State* (Austin: University of Texas Press, 2005), 157–169. Saudi Arabia's King Saud refused to join because he did not want to partner with Hashemite King Faysal.

[34] Malcolm H. Kerr, *The Arab Cold War: Gamal 'Abd al-Nasir and His Rivals, 1958–1970*, 3rd ed. (Oxford: Oxford University Press, 1971); Khalidi, *Sowing Crisis*, 101–158.

Defense Organization (MEDO), which would have included Egypt. Betraying his own analytical blind spots, Dulles complained about "the complete preoccupation of [most] Arab states with their own local problems" and their refusal to view the world in terms of the U.S.–Soviet rivalry.[35] As the decade wore on, the Secretary eschewed formal pacts, preferring informal bilateral support for friendly countries and various forms of intervention in less-friendly countries.[36]

If the entire Middle East could not be subsumed into a formal security alliance, how else could the United States project its power onto the region? Under Truman, the U.S. offered funding for development projects to pro-western governments through the Point IV aid program. In many ways, this approach was a precursor to the modernization theory, which was premised on promoting order through economic development in the Global South.[37] However, despite previously serving on the board of the Rockefeller Foundation – a prominent NGO that doled out millions in aid for development projects around the globe – Dulles felt that distributing aid was not enough to counter the threat of Soviet Communism in the Global South.

Instead, Dulles turned to dictators and covert operations. While debriefing Eisenhower and the rest of the National Security Council on his trip to the Middle East in June 1953, Dulles lavished praise on Syria's military dictator, Adib Shishakli (r. 1949–54) – an "impressive figure" and "a man of much broader vision and deeper understanding of the relation of his country to world problems" than other leaders in the region. Where dictators did not exist, they could be produced. In Iran, for example, Dulles lamented the leftist (though not communist) leadership of Prime Minister Mosaddegh and insisted that the administration act immediately to change the country's internal politics.[38] Two months later, Mossadegh was deposed in a coup orchestrated by the CIA and Britain's MI6, which greatly enhanced the autocratic powers of the Shah[39]

---

[35] "Memorandum of Discussion at the 147th Meeting of the National Security Council, Monday, June 1, 1953," *FRUS 1952–54, The Near and Middle East*, Vol. IX, Part 1, United States Department of State (Washington, DC: US GPO, 1986), document 137.

[36] Salim Yaqub, *Containing Arab Nationalism: The Eisenhower Doctrine and the Middle East* (Chapel Hill: University of North Carolina Press, 2004), 74–80.

[37] "The Point Four Program," *Department of State*, Publication 3347 (Washington, DC: US Government Printing Office, 1949); Jacob Shively, "'Good Deeds Aren't Enough': Point Four in Iran, 1949–1953," *Diplomacy & Statecraft* 29:3 (2018), 413–431. On development more broadly, see Nathan J. Citino, *Envisioning the Arab Future: Modernization in US-Arab Relations, 1945–1967* (Cambridge: Cambridge University Press, 2017).

[38] "Memorandum of Discussion at the 147th Meeting."

[39] Abrahamian, *The Coup*.

Dulles's appetite for covert operations presupposed a world order where national sovereignty was porous. As early as 1939, Dulles argued that "the sovereignty system violates fundamental political principles ..." and was ultimately responsible for the outbreak of the war.[40] He was hardly alone in this. A system of binding international laws, arbitration, or human rights covenants would theoretically require states to comply with decisions that may conflict with decisions they made as sovereign nations. But because Cold War liberalism rejected a rules-based world order, decisions of whether to violate national sovereignty in the Global South turned not on universally applicable legal principles but on American perceptions of threats to the global order and the preponderance of American power – "emergencies," in which ends almost always justified means.

The Anti-imperial Empire

Although the paradigm of the United States as a liberal empire offers important insights for the Cold War era, it is crucial to understand that Cold War liberals saw themselves as making a decisive, historic break from empire – at least as it operated in the nineteenth and early twentieth centuries. Wilson, again, was an important antecedent. To be sure, Wilson did almost nothing to undo imperialist endeavors undertaken by the United States since the McKinley administration. Like his predecessors, Wilson maintained colonial control over the Philippines, Guam, and Puerto Rico. He also invaded Cuba, Mexico, and the Dominican Republic. However, many of Wilson's progressive allies, including social reformers such as Jane Addams and Lillian Wald, and populists such as William Jennings Bryan opposed European *and* American imperialism.[41] Rhetorically, at least, they rubbed off on Wilson.

Wilson channeled the progressive, anti-imperialist ethos repeatedly while in office. Perhaps most famous was the fifth of his fourteen points, which called for "a free, open-minded and absolutely impartial adjustment of all colonial claims" that kept in mind the interests of colonized peoples.[42] He even invoked anti-imperialist principles to justify America's continued involvement in World War I. In a Baltimore address on April 6, 1918, Wilson condemned Germany as "an empire of force" that sought "an empire of gain and commercial supremacy ..." Germany's rapacious

---

[40] John Foster Dulles, "The Church's Contribution toward a Warless World," *Bushnell Memorial Hall Sessions*, Hartford, CT. Oct. 11, 1939, *DP*, Box 289.

[41] Thomas J. Knock, *To End All Wars: Woodrow Wilson and the Quest for a New World Order* (Princeton: Princeton University Press, 1992), 15–30, 48–69.

[42] *The Bases of Durable Peace as Voiced by President Wilson* (Chicago: The Union League Club of Chicago, 1918), 15.

imperial designs left the United States with no choice but to respond with force, Wilson argued.[43] The fate of the world depended on it.

Arguably even more so than Wilson, Dulles opposed formal systems of empire – a position that meshed well with the Global South's anti-imperialist *zeitgeist* after World War II. As chairman of the Federal Council of Churches' Commission for a Just and Durable Peace, Dulles argued in favor of self-determination for colonized peoples even before the end of the war. The Commission called for "autonomy for subject peoples" and for an "international organization to assure and to supervise the realization of that end."[44]

Dulles should not be mistaken for an anti-imperial crusader: He supported the League of Nations Mandate system as it trampled over the self-determination of millions and expanded the British and French empires to their peaks during the interwar period. Even with the benefit of hindsight, Dulles accepted the dubious proposition that, in his words, under the Mandate system, "colonial control was not an opportunity for selfish national exploitation, but a 'sacred trust' to be administered first to advance the well-being of the native inhabitants, and secondly to insure, to others, economic access on terms of equality." The problem with the Mandate system, Dulles suggested, was in its execution: in practice, the system had come to resemble older forms of colonialism.[45]

In a 1946 article for *LIFE* magazine, Dulles conceded that racism was a by-product of British and American imperialism.[46] But in actuality, his opposition to formal empire was more about global order than altruism. With the Commission for a Just and Durable Peace, Dulles warned that there was a "ferment" among many colonized peoples. A lasting peace would be "unattainable unless such peoples are satisfied that they can achieve self-rule without passive or active resistance to the now constituted authorities."[47] In other words, colonialism created intolerable conditions that could (and sometimes did) erupt into destabilizing and unpredictable revolutions.

---

[43] Ibid., 22, 28–30.
[44] Federal Council of Churches in America, "A Just and Durable Peace: Statement of Political Propositions" (New York, 1943), 9. A copy can be found in *DP*, Box 283. For broader context, see Anthony Clark Arend, *Pursuing a Just and Durable Peace: John Foster Dulles and International Organization* (New York: Greenwood Press, 1988).
[45] Dulles, "The United States and the World of Nations," 4–5. Dulles was ambivalent about the UN Trusteeship system, which succeeded the League's Permanent Commission on Mandates. See "Statement of John Foster Dulles to the plenary meeting of the Federal Council," undated, *DP*, Box 29.
[46] John Foster Dulles, "Thoughts on Soviet Policy and What to Do about It," *LIFE*, June 3 and 10, 1946, 17.
[47] Federal Council of Churches, "A Just and Durable Peace," 9.

As Cold War battlelines began to crystallize, Dulles also realized that anti-imperialist rhetoric could be deployed against geopolitical foes, just as Wilson had demonstrated in his denunciations of Germany. In a 1951 speech to the Advertising Council in Detroit, Dulles framed Soviet foreign policy as explicitly imperialist. After painting a picture of an insatiable Soviet Union that sought to dominate Europe, Africa, the Middle East, East Asia, and possibly even the Americas, he told his audience that "Russian imperialism can be stopped" and that "evil is never irresistible."[48]

Dulles's anti-imperialism involved more than rhetorical flourishes, particularly as Middle Eastern leaders realized they could leverage the omnipresent "emergency" of Communist penetration into the Middle East to press for greater decolonization. This was most vividly on display in Egypt when Dulles met with leaders of the Free Officers movement in Cairo during his May 1953 tour. Egyptian Minister for Foreign Affairs, Mahmoud Fawzi complained to his American counterpart about the continued presence of British troops in Egypt, particularly in the Suez. Having just deposed Egyptian King Farouk, who had long been seen as a patsy for British imperial interests, Fawzi demanded that all British troops leave the country and that any foreign engineers who remained be placed under Egypt's jurisdiction.[49]

Minister Fawzi and Egyptian President Muhammad Naguib astutely played to Dulles's anti-imperialism and Cold War liberalism. Acceding to the preponderance of American power, Fawzi told Dulles that he "would like to see the US measure up to its role of leadership" in the world.[50] He also warned the Secretary that Britain's refusal to evacuate from Egypt could affect Egypt's neutrality. "Perhaps we are not Communists now. We do not want to be, but this situation might change ..."[51] Naguib agreed, noting that he was "aware of the many anti-Communist measures undertaken by the US but ... that many people feel that delay in solving the problems in the Middle East is one of the best ways to make Communists."[52]

---

[48] John Foster Dulles, *"Can We Stop Russian Imperialism?"* Advertising Council, Nov. 27, 1951, Detroit, Michigan, *DP*, Box 305.

[49] "Statement by the Honorable John Foster Dulles, Secretary of State, at a Press Conference Held at the United Nations Headquarters: Trip to the Near East and South Asia," Press Release No. 1652, Mar. 9, 1953, and "Schedule: Monday, May 11," in *DP* Box 71, Reel 26; "*Dalās Yughādir Nīyū Yūrk ʿila al-Qāhira fī Riḥla ʿila al-Sharq al-Awsaṭ Tastaghriq ʿAshrīn Yawmān*" ["Dulles Departs from New York to Cairo for a Twenty-Day Trip to the Middle East"] *Al-Ahrām*, May 11, 1953, 6.

[50] "Memorandum of Conversation, Prepared in the Embassy in Cairo," May 11, 1953, *FRUS*: 1952–1954, Vol IX, The Near and Middle East, part 1, document 3, p. 6.

[51] Ibid., 5.

[52] Ibid., 6–7.

Dulles told Egypt's leaders that "the US is not ashamed of its close ties of alliance with the UK" but quickly added that "the US does not automatically accept British policy." He reiterated his long-standing anti-colonial views and promised that "the United States does not believe in colonialism." Dulles told Naguib that the Eisenhower administrated agreed that "British troops must be evacuated and Egyptian sovereignty must be restored ..." and reiterated this position upon returning to the United States in a public news broadcast.[53] Dulles remained consistent in a meeting of the National Security Council, reporting that "the United States suffered from being linked with British and French Imperialism."[54] Facing financial and diplomatic pressure, British troops left the Suez the following year.

The most famous display of American anti-imperialism during Dulles's tenure was during the Suez Crisis, when Britain, France, and Israel invaded Egypt on October 29, 1956. The invasion, which American officials had no prior knowledge of, was primarily in response to Egyptian President Gamal Abdel Nasser nationalizing the Suez Canal after failing to receive American financing to build a dam at Aswan. Despite souring relations with Nasser, Eisenhower publicly rebuked his allies and shepherded a resolution through the UN General Assembly demanding a ceasefire and a withdrawal of Israeli troops from Egypt. They complied shortly after.[55]

The American position in Suez is best explained by the anti-imperialist imperialism of Cold War liberalism. Dulles was not wholly unsympathetic to Nasser's pursuit of economic development after decades of British colonialism. In fact, he reportedly supported Nasser's Aswan Dam loan request before realizing that it would be politically impossible to secure Congressional support. Drawing on his experience as an international lawyer, Dulles also spearheaded efforts to negotiate an agreement for shared use of the Suez Canal that he felt would balance Egyptian national sovereignty with the demands of global interdependence. The overt military operation was clumsy and threatened to push Nasser further into the Soviet sphere. Unbeknownst to the American public, it also interrupted a delicate CIA operation to overthrow Syria's

---

[53] "Memorandum of Conversation, Prepared in the Embassy in Cairo," May 11, 1953, document 4, pp. 14–15; "Dulles reports on 12 Nation Visit, 195[3]," Footage Farm 221628-10. https://footagefarm.com/reel-details/cold-war/generic/dulles-reports-on-12-nation-visit-195#/ (accessed Oct. 22, 2022).

[54] "Memorandum of Discussion at the 147th Meeting," 383.

[55] Yaqub, Containing Arab Nationalism, 51–55. For fuller accounts, see Herman Finer, *Dulles over Suez: The Theory and Practice of His Diplomacy* (Chicago: Quadrangle Books, 1964) and David A. Nichols, *Eisenhower 1956: The President's Year of Crisis – Suez and the Brink of War* (New York: Simon & Schuster, 2011).

left-leaning government.⁵⁶ Finally, the invasion of Egypt overlapped with a similar Soviet campaign to crush dissidents in Hungary, making it hard for the U.S. to lob credible charges of "imperialism" at the Soviet Union.⁵⁷ In short, the tripartite invasion of Egypt by Israel, France, and the UK too closely resembled an old-school imperialism that did not align with Cold War liberalism.

Safe for Democracy?

For both Wilson and Dulles, opposition to formal expressions of imperialism did not translate into support for genuine democracy and self-determination in the rapidly decolonizing Global South. Embedded within this paradox is the final pillar of Cold War liberalism in the Middle East: a perennial distrust of the masses. With little awareness of the political or intellectual currents in the Middle East, American foreign policymakers felt that peoples in the Middle East were ill-equipped to govern themselves.⁵⁸ Rather than encouraging the organic development of postcolonial public and political spheres in the region, the United States repeatedly undermined fragile parliamentary democracies through covert action. Dulles and others discounted popular sovereignty in the Middle East with paternalistic rhetoric about Middle Eastern peoples whose aspirations and perspectives were often seen as out-of-step with American conceptions of global order.

Initially, greater U.S. involvement in the Middle East seemed to portend greater respect for self-determination and the fledgling democracies emerging in Egypt and the Levant after the fall of the Ottoman Empire. To ascertain how people in the region felt about self-governance, colonial "tutelage," and Zionist settlers, Wilson appointed Oberlin College Professor Henry King and prominent Democratic Party donor Charles Crane to oversee the Inter-Allied Commission on Mandates in Turkey – or the "King-Crane Commission."⁵⁹ For several weeks, the group travelled through present-day Syria, Lebanon, Palestine, Israel, Jordan, and southeastern Turkey and met with hundreds of delegations, including religious leaders, businessmen, democratically elected

---

⁵⁶ Eveland, *Ropes of Sand*, 206–230.
⁵⁷ This is the primary justification offered by the State Department. See "The Suez Crisis, 1956," *Office of the Historian, United States Department of State*, https://history.state.gov/milestones/1953-1960/suez (accessed Aug. 10, 2022).
⁵⁸ See Elizabeth Thompson's aptly named, *How the West Stole Democracy from the Arabs*, for example.
⁵⁹ For detailed overviews of the Commission's work, see Harry N. Howard, *The King-Crane Commission: An American Inquiry in the Middle East* (Beirut, 1963); and Andrew Patrick, *America's Forgotten Middle East Initiative* (London: I.B. Tauris, 2015).

officials, representatives from women's groups, other prominent members of society, Syria's would-be-king Faysal (a Hashemite Emir), and Faysal's entourage.[60] They also collected nearly 2,000 petitions with scores of signatures from people hopeful that they would have a say in their region's future.[61]

Ultimately, Wilson suppressed the publication of the King-Crane Commission's report and negotiators at Versailles ignored its contents. Instead, they partitioned the region into "Mandates," which were then placed under the control of Britain and France. Less often appreciated is that Wilson and his Secretary of State, Robert Lansing, both harbored racist views about Arabs, which shaped their views on colonial governance in the Middle East. For example, Lansing argued that Wilsonian self-determination did not apply to "races, peoples, or communities whose state of barbarism or ignorance deprive them of the capacity to choose intelligently their political affiliations," such as "the Mohammedans of Syria and Palestine." To do otherwise, he argued, would only "breed discontent, disorder, and rebellion."[62]

Concerns about order also shaped Wilson's views on Zionism and Palestine. Proponents of Zionism, including Arthur Balfour and Edward House, ironically relied on anti-Semitic fears to persuade Wilson to support Jewish migration to Palestine. Balfour claimed that "nearly all Bolshevism and disorder of that sort is directly traceable to Jews," leading House to suggest "putting them, or the best of them, in Palestine, and holding them responsible for the orderly behavior of Jews throughout the world."[63] Wilson agreed, over the objections of his former Ambassador to the Ottoman Empire and the vast majority of the region's inhabitants.[64]

---

[60] Records of schedules, meetings, and some petitions can be found online in the King-Crane Commission Digital Collection of the Oberlin College Archives at: www2.oberlin.edu/library/digital/king-crane/ (accessed Aug. 2, 2022). Especially useful is the "Transcript of Albert Lybyer's Diary, March to September 1919," in Albert H. Lybyer Papers, 1876–1949, Record Series 15/13/22, Box 16: King-Crane Commission (May–Aug. 1919), University Archives, The University of Illinois Urbana-Champaign. For a firsthand Syrian account, see Yusuf al-Hakim, *Sūriyya wa al-ʿAhd al-Fayṣalī [Syria and the Faysal Era]* (Beirut: al-Maṭbaʿa al-Kāthūlīkīyya, 1966), 98–104.

[61] James Gelvin, "The Ironic Legacy of the King-Crane Commission," in David W. Lesch and Mark L. Haas, *The Middle East and the United States: History, Politics, and Ideologies*, 6th ed. (New York: Routledge, 2018), 30–46. Petitions are summarized in the published report: "First Publication of King-Crane Report on the Near East: A Suppressed Official Document of the United States Government," *Editor & Publisher*, Dec. 2, 1922.

[62] Robert Lansing, *The Peace Negotiations: A Personal Narrative* (New York: Houghton Mifflin Company, 1921), 97, 102.

[63] Arthur Walworth, *Wilson and His Peacemakers: American Diplomacy at the Paris Peace Conference, 1919* (New York: W.W. Norton & Company, 1986), 478.

[64] Morgenthau, himself, was Jewish and served as ambassador from 1913 to 1916. His fullest critique of Zionism was published as an addendum to an issue of *The World's Work*

Wilson's solution for all of this was borrowed from his own approach to the Philippines and the French protectorate in Morocco, which received his blessing in 1917. That is, he believed that with "proper guidance," nonwhite races could become "civilized."[65] This logic undergirded the League of Nations Mandates system, which kept Syria, Lebanon, Transjordan, Palestine, and Iraq under European control, along with several other countries in Africa and the Pacific.[66] At the heart of these concerns about self-determination in the Middle East was a preoccupation with global order and, in the final analysis, a distrust of non-white peoples including Arabs, Latin Americans, Asians, and even Eastern European Jews to fit within that order.

When Dulles became Secretary of State, the Mandates system in the Middle East had ended, but unease about unbridled popular sovereignty in the region remained a keystone of U.S. foreign policy. As discussed previously, Dulles was skeptical of national sovereignty as a general principle. He recognized that highly industrialized nations coveted their sovereignty and would only surrender it in limited circumstances. Colonized and newly decolonized countries, however, were a different story: Dulles envisioned a two-tiered system of national sovereignty. Even before the end of World War II ended imperial control in most of the Middle East, Dulles argued that "when emancipation occurs, it should be on terms which will preclude reversion to the outmoded features of the present sovereignty system."[67] Decolonization, in other words, would have to remain incomplete; sovereignty for newly independent Middle Eastern countries would not be as inviolable as the sovereignty of great powers.

We have already seen that Dulles's contempt for national sovereignty justified, in his mind, a covert operation in 1953 to oust Iran's democratically elected Prime Minister, Mohammad Mosaddegh. He also worked to overthrow or undermine Middle Eastern governments that sought to chart a course of "positive neutrality" vis-à-vis the United States and the Soviet Union. Even if they were not overtly aligned with

---

in 1921 and reprinted in *The New York Times*, although his opposition was long known. See Henry Morgenthau, "Zionism a Surrender, Not a Solution," *The World's Work*, Vol. XLII (May–Oct. 1921), i–viii.

[65] Erez Manela, *The Wilsonian Moment*, 26–30; "Morocco: United States capitulatory rights in Morocco – French and Spanish protectorates in Morocco," in Papers relating to the Foreign Relations of the United States with the address of the President to Congress December 4, 1917, *United States Department of State* (Washington, DC: US GPO, 1926), 1093.

[66] Susan Pedersen, *The Guardians: The League of Nations and the Crisis of Empire* (Oxford: Oxford University Press, 2015), 1–3, 23–32. Pedersen explains that the idea of imperial "tutelage" also a long history in British politics.

[67] Dulles, "The United States and the World of Nations," 11.

the Soviet Union, Dulles believed that revolutionary nationalist governments were incapable of resisting Communist infiltration and thus constituted a threat to global order. If formal imperialism had ended, western "tutelage" had not.

Dulles's approach to Syria is particularly instructive. In 1949, the CIA helped organize its first coup in the region, toppling a democratically elected government in Syria. Five years later, during Dulles's tenure, Syria's U.S.-backed military dictator was deposed and democracy was restored. However, shortly after the Arab Socialist Ba'th Party's strong show of support in Syria's 1954 Parliamentary elections, Dulles sent a frantic cable to the American embassy in Syria, telling Ambassador James Moose that he had been warned by pro-western statesmen from the Middle East (including Charles Malik) that the Ba'th Party would likely win a plurality of seats in Parliament.[68] In his reply, Ambassador Moose incorrectly claimed that the Ba'th was "communist-infiltrated" and closely aligned with a Kremlin-directed Communist Party.[69] Dulles and Moose agreed that something had to be done.

In reality, the Ba'th Party's cofounder, Michel 'Aflaq, took great pains to differentiate his revolutionary socialist party from Soviet communism. As early as 1936, 'Aflaq clarified: "If I was asked to define socialism, I would not seek its definition in the books of Marx and Lenin, but I would answer: It is a religion of life ... opening the door of employment for everyone, and allowing all the gifts and virtues of humans to blossom and launch and be used."[70] 'Aflaq also expressed a deep concern over Soviet imperialism, specifically, citing Tito's Yugoslavia as an example of the Soviet Union seeking to subordinate a nation's will to the directives of Moscow.[71] To be sure, part of the disconnect between Dulles's understanding and

---

[68] "Telegram from the Department of State to the Embassy in Syria," in *FRUS*, 1955–1957, Near East: Jordan-Yemen, Vol. XIII, United States Department of State (Washington, D.C.: Government Printing Office, 1988), document 296.

[69] "Telegram from the Embassy in Syria to the Department of State," in *FRUS*, 1955–1957, Near East: Jordan-Yemen, Vol. XIII, document 297. Not only does the Ambassador's claim ignore the number of stark ideological differences that kept the Ba'th from close cooperation with the Syrian Communist Party, but it also incorrectly implies that Akram al-Ḥawrānī was the primary leader of the Party. While he was a member of the Party's Executive Committee, the distinction of leader more appropriately belongs to co-founders 'Aflaq (who was the Party's Secretary-General until 1966) or Salāḥ al-Dīn al-Bīṭār.

[70] Michel 'Aflaq, "*Thawrat al-Ḥīyā*" [The Revolution of Life] in *Fī Sabīl al-Ba'th* [*The Way of Resurrection*] ed., Sa'dūn Hamacī (Beirut: *Dār al-Ṭalī'a*, 1959), 22. Unless otherwise noted, all translations from Arabic are mine.

[71] Michel 'Aflaq, "*Bayna Ishtirākītina wa al-Shīyū'iyya wa al-Ishtirākīyya al-Wataniyya*" [Between Our Socialism, Communism, and National Socialism] in *Fī Sabīl al-Ba'th*, 96–97.

the reality of the Ba'th Party represented an intelligence failure. But equally to blame was Dulles's paternalistic epistemology that could not countenance peoples in a newly-independent Arab country being capable of developing an ideology both independent of the West *and* Soviet Communism.

Shortly after the above exchange between Secretary Dulles and Ambassador Moose, the CIA began work on a series of unsuccessful attempts to overthrow the democratically-elected government of Shukri al-Quwatli, which had managed to restore Syria's fragile democracy after four years of military dictatorship. While these covert operations are still shrouded in some degree of mystery, evidence has shown that the United States pursued a broad effort to undermine leftist actors in Syria, planned ultimately unsuccessful attempts to overthrow Quwatli's government in 1956 and 1957, and conspired with British officials to assassinate Syrian politicians.[72] As mentioned earlier, a lesser-known reason that the Eisenhower administration sided with Nasser over Suez was because the 1956 invasion of Egypt disrupted efforts of a CIA asset named Mikhail Ilyan to foment a conservative coup in Syria with CIA funding. Ilyan reportedly told his handler, Wilbur Eveland, that no "amount of money can help us unless you can restrain your allies."[73] Although the coup attempts were ultimately unsuccessful, they severely damaged U.S.–Syrian relations and undermined democracy in Syria in the long term.[74]

One of the most formal expressions of Dulles's Cold War Liberalism in the Middle East was the so-called Eisenhower Doctrine. Drafted largely by Dulles and announced in a special 1957 presidential address to Congress, the Doctrine promised American economic or military assistance to any country in the Middle East that felt threatened by "international communism." Importantly, it allowed for the illusion of respecting sovereignty – assistance had to be requested – and preemptively framed any intervention by the United States as strictly

---

[72] Anthony Gorst and W. Scott Lucas, "The Other Collusion: Operation Straggle and the Anglo-American Intervention in Syria, 1955–56," *Intelligence and National Security* 4:3 (1989), 179–93; Douglas Little, "Cold War and Covert Action: The United States and Syria, 1945–1958," *Middle East Journal* 44:1 (Winter, 1990), 51–75; Matthew Jones, "The 'Preferred Plan': The Anglo-American Working Group Report on Covert Action in Syria, 1957," *Intelligence and National Security* 19:3 (Autumn 2004), 401–415; Eveland, *Ropes of Sand*, 206–230.

[73] Eveland, *Ropes of Sand*, 207.

[74] David W. Lesch, *Syria and the United States: Eisenhower's Cold War in the Middle East* (Boulder, CO: Westview Press, 1992); Sami Moubayed, *Syria and the USA: Washington's Relations with Damascus from Wilson to Eisenhower* (New York: I.B. Tauris & Co. Ltd. 2012).

defensive. At the same time, the Doctrine offered wide latitude for the United States to meddle in the internal affairs of other countries by not clearly defining what constituted a Communist threat.[75]

The Eisenhower Doctrine proved controversial in the Middle East. Many balked at the idea of western meddling; others, however, embraced it. Having given up on the prospect of a rules-based world order, Charles Malik, for example, actively courted American intervention in Lebanon. Like Dulles, Malik too believed that national sovereignty should be porous – if not for the sake of a binding human rights covenant, then at least for U.S. meddling. First, Malik worked with the Dulles brothers and American operatives to orchestrate a pro-western majority in the 1957 Lebanese Parliamentary elections and ensure that a pliant president would be elected in 1958. As part of the election-rigging operation, CIA operative Wilbur Eveland recalled delivering briefcases of Lebanese pounds to the Presidential Palace and returning to the U.S. embassy each night with an empty case to be replenished throughout the election. Malik, himself, relied on such funds to oust an incumbent and win a seat in Parliament.[76]

The U.S. did not interfere in Lebanon's elections because of an imminent Communist takeover – there was none. Rather, it did so because Cold War liberals believed that Lebanese President Camille Chamoun's Arab nationalist opponents were incapable of governing Lebanon and that the Lebanese public could not be trusted with choosing their own leaders. The United States followed up its election meddling with millions of dollars in military aid as tensions between opposition and government groups escalated. At the UN, Malik swept aside local factors driving the escalating political crisis and reduced the conflict to little more than a proxy war between the West and the Soviet Union.

Dulles similarly misrepresented the situation publicly, including to members of Congress, exaggerating the threat posed to Lebanon by the newly constituted United Arab Republic and claiming a close connection between regional power brokers such as Nasser and the Soviet Union despite CIA assessments to the contrary. Finally, the U.S. famously deployed marines to Beirut in 1958 after Chamoun attempted to unconstitutional extend his presidency another term, backing down only when it became clear that his government could no longer be

---

[75] Dwight D. Eisenhower, "Address of the President of the United States Delivered before a Joint Session of the Two Houses of Congress Relative to the Middle East Situation," Committee on Foreign Affairs, House, Jan. 5, 1957, 85th Cong., 1st Sess. H.doc.46. ProQuest Congressional.

[76] Eveland, *Ropes of Sand*, 248–253.

propped up.⁷⁷ The episode exemplified disdain for democratic governance – a hallmark of Cold War liberalism.

After Dulles: The Persistence of Cold War Liberalism in the Middle East

On November 17, 1962, President Kennedy officially dedicated a new international airport in Chantilly, Virginia to the late John Foster Dulles, despite belonging to a different political party. A few months later, the Kennedy administration celebrated a violent coup in Iraq that toppled 'Abd al-Karim Qasim's leftist government and brought the Ba'th Party to power.⁷⁸ Although the CIA's involvement in the coup itself remains a matter of some debate among historians, declassified documents show that Kennedy quickly moved to supply the Party with clandestine military, financial, and logistical support, which it then used to launch brutal attacks against the Kurdish Democratic Party and leftist intellectuals in Iraq.⁷⁹

The Ba'th Party, which came to power in the aftermath, conducted brutal purges of leftists in Iraqi civil society with the blessing of the Kennedy administration, effectively "finishing off any and all forms of participatory politics in postcolonial society," in the words of historian Samira Haj.⁸⁰ Thus, in different ways, both Kennedy's airport dedication and his Dulles-style approach to Iraq were testaments to the Secretary's outsized and bipartisan influence on U.S. foreign policy. While much has changed since Dulles's tenure as Secretary of State, the three pillars of his Cold War liberalism discussed in this chapter continued to undergird U.S. foreign policy in the Middle East even after Dulles's death in 1959.

Cold War liberalism in the Middle East has even persisted past the end of the Cold War as such. This dismal reality was thrown into sharp relief after October 7, 2023. On that day, Hamas, Palestinian Islamic Jihad, and other militant groups in Gaza killed over 1,100

---

⁷⁷ Irene L. Gendzier, *Notes from the Minefield: United States Intervention in Lebanon and the Middle East, 1945–1958* (Boulder, CO: Westview Press, 1999), 209–212, 224–226, 284–292.

⁷⁸ Kennedy also welcomed a Ba'thist coup in Syria one month after the coup in Iraq, but the US was not as closely connected to the Syrian branch.

⁷⁹ Weldon C. Matthews, "The Kennedy Administration and Arms Transfers to Ba'thist Iraq," *Diplomatic History* 43:3 (2019), 469–492. Brandon Wolfe-Hunnicutt makes a compelling case for CIA collusion in the 1963 in *The Paranoid Style in American Diplomacy* (Stanford: Stanford University Press, 2021), 110–121.

⁸⁰ Samira Haj, *The Making of Iraq, 1900–1963: Capital, Power, and Ideology* (Albany: State University of New York Press, 1997), 137.

Israel civilians and soldiers, wounded over 3,000 more, and took 250 people hostage. Israel's response was swift and fierce. Israel's Defense Minister, Yoav Gallant, announced a "complete siege on Gaza" in which there would be "no electricity, no food, no water, [and] no fuel." He added that he had "released all the restraints" on Israeli soldiers heading into Gaza. Shortly after, Israeli President Isaac Herzog blurred the lines between civilians and combatants in a public press conference, saying "it's an entire nation out there that's responsible." Meanwhile, Prime Minister Benjamin Netanyahu repeatedly invoked a genocidal Biblical story of the Israelites eradicating the Amalekites in messages to Israeli forces.[81]

Before long, several humanitarian organizations, UN organizations and officials, human rights watchdogs, and scholars raised grave concerns about Israel's conduct in Gaza. Citing the staggering loss of civilian life wrought by Israel's disproportionate use of force, the large-scale destruction of Gaza's civilian infrastructure and agricultural land, repeated episodes of forced displacement, and severe restrictions on the flow of humanitarian aid into Gaza, which precipitated famine-like conditions, many argued that Israel was violating International Humanitarian Law.[82]

In December 2023, South Africa went a step further and filed a case at the International Court of Justice (ICJ) accusing Israel of violating the Genocide Convention of 1948. After a preliminary hearing the following month, the ICJ – then headed by an American judge – issued provisional measures. Without ruling on the merits, the Court expressed horror at the humanitarian crisis in Gaza and held that Palestinians in Gaza had a plausible right "to be protected from acts of genocide." Finding that there was a "real and imminent risk" of that right being violated, the Court ordered Israel to "take all measures within its power" to prevent genocide in Gaza, to "prevent and punish the direct and public incitement to commit genocide," and to "enable the provision of urgently needed basic services and humanitarian assistance to address the adverse conditions of life faced by Palestinians in the Gaza Strip."[83] Implicitly acknowledging that its initial order was

---

[81] Quoted in South Africa's "Application Instituting Proceedings and Request for the Indication of Provisional Measures," to the International Court of Justice, Dec. 29, 2023, pp. 60–61; 1 Samuel 15:1–34.

[82] See inter alia, Human Rights Watch, "World Report 2024: Events of 2023" (New York: Human Rights Watch, 2024), 324–335.

[83] Application of the Convention on the Prevention and Punishment of the Crime of Genocide in the Gaza Strip (South Africa v. Israel), Provisional Measures, Order of January 26, 2024, I.C.J. Reports 2024, pp. 18, 24–25.

not implemented, the ICJ ordered additional measures on March 28 and May 24, 2024.[84]

Despite being a party to the UN Charter and the Genocide Convention of 1948, the United States was unmoved by the ICJ's legally binding orders.[85] While other countries began to rethink their military support for Israel, the Biden administration doubled down with additional weapons transfers.[86] Reviving a Trump-era policy, Biden also suspended aid to the United Nations Relief and Works Administration (UNRWA), which was widely recognized as the largest and most effective humanitarian organization operating in Gaza.[87] It is difficult to square these actions with the ICJ's orders or, for that matter, the basic precepts of international law. Cold War liberalism offers some helpful context.

Over several decades, the approach of U.S. foreign policymakers toward a "rules-based international order" has morphed from skepticism and ambivalence under Dulles to contempt and defiance in the twenty-first century. More precisely, the United States Government supports a "rules-based international order" only insofar as the rules align with its interests. So, for example, the Biden Administration welcomed efforts by International Criminal Court (ICC) Prosecutor, Karim Khan, to investigate and prosecute Vladimir Putin for war crimes committed in Ukraine.[88] The State Department, however, did not welcome Khan's decision to issue arrest warrants for Prime Minister Netanyahu and Defense Minister Gallant (along with three leaders of Hamas) for war crimes in Gaza. Instead, Secretary Blinken denounced the warrants against Israeli officials as "wrong-headed" and, at least

---

[84] Application of the Convention on the Prevention and Punishment of the Crime of Genocide in the Gaza Strip (South Africa v. Israel), Provisional Measures, Orders of March 28, 2024 and May 24, 2024, I.C.J. Reports 2024.

[85] Under Reagan, the US asserted a right to exempt itself from the ICJ's jurisdiction of cases involve claims that the US is committing genocide. However, it is not exempt from its broader obligations to prevent genocide and abide by the Court's orders as applied to other countries. For more, see Sean D. Murphy, "The United States and the International Court of Justice: Coping with Antinomies," in Cesare Romano, ed., *The Sword and the Scales: The United States and International Courts and Tribunals* (New York: Cambridge University Press, 2008), 59–68.

[86] Branko Marcetic, "International Legal Rulings Are Helping Block Arms to Israel," *Jacobin*, Mar. 19, 2024.

[87] "Withholding Funding to UNRWA a "Moral and Strategic Failure," *International Refugee Assistance Project*, Apr. 29, 2024. https://refugeerights.org/news-resources/letter-from-100-refugee-and-human-rights-organizations-to-u-s-government-withholding-funding-to-unrwa-a-moral-and-strategic-failure

[88] Beth Van Schaack, "Statement of the United States at the 22nd Session of the Assembly of States Parties of the International Criminal Court," New York City, New York, Dec. 8, 2023.

initially, even expressed support for Congressional sanctions against the ICC.[89] In January 2025, a bipartisan majority in the U.S. House of Representatives voted to do just that. Trump announced sanctions against the ICC the following month.[90]

Eschewing enforceable human rights laws and norms, the United States still relies primarily on informal regional security alliances to project its power abroad, just as Dulles had done. American diplomats prioritized bilateral treaties between Israel and its Arab neighbors over – and often at the expense of – a just resolution to the Palestinian question.[91] President Trump continued this tradition during his first term through the "Abraham Accords," which normalized diplomatic relations between Israel and the United Arab Emirates, Bahrain, Morocco, and Sudan. The Biden Administration picked up where Trump had left off, pursuing a normalization agreement between Saudi Arabia and Israel. Although Hamas's attack on October 7th temporarily derailed these efforts, normalization remarkably remained a primary objective of Biden's administration, over and above the much-vaunted two-state solution.[92]

Official rhetoric aside, contemporary normalization agreements should not be understood as peace treaties. Countries involved in these efforts have either never declared war on Israel (the UAE, Bahrain, and Sudan) or have not done so since the 1970s (Morocco and Saudi Arabia). Rather, the Abraham Accords and similar efforts buttress a security alliance positioned in opposition to America's geopolitical rivals like Russia and regional foes such as Iran, Hezbollah, and *Ansar Allah* ("Houthis"). This informal security alliance does little to end actual conflict or instability in the region, whether in Sudan, Yemen, Libya, Palestine, or elsewhere. It does, however, undergird American neo-imperialism in a postcolonial world. This informal empire includes other mechanisms

---

[89] "American Diplomacy and Global Leadership: Review of the FY25 State Department Budget Request," 118th Cong. (2024). www.foreign.senate.gov/hearings/american-diplomacy-and-global-leadership-review-of-the-fy25-state-department-budget-request. Ultimately, the Biden Administration decided not to impose sanctions, but maintained its opposition to prosecuting Israeli officials for war crimes.

[90] House Roll Call Vote No. 7, "Illegitimate Court Counteraction Act" (H.R. 23), 119th Cong., 1st sess., January 9, 2025. Office of the Clerk, U.S. House of Representatives;" and Exec. Order. No. 14203. 90 Federal Register, 9369 (Feb. 6, 2025).

[91] Seth Anziska convincingly argues that this approach dates back to the Camp David Accords negotiated by President Carter between Israel and Egypt in 1978–79. See Anziska, *Preventing Palestine: A Political History from Camp David to Oslo* (Princeton: Princeton University Press, 2018), 1–161.

[92] "Remarks by President Biden on the Middle East," May 31, 2024. www.whitehouse.gov/briefing-room/speeches-remarks/2024/05/31/remarks-by-president-biden-on-the-middle-east-2/

that would have been familiar to Dulles, from carefully cultivated, pliable regional clients to economic arrangements favorable to American business interests.

One notable difference is the now expansive "pointillist" U.S. military network based primarily in the Persian Gulf.[93] But if Dulles and other early Cold War liberals had less of an appetite for overt military intervention than some of their twenty-first century counterparts, the justifications that underpin America's vast military footprint in the Middle East still spring from the same Cold War liberal playbook: namely, invoking the language of emergency to justify extraordinary countermeasures. The perceived, omnipresent threat of Communism emanating specifically from the USSR and China has given way to an even more pliable threat of terrorism since the end of the Cold War.

American militarism in the Middle East also rests on Dulles's presumption of a two-tiered system of sovereignty. The U.S.-led invasion of Iraq (2003), the dramatic and bipartisan expansion of drone warfare, and the still-largely classified covert operations in the region all reflect a global order in which the sovereignty of Middle Eastern states is porous and easily discarded as American presidents see fit.

Finally, with the memory of formal empires receding into the sands of time, anti-imperialist rhetoric has given way to new liberal alibis for empire, such as nation-building, democracy promotion, and humanitarian assistance – all ironically solutions to problems exacerbated by decades of American Cold War liberalism in the region.

The Cold War liberalism paradigm offers a more honest appraisal of the United States' approach to democracy and self-determination in the Middle East. Wary of unpredictable mass movements and popular sovereignty, Dulles and his successors routinely supported military dictators and monarchs who quashed fragile democracies and stifled dissent during the formative postcolonial period. Robust public spheres and incipient democratic institutions in the Middle East were often sacrificed on the altar of "reliable" autocracies or, in some cases, Islamist insurgents who morphed from American assets to threats over time.[94] Of course, authoritarianism in the Middle East has its own history apart

---

[93] On military bases, see Daniel Immerwahr, *How to Hide an Empire: A History of the Greater United States* (New York: Farrar, Strauss, and Giroux, 2019), part two.

[94] On autocracies, see Fawaz A. Gerges, *What Really Went Wrong: The West and the Failure of Democracy in the Middle East* (New Haven: Yale University Press, 2024); Kevin W. Martin, *Syria's Democratic Years: Citizens, Experts, and Media in the 1950s* (Bloomington: Indiana University Press, 2015); on Islamist groups, Paul Thomas Chamberlin, *The Cold War's Killing Fields*, part III (New York: HarperCollins, 2019).

from American meddling.[95] Still, the United States' strong material support for governments with appalling human rights records in the Middle East has contributed to an atmosphere of impunity.

So too in the Occupied Palestinian Territories. Although Palestinians without Israeli citizenship have elected representatives in the Palestinian National Authority (PNA), the PNA's independence is severely circumscribed by the state of Israel. Several scholars and human rights organizations have long observed the one-state reality within Israel–Palestine. Put simply, since 1967, there is only one political entity that possesses what Max Weber called "the monopoly of the legitimate use of physical force within" Israel–Palestine.[96] Yet, millions of Palestinians have no say in how that entity exercises its monopoly over their daily lives. The separate and unequal categories of citizenship and non-citizenship that exist within Israel and the OPT cannot be reconciled with genuine principles of democracy, and yet successive American administrations have embraced this status quo.

Cold War liberalism undermines American democracy at home too. While the Executive Branch is given wide latitude in foreign policy decisions, Congress has passed laws ostensibly designed to reign in the worst excesses. One example is a series of amendments to the Foreign Assistance Act of 1961 (often called the "Leahy Amendments"), which bans U.S. aid to foreign military units found to have violated human rights or to a country that "prohibits or otherwise restricts, directly or indirectly, the transport or delivery of United States humanitarian assistance."[97] But despite overwhelming evidence from journalists, scholars, humanitarian workers, and foreign governments that Israel repeatedly contravened both principles in Gaza, weapons transfers remained largely unabated in violation of U.S. law.[98]

---

[95] Some autocrats weathered the storm; others were deposed but replaced with new autocrats after a brief democratic interregnum. See Joseph Sassoon, *Anatomy of Authoritarianism in the Arab Republics* (New York: Cambridge University Press, 2016); and Roger Owen, *The Rise and Fall of Arab Presidents for Life* (Cambridge, MA: Harvard University Press, 2012) both offer good comparative overviews.

[96] Michael Barnett, et al., eds. *The One State Reality: What Is Israel/Palestine?* (Ithaca: Cornell University Press, 2023); Max Weber, "Politics as a Vocation," in H. H. Gerth and C. Wright Mills (trans. and ed.), *From Max Weber: Essays in Sociology* (New York: Oxford University Press, 1946), 77–78.

[97] 22 U.S. Code § 2378–1; 22 U.S. Code § 2378d; and 10 U.S. Code § 2249e.

[98] Noura Erakat, Josh Paul, et al., "Report of the Independent Task Force on the Application of National Security Memorandum-20 to Israel," published by *Just Security* on April 24, 2024. www.justsecurity.org/94980/task-force-national-security-memorandum-20/ and "Thematic Report: Indiscriminate and Disproportionate Attacks during the Conflict in Gaza (Oct.–Dec. 2023), *United Nations Human Rights Office of the High Commissioner*, June 19, 2024. www.ohchr.org/sites/default/files/documents/countries/opt/20240619-ohchr-thematic-report-indiscrim-disprop-attacks-gaza-oct-dec2023.pdf

Concerning the provision of aid to Israeli military units, Secretary of State Antony Blinken conceded in a letter to Speaker of the House Mike Johnson that multiple units operating in the West Bank were found to have committed "gross human rights violations," even before October 7, but that the administration would not suspend military aid. Blinken justified the decision by claiming that most (though not all) of the units had taken "satisfactory remediation or accountability measures." No details, however, about these reported measures were made available to the American public.[99]

The Biden Administration was similarly evasive over Israel's blockade of humanitarian aid. In February 2024, President Biden ordered the State Department to assess whether Israel's blockade of food, water, and humanitarian assistance into Gaza violated U.S. law. Several months later, the State Department shared its assessment with Congress acknowledging that Israeli actions "delayed or had a negative effect on the delivery of [U.S.] aid to Gaza" and that "the overall level reaching Palestinian civilians – while improved – remains insufficient." But with little explanation, the report bizarrely concluded that the Department did not assess the Israeli government to be in violation of the Foreign Assistance Act.[100] Lofty rhetoric notwithstanding, Cold War liberalism prioritizes aspirations of American global hegemony over genuine democratic governance abroad and democratic accountability at home.

What explains the persistence of Cold War liberalism in the Middle East? First, as I have shown, Cold War liberalism is fundamentally Wilsonian at its core. As such, it is deeply enmeshed within the broader U.S. liberal tradition. Except for a small cadre of libertarians, leftists, and perhaps some isolationist supporters of Donald Trump, the general precepts of Cold War liberalism are embraced by a bipartisan foreign policy establishment. Second, this establishment consensus is bolstered by an array of lobbyists and special interest groups who play an outsized role in U.S. elections.[101] Finally, the Cold War liberal framework has long been accepted and exploited by some actors in the Middle East – from Arab dictators to Israel's far-right – who have relied on it

---

[99] Anne Flaherty, "US Holds Off on Sanctioning Israeli Military Units Accused of Human Rights Violations in the West Bank before Start of War with Hamas," *ABC News*, Apr. 26, 2024. https://abcnews.go.com/Politics/biden-sanction-israeli-military-units-accused-human-rights/story?id=109651562

[100] Unclassified version of "Report to Congress under Section 2 of the National Security Memorandum on Safeguards and Accountability with Respect to Transferred Defense Articles and Defense Services (NSM-20)," published by *Just Security* on May 10, 2024. www.justsecurity.org/95584/nsm-20-report-israel-us/

[101] For example, John Mearsheimer and Stephen Walt, *The Israel Lobby and U.S. Foreign Policy* (New York: Farrar, Straus, and Giroux, 2007).

to promote their own interests and further solidify their power at the expense of political pluralism.

Recognizing its failures in a primarily domestic political context, Michael Brenes and Daniel Steinmetz-Jenkins called Cold War liberalism a "zombie ideology." In the formulation of U.S. foreign policy in the Middle East, too, it lives on as an intellectual straightjacket, frustrating efforts to confront global challenges and build a more egalitarian body politic.[102] Even as the ignominious end of wars in Afghanistan and Iraq have shown the limits of U.S. power, American policymakers and intellectuals alike appear incapable of envisioning ways to engage the region based on something other than a preponderance of American power. Neither the United States nor its unscrupulous regional allies actually wants a "rules-based" order predicated on democratic governance and a genuine decolonization of political and economic institutions.

Ideologically, Cold War liberalism has always been wrought with contradictions: a chaotic and destructive regional order, an anti-imperial empire, antidemocratic democracy promotion, and so on. Recently, the ugly contradictions of Cold War liberalism have been laid bare by the combination of war weariness from the American public and new forms of social media that have granted an unprecedented number of people in the Middle East what Edward Said called the "permission to narrate" their own experiences to global audiences.[103]

Biden's handling of Gaza vividly and painfully heightened these contradictions. Tens of thousands of Palestinians were killed, the majority of Gaza's civilian infrastructure is in ruins, fears abound of greater regional instability, and the United States stands increasingly isolated on the international stage in its position on Israel–Palestine. A man whose 2020 presidential campaign centered decency and respect for the rule of law now stands complicit in genocide. The situation has only worsened under Donald Trump's second term as president.

From Dulles to the present, Cold War liberalism has yielded little more than destruction, chaos, and injustice in the Middle East. The question remains whether actors in the United States can dismantle the pillars of Cold War liberalism and instead meaningfully promote freedom, self-determination, and human rights in the region, not only in word but also in deed.

---

[102] Michael Brenes and Daniel Steinmetz-Jenkins, "Legacies of Cold War Liberalism," *Dissent* 68:1 (Winter 2021), 118–119.
[103] Edward Said, "Permission to Narrate," *Journal of Palestinian Studies* 13:3 (Spring 1984), 27–48.

4 Walter Lippmann
The Cold War Liberal as Conservative Isolationist

Mark Edwards

Cold War liberalism did and did not exist. The phrase and its companion, "liberal consensus," were barely noticeable in public life until historians began to mourn the "fall of the New Deal order" just before, during, and after the Reagan revolution. Even the word "liberalism" was a late-blooming political logo in the twentieth century. There seems to be a problem, then, in assuming the existence of any "vital center," as historian and prototype Cold War liberal Arthur Schlesinger, Jr., termed it. Perhaps Cold War liberalism is best approached as a useful fiction.[1]

Nevertheless, following World War II, enterprising networks of intellectuals, policymakers, and activists did become indentured to more "guns" (a large military establishment), more "butter" (an expansive welfare state), and more economic growth to sustain them. Those self-appointed "responsible men" inhabited organizations like Americans for Democratic Action (ADA) and the Congress for Cultural Freedom (CCF). As fellow travelers with what sociologist C. Wright Mills would call the "power elite," Schlesinger, Jr., and associates lambasted the inertia of American mass society. They advanced alternatively a "politics of emergency" and vision of "liberal empire," as outlined by Daniel Bessner and Michael Brenes in this book's introduction. The ADA and CCF members valorized frontier masculinity, eschewing McCarthyism while more subtly endorsing the red and pink scares of the 1950s. Though hardly unsympathetic to the Civil Rights Movement as a diplomatic priority, the new welfare-warfare

---

[1] See Gary Gerstle and Steve Fraser, eds., *The Rise and Fall of the New Deal Order, 1930–1980* (Princeton: Princeton University Press, 1989); and Arthur M. Schlesinger, Jr., *The Vital Center: The Politics of Freedom* (New York: Houghton Mifflin, 1949). According to a Ngram search, "liberal consensus" began to be mentioned in the early 1960s, grew throughout the 1980s, and peaked around 2000. "Cold War liberalism" got a later start but also spread during the 1980s and peaked around 2000. "Liberalism" enjoyed some popular circulation by the 1930s but did not really take off until the 1980s.

class coveted whiteness as a privilege as well as a protection against anti-Semitism (many were of Jewish descent).[2]

If the "Cold War liberal" branding was appropriate for such persons and communities, you would think the political journalist Walter Lippmann was deserving of it. Lippmann's thousands of articles and editorials, his weekly readership of eight-to-twelve million, his several bestsellers, and his advisory relationship to U.S. Presidents from Woodrow Wilson through Lyndon Johnson all testify to his unparalleled influence as a public intellectual. Lippmann is generally overlooked in surveys of Cold War liberalism, and not without good reason. He had only tenuous connections to the ADA and the Congress for Cultural Freedom (CCF). With the exception of political theologian Reinhold Niebuhr, he was quite a bit older that Schlesinger, Jr., and other Cold War liberals. Lippmann was Jewish yet looked to Christianity rather than the secular state for a sense of belonging (although he never converted). At the same time, Lippmann coined the term "Cold War," was dubbed the "Moses" of twentieth-century American liberalism, and had long indulged the heterosexual white male benefits of the East Coast establishment that Cold War liberals came to occupy.[3]

This essay contends that Lippmann should be ranked among the Cold War liberals. As soon as he is placed in that category, however, he blows it up. A survey of Lippmann's writings on foreign and domestic policymaking will show the necessity and yet impossibility of generalizing about America's strong-state liberal consensus, especially its Cold War period. Part I of this essay considers Lippmann's affirmative-negative response to the superpower showdown between the United States and the Soviet Union. Lippmann endorsed the country's military-industrial complex and supported most efforts to halt communist advances. Yet he did that while positioning himself as an isolationist critic of "globalism." Lippmann was no simple advocate for liberal empire, in other words. Lippmann offered a similar yes-no to the New Deal and its post–World War II expansion, as will be examined in part II. Lippmann appeared to dismiss most of the New Deal from the standpoint of (Edmund) Burkean conservatism as he understood it. At the same time, he was a key apologist for the British economist John Maynard Keynes, one of Cold War liberalism's godfathers. Like Keynes, Lippmann advocated

---

[2] See Kevin Mattson, *When America Was Great: The Fighting Faith of Liberalism in Post-War America* (New York: Routledge, 2004); and Steven M. Gillon, *Politics and Vision: The ADA and American Liberalism, 1947–1985* (New York: Oxford University Press, 1987).

[3] *Time* magazine called Lippmann a "Moses" to liberals in 1931. See Ronald Steel, *Walter Lippmann and the American Century* (Piscataway, NJ: Transaction, 1980), 276. Gillon, *Politics and Vision*, mentions Lippmann a few times.

faithfully for federal investment in cities, education, and health care. While championing a strong executive, even a monarchy, Lippmann rejected emergency policymaking in favor a pragmatic statecraft guided by Western heritage. Finally, part III looks at Lippmann's legacy as well as what we mean when we talk about liberalism. The aim is to consider Lippmann in all his irreducible messiness. He had a remarkable capacity to tolerate disorder in his cultural-political life that he could never bear in his interpersonal and professional associations.

Much the same could be said of Cold War liberalism. Just as its early twentieth-century parentage, Progressivism, had included so many diverse and conflicting yet connected and cooperative actors, so Cold War liberalism often existed without Cold War liberals. That is not to say we should dispense with the term, as some in the past have wanted to do with Progressivism. It is true that Lippmann opposed many of the ideals that this collection suggests were constituent of Cold War liberalism. He still raised that opposition from within, among, and on behalf of Cold War liberal circles. If Lippmann represented the diversity of the Cold War liberalism, he also highlighted its durability as an analytical category. That Lippmann betrayed the illiberality of the broader twentieth-century liberal consensus must also not be forgotten.

The Neo-isolationist as Cold Warrior, the Cold Warrior as Neo-isolationist

Regarding his country's conflict with the Soviet Union, Lippmann named names as an act of defiance. He had been fighting irrationality and overreaction in politics since the first red scare following World War I. It was that fight that had led to his critique of the Jeffersonian "omnicompetent citizen" in *Public Opinion* (1922). Lippmann's book unfairly marked him as an elitist champion for expert-managed democracy and world order. In truth, Lippmann would track closely with politicians and political activists who believed in liberal American imperialism. Yet he was one of their harshest detractors. In Lippmann, we witness both the continuities and contradictions of Cold War liberal worldmaking.

Lippmann recalled having first used the term "Cold War" during the 1930s. He dusted it off and repurposed it after reading Russian expert George Kennan's *Foreign Affairs* article (1947) on the need to contain Soviet aggression. Kennan's proposed "counterforce," Lippmann argued, was a "strategic monstrosity." No country, let alone the United States, had enough weapons, wisdom, or will to fight the Soviets and their satellites everywhere for the ten years or more that it would take to wear them down. The U.S. military was not built to occupy foreign territory indefinitely, and the American people were not and should not be patient enough to wait on communism's next move. Lippmann challenged countrymen to focus on the preservation of the "Atlantic Community" and on the construction of a united Europe through the "evacuation" of both the American and Soviet armies from the continent. Asia and the Middle East should be considered "secondary."[4]

Lippmann believed an America with lowered expectations of its irresistibility might still have a date with destiny. If the United States could orchestrate a withdrawal from Europe, "we shall have written off the liabilities of the Truman Doctrine which must in practice mean inexorably an unending intervention in all the countries that are supposed to 'contain' the Soviet Union," Lippmann concluded.

> We shall be acting once more in the great American tradition which is to foster the independence of other countries, not to use other countries as the satellites of our own power, however beneficent, and as the instruments of our own policy, however well meant. Our aim will not be to organize an ideological crusade. It will not be to make Jeffersonian democrats out of the peasants of Eastern Europe, the tribal chieftains, the feudal lords, the pashas, and the warlords of the Middle East and Asia, but to settle the war and to restore the independence of the nations of Europe by removing the alien armies – all of them, our own included.[5]

Lippmann set himself against the Cold War creed for the same reason his Harvard mentor William James had opposed the annexation of the Philippines in 1899: Their anti-imperialist conviction that no person or group could ever possess enough knowledge or virtue to rule over another. Lippmann quickly won Kennan over to his side, and the two remained mutually cranky confidants well into the 1960s.[6]

Kennan and Lippmann like James were part of the realist vein within American diplomacy, which advocated for maintaining balances of power over utopian schemes for world government. Lippmann's pragmatic foreign policymaking was evident as early as 1915 when he published *The Stakes of Diplomacy*. Well before the Truman administration sought to unite all religions in an interfaith front against international communism, World War I had pitted Christian "civilization" against

---

[4] Walter Lippmann, "Interview," Columbia Oral History Project, conducted by Allan Nevins and Dean Albertson, Apr. 3–8, 1950, 260, in The Walter Lippmann Papers (hereafter WLP), Manuscripts and Archives, Sterling Memorial Library, Yale University, Reel 111; Walter Lippmann, *The Cold War: A Study in U. S. Foreign Policy* (New York: Harper and Brothers, 1947), 18, 20, 24–28, 38–39, 56–57.
[5] Lippmann, *Cold War*, 44–45.
[6] See Christopher McKnight Nichols, *Promise and Peril: America at the Dawn of a Global Age* (Cambridge: Harvard University Press, 2015), on the linkage of isolationism and anti-imperialism in James and Lippmann.

German "barbarism." The young Lippmann was weary and wary of holy wars and all talk of "manifest destiny" and the "white man's burden." The world war, he argued, emanated from imperialist adventures to control and exploit the planet's "weak" states. While the desire to subdue "anarchy" internationally – to "make civilization march" in the interests of capital expansion and protection – was inevitable and even understandable, imperialism necessarily produced reactionary "primitive" nationalisms. Those nationalisms then crushed democratic aspirations the world over.[7]

The only way to avoid global catastrophe was to organize "industrially backward" and "politically incompetent" peoples through international institutions. Lippmann prefigured the modernization theory that, for a season, became Cold War orthodoxy. However, beneath Wilsonian talk of "world government," readers could already witness Lippmann's realist commitments to regionalism or "local world governments." Lippmann went on to write several of Wilson's Fourteen Points while serving as a military intelligence officer. Following the war, Lippmann counselled against U.S. interventions in Russia and Central and South America.[8]

The sturdier roots of Lippmann's critique of the Truman Doctrine lay in his World War II bestseller, *U.S. Foreign Policy: Shield of the Republic* (1943). The fundamental problem with the United States, he argued, was that the country had embarked upon market and moral expansion after 1898 yet never formed a foreign policy. Lippmann laid out a cardinal anti-globalist principle that a nation's foreign policy commitments must not extend beyond their power to fulfill them (that became known as the Lippmann gap). Teddy Roosevelt had understood that, but every president since Wilson had preferred to govern by "persisting illusion." Lippmann challenged his Washington disciples to dedicate themselves to realizing the "Atlantic Community" as a "community of interest" rather than as a "scheme for empire." Lippmann's *U.S. War Aims* (1944) reiterated his conviction that only regional pacts could guarantee the success of superpower cooperation through a United Nations.[9]

---

[7] Walter Lippmann, *The Stakes of Diplomacy* (New York: Henry Holt, 1915), 66, 87–88, 98, 170–172. On Truman's religious Cold War, see William Inboden, *Religion and American Foreign Policy, 1945–1960: The Soul of Containment* (New York: Cambridge University Press, 2008). See also Philip Jenkins, *The Great and Holy War: How World War I Became a Religious Crusade* (New York: HarperOne, 2014).

[8] Lippmann, *Stakes of Diplomacy*, 129, 144, 152, 170–172.

[9] Walter Lippmann, *U. S. Foreign Policy: Shield of the Republic* (Boston: Little, Brown, 1943), 4–5, 7–10, 30, 130, 173; Walter Lippmann, *U. S. War Aims* (Boston: Little, Brown, 1944). On the "Lippmann gap," see Patrick Porter, "Beyond the American Century: Walter Lippmann and American Grand Strategy, 1943–1950," *Diplomacy & Statecraft* 22 (2011): 557–577.

Lippmann's outlook is best characterized as realistic Wilsonianism, but that did not stop him from condemning the entire Wilson project while trashing Truman and Kennan. "The Wilsonian ideology is American fundamentalism made into a universal doctrine," Lippmann complained to British audiences in 1952. Wilsonianism was simultaneously the creature and creator of imperial overreach. It was "an impossible foundation" for U.S. diplomacy. Lippmann thereby condemned American Cold Warriors who imagined a liberal empire was possible or even desirable.[10]

At the same time, Lippmann's "no" to the deadly abstraction he had dubbed the Cold War frequently contained a "yes." Lippmann hated Truman's Doctrine but still approved of the president's request for aid to Greece and Turkey which launched American leadership of the "free world." Lippmann could apologize for Soviet expansionism while remaining an anti-communist, which Peter Slezkine stresses was the real meaning of "free world" in his essay in this collection. Perhaps that explains why Lippmann also backed the Marshall Plan and a limited version of NATO. In his mind, both were rejections of containment theory universalism. They were approximations of the provincial "communities of states" that he and Republican operative John Foster Dulles had agreed were necessary to give coherence and, thus, legitimacy to the United Nations. In Europe, United States and Soviet "zones of power" were the best that could be hoped for until the former forced, bought, or begged the latter out of the continent.[11]

Lippmann thereby backed his way into support for Kennan's "counterforce" well into the 1950s and 1960s. No wonder that Ronald Steel, Lippmann's chief biographer, concluded, "whenever containment was put to the test as a policy choice rather than as an abstract doctrine, he went along with it." Lippmann might have considered Truman a "warlord," and he became one of Dulles's most vocal critics, but the Soviets themselves had decided as early as 1946 that Lippmann was a "representative of imperialist ideology."[12]

Lippmann was similarly equivocal toward the East. "We have very little power in Asia," Lippmann wrote a friend in 1949, "and we must not think of ourselves as lords of creation." Democracy and free enterprise might never take root there. Rather, "a totalitarian system is normal in Asia," Lippmann concluded after interviewing Indian Prime Minister

---

[10] Walter Lippmann, *Isolation and Alliances* (Boston: Little, Brown, 1952), 24, 26.

[11] Walter Lippmann, to John Foster Dulles, Apr. 25, 1949, in *Public Philosopher: Selected Letters of Walter Lippmann*, ed. John Morton Blum (New York: Ticknor and Fields, 1985), 537; Walter Lippmann, to Lewis Douglas, Aug. 31, 1948, in WLP, Reel 58.

[12] Steel, *Walter Lippmann*, 489; Walter Lippmann, to Arthur Vandenberg, Aug. 8, 1949, in WLP, Reel 97. On the Soviet's criticism of Lippmann, see Steel, *Walter Lippmann*, 427.

Jawaharlal Nehru. Still, Lippmann told British listeners that it had been a "mistake" for the United States to not have built up South Korean defenses before exiting after World War II. He decided the Korean War was good if for nothing else than that it stabilized the Atlantic Community after a period of benign neglect. Ultimately, Lippmann hoped the West would pivot toward Nehru and India as allies in the fight against international communism. Lippmann caught the developmental bug along with Walt Whitman Rostow and other Cold War modernization theorists, believing that Africa and Asia might still be lured away from communism and brought peacefully and rapidly into an urban–industrial capitalist world community. Lippmann's commentary on his two Pulitzer Prize–winning interviews with Soviet Premier Nikita Khrushchev reiterated his better-fed-than-red approach to outliving communism.[13]

Lippmann was a more standard Cold Warrior regarding the Middle East. He grumbled about Dulles, now Eisenhower's Secretary of State, as a Christian nationalist zealot. He endorsed Khrushchev's warning about the danger of America's "militarists." He juxtaposed his own "quiet diplomacy" with the "loud-mouthed diplomacy" – the "pretension to know and to speak for the universal order of things" – of the Eisenhower administration. But Lippmann was hardly silent on the need to disrupt any sort of Arab agreement that the Soviets might then take advantage of. "Our aim should be not to encourage the unity of the Arab world and of Islam," Lippmann counselled one naval commander, "but to keep it divided .... A united Mohammedan world must in the end expel the western powers from all its territories, not only in the Middle East, but in North Africa." Like most of his friends in New York and Washington, Lippmann thought an independent Israeli state was impossible. He favored a Palestinian protectorate, backed by the Atlantic Community, within an integrated Jewish-Palestinian economic zone. But that did not stop him from going beyond Dulles in supporting Israel's attack with Britain and France on the "typical aggressor-dictator," the Arab nationalist leader of Egypt Gamal Abdel Nasser. Lippmann did not always stand outside the Cold War globalism he so often railed against.[14]

[13] Walter Lippmann, to Russell C. Leffingwell, Dec. 29, 1949, in *Public Philosopher*, ed. Blum, 1949; Walter Lippmann, to Bernard Berenson, Dec. 22, 1949, in WLP, Reel 45; Lippmann, *Isolation and Alliances*, 43–44, 49; Walter Lippmann, to Forrest P. Sherman, Feb. 16, 1950, in *Public Philosopher*, ed. Blum, 548; Walter Lippmann, *The Communist World and Ours* (Boston: Little, Brown, 1958), 41–43; Walter Lippmann, *The Coming Tests with Russia* (Boston: Little, Brown, 1961), 37.

[14] Lippmann, *Communist World and Ours*, 28–29; Walter Lippmann, "Today and Tomorrow: Quiet Diplomacy, for Now, Is Hope of the World," Jan. 26, 1961, in the Robert O. Anthony Collection of Walter Lippmann (hereafter RAC), Manuscripts

Cuba and Vietnam brought Lippmann back to his anti-imperialist senses and led to his neo-isolationism. Lippmann rejected attempts to overthrow Castro as un-American and unnatural ("like a cow that tried to fly"). His developmentalism inclined him rather toward something like the Kennedy administration's Alliance for Progress for Central and South America. Indeed, Lippmann served as an unofficial advisor for the Kennedy and Lyndon Johnson presidencies. In public and behind closed doors, he repeated his foreign policy life lessons: that a country should not make promises it did not have the power to fulfill; that the U.S. military was not built for long-term occupations; and that ideology inevitably corrupted diplomacy.[15]

After the Bay of Pigs, Lippmann repented of his earlier support for Western intervention in Vietnam and preached reunification and neutralization of the country (under Christian anti-communist Ngô Đình Diệm, of course). "Our security and well-being are not involved in Southeast Asia or Korea and never have been," Lippmann told readers in 1964. "If it is said that this is isolationism, I would say yes. It is isolationism if the limitation of our power is isolationism. It is isolationism as compared with the globalism which became fashionable after the Second World War." Lippmann backed Johnson's Operation Rolling Thunder bombing campaign in 1965 because he thought it would force North Vietnam to the negotiating table. When the president started ordering more troops, however, Lippmann went on his own offensive.[16]

Washington's consensus columnist quickly fell out of favor. Lippmann impugned American exceptionalism, chiding Schlesinger, "the search for security and the assembling of an empire are two sides of the same coin." Lippmann was even harsher in print. "The time has come to stop beating our heads against stone walls under the illusion that we have been appointed policeman to the human race," Lippmann charged. Johnson was suffering from "messianic megalomania" and believed that he could "kill mosquitoes with tanks and build a Great Society with B-52s." America under Johnson was becoming a "bastard empire which relies

---

and Archives, Sterling Memorial Library, Yale University, Reel 11; Walter Lippmann, "Today and Tomorrow: Dulles and the Churchmen," Nov. 27, 1958, in RAC, Reel 11; Walter Lippmann, to Forrest P. Sherman, Apr. 5, 1948, in *Public Philosopher*, ed. Blum, 508; Walter Lippmann, "Today and Tomorrow: Disaster in the Middle East," Nov. 1, 1956, in RAC, Reel 11.

[15] Lippmann, *Coming Tests*, 33–34. On Lippmann's involvement in the Kennedy and Johnson administrations, including debates over Vietnam policy, see Steel, *Walter Lippmann*, 521–584.
[16] Walter Lippmann, "Today and Tomorrow," Dec. 29, 1964, in RAC, Reel 11. On Lippmann's involvement in the Kennedy and Johnson administrations, including debates over Vietnam policy, see Steel, *Walter Lippmann*, 521–584.

on superior force to achieve its purposes, and is no longer an example of the wisdom and humanity of a free society .... the American promise has been betrayed and abandoned."[17]

Lippmann was a Cold Warrior who rejected Cold War statecraft in favor of fidelity to longstanding American principles of isolationism. Yet less one think he had joined the ranks of antiwar New Leftists, his turn against liberal empire combined the philosophical anti-imperialism of James with the middlebrow nativism of a Charles Lindbergh. Lippmann ended his journalistic career a self-described "neo-isolationist" opposed to the "foolish globalism" he had been fighting at least since World War II. "Nobody is wise enough or clever enough or strong enough to arrange it all for the world," he explained while recommending that U.S. policymakers let majority world revolutions play themselves out. Lippmann went on to endorse Nixonian détente because he had been championing it since 1945 if not 1915.[18]

The Conservative as Liberal, the Liberal as Conservative

"I am a conservative; I think I always have been," Lippmann confessed shortly before his death. "But that doesn't mean that I'm a conservative who agrees with William Buckley. I hope and trust I am a conservative in the line of Edmund Burke. I believe in certain fundamental things in philosophy and constitutional law which are conservative as against the Jacobins." By "Jacobins," Lippmann meant those who believed human nature could be perfected (he named progressive presidential candidate George McGovern as a representative). Lippmann's profession seemed to be yet one evidence that was no longer a strong-state liberal – or that he had never been one to begin with. In fact, Lippmann's heterodox conservativism placed him within the mainstream of Cold War liberal musings on state and society.

Lippmann had been praising Burke at least since the 1930s. Lippmann saw in the conservative icon a fellow Jamesian, opposed to ideological crusades. Given Lippmann's foreign policy views, one can imagine why he felt like he could never go along with William F. Buckley, Jr., and the New Right, including Barry Goldwater whom Lippmann

---

[17] Walter Lippmann, to Arthur Schlesinger, Jr., Sept. 25, 1967, in WLP, Reel 90; Walter Lippmann, "Today and Tomorrow," Feb. 2, 1965, in RAC, Reel 11; Walter Lippmann," Today and Tomorrow," Nov. 7, 1966, in RAC, Reel 11; Walter Lippmann," Today and Tomorrow," Jan. 19, 1967, in RAC, Reel 11; Walter Lippmann, "The American Empire," *Newsweek*, Oct. 9, 1967, 21.

[18] Ronald Steel, "The World We're In: An Interview with Walter Lippmann," *New Republic*, Nov. 13, 1971, 20–21.

routinely roasted. Yet Lippmann's break with Buckley was just as much about domestic concerns. Lippmann was one of many heterodox conservatives during the 1950s and 1960s – aligned with persons such as the historians Peter Viereck and Clinton Rossiter. Together, their "liberal conservativism" or "conservative socialism" won the appreciation of realist liberals such as Schlesinger and the theologian Reinhold Niebuhr.[19]

Lippmann's social conservativism first appeared in the 1920s in reaction to the flapper as well as to fascism. *Public Opinion* and its companion piece, *The Phantom Public* (1925), betrayed a thinker ill at ease with mass electorates. Lippmann was worried that William Jennings Bryan's fundamentalists intended to bring to America the kind of totalitarian takeover Benito Mussolini was then affecting in Italy (Lippmann first introduced the term "totalitarianism" to American audiences during these years). Someone had to put a stop to Jeffersonian majoritarianism, and Lippmann believed it was him. For a book heralded as a liberation from Protestant Christian moralism, Lippmann's best-selling *A Preface to Morals* (1929) spent a lot of time arguing that "modern man" needed a moral equivalent of the old religious restraints on desire. Lippmann then expanded on that traditionalist talking point in his first sequel, *The Good Society* (1937). He bid readers to give up worship of the state and renew their commitments to what he called the "higher law." Lippmann's higher law was a makeshift personalism, a "denial that men may be arbitrary in human transactions."[20]

American Catholics believed they had found a new convert and champion, and Lippmann did not disappoint. He began to lambast "secular man" before religious groups and compared fellow countrymen to a "horde of beings" no longer capable of self-control. Lippmann – a self-described agnostic, humanist, and secular Jew – urged his World War II audiences to come to Jesus (or maybe to Aristotle). "As perfected in the religious tradition of the West," he boasted, "the good life is an imitation of God – that is to say, the cultivation of the reason, which is an imitation of His omniscience, and of the only true freedom – the freedom to follow the dictates of reason – which is an imitation of His

---

[19] Ronald Steel, "Walter Lippmann: An Interview with Ronald Steel," *New Republic*, Apr. 14, 1973, 16–17. Viereck's and Rossiter's feelings toward Lippmann are captured in *The Essential Lippmann: A Political Philosophy for Liberal Democracy*, edited Clinton Rossiter and James Lare (New York: Vintage, 1965). See also Jennifer Burns, "Liberalism and the Conservative Imagination," in *Liberalism for a New Century*, edited Neil Jumonville and Kevin Mattson (Berkeley: University of North Carolina Press, 2007), 58–72.

[20] Walter Lippmann, *A Preface to Morals* (New York: Macmillan, 1929 [Reprint: Time Incorporated, 1964]), 129–130, 136, 178–180; Walter Lippmann, *The Good Society* (Boston: Little, Brown, 1937), 346.

omnipotence." Lippmann might be counted one of the architects of the synthesis between American Catholicism and Cold War liberalism described by Chris Schaefer in this volume.[21]

Lippmann continued to lay foundations for religious rights with his Cold War credo, *The Public Philosophy* (1955). America's foreign policy misadventures suggested to Lippmann that the cancer of secularism, the "practical neutrality in ultimate issues," was spreading throughout the body politic. Lippmann marshalled an array of characters – from the founding fathers and William James to the Stoics and St. Paul – against the Nietzschean (and Existentialist) assault on an "objective order" of human being. What Lippmann called "traditions of civility," or the "Mandate of Heaven" after Chinese sources, persisted despite the "acids of modernity." On that point, Lippmann sounded a lot like the conservative philosopher Leo Strauss in his defense of natural law. Lippmann, too, believed his "objective order" could cure countrymen of their "public agnosticism." His portrait of an American "mass society" – the result of "large mass electorates" – betrayed Lippmann's discomfort with women's liberation. His call for a stronger executive was intended to end the "progressive barbarization" of emancipated moderns and replace it with something akin to divine right monarchy.[22]

Lippmann's combined his elitist Christian culture warring against populism with an assault on the strong state liberalism of the New Deal. That made sense, given Lippmann's conviction that the uprooted interwar masses had exchanged the love of "God" (whatever that meant to him) for the worship of government. Lippmann never really feared Franklin Roosevelt as a "political messiah" like several of his contemporaries, but he did find him inept and prone to overstretch. Lippmann directed much of his ire at the National Recovery Association for trying, as he saw it, to control prices and wages. He also became critical of Social Security and especially the National Labor Relations Act for, in his understanding, compelling workers to unionize. By 1936, Lippmann abandoned his ambivalent support for Roosevelt and endorsed his Republican opponent.[23]

---

[21] Walter Lippmann, "Man's Image of Man," Address, Seventeenth Annual Meeting of the American Catholic Philosophical Association, Philadelphia, Dec. 29 and 30, 1941, in *Essential Lippmann*, ed. Rossiter and Lare, 162–168.

[22] Walter Lippmann, *The Public Philosophy* (Boston: Little, Brown, 1955), 14, 28–40, 47–57, 96–97, 110–111, 172–181. On women's rights and Lippmann's perceived "crisis of authority," see Sarah Imhoff, "My Sons Have Defeated Me: Walter Lippmann, Felix Adler, and Secular Moral Authority," *Journal of Religion* 92 (Oct. 2012): 536–550.

[23] Of Lippmann's public references to the New Deal between 1933 and 1938, 70 percent were unfavorable while only 9 percent were favorable. See David Elliott Weingast, *Walter Lippmann: A Study in Personal Journalism* (Westport, CT: Greenwood, 1949), 61.

In *The Good Society*, Lippmann tied his emerging personalism to blanket condemnation of "collectivism," including the New Deal's "overhead planning." Put simply, "a democratic people cannot have a planned economy." The "Providential State" was no substitute for the "higher law" of personal liberty and responsibility. Lippmann imagined a "renascence of liberalism" in America as Roosevelt's regulatory apparatus decreased so that the court-administered "common law" increased. Lippmann's book was influenced by as well as inspired the Austrian-British economist Friedrich von Hayek, one of the founders of modern American libertarianism. The two even began collaborating on an international think tank of anti-collectivists that became the Mont Pelerin Society. Their first meeting in August of 1938 in Paris, where the term "neoliberalism" was coined, was entitled the "Walter Lippmann Colloquium."[24]

Lippmann never became an active member in Mont Perelin, but he did help promote their understanding of "free society" during the early Cold War. Lippmann joined the chorus of public intellectuals who believed that the United States alone had escaped the iron logics of history to build a Jeffersonian Empire of Liberty. Yet American exceptionalism could survive only on the basis of limited government. Lippmann criticized the "fatty degeneration" of the Truman administration's growing military–industrial bureaucracy. "It is the inevitable, unavoidable, incurable tendency of all modern governments to expand," Lippmann warned, "and the need to contract and to reduce them is therefore never finished." Buckley and the upstart *National Review* could not have said it any better.[25]

And yet, by Lippmann's own admission, he never spoke for their New Right. Lippmann was rather a close friend and fervent admirer of the conservative libertarian foil John Maynard Keynes. Lippmann's missives against "planning" aside, he had also insisted that government intervention in the economy was the new normal. Keynes, whom Lippmann corresponded and spent time with, pointed Lippmann to ways that governments might bend but not break free markets through crisis relief measures. What the world would soon call Keynesianism Lippmann

---

[24] Lippmann, *Good Society*, 6, 52, 108, 207, 260–266; Walter Lippmann, to Friedrich von Hayek, Mar. 12, 1937; Friedrich von Hayek, to Walter Lippmann, Apr. 6, 1937, both in WLP, Reel 66. On the Lippmann Colloquium and Mont Perelin Society, see Angus Bergin, *The Great Persuasion: Reinventing Free Markets since the Depression* (Cambridge: Harvard University Press, 2015).

[25] Walter Lippmann, "Today and Tomorrow: The Election Explained," Nov. 3, 1952, in *Essential Lippmann*, ed. Rossiter and Lare, 303; Walter Lippmann, "Today and Tomorrow: Morale and Discipline," Dec. 2, 1952, in *Essential Lippmann*, ed. Rossiter and Lare, 53.

initially termed a "Compensated Economy," or "Free Collectivism." In advocating for a nonsocialist economic role for the state, Keynes joined James in the repudiation of ideology. But that also made Keynes a Burkean conservative in Lippmann's eyes (an identification that Keynes himself appreciated). Building upon Keynes, Lippmann imagined networks of federally funded public works programs ready to be mobilized in response to future market collapses. As he told the historian Henry Steel Commager in 1947, he had objected to the technique, not the substance, of the New Deal. Lippmann believed the promises of both liberalism and socialism could be realized through the right method of intermingling free enterprise and compensatory government action.[26]

Lippmann was never a resolute anti-communist in foreign affairs, and he definitely was not so in domestic ones. It is easy to read *The Good Society* as Lippmann's statement that fascism and communism could happen here. But Lippmann went out of his way to argue that both were "alien stereotypes" that clouded rather than clarified America's unique (as he saw it) economic development. He continued to do so into the 1950s and 1960s. "The so-called socialism which is supposed to be creeping up on us," Lippmann mocked, "is in fact nothing more than the work of making life safe and decent for a mass society collected in great cities." Modernity was expensive, but it was well worth it. Lippmann worried that Cold Warriors were too amorous of guns and were not willing to spend commensurate or even greater amounts on butter.[27]

In fact, no self-identifying conservative was more committed than Lippmann to increasing public expenditures. Responding to the "militarist danger" expressed in Eisenhower's farewell address, Lippmann called for renewed civilian control over the military. He held the federal government responsible to make cities great again as well as maintain a large defense establishment. That meant more public dollars going to schools and universities, to highway construction, to health care, and to urban renewal. Lippmann had little patience for the tax revolt being

[26] Walter Lippmann, *The Method of Freedom* (New York: Macmillan, 1934), 38; Walter Lippmann, to Henry Steel Commager, May 31, 1947, in WLP, Reel 53. See Walter Lippmann, to John Kenneth Galbraith, Dec. 23, 1965, in WLP, Reel 63, where Lippmann describes himself as an "ardent, amateur Keynesian." See also Lippmann, "Interview," 152–155. For Lippmann's thoughts on public works, see Lippmann, *Method of Freedom*, 106–110; Walter Lippmann, *Interpretations, 1931–1932*, ed. Allan Nevins (New York: Macmillan, 1932), 79–82; and Walter Lippmann, *Interpretations, 1933–1935*, ed. Allan Nevins (New York: Macmillan, 1936), 228–248. On Keynes as a Burkean, see Zach Carter, *The Price of Peace: Money, Democracy, and the Life of John Maynard Keynes* (New York: Random House, 2020).

[27] Walter Lippmann, *The New Imperative* (New York: Macmillan, 1935), 5; Walter Lippmann, "Today and Tomorrow: Big Money," Jan. 2, 1962, in *Essential Lippmann*, ed. Rossiter and Lare, 348.

propagated by both parties, which he equated with preferring "private self-indulgence" over "public responsibilities." Been there, done that, during the Jazz Age. The imperative need now was to outlive the communists. "In the real world," Lippmann cautioned, "we are up against great mass societies of powerfully disciplined people, and unless we can restore and concentrate our own energies to outdo them, it will not matter at all how many adjectives we hurl at them in the battle of words."[28]

The name of the Johnson administration's attempt to outlive communism, the Great Society, would be drawn from several of Lippmann's writings over the years. Lippmann, in turn, had borrowed it from his friend and other mentor, the ex-socialist Graham Wallas. Armed with Keynesianism and its diplomatic compliment, modernization theory, Lippmann foresaw America building brotherhoods of free men at home and enjoying peaceful conquests of the majority world abroad. This was a Cold War liberal vision if there ever was one.

Walter Lippmann and the End of Ideology

But was there ever one? Is it right to talk about Cold War liberalism as a common creed? In many ways, Cold War liberals in the ADA and CCF were bound to transcend the impasse between laissez faire/libertarianism and socialism/communism, as reflected in Daniel Bell's *The End of Ideology* (1960). Yet those same liberals were hamstrung, even self-defeated, by their anticommunism. This brings us to Walter Lippmann's legacy: He was the most influential, outspoken, and consistent anti-ideologue of the American Century. To remember him exclusively as a political realist or a cultural reactionary is to miss a lot. Lippmann frequented Schlesinger's "vital center" even as he was skeptical that such a consensus could and should exist. Lippmann's final self-understanding as a conservative isolationist did not prevent him from endorsing the major Cold War and strong-state liberal policies of the 1950s and 1960s. In both domestic and foreign policymaking, Lippmann was the Jamesian prophet of limits.

---

[28] Walter Lippmann, "Today and Tomorrow: Eisenhower's Farewell Warning," Jan. 19, 1961, in *Essential Lippmann*, ed. Rossiter and Lare, 55; Walter Lippmann, "America Must Grow," *Saturday Evening Post*, Nov. 5, 1960, in *Essential Lippmann*, ed. Rossiter and Lare, 330–331; Walter Lippmann, "Today and Tomorrow: The Size of the Problem," Mar. 8, 1960, in *Essential Lippmann*, ed. Rossiter and Lare, 365–367; Walter Lippmann, "Today and Tomorrow: The Incoming Tide," Nov. 20, 1958, in *Essential Lippmann*, ed. Rossiter and Lare, 362–363; Walter Lippmann, "Today and Tomorrow: Public Need and Private Pleasure," Sept. 5, 1957, in *Essential Lippmann*, ed. Rossiter and Lare, 361–362; Walter Lippmann, "Today and Tomorrow: Crucial Internal Question," Dec. 11, 1958, in *Essential Lippmann*, ed. Rossiter and Lare, 365.

Paradoxically, it was ideology that wrecked Cold War liberalism. Not merely the Domino Theory, but also the liberal defense of white male privilege. Lippmann's career spanned the failure of New England pragmatism to live up to its radical racialized and gendered potential. Lippmann had made war on the Ku Klux Klan and white supremacy during and after World War I. But between 1931 and 1957, he only wrote ten articles on African Americans, including his feeling that the *Brown* Supreme Court decision had been a tragic mistake. Lippmann supported the civil rights movement during the 1960s because he believed that racial violence threatened America's moral standing in the world. He endorsed Black Power to the extent that it represented an effort by minorities to uplift themselves independent of redistributionist tax policies. Lippmann opposed the Equal Rights Amendment from its inception and came to believe that universal suffrage had severely weakened American democracy. He rarely credited the army of women who helped research and produce much of his daily editorial output, including his second wife Helen, who translated a lot of Lippmann's interviews with Khrushchev. Lippmann was once pressed by the historian and international correspondent Mary Blume for his opinion on the women's movement, to which he admitted, "there have been so many liberation movements. I'd flunk out on that question. I haven't had any particular contact with it. I hadn't really thought that women were a deprived part of mankind. There is a great deal of discrimination in jobs, but that's a fairly simple problem to settle."[29]

Lippmann offered little challenge to the moral limitations of New Deal and Great Society liberalism. He did not think the Vietnamese would or could submit to American democratic procedure, and he grew increasingly doubtful that Americans could, either. "I wrote a book back in the beginning of the century about the dissolution of the ancestral order," Lippmann reminded Steel about *A Preface to Morals*. "Clearly, the ancestral order of the family, for instance, has been much more affected by the contraceptive pill than it has by anybody's speeches or by the war."[30]

Lippmann's lament for family values was not the only provocative thing he said in the 1970s. "I think it's going to be a minor Dark Age," he confessed of his fears about growing populations, pollution, and promiscuity. In his final unpublished manuscript, "The Ungovernability of

---

[29] Walter Lippmann, "The Race Report," *Newsweek*, Mar. 25, 1968, 19; Mary Blume, "Walter Lippmann at 80: The Hopeful Skeptic," *Washington Post*, May 31, 1970, B3. On Lippmann and civil rights, see Steel, *Walter Lippmann*, 551–555.

[30] Steel, "Walter Lippmann," 17.

Man," Lippmann warned that America would become "anarchical and barbarian unless there is an ordered moral, political, religious consensus which the preponderant mass of men accept and obey and enforce." Lippmann voted for Nixon in 1968 and 1972 for his amalgamation of anti-globalism, Keynesianism, and law and order. On Watergate, Lippmann concluded, "The President of the United States is like a King with all the powers and limitations inherent in a King."[31]

It is tempting, but also wrong, to conclude that Lippmann made the neoconservative turn with Bell and other disaffected Cold War liberals. Nor was Lippmann a fellow traveler with Billy Graham and evangelical conservatism. Since Lippmann despised Goldwater, it is hard to imagine him liking Ronald Reagan very much. Lippmann was a halfhearted Christian humanist in ideas, a Keynesian in economics, and a Hamiltonian in politics. Lippmann fought our so-called age of fracture more than he joined in it. But whatever names we might want to impress upon him, this much seems true: Lippmann's career highlights the diversity within the uniformity – the heterodoxy within the orthodoxy – of Cold War liberalism. He suggests the need for, simultaneously, more splitting and more lumping in our studies of midcentury public intellectuals.

---

[31] Steel, "The World Were In," 21; Walter Lippmann, "The Ungovernability of Man," undated, unpaginated manuscript, in WLP, Box 223, Folders 326–327; Steel, "Walter Lippmann," 17.

5 Catholic Internationalism and American Empire
The Cold War Liberalism of William Pfaff

Christopher Schaefer

William Pfaff was convinced that Charles R. Morris had not accurately captured the nuances of midcentury American Catholicism. Morris, a lawyer and banker by trade, had written popular books about the arms race, IBM, and the AARP before turning his attention in the early 1990s to American Catholicism. Pfaff, for his part, began his long career as a foreign affairs commentator over four decades earlier at *Commonweal*, a liberal Catholic magazine with a unique position in the American political and religious firmament. In 1994, Morris sent Pfaff early drafts of a book, which a few years later, would become *American Catholic: The Sinners and Saints Who Built America's Most Powerful Church*.[1] After reading the draft, Pfaff, who at the time was writing foreign affairs columns for *The New Yorker* and the *International Herald Tribune*, felt that Morris had misunderstood *Commonweal*. So Pfaff wrote Morris to set him straight regarding his magazine's politics during the early Cold War.

Pfaff had an excellent vantage point since he wrote "most of the foreign policy editorials [at *Commonweal*] between 1949 and 1955." Virtually all Catholics at the time were anti-communist. Many were conservative and followers of Joseph McCarthy, of course, but not all. Pfaff explained, "Our position in general was the one which today is usually identified (more often condemned, in the present politically correct climate) as 'Cold War Liberalism.'" On a comparative note, he added that *Commonweal* and the *New Leader* were anti-communist at a time "when the *Nation* was fellow-travelling and the *New Republic* was running Henry Wallace, a captive of the Communist Party, for president." *Commonweal* was "liberal on social issues" but also "against McCarthy and the House Un-American Activities Committee." In fact, in the early 1950s, McCarthy had explicitly denounced *Commonweal* as "Communist

---

[1] Charles Morris, *American Catholic: The Saints and Sinners Who Built America's Most Powerful Church* (New York: Penguin Random House, 1998).

dupes." One of Pfaff's colleagues was subpoenaed to appear before the committee to defend both himself and the magazine. "Acquitted with honor," Pfaff proudly informed Morris.[2]

Commonweal Catholics such as Pfaff were not just Cold War liberals. In some sense, they were Cold War liberals *avant la lettre*. In the interwar period, when the American liberal view of the Soviet Union had not yet settled, Catholics were already resolute anti-communists. They were guided by anti-totalitarian theory, which had been first developed in part by Waldemar Gurian, later one of Pfaff's professors at the University of Notre Dame.[3] Additionally, before a wave of Progressive and New Deal reforms inflected American liberalism, the Roman Catholic Church had already articulated doctrine on the "social question" in nineteenth-century papal encyclicals that far surpassed what nineteenth-century liberalism offered to workers. At the same time, Catholicism had a long-standing skepticism concerning democracy – a source of some tension between liberals and Catholics – although, arguably, in the United States, the coexistence of the hierarchical church with democratic political norms was further developed than anywhere else.[4] Finally, Catholics were internationalists. The Church, after all, was a transnational institution with an uneasy relationship to nationalism.

Shifts in both American liberalism and Catholicism in the first half of the twentieth century allowed a political and ideological convergence between the two in a way that would have been impossible in earlier decades. That convergence occurred as Pfaff was coming of age, ultimately allowing Commonweal Catholics like him to both integrate into the intellectual elite and become Cold War liberals. American liberalism, with its "protean character," evolved to include Progressive reforms and the New Deal, and then anti-communism and American primacy on the international stage.[5] American Catholicism, for its part,

---

[2] William Pfaff to Charles Morris, June 7, 1994, William Pfaff Papers, Hesburgh Libraries, University of Notre Dame, South Bend, IN (hereafter WPP). I personally preprocessed the William Pfaff Papers in his family's apartment in Paris, France, during which time I consulted them. As I did so before they were fully processed at the Hesburgh Libraries, the box and folder numbers are absent here.
[3] James Chappel, "The Catholic Origins of Totalitarianism Theory in Interwar Europe," *Modern Intellectual History* 8, no. 3 (September 2011), 561–590. See also Udi Greenberg, *The Weimar Century: German Émigrés and the Ideological Foundations of the Cold War* (Princeton: Princeton University Press, 2014), chapter 3.
[4] Paul Blanshard, *American Freedom and Catholic Power* (Boston: Beacon Press, 1949); John T. McGreevy, *Catholicism and American Freedom: A History* (New York: W.W. Norton, 2003).
[5] Gary Gerstle, "The Protean Character of American Liberalism," *American Historical Review* 99, no. 4 (October 1994), 1043–1073.

also increasingly became part of the American mainstream.[6] On the other side of the Atlantic, evolutions in European Catholic thought led to a greater embrace of modernity, much closer to the liberal relationship between church and state in the United States. This current of Catholicism, which James Chappel has termed "Catholic Modern," was well received in the United States at institutions such as Notre Dame and *Commonweal*, where Pfaff spent his formative years.[7] In the wake of World War II, the shared anti-communism of the United States and the Vatican also led to a convergence regarding the geopolitical role of the United States as a bulwark against Soviet expansion.[8] On a domestic level in the United States, all these ideological developments accompanied and encouraged a greater integration of American Catholics into the structures of the American mainstream, including political and intellectual elites.

William Pfaff was one of those elites, formed in this midcentury crucible of Americanism, Catholicism, and liberalism. His early career alternated between the liberal Catholic magazine *Commonweal* and several organizations of the American national security state. His formative experiences occurred in a liberal Catholic milieu, first as a precocious undergraduate at the University of Notre Dame from 1945 to 1949 and then as an editor at *Commonweal* after 1949.[9] During the Korean War, Pfaff's firm anti-Stalinism led him to leave *Commonweal* and join the Army. He later rejoined *Commonweal*, worked for the Free Europe Committee (FEC), a CIA-funded anti-communist front organization, and was one of the very first hires at the Hudson Institute, a think tank, in 1961. Geopolitical changes from the late 1950s on, including most notably the American war in Vietnam, caused Pfaff to become an ever-harsher critic of American liberalism, even as he himself hewed to the particular midcentury liberal synthesis that had shaped him. Pfaff's disillusionment over the course of the 1960s led him to develop an eclectic critique of the U.S. imperial project. And then, in 1971, after two decades in institutions at the heart of the American national security

---

[6] McGreevy, *Catholicism and American Freedom*.
[7] James Chappel. *Catholic Modern: The Challenge of Totalitarianism and the Remaking of the Church* (Cambridge, MA: Harvard University Press, 2018); Sarah Shortall, *Soldiers of God in a Secular World: Catholic Theology and Twentieth Century French Politics* (Cambridge, MA: Harvard University Press, 2021).
[8] Giuliana Chamedes, *A Twentieth-Century Crusade: The Vatican's Battle to Remake Christian Europe* (Cambridge, MA: Harvard University Press, 2019); Peter Kent, *The Lonely Cold War of Pope Pius XII* (Montreal: McGill-Queen's University Press, 2002); Patrick McNamara, *A Catholic Cold War: Edmund A. Walsh, SJ, and the Politics of American Anticommunism* (New York: Fordham University Press, 2005).
[9] Until the 1960s, the magazine was known as *The Commonweal*.

state, he consciously chose to move to its margins. He left the United States to establish residency in France, where he lived the rest of his life, serving first as the deputy director of the Hudson Institute Europe and then as a commentator on foreign affairs for publications such as the *New Yorker*, the *International Herald Tribune*, *Foreign Affairs*, and the *New York Review of Books*.

This chapter examines Pfaff's early career, as a window on the Catholic contribution to Cold War liberalism and the American empire that accompanied and reinforced it. As the most prominent foreign policy intellectual to emerge from this midcentury liberal Catholic world, Pfaff's thought is indicative of the tenuous nature of that liberal Catholic synthesis. His eclectic liberalism over the course of his writing career is best read as an idiosyncratic – and ultimately failed – attempt to integrate the modern Catholic principles he imbibed at Notre Dame and *Commonweal* within the ideology and institutions of American liberalism. Notably, the American imperial project proved a sticking point. Despite Pfaff's disenchantment with his early Cold War liberalism, in later decades he was steadfast in his refusal to fully embrace either the New Left or neoconservatism, unlike many of his colleagues and friends.[10] By following Pfaff's career from its 1949 beginning at *Commonweal* magazine up to his permanent departure from the United States in 1971, this chapter sheds new light on the integration of Catholics into the institutions and debates of midcentury American liberalism and the particular postwar conjunction that produced Cold War liberalism.

Commonweal Catholic, Cold War Liberal

During the years he was on the masthead, Pfaff's personal positions on political issues and *Commonweal*'s editorial line were virtually indistinguishable. As Pfaff told Morris in the 1990s, he wrote most of the foreign policy editorials between 1949 and 1955. Those editorials were unsigned. Even if one person had the primary responsibility for drafting them, the editorial process was collaborative and consensual.[11] Pfaff's other responsibilities in those early years were primarily editorial. When they did involve writing, it largely consisted of short reviews of books and films. The editorial team in the early Cold War rarely disagreed. "In retrospect it was surprisingly easy to form a consensus,"

---

[10] Michael Novak and Michael Harrington are perhaps the most representative examples. Both wrote regularly for *Commonweal* before their ideological shifts toward, respectively, neoconservatism and the New Left. Novak was a close friend of Pfaff before 1971.

[11] Peter Steinfels, Correspondence with the Author, November 2, 2020.

one former editor remembers, largely because the close-knit group discussed issues constantly throughout the week.[12] As the youngest editor on staff, Pfaff's writing was thus symptomatic of the intellectual currents the magazine represented. The political positioning of Commonweal Catholics such as Pfaff may have not been characteristic of the majority of American Catholics, but they were representative of a very important transatlantic current within Catholicism. The same ideas, arguments, and people that appeared in *Commonweal* also animated the education that Pfaff received at the University of Notre Dame. The values, frameworks, and analytic approaches that he learned in both institutions shaped his work throughout his career.

Francis O'Malley, Pfaff's favorite professor at Notre Dame, was a notable individual in the *Commonweal* orbit who played a role in both of Pfaff's early formative experiences. O'Malley, who served as the managing editor of *Review of Politics* alongside Waldemar Gurian, designed and taught Pfaff's degree, and also recommended Pfaff for a job at the magazine in 1949, launching the lower-class boy from Iowa on his career as a journalist and foreign policy intellectual.[13] Throughout his long career, Pfaff recognized the influence of O'Malley on his own life and thinking. Over half a century afterwards, he was still making the debt explicit. In the acknowledgment section of his last book, he ended with a recognition of "the crucial moral and philosophical influence of Frank O'Malley at Notre Dame so many years ago."[14] Pfaff's lasting gratitude went not to a history or political science professor but to someone who taught English. Written as it was in a book on American foreign policy, this unusual sign of respect for an English professor whose direct influence ended over sixty years earlier deserves further comment.

O'Malley had a profound influence on more than one generation of young Midwestern Catholic boys such as William Pfaff. O'Malley was a "bachelor don" at Notre Dame, an instructor who had never obtained his PhD, but lived in the university dorms in close contact with students, like in other elite universities' collegiate or house systems. Without specialized study, he was an inveterate generalist, which showed in the English course of study he designed at Notre Dame. In "The Lay

---

[12] Ibid. Steinfels is speaking of the editorial process a decade later (he arrived in 1964), but he worked under the same editor as Pfaff with several other key staff members. Given that continuity, we can safely assume the process had changed little.

[13] Note, *The Commonweal* (October 28, 1949), 61; William Pfaff, "Trying My Hand: How I Got Started in Journalism," *Commonweal* (October 10, 2014), www.commonweal magazine.org/trying-my-hand (accessed: January 6, 2023).

[14] William Pfaff, *The Irony of Manifest Destiny: The Tragedy of America's Foreign Policy* (New York: Walker & Company, 2010), 191.

Intellectual," Pfaff mentioned that the Notre Dame English curriculum included "studying the Greeks, aesthetics, Dante, Shakespeare, Kierkegaard, Rimbaud and Baudelaire, Maritain, Bernanos, Mauriac, Hermann Broch, Romano Guardini," among many others.[15] Each year, O'Malley distributed a reading list of hundreds of books, which captured his own idiosyncratic reading of the Western tradition and highlighted the Catholic ideas and values that flowed throughout it.[16] In addition to the standard course – something along the lines of "The Greats" and "The Moderns" one might find at Oxford at the time – O'Malley's also designed and taught Notre Dame's most popular English class: "Catholic Writers."

O'Malley's devoted following among the young midwestern Catholic boys at Notre Dame came to be known as the O'Malley Boys. Taking their cues from the popular English professor, they wore dapper clothing and took an intense interest in writing, politics, and the liturgical movement.[17] O'Malley also was the faculty sponsor of a selective debating society called "The Wranglers," which Pfaff joined. Many of the O'Malley Boys commented that they got most out of regular discussion sessions at a local bar, where their professor would hold forth on politics, art, and literature late into the night. Several of O'Malley's students remarked that he gave a religious education but in literary form.[18] As his biographer notes, O'Malley had "somehow broken free" from the "garrison mentality" of Tridentine Catholicism.[19] His program for young Catholic boys provided them a social and religious identity that was Catholic and yet somehow more liberated, even attuned to the European avant-garde.[20] Pfaff was only one of several notable graduates of the O'Malley's program. Others included the longtime religion editor at *Newsweek*, a Pulitzer Prize–winning novelist, and a governor of Ohio.[21] Decades after graduating from his program, all credited O'Malley with providing them an integrated view of religion, politics, art, and literature.

---

[15] William Pfaff, "The Lay Intellectual (Apologia Pro Vita Sua)," *Salmagundi* no. 70/71 (Spring–Summer 1986), 341.

[16] John William Meaney, *O'Malley of Notre Dame* (South Bend, IN: University of Notre Dame Press, 1991), 46–50. See also Arnold Sparr, *To Promote, Defend, and Redeem: The Catholic Literary Revival and the Cultural Transformation of American Catholicism, 1920–1960* (New York: Greenwood Press, 1990), chapter 8.

[17] Pfaff and others often attended mass in the evenings with O'Malley. William Slavick, Personal Interview, September 21, 2019.

[18] Meaney, *O'Malley of Notre Dame*, 249.

[19] Ibid., 14.

[20] Sparr, *To Promote, Defend, and Redeem*, chapter 8.

[21] For recollections from a wide variety of devoted O'Malley students, see Meaney, *O'Malley of Notre Dame*, chapter 6.

This wide-ranging curriculum in the humanities with a strong Catholic inflection opened Pfaff's eyes to the broader world, gave him pride in his Catholic identity, and provided an education in the "Western canon."[22] It was not, Pfaff admitted, "a bad education to offer provincial boys from the Catholic immigration; but it was not exactly an education calculated for success in the American Dream."[23] For Pfaff, O'Malley's curriculum also cultivated a particular set of values and analytic tools that he used throughout his career. The Notre Dame professor often read texts against the grain, in ways that specialists would not, filtering them through Catholic beliefs on psychological and social questions.[24] It provided students like Pfaff a willingness to similarly read texts against the grain, even against American values at times (if they were portrayed as in conflict with deeper Catholic truths). More generally, it gave Pfaff an introduction to the literary and cultural zeitgeist of countries across Europe and a deep ability to seek out motivating principles in that writing. An attention to religious motivations in fictional texts and their political and social implications, cultivated in O'Malley's classroom, served Pfaff in great stead throughout his career.[25]

Pfaff's education also provided the conditions to accomplish something else rather significant: It enabled him to reconcile his American nationalism and his Catholic internationalism.

My education would be irreproducible today ... A Catholic education in the United States before Vatican II was necessarily an education in what Scott Fitzgerald described as the true capacity of the intelligent person – the capacity to simultaneously entertain two conflicting ideas. One was a Catholic and one was an American: but the Catholic was an internationalist when the American was a nationalist. The American was a democrat but the Catholic was committed to making Catholicism the state religion and suppressing other religions. ... It was an uneasy internationalism precisely because it challenged the American conviction that America was best and the culmination of good things in history while Europe was bad and dangerous. ... The Catholic knew that he was implicated in Europe and found it awkward that Italy and Germany were supposed to be Catholic nations, or part Catholic, while England was defiantly

---

[22] See Sparr, *To Promote, Defend, and Redeem*, chapter 8.
[23] William Pfaff, "The Lay Intellectual (Apologia Pro Vita Sua)," 341.
[24] It also made graduate study more difficult. More than one of O'Malley students struggled to master other modes and methods in approaching texts when they attempted to continue their education at the graduate level. Kenneth Woodward, Personal Interview, August 9, 2019.
[25] In the late 1970s, Steve Wasserman, an editor at the *Los Angeles Times*, invited Pfaff to become a regular contributor after reading his "brilliant commentary on the eschatological underpinnings of the debacle that was the Jim Jones suicides and murders in the Guyanese jungle." Steve Wasserman, Personal Correspondence, February 24, 2017; William Pfaff, "The People's Temple," *The New Yorker* (December 10, 1978), 57.

Protestant, imperialist, and in the eyes of the Catholic Irish immigration the hereditary enemy. The German Catholic immigration had its own recollections of the first world war, when the Germany in which they or their parents had grown up was demonized by English propaganda.[26]

Commonweal Catholics exhibited the most refined vision of this synthesis. Being a Commonweal Catholic resolved – or at least seriously diminished – the tensions between American nationalism and Catholic internationalism. And it did so largely because of what one might consider liberal political ideology. James Chappel has used the case of German Catholic intellectual Eugen Kogon to argue that Cold War liberalism was not an "elitist ideology designed to further American hegemony" so much as "a diverse thought collective that brought together those who believed in individual rights, social justice, and mass enlightenment."[27] Like Kogon in Germany, Pfaff's experience as a Commonweal Catholic demonstrates that Cold War liberalism in the United States was also a contingent coalition made possible by a series of simultaneous convergences.

Commonweal was a lay magazine. Unlike most Catholic magazines at the time, there were no clerics in positions of authority at the publication. It was not a mouthpiece for the ecclesiastical hierarchy but rather a forum for democratic expression and debate that was inflected – but not dictated – by Catholic dogma. It sought to form Catholic opinion on key issues, staking out a place for principled democratic debate that was heavily influenced but not entirely determined by the Catholic hierarchy – a stance that in theory, if not in practice, could mollify liberal concerns about the compatibility of Catholicism and democracy. In its content, whether debates between (non-)Catholic) liberals and Catholics or in the publication of speeches by philosophers such as Jacques Maritain, it also sought to do the work of reconciling Catholicism with America's liberal state and society.[28] The independence from the Catholic hierarchy meant that they often staked out a political line that differed from the American Catholic mainstream. Before Pfaff arrived at the magazine, they had refused to support the Francoist side during the Spanish Civil War, in opposition to the vast majority of American Catholics.[29] They

---

[26] William Pfaff, Unpublished Manuscript ["John Casey, a fellow ..."], WPP, 1. The digital document seems to be preparatory notes for a memoir that was never completed.

[27] James Chappel, "The God That Won: Eugen Kogon and the Origins of Cold War Liberalism," *Journal of Contemporary History* 55, no. 2 (April 2020), 345.

[28] Unsigned Editorial, "Catholics and Liberals," *The Commonweal* (February 3, 1950), 452–453; Jacques Maritain, "America's Role in the New Europe" *The Commonweal* (February 26, 1943), 462–464.

[29] Van Allen, *The Commonweal and American Catholicism*, 60–65.

had also raised questions about whether the American use of the atom bomb at the end of World War II corresponded with Catholic just war theory.[30] Five years later, after the first hydrogen bomb test, *Commonweal* again expressed reservations. Nuclear weapons "will continue deeply to trouble the individual Christian conscience," *Commonweal* wrote.[31]

In Pfaff's first year as an editor, *Commonweal* observed its twenty-fifth anniversary by publishing a statement of its program and approach. The magazine defined that approach as "personalist" and "social," which, for the magazine's editors, meant "working essentially for the extension of social justice and for the protection of the human person in a period when he is threatened by impersonal, inhuman bigness, by machine-like institutions of government, industry, education and propaganda."[32] This implied a support for the welfare state as well as the civil rights movement.[33] Unlike Father Coughlin and other Catholics, they were not anti-Semitic. In fact, *Commonweal* editors actively engaging in meals, drinking sessions and pilgrimages with the Jews at *Commentary* (as well as with the Protestants at *Christian Century* and *Crisis*, an ecumenical grouping called the 4 C's). Of course, *Commonweal* editors' leftist leanings did not extend so far as anarchism or socialism. Although they occasionally associated with the Catholic Worker movement in New York centered around Dorothy Day and Peter Maurin, Commonweal Catholics were not pacifists.

In its support for these positions, however, the magazine regularly found itself on the defensive – nuancing positions or taking a stand based on means rather than ends. The welfare state was "potentially a serious threat to a free society, to the liberal tradition of personal independence," insisted one *Commonweal* editorial in Pfaff's first year, but Democratic policy, it also opined, was not socialism or communism.[34] The magazine's editorials acknowledged concerns that a greater centralization and bureaucratization might violate subsidiarist principles, but in practice they found that the government programs of the New Deal and the Fair Deal allowed Americans to preserve their personal freedoms.[35] In similar form, *Commonweal* expressed strong support for labor as a general principle, articulating an application of papal encyclicals to a

---

[30] Ibid., 92.
[31] Unsigned Editorial, "The H-Bomb," *The Commonweal* (February 17, 1950), 499.
[32] Unsigned Editorial, "Program and Approach," *The Commonweal* (December 2, 1949), 230.
[33] Unsigned Editorial, "Statement on the Welfare State," *The Commonweal* (February 10, 1950), 476.
[34] Ibid.
[35] Unsigned Editorial, "Commonweal Statement III: The Fair Deal," *The Commonweal* (March 31, 1950), 644.

steel workers' strike in September 1949, for instance, but also aired skepticism about labor's strategy.[36] Notably, *Commonweal* found McCarthy's anti-communist crusade excessive. His anti-communist aims were important and necessary, they wrote, but his means were dishonorable. The country needed to find a middle way, the magazine wrote, between "reckless smearing of honest liberals" and "ignoring the dangers of Communist infiltration."[37] In June 1950, an editorial denounced McCarthy as a "reckless, irresponsible bogey-man."[38]

Commonweal's political vision was firmly internationalist. In the same twenty-fifth anniversary issue, it articulated its position on foreign policy: "As in domestic affairs, so in assessing international relations the editors have held to the same two social and personalist objectives. Full employment, distribution of wealth and a condition of general prosperity in this country depend on the existence of similar conditions in foreign countries."[39] The magazine's own contributors as well as its topics were almost evenly distributed between American and international (primarily European), with a strong prominence of U.S.-based European *émigrés* writing in its pages.[40] Consequently, its positioning was firmly anti-isolationist.[41] Like many others, *Commonweal* was deeply concerned about the communist victory in the Chinese Civil War, provoking introspection about the American role in east Asia. However, *Commonweal*'s editorial went out of its way to pin the blame in part on American racism, arguing that too many Americans thought of the Chinese as "laundrymen and houseboys" in a "slum of the world," and not of their culture or what was going on in their minds.[42] The personalist commitment to the dignity of all humans lent

---

[36] Unsigned Editorial, "The Labor Movement: The Steel Dispute and the Encyclicals," *The Commonweal* (September 2, 1949), 509.

[37] Christopher Emmet, "The McCarthy Muddle," *The Commonweal* (April 7, 1950), 673. A separate editorial on the census included this brilliant yet entirely unnecessary aside: "In the week when Senator McCarthy was shooting away at political records and personal reputations like a drunken sailor attacking the rotary ducks at Coney Island, more and more Americans were in no hospitable mood to receive the imminent visit from the census taker." Unsigned Editorial, "... And I'll Tell You No Lies," *The Commonweal* (March 31, 1950), 646.

[38] Unsigned Editorial, "The Long Road," *The Commonweal* (June 2, 1950), 188.

[39] Unsigned Editorial, "Program and Approach," *The Commonweal* (December 2, 1949), 230.

[40] In addition to Jacques Maritain, among many others, there were Pfaff's professors Waldemar Gurian and Yves Simon, as well as the antidemocratic monarchist Erik von Kuehnelt-Leddihn, who wrote political reports about his native Austria. He moved to *National Review* after it was founded in 1955.

[41] Unsigned Editorial, "Isolationism Is Just around the Corner," *The Commonweal* (May 12, 1950), 118.

[42] Unsigned Editorial, "Playing for Keeps," *The Commonweal* (March 24, 1950), 622.

itself to greater empirical investigation and a greater openness to the experiences of colonized peoples.[43] It was an intellectual trait that Pfaff would carry with him throughout his career.

In most cases, this social and personalist, prolabor, internationalist anti-communism was indistinguishable from midcentury American liberalism. The convergence, however, was not without contradictions or tensions. The greatest shift was in the way that Catholic anti-communist thought created a place for the American state – and for American empire – unthinkable for earlier Catholics. The opening for American empire as a bulwark against global communism required an acceptance of the secular, liberal nature of the American state – one that may have approximated but did not fully incarnate the idea of a new "Christian civilization" for which Jacques Maritain called in the pages of *Commonweal* during World War II.[44] A *Commonweal* foreign policy editorial on Czechoslovakia from late 1949, which we can presume Pfaff wrote, illustrates the ways in which the motivations for the same political positions might differ. *Commonweal* argued that the "most essential right of man is the right to know and love God," which requires "certain political and social guarantees."[45] It also implied an obligation for Catholics in the United States – and in the West more generally – to stay engaged in European affairs. The arrest of hundreds of priests in Czechoslovakia, including the second-ranking prelate in the country, obliged the West to stay interested. It was the Catholic concern with freedom of religion in communist countries that translated into a direct defense of liberal rights.

Commonweal's foreign policy editorial on the beginning of the Korean War in the summer of 1950 praised the American entry in the war: "Politically, Mr. Truman's second historic decision was almost inevitable. To let Korea go would be to encourage sorties against the other weak spots adjacent to Soviet territory and spur on Soviet aggressiveness and enslavement."[46] It called for a "spirit of resistance" against the monolithic communist threat, and it exhorted its readers to fight against the disappearance of freedom for even more of their fellow humans. In the

---

[43] For a thoughtful exploration of the variegated relationship of Catholic personalism to colonialism, see Elizabeth Foster, *African Catholic* (Cambridge, MA: Harvard University Press, 2019).

[44] Jacques Maritain, "America's Role in the New Europe," *The Commonweal* (February 26, 1943), 462–464.

[45] Unsigned Editorial, "The Church in Czechoslovakia," *Commonweal* (October 7, 1949), 620.

[46] Unsigned Editorial, "Taking a Stand," *The Commonweal* (July 7, 1950), 307. As noted earlier, Pfaff presumably wrote this unsigned foreign policy editorial as well as the others mentioned here.

foreign policy editorials that followed that month, *Commonweal* praised the UN for choosing "to stand up to tyranny and fight for peace" and the United States for reassuring Europeans while also decrying Senator Taft's lack of bipartisanship.[47] Two articles in late July 1950 further fleshed out *Commonweal*'s thinking on communism and the Cold War. Pfaff's colleague John Cogley, whom Pfaff praised in his letter to Morris, argued that the anti-communist efforts of the past half decade were wasted because Americans were "half-materialists ourselves."[48] Waldemar Gurian, Pfaff's professor at Notre Dame, expressed concerns about strategic mistakes in the American policy of containment, highlighting doubts about the true path of Communist expansionism.[49] Korea could be a diversionary tactic in preparation for a push into western Europe. Later that same year, a foreign policy editorial fretted that the Cold War was in its final stages as a merely cold war. The "risk we are taking is enormous."[50] Another editorial rebutted Dorothy Day's pacifism, arguing that American military force was necessary to constrain evil in the world.[51] The war in Korea was a just one, an important criterion for the Catholic magazine.

Pfaff did not just argue for the war; he also chose to fight himself. As was the case for so many others, Pfaff's Korean War engagement was a reflex cultivated in the previous decade. During World War II, his father worked at the Army base in Fort Benning, Georgia, and Pfaff himself joined the Junior ROTC. With the outbreak of war again in the early 1950s, Pfaff felt so strongly about the events in the Korean peninsula that he decided to leave his editorial job at *Commonweal* and enlist. The magazine kept him on the masthead, adding a note next to his name: "On leave with the armed forces," a weekly reminder that their own editor was doing his part in the fight against global communism.[52] By implication, it communicated that participating in the anti-communist struggle and serving the nation were of one piece with living out Catholic ideals. In 1952, Pfaff left the magazine for basic training, when the war had already entered its stalemate phase. The next year he was finally

---

[47] Unsigned Editorial, "UN," *The Commonweal* (July 14, 1950), 331; Unsigned Editorial, "It's an Ill Wind ...," *The Commonweal* (July 14, 1950), 333; Unsigned Editorial, "Politics as Usual," *The Commonweal* (July 21, 1950), 355.
[48] John Cogley, "The Failure of Anti-Communism," *The Commonweal* (July 21, 1950), 358.
[49] Waldemar Gurian, "After Korea, What?" *The Commonweal* (July 21, 1950), 359–361.
[50] Unsigned Editorial, "Next," *The Commonweal* (December 29, 1950), 293.
[51] Unsigned Editorial, "The Use of Force," *The Commonweal* (December 29, 1950), 293–294.
[52] It first appeared on February 15, 1952. Masthead, *The Commonweal* (February 15, 1952), 2.

deployed to east Asia. During that time, Pfaff found time to review books by American General George Marshall and German Field Marshall Rommel for *Commonweal*. In his review, he commented on war's tragic necessity: "War is not a perverse game, nor an aberration. That is the tragedy of it."[53] Implicitly or explicitly, his comments echoed Reinhold Niebuhr, embracing the pessimistic view of humanity and society that served as the backbone of Cold War liberalism.

After the war, Pfaff moved back into journalism and began to travel more extensively. He never saw action during the Korean War, since he was on a transport ship when the armistice was signed in the summer of 1953. After decommissioning, he returned to *Commonweal* to become an associate editor. In 1955, as the magazine faced financial difficulties, he became a contributing editor and moved to an editorial job at ABC News. Between 1955 and 1957, he traveled extensively, including to the Belgian Congo, Egypt, Syria, Iraq, and Lebanon, writing trenchant commentary for *Commonweal* on each visit. Pfaff increasingly nuanced the abstract concepts of atheistic communism, domino theory, and just war with perceptive descriptions of the decolonizing world. In 1954, Pfaff attempted to grapple with how the particularities of Asian culture and history fit into the American anti-communist struggle. "The major problem in Asia is one of culture and history," he wrote.[54] Pfaff explicitly compared the tenuous nature of political development in Asian countries with the fragility of Western democracies. "Thus Asia is in a revolution whose outcome is more than a little doubtful. Even in the West, with its rather long tradition of the rule of law and of representative government, democracy is not a sure thing. It has collapsed in certain countries and may do so again."[55] In the same essay, Pfaff broached the possibility of capitalizing on the U.S.'s anti-colonial past and embracing the revolutions in Asia, before concluding that Americans were too conservative and thus fundamentally incapable on a political level of doing so. As was typical for *Commonweal* as a whole, a pragmatic argument based on means rather than ends led him to discard a radical option. He also expressed a deep concern that the anti-American effects of racial discrimination and McCarthyism would undermine the anti-communist struggle.[56]

In 1957, Pfaff moved to the FEC, a CIA-funded front organization engaged in political warfare in eastern Europe. In his papers, there are

---

[53] William Pfaff, "Two Kinds of War," *The Commonweal* (June 26, 1953), 300.
[54] William Pfaff, "The Asian Horizon" *The Commonweal* (September 3, 1954), 527.
[55] Ibid., 528.
[56] For a full treatment of this dynamic, see Mary L. Dudziak, *Cold War Civil Rights: Race and the Image of American Democracy, Politics and Society in Twentieth-Century America* (Princeton: Princeton University Press, 2011).

no contemporaneous records of his work at the FEC, although, later in life, he described his work as helping to promote intellectual and artistic freedom in eastern Europe. It seems he played some role in the publication, translation, and distribution of *The New Class: An Analysis of the Communist System* by Milovan Đilas. His choice to work at FEC, as shown by his writing on the experience later in life, expresses a commitment to the anti-communist cause and, like many involved in the cultural Cold War, strong support for free artistic and intellectual production and distribution.

The Emergence of a Critic

During the 1950s, Pfaff began to develop his own voice. While still a deeply committed anti-communist, there were moments when Pfaff displayed a willingness to grapple with the blind loyalty that anti-communism engendered or the power that the United States was accumulating. Hints of this skepticism appear early on. In 1950, Pfaff accompanied an American Catholic group to Rome for a pilgrimage. While at a Catholic youth rally at the Colosseum in Rome with Germans and Italians, he distanced himself from the crowd, bothered by the "interminable triple translation" and the general tenor of the proceedings. He felt "that in the marches and noise of the rally, in this business of demonstrations, in what was being said, there was not being made an appeal to spiritual strength and charity, but to loyalty."[57] In a meditative reflection on the differences between Americans and Europeans, he worried about the military, political, and economic force that the United States was accumulating and the effect it might have. While not budging on his anti-communist principles or his belief in the justice of the war effort in Korea, he argued, echoing Kennan in the Long Telegram, "we have to walk the knife edge, building material power, and still refusing to permit our minds and our faith to be corrupted by the power we control."[58]

Pfaff also began to flesh out a critique of the American national security state's overreliance on quantitative methods. In 1961, Pfaff and his FEC colleague Edmund Stillman reviewed Herman Kahn's *On Thermonuclear War*.[59] In contrast to other critics, the two FEC colleagues found that the discussion of thermonuclear war was not immoral and evil in and of itself. They did however take exception to the large

---

[57] William Pfaff, "Force," *The Commonweal* (October 20, 1950), 31. It is worth mentioning that he was twenty-one when he wrote this reflection.
[58] Ibid.
[59] Edmund Stillman and William Pfaff, "Ready for Extinction," *Problems in Communism* (July 1961), 37–39.

amount of "strategic and politico-strategic speculation using mathematical and statistical techniques."[60] The psychological and political elements of a potential nuclear war were not always "susceptible to such analysis," they argued.[61] Kahn, they observed, was representative of the failure of his entire class of defense intellectuals, "those civilian and quasi-civilian experts who are legion and who provide the cadres of the military and ideological agencies that have been engendered by the cold war."[62] These defense intellectuals failed on a very basic level "to grasp the true passions and motives in the lives of men and nations." Stillman and Pfaff admitted that their review was "harsh," but, they added, "it must be said that he invites harshness."[63] Their critique of Kahn's argument did not seem to disturb Kahn. He decided to hire Stillman and Pfaff as two of the first hires at his new think tank, the Hudson Institute, convinced that such internal critique could only be beneficial. The FEC colleagues, for their part, were more than willing to add two more to the legions of defense intellectual they had criticized. Stillman and Pfaff eventually stayed for a decade at the New York think tank, leaving in the early 1970s to establish the Hudson Institute Europe in Paris.

Beginning in that same year, Pfaff and Stillman cowrote the first of three books criticizing American foreign policy, *The New Politics* (1961), *The Politics of Hysteria* (1964), and *Power and Impotence* (1966).[64] Collectively, the trilogy made the argument that American foreign policy was failing because it ignored geopolitical shifts since the mid-1950s, was reliant on a "defective sense of history," and was carried out in a Manichean and messianic fashion. Additionally, it misunderstood the impact of Western civilization on other societies. The books brought the two men fame and attention.[65] John F. Kennedy was photographed with *The New Politics* under his arm. After their first success, Stillman and Pfaff received a Rockefeller Grant to write the second book, enabling them to travel extensively and then write at the Rockefeller retreat at Lake Como.

During that time, Pfaff also regularly wrote foreign affairs commentary in *Commonweal*, *Commentary*, and *Foreign Policy*, with almost monthly

---

[60] Ibid., 38.
[61] Ibid., 38.
[62] Ibid., 37.
[63] Ibid., 39.
[64] Edmund Stillman and William Pfaff, *The New Politics: America and the End of the Postwar World* (New York: Harper Colophon, 1961); Edmund Stillman and William Pfaff, *The Politics of Hysteria: The Sources of 20th Century Conflict* (New York: Harper Colophon, 1964); Edmund Stillman and William Pfaff, *Power and Impotence: The Failure of America's Foreign Policy* (New York: Vintage Books, 1966).
[65] *Power and Impotence* was blurbed by no less than three U.S. senators: Frank Church, George McGovern, and Ernest Gruening.

articles in his former employer's publication from 1964 until 1970. The vast majority dealt with Vietnam, an ever-increasing obsession. He insisted on the complex nature of the conflict in Vietnam and deplored the American urge to simplify. "This war in Vietnam has been made into a symbolic confrontation of American power with Asian Communism. We are responsible for having given it this terrible symbolic weight, stubbornly refusing to see it in its tormented singularity."[66] He also deplored the determinism behind development theory as well as the "belief that the North American political and social experience is of general validity and relevance" to developing nations.[67] Pfaff visited Vietnam himself in 1962 during the Rockefeller-funded research trip for *The Politics of Hysteria* and then again in 1966.[68] After his first visit, the discrepancy between his observations and the official narrative made him suspicious. He looked to any writer who could provide useful background and trustworthy information. He took a particular interest in the writings of Bernard Fall, who he regularly cited in his own work.[69] Pfaff also became increasingly pugnacious when the subject of the war in Vietnam arose. His wife remembers having to drag him out of a cocktail party, where he got into a heated argument on the subject with a member of the *New York Times* editorial board.[70]

Pfaff pinned the fault of Vietnam fully on American liberals. Some argued that it was the conservative men in the Pentagon determining American foreign policy, but, in truth, Pfaff insisted, it was the liberals themselves. "The Pentagon today is a triumph of the applied rationalism of modern American engineering."[71] This produced a "disorientation in attempting to deal with the non-military elements in the Vietnamese problem."[72] The English major decried the management consultants and technical theorists, positions that he viewed as firmly rooted in liberalism itself. "The Defense Department does not pose a rightist or militarist threat to American policy. The threat it poses is the threat of unanalyzed liberal cant earnestly and tirelessly and unskillfully applied to tormented and complex conflicts."[73] Pfaff refused to countenance assertations that there were differences between the earlier

---

[66] William Pfaff, "No Victory in Vietnam," *The Commonweal* (April 23, 1965), 137.
[67] William Pfaff, "Yankees vs. Latins," *The Commonweal* (May 28, 1965), 310.
[68] His letters to his parents from the 1962 visit are preserved in his papers. The 1966 visit generated a series of discussion papers at the Hudson Institute. Both are found in WPP.
[69] William Pfaff, "Vietnam: The Roots of the Chaos," *The Commonweal* (November 6, 1964), 187–188.
[70] Carolyn Pfaff, Personal Interview, Paris, France, September 11, 2020.
[71] William Pfaff, "Computerized Diplomacy," *Commonweal* (July 23, 1965), 520.
[72] Ibid., 521.
[73] Ibid.

American engagement in Vietnam and the escalation under Johnson. When Robert Kennedy declared that the whole moral position of the United States in Vietnam had shifted since his brother was President, Pfaff insisted, "Actually Vietnam is American liberalism's war, which most liberals now want to disavow."[74] Within the Hudson Institute, the division regarding social scientific methods between Stillman and Pfaff, on the one hand, and Kahn, on the other hand, only grew over the 1960s. They took the opposing side to Kahn and several other colleagues in the think tank's 1968 publication *Can We Win in Vietnam?*[75] In a review of the debate by RAND analyst Daniel Ellsberg, he praised Pfaff and Stillman's contribution, arguing that a tragedy could have been averted had they been listened to earlier.[76]

American liberal foreign policy was not just failing in Vietnam because of liberals' poor choices and methods; it was also tainted by a secularized puritanism. "Cromwellian" and "puritan" reoccur as epithets in his writing about American foreign policy. Despite claims to the contrary, U.S. policy was not the tough realism of Talleyrand or Metternich. "Our foreign policy has always reflected a puritan view, with little sympathy for the aberrations or selfishness of other nations, and little attention to our own."[77] Its view of history was similarly flawed: "It has also expressed a progressive or perfectionist view of history, originally Enlightenment, latterly a Wilsonian romanticism about world organization and order."[78] Like Daniel Patrick Moynihan and Richard Rovere, Pfaff was willing to be a "serious" liberal who was capable of self-criticism in contrast to these progressives. Increasingly, Pfaff sought out different political categories to correspond with the divide he observed. Like others trying to grapple with the events of the 1960s and postindustrial society, Pfaff wanted to dispense with categories of right and left. At one point, he indicated an interest in labeling political movements based on whether they were "romantic" or not.[79]

The centrality of the United States in Pfaff's internationalism had always been contingent. At the beginning of the Cold War, the United States happened to be the most powerful and best placed to

---

[74] William Pfaff, "Foreign Affairs: The Liberals' War," *Commonweal* (December 15, 1967), 350.
[75] Frank E. Armbruster, Raymond D. Gastil, Herman Kahn, William Pfaff, Edmund Stillman, *Can We Win in Vietnam?* (Greenwood, CT: Praeger, 1968).
[76] Daniel Ellsberg, "Kahn on Winning in Vietnam: A Review," November 1968. The publication is not clearly marked in the copy found in WPP. It was either a draft for the *American Political Science Review* or a speech given based on it.
[77] William Pfaff, "On Being Tough," *Commonweal* (June 25, 1965), 431.
[78] Ibid., 431.
[79] William Pfaff, "Right and Left," *Commonweal* (March 11, 1966), 655.

oppose communism. By the end of the 1960s, Pfaff was not so sure. If American liberalism and its methods were at fault for the quagmire in Vietnam, then perhaps American primacy required a rethinking. He increasingly looked for counterbalances to American hegemony, drawing hope from De Gaulle's foreign policy. In response to the French President's decisions in the mid-1960s, Pfaff encouraged the U.S. to move away from a position of primacy. It would not be "isolationism" or "neo-isolationism" to accept a multipolar world, he argued. It could be liberating. The United States could "acknowledge and even welcome this attenuation of the responsibilities we have borne since the Second World War, this opportunity to play a new and freer role in world affairs."[80]

At times, Pfaff could echo neoconservative points. He noted that the last three decades of liberal consensus "are coming apart and liberalism finds itself at a dead stop."[81] He spoke kindly about an ADA talk that Daniel Moynihan delivered in 1967 which called for liberal alliance with moderate conservatives "to defend the social fabric, the social peace, of the United States."[82] He worried that the repudiation and abdication of the center would extend, and in a "growing sense of powerlessness and humiliation," the U.S. would live through its own crisis of liberal civilization, as Europe had in the 1920s and 1930s.[83] More generally, he was concerned that all these developments could upend something even more crucial, "the commitment to constitutional government."[84] In a 1967 *Commonweal* column entitled "Star-Spangled Fascism," he fretted that American liberal governance was not matching societal change, and if something was not done to change course, the liberal government could become "the prisoner of assumptions about international society and international relations that prompt it into wars and crises that amount to violent attempts to resolve problems that are insoluble on liberal terms."[85] In such cases, the United States might follow a "romantic retreat from reason" and the elites and masses might seek "solutions which promise to short-cut the normal political process of compromise and conciliation."[86] In that case, it would not be called it fascism, but the evolution of American politics would be on the same order.

[80] William Pfaff, "Return to Isolation?" *The Commonweal* (March 26, 1965), 7.
[81] William Pfaff, "The Liberal Crisis," *Commonweal* (January 19, 1963), 463.
[82] Ibid., 463.
[83] Ibid., 463.
[84] William Pfaff, "Muddied American Messianism," *Commonweal* (March 22, 1963), 9.
[85] William Pfaff, "Star-Spangled Fascism," *Commonweal* (August 11, 1967), 488.
[86] Ibid., 488.

Pfaff's first and only sustained engagement with liberalism per se came in his 1971 book *Condemned to Freedom*.[87] His only book to exclusively address domestic policy as well, it made the case for saving liberalism from itself. After detailing his view of liberalism's contemporaneous crisis, Pfaff proposed limited, technocratic, yet simultaneously "radical" solutions to save it from itself. According to Pfaff, class and religion were no longer pertinent categories. The bigger issue was that too many were seeking utopian and transcendent goals via politics. If politics could only be limited to what was truly attainable and then guided by reason, then liberalism might self-correct. It was an idiosyncratic attempt to do what many were attempting around the same time. The book emerged from a series of discussion groups at the Council on Foreign Relations in 1969 and 1970.[88] Arthur Schlesinger, Jr., who had recently published his own diagnosis of the problems facing American liberalism, was one of the participants in the CFR discussion group.[89] Pfaff was less dismissive of the student protesters and less focused with the American presidency than Schlesinger, but their assessments of the political landscape in their respective books resembled each other. Both emphasized the role of rationality in liberalism and believed intellectuals ought to play a prominent role. In short, both assumed a certain kind of elitism. Naturally, the war in Vietnam loomed large in their depictions of the crisis enfolding American liberalism.

The year 1971 was significant for Pfaff for more than one reason. In addition to the publication of his first book as a solo author, that year he also moved to Paris. Ed Stillman, Pfaff's coauthor and longtime colleague at the FEC and the Hudson Institute, had opened a European branch of the Hudson Institute with plans to gain full operational independence from Herman Kahn and New York, and Pfaff was given the opportunity to be Stillman's deputy. He immediately found that he enjoyed the intellectual climate in France. Unlike in the United States, he felt that French intellectuals were held in greater esteem and played a more important role in public debate.[90] Although his stay in Paris was meant to be temporary, Pfaff lived in Paris until his death, forty-four years later, in 2015.[91]

---

[87] William Pfaff, *Condemned to Freedom* (New York: Random House, 1971).

[88] William Pfaff, "Background Paper No. 6, The Quest for a Conclusion," May 21, 1970, Discussion Group on New Forces in World Politics, Council on Foreign Relations, WPP.

[89] Arthur Schlesinger, Jr., *The Crisis of Confidence; Ideas, Power, and Violence in America* (Boston: Houghton Mifflin, 1969).

[90] William Pfaff, "The Lay Intellectual (Apologia Pro Vita Sua)," 334–342.

[91] His widow says that they rented out their Connecticut home at first, only selling it at a later date. Carolyn Pfaff, Personal Interview, Paris, France, September 11, 2020.

As Deputy Director of the Hudson Institute Europe (1971–78) and then as an opinion columnist at the *International Herald Tribune* (1978–2005), Pfaff engaged extensively with European political and business elites. *Le Monde*, *Le Figaro*, and *Le monde diplomatique* became a part of his information diet, and the American news he read was filtered through the Paris-based editors at the *International Herald Tribune*. Like many Americans in the twentieth century, he took stock of his American identity from the vantage point of Paris.[92] The resulting perspective was decidedly negative. Despite a brief burst of enthusiasm at the end of the Cold War, Pfaff largely soured on the American project. By the new century, he was complaining that George W. Bush's policymakers had completed a process begun at midcentury. They had turned liberalism into a utopian political project in line with fascism or communism.[93] As an inveterate anti-utopian, he felt strongly that liberalism – and the United States more generally – had deserted him. The anti-intellectual and consumerist characteristics of American society rendered the people incapable of reinvigorating the American values he had known at midcentury, and no better experts were on hand. By the 2010s, he saw no way to right the course.

Cold War Afterlives

Despite William Pfaff's critiques of American foreign policy, his early Cold War engagement in the Army and the FEC remained meaningful to him throughout his life. The Pfaff apartment in Paris contained mementos of his time in the Army, including a designer ashtray with the insignia of his U.S. Army division. As his friend David Rieff notes, such an attachment to the military "takes a certain type."[94] Pfaff was far from an "anti-American" to his own mind, despite being tagged with the label for his criticism of American foreign policy.[95] Yet even if Pfaff embraced a certain idea of the United States, he rarely spoke about his time fighting the cultural Cold War at the FEC. In the decades that followed his employment there, his four years at the FEC were regularly omitted from

---

[92] Brooke L. Blower, *Becoming Americans in Paris: Transatlantic Politics and Culture between the World Wars* (Oxford: Oxford University Press, 2011).
[93] William Pfaff, *The Irony of Manifest Destiny: The Tragedy of America's Foreign Policy* (New York: Walker & Company, 2010).
[94] David Rieff, Personal Interview, Paris, France, January 25, 2017.
[95] His longtime residency in Paris provided easy fodder when he critiqued George W. Bush's foreign policy in the lead-up to the 2003 invasion of Iraq. In early 2003, Bill O'Reilly devoted a ten-minute segment of his show to denounce Pfaff as "anti-American." Peter Hart, *The Oh Really Factor: Unspinning Fox News Channel's Bill O'Reilly* (New York: Seven Stories Press, 2003), 150.

biographies he submitted for conferences and publications. In the words of his widow, "he just didn't go there."[96]

The end of the Cold War, however, opened a space for him to publicly address his work at the FEC and grapple with its role in the American imperial project. Both in columns and in correspondence with former colleagues in the 1990s, he opined on the relative merits of those early years of engagement as a Cold War liberal. The 1991 nomination of Robert Gates as the Director of Central Intelligence provided one such opportunity. Gates was suspected of involvement in the Iran–Contra affair a few years prior to his nomination while serving as deputy to then Director William Casey. In late July 1991, Pfaff chose to intervene in the political controversy in the *International Herald Tribune*. He acknowledged his own Cold War service and then used it as a legitimating experience to argue that the CIA should be shuttered: "In this writer's view, political operations and political warfare could and should simply be shut down," he wrote, staking out a position that easily could have come from the New Left.[97] "This is an area in which I was involved in the 1950s, and I would argue that then, and certainly now, U.S. interference in other peoples' elections, colonial wars and internal government struggles has done more harm than good."[98] Pfaff did carve out at least a partial exception for certain programs of the Cultural Cold War, however. "Radio Free Europe and the Congress for Cultural Freedom were sound programs, but even the latter was carried on far too long, and backfired when the CIA's sponsorship was eventually revealed."[99] Among several laudatory responses from former colleagues and friends, Senator Daniel Patrick Moynihan wrote to tell him, "You are dead right on the CIA."[100]

The 1999 publication of Frances Stonor Saunders's book *Who Paid the Piper? The CIA and the Cultural Cold War* provided another occasion for Pfaff and his former colleagues to revisit their service at the FEC.[101] Pfaff made a full-throated defense of their work during the

---

[96] Carolyn Pfaff, Personal Interview, Paris, France, September 11, 2020.
[97] William Pfaff, "Casey's Agency Is Probably Too Old to Change Stripes," *International Herald Tribune* (July 31, 1991), 5.
[98] Ibid., 5.
[99] Ibid., 5.
[100] Daniel Patrick Moynihan to William Pfaff, August 14, 1991, WPP. Svetlana Alliluyeva, Stalin's only daughter, also wrote in response to the column, complimenting him and asking his advice on her relationship with the agency. Christopher Schaefer, "Covering the World with the International Herald Tribune" (PhD diss., University of Cambridge, 2023).
[101] Frances Stonor Saunders, *Who Paid the Piper? The CIA and the Cultural Cold War* (London: Granta Books, 1999).

1950s in an unambiguously titled *IHT* column, "We Cultural Cold Warriors Fought a Good Fight for Liberty."[102] He defined the CCF as a "counterattack against Soviet-funded propaganda organizations founded under prewar Comintern auspices."[103] Pfaff contrasted current disapproving views with those of his cohort, who believed "they were defending liberal political civilization."[104] In the most detailed description of his work at the FEC in any of his writing, Pfaff acknowledged traveling to the Middle East and India to arrange subsidized translations of Milovan Djilas's "The New Class" and later helping to publish a book on abstract expressionism for the Soviet and East European delegates to the 1956 Communist Youth Festival.[105] He went on to muse whether it was this book, rather than the MoMa connections, that had generated the popular thesis concerning the CIA-abstract expressionism connection. Pfaff defended these projects as far from "sinister." After providing anonymous descriptions of his colleagues from eastern Europe, Pfaff concluded the column, "You will understand that such colleagues left their influence on an American provincial then in his 20s, and that the influence has lasted."[106] Other former FEC colleagues praised him in response, concurring with his thesis: it was "balanced," they said, they were "touched," sharing "very similar feelings."[107]

Pfaff's 2004 book *The Bullet's Song* allowed him a final opportunity to refine his apology for the liberal Cold War actions of his youth.[108] *The Bullet's Song* consists of a series of profiles of intellectuals drawn to romance, adventure, and violence. These figures, which included Gabriele D'Annunzio, T. E. Lawrence, Ernst Jünger, André Malraux, were often motivated by utopian visions. Each was seemingly at odds with modernity, and yet those modern men of arms and letters exercised an influence on geopolitics, if only temporarily and often tragically. In an appendix entitled "Out-Münzenberging Münzenberg," Pfaff attempted to fit his own early Cold War engagement within the framework he had applied to the other intellectuals.[109] He argued that the development of the Congress for Cultural Freedom (CCF) was a

---

[102] William Pfaff, "We Cultural Cold Warriors Fought a Good Fight for Liberty," *International Herald Tribune* (August 9, 1999), 8.
[103] Ibid., 8.
[104] Ibid., 8.
[105] Ibid., 8.
[106] Ibid., 8.
[107] John Foster Leich to William Pfaff, August 22, 1999, WPP; Abraham Rothberg to William Pfaff, December 4, 1999, WPP.
[108] William Pfaff, *The Bullet's Song: Romantic Violence and Utopia* (New York: Simon & Schuster, 2004).
[109] Ibid., 321–335.

direct but more controlled outgrowth of Soviet propaganda campaigns under Willi Münzenberg (focusing in particular on the role of Arthur Koestler in both the Soviet and the American operations). For Pfaff and his FEC colleagues from eastern and central Europe, the revelation about CIA funding did not merit the angry denials of Stephen Spender and Dwight Macdonald. According to Pfaff, the East European exile staff of the FEC were "not born yesterday ... Nearly all had been in influential governmental, intellectual, academic, or political positions in their home countries before Communist occupation"[110] From their perspective, government funding or interference did not undermine or even taint the art. Rather, they "were delighted that this was so, since this implied official American commitment to the cause of their countries' national independence."[111] In a footnote, Pfaff mentions that the CIA daily bulletin that analyzed "Communist crime and duplicity and demonstrated America's virtue" was "the object of general mockery" by the staff of the FEC.[112] A mark of civilized people everywhere, the FEC staff demonstrated the capability of ironic detachment.

If the FEC, with its large European staff, was fighting the good fight of liberty, he could not consistently say the same of the CCF and the CIA. As Pfaff put it, "The CCF eventually collapsed not only because of the falsehood at the center, corrupting and unsustainable in the long run (and even eventually unnecessary) but also because the enterprise proved too much of a good thing."[113] Pfaff pinned this change to the 1960s, "as part of a larger corruption of the CIA, and under pressure of the Vietnam War."[114] Pfaff further argued that the CCF succeeded because it did not become the "crusading anti-Communist organization Koestler wanted."[115] Instead, the organization maintained its commitment to "the values of intellectual and artistic freedom" just as those values were "being aggressively suppressed in the Soviet Union and in the central and Eastern European countries under obscurantist Soviet-controlled police regimes."[116]

For William Pfaff, liberal political civilization was never tied to the American imperial project. America's place in Western civilization, like so much within the "thought collective" of the Cold War liberal synthesis, was a contingency of the mid twentieth century. Pfaff's liberal

---

[110] Ibid., 333.
[111] Ibid.
[112] Ibid., 327.
[113] Ibid., 335.
[114] Ibid.
[115] Ibid.
[116] Ibid.

Catholic formation, with its thick transatlantic ties, meant that a simple conflation of American hegemony with Western civilization was impossible. And the Catholic principle of subsidiarity provided a bulwark against American primacy in his thought. Even if he had fond memories of his own early engagement as a Cold War liberal, he was all too aware of the broader failures. And the abstract concepts of liberal civilization and freedom of expression, which undergirded so much Cold War commentary about American foreign policy, eventually provided Pfaff with a rhetorical arsenal to critique his own country. By the end of his career, he was convinced that the problems lay with American imperial ambitions accompanied by a crusading, even utopian, liberalism that had shown itself utterly incapable of self-correction. His career in America's liberal empire, first as a participant and then as a commentator, was made possible by the early Cold War synthesis between his American nationalism and his Catholic internationalism. For decades afterwards, Pfaff clung to the exhilaration of those formative moments and the liberal Catholic principles he thought it represented. The synthesis, however, was far from stable.

6 The Productive Character
Cold War Liberal Social Psychology from Totalitarianism to Entrepreneurship

Erik Baker

One day in December 1941, shortly after Pearl Harbor, Abraham Maslow had an epiphany. He was driving home from Brooklyn College, where he worked as an assistant professor of psychology, when he came across a "poor, pathetic parade" of Boy Scouts and World War I veterans. "As I watched, the tears began to run down my face," Maslow recalled. "I felt we didn't understand – not Hitler, nor the Germans, nor Stalin, nor the Communists. We didn't understand any of them. I felt that if we could understand, then we could make progress." Maslow became convinced that his vocation as a scholar was to furnish the "understanding" so conspicuously missing from the contemporary world. While traditional political doctrine had failed to grasp the reasons for the rise of Nazism and Stalinism, modern psychological science could provide a more sophisticated explanation and illuminate a pathway forward.[1]

In the decades following his Damascus moment, Maslow became one of the most visible representatives of a movement that used social and personality psychology to articulate the core themes of Cold War liberalism. Cold War liberalism, in Jan-Werner Müller's phrase, was a "liberalism after the failure of liberalism." As the introduction to this volume explores, it was haunted above all by a sense of the fragility of democracy – a fragility that many contemporary psychological theorists sought eagerly to explain. Cold War liberal intellectuals believed that if they were able to grasp the reasons for classical liberalism's failure to prevent the rise of fascism and Stalinism, it would be possible to forge a new liberalism capable of preventing the spread of "totalitarianism" in their own time. In the light of the catastrophe of the mid twentieth century, many mainstream intellectuals were prepared to resolve any

---

[1] "Overcoming Evil: An Interview with Abraham Maslow, Founder of Humanistic Psychology," *Psychology Today* (1992 [1968]), www.psychologytoday.com/us/articles/199201/abraham-maslow.

dispute between modern psychological theory and the assumptions of classical liberalism in favor of the former.²

As this volume shows, Cold War liberals felt acutely the need to distinguish between elites capable of guiding liberal rule and the masses who menaced its stability. Contemporary social scientists turned to the tools of developmental and personality psychology to rearticulate this distinction in an ostensibly more rigorous, scientifically sophisticated vocabulary. Classical liberalism, these psychologists claimed, assumed that traits such as rationality and autonomy were universal anthropological attributes, when they were really the fruits of psychological development and health. As a result, liberal societies foisted a degree of freedom and self-governance upon their citizens that they were not psychologically equipped to handle. Overwhelmed and neurotic, such citizens sought the supposed psychological comforts of authoritarian and totalitarian movements. The psychological diagnosis of what had gone wrong with classical liberalism implied that societies around the world needed to be led systematically to a higher degree of psychological development: to what was often called the "productive" character or personality.

Developed during World War II and the early Cold War period, the discourse of the productive character held that individuals who were too psychologically frail to stand up to totalitarian movements were distinguished by an inability to pursue work that was "productive" in a particular psychological sense: psychologically "productive" work was creative and functioned as an expression of the self. By the 1960s, this logic led liberals to hope that by developing psychologically healthy populations around the world, U.S. global leadership would not only create a bulwark against the seductions of totalitarianism but would also foster economic growth and "entrepreneurship," driven by productive individuals. What began as a political imperative to prepare individuals psychologically for freedom ultimately became an economic license for military interventionism and American-led economic development policy. The conceptual apparatus of Cold War social psychology was thus crucial to the reformulation of the justification for liberal empire in the aftermath of the defeat of fascism documented throughout this

---

² Jan-Werner Müller, "Calming the Ideological Storms? Reflections on Cold War Liberalism," in *Ideological Storms: Intellectuals, Dictators, and the Totalitarian Temptation*, ed. Vladimir Tismaneanu and Bogdan C. Iacob (Budapest: Central European University Press, 2019), 471; Edward Purcell, Jr., *The Crisis of Democratic Theory: Scientific Naturalism and the Problem of Value* (Lexington: University Press of Kentucky, 2013 [1973]). Today "social psychologists" are predominantly concerned with the dynamics of interpersonal interaction, but at midcentury, the label was also used for social theorists who deployed psychological methodologies.

volume. Psychological science was the medium in which the immutable racial inferiority postulated by classical imperialist ideology evolved into what Étienne Balibar describes as the "neo-racist" doctrine of rectifiable "cultural" backwardness that emerged triumphant in the late twentieth century.[3]

This chapter contributes to an ongoing scholarly reassessment of the origins of late twentieth-century neoliberalism in the political economy, culture, and society of the postwar decades. Many contemporary and subsequent assessments of Cold War society imagine a "closed world" in which sophisticated social management, aided by psychological expertise, smoothed over contradictions and maintained hegemonic homeostasis. But as I show here, postwar psychology, in theory and practice, was no less riven by contradiction than the welfare-state frameworks investigated by Amy Offner and Gabriel Winant or the rural economies analyzed by Bethany Moreton and Shane Hamilton. Cold War liberal psychologists tried to hold in one hand social democracy and individualism; self-expression and the work ethic; and political liberty and U.S. global dominance. In the end, it was the right-wing elements of this attempted synthesis whose staying power proved most robust.[4]

Diagnosing Totalitarianism

The theory of totalitarianism was arguably the conceptual centerpiece of Cold War liberalism, and social psychologists developed its most influential formulation. For Cold War liberal social psychologists, fascism and Communism were both manifestations of the same underlying phenomenon, totalitarianism or authoritarianism, which responded to a set of psychological needs that classical liberal theory neglected. Individuals joined totalitarian movements when their sense of self was inadequately developed. The healthy individual was secure enough in their ego or selfhood to be "productive," extending the self into the

---

[3] Etienne Balibar, "Is There a 'Neo-Racism'?" in Balibar and Immanuel Wallerstein, *Race, Nation Class: Ambiguous Identities* (New York: Verso Books, 1991).

[4] Amy C. Offner, *Sorting Out the Mixed Economy: The Rise and Fall of Welfare and Developmental States in the Americas* (Princeton: Princeton University Press, 2019); Gabriel Winant, "'Hard Times Make for Hard Arteries and Hard Livers': Deindustrialization, Biopolitics, and the Making of a New Working Class," *Journal of Social History* 53, no. 1 (2019), 107–132; Bethany Moreton, *To Serve God and Wal-Mart: The Making of Christian Free Enterprise* (Cambridge, MA: Harvard University Press, 2009); Shane Hamilton, *Trucking Country: The Road to America's Wal-Mart Economy* (Princeton: Princeton University Press, 2008). For the "closed world" idea, see Paul N. Edwards, *The Closed World: Computers and the Politics of Discourse in Cold War America* (Cambridge, MA: MIT Press, 1996).

world through creative work. The unproductive individual, in contrast, was dependent on external authorities to provide the sense of security they lacked on a psychological level. Totalitarianism was a movement of takers – liberal societies required givers.[5]

The social-psychological diagnosis of totalitarianism synthesized two streams of post-Freudian theorizing that developed in the years before the Cold War, one incubated in the New York emigre intellectual community and the other in the social science research apparatus of the wartime Office of Strategic Services (OSS). In New York, one of the most important outposts of social-psychological theorizing about totalitarianism was the New School for Social Research. The Gestalt psychologist Max Wertheimer, for instance, argued that totalitarian movements attracted individuals who were not able to achieve the psychological coherence that underpinned what he called "productive thinking." Movements such as Nazism promised to recapitulate the missing unity of the psychological *Gestalt* on the level of the nation or *Volk*.[6] Wertheimer's neo-Freudian colleague Karen Horney also claimed that individuals became psychologically susceptible to totalitarianism when they failed to achieve what she called "self-development." For Horney, it was parenting above all that determined whether or not a child would be "strong, courageous, independent, capable of dealing with all sorts of situations." Horney warned that too many parents instead tended "to shelter the child, to make it obedient, to keep it ignorant of life as it is, or in short to infantilize it up to twenty years of age or longer," creating an insecure, dependent subject for totalitarian mass movements.[7]

---

[5] I use "totalitarianism" and "authoritarianism" more or less interchangeably in this section. Some theorists at the time distinguished between the two, but most readers would have understood remarks on "authoritarianism" to apply *mutatis mutandis* to "totalitarianism" and vice versa. On the broader history of the "totalitarianism" idea, see William D. Jones, *The Lost Debate: German Socialist Intellectuals and Totalitarianism* (Champaign: University of Illinois Press, 1999); Benjamin L. Alpers, *Dictators, Democracy, and American Public Culture: Envisioning the Totalitarian Enemy, 1920s–1950s* (Chapel Hill: University of North Carolina Press, 2003).

[6] Max Wertheimer, *Productive Thinking* (New York: Harper, 1945); Peter Rutkoff and William B. Scott, "Democracy and Fascism: From Europe to America," *State, Culture, and Society* 1, no. 1 (Autumn 1984), especially 54–55; Abraham S. Luchins and Edith H. Luchins, "Max Wertheimer in America, 1933–1943," *Gestalt Theory* 9, no. 2 (1987), 70–101; D. Brett King and Michael Wertheimer, *Max Wertheimer and Gestalt Theory* (London: Routledge, 2017). On the New School intellectual community, see Judith Friedlander, *A Light in Dark Times. The New School for Social Research and Its University in Exile* (New York: Columbia University Press, 2019); Daniel Bessner, *Democracy in Exile Hans Speier and the Rise of the Defense Intellectual* (Ithaca, NY: Cornell University Press, 2018), chapter 2.

[7] Karen Horney, *The Neurotic Personality of Our Times* (New York: Norton, 1937), 85; Bernard J. Paris, *Karen Horney: A Psychoanalyst's Search for Self-Understanding* (New Haven, CT: Yale University Press, 1994).

Uptown from the New School, the emigre representatives of the Institute for Social Research – more commonly known as the Frankfurt School – also encouraged New York's sociologists to adopt a more psychological focus. Institute researchers sought to supplement Marxism with Freudian psychoanalysis to understand two striking social developments that they felt more economistic strands of Marxism could not explain: the movement of German workers away from revolutionary socialism and into right-wing nationalism following World War I, and the descent of the Communist project in the Soviet Union into Stalinist tyranny. After the core Institute members fled Nazism for an outpost at Columbia University, they discovered that New York was home to a community of young American ex-communist and Trotskyist intellectuals who were struggling to explain exactly the same phenomena. Young sociologists such as Daniel Bell, Lewis Coser, and Nathan Glazer helped translate and edit the Institute's German prose. *Partisan Review* editors William Phillips and Phillip Rahv as well as *politics* editor Dwight Macdonald used their "little magazines" to bring Frankfurt ideas to an American audience.[8] The Institute's former chief Freudian revisionist, Erich Fromm, made independent inroads into the city's psychological community. In 1941, Fromm decided to release a comprehensive statement of his intellectual approach for a mainstream English readership: *Escape from Freedom*.

Fromm was the most important influence on the Cold War liberal concept of the productive character. In Fromm's view, healthy psychological development required individuals to engage with the outside world through "the spontaneity of love and productive work." The productive individual had a fully developed sense of themselves and the difference that their selfhood made in the world. But Fromm claimed that in the "monopolistic phase of capitalism," individuals lacked the opportunity to develop productive relationships with the world and had failed to develop a substitute for the primal ties with nature and tradition dissolved by processes of modernization. Fromm argued that without the ability to grow into productive, self-reliant individuals, people were forced to turn to other "mechanisms of escape." One mundane form of escape, common in the nontotalitarian nations, was what Fromm called "automaton conformity," in which the individual "adopts entirely the kind of personality offered to him by cultural patterns." But automaton conformity was one end of a spectrum that ran all the way to

---

[8] Thomas Wheatland, *The Frankfurt School in Exile* (Minneapolis: University of Minnesota Press, 2009). On the "New York Intellectuals," see Alan M. Wald, *The New York Intellectuals: The Rise and Decline of the Anti-Stalinist Left from the 1930s to the 1980s* (Chapel Hill: University of North Carolina Press, 2017 [30th Anniversary Edition]).

full-blown "authoritarianism," or "the tendency to give up the independence of one's own individual self and to fuse one's self with somebody or something outside oneself in order to acquire the strength which the individual self is lacking." Despite placing the blame on monopoly capitalism rather than on parenting or German cultural pathology, Fromm's approach harmonized with the theories of Horney and Wertheimer. Totalitarianism ultimately sprang from the failure of individuals to develop an integrated, productive, independent personality.[9]

As a young psychologist, Abraham Maslow became friends with both Horney and Fromm, attending Horney's New School lectures and discussion group meetings and regularly socializing with Fromm at his Central Park West apartment.[10] In a series of papers in 1943, Maslow developed his famous concept of the hierarchy of needs to articulate his own version of the basic psychological story that Horney and Fromm each told. Maslow theorized that all humans possessed a basic set of psychological needs that were arranged "in hierarchies of pre-potency." When "lower" needs for physiological and emotional security were satisfied, they more or less permanently receded, allowing the emergence of "higher" needs for esteem and "self-actualization" – that is to say, for the kind of creative achievement that Fromm saw as distinguishing the productive character. Maslow warned, however, that "in certain people the level of aspiration may be permanently deadened or lowered." A person who experienced chronic insecurity, especially in youth, might never develop esteem or self-actualization needs, even if the resources to satisfy the security needs in a normal person later materialized. Maslow conceptualized "authoritarian individuals" as having this kind of insatiable need for security. In the mind of the authoritarian, "the whole world is conceived of as dangerous, threatening, or at least challenging." Driven by this overwhelming perception of danger, the authoritarian had to seek either to develop the "power" to defend himself or, more frequently, to find a sufficiently powerful external protector. For the authoritarian person, "peace" was possible only "if this protector is strong enough and can be relied upon." Authoritarians were therefore characterized, above all, by "the tendency to avoid responsibility for one's own fate." They were unproductive, taking what was given to them by their protectors rather than making their own way in the world.[11]

---

[9] Erich Fromm, *Escape from Freedom* (New York: Rinehart & Company, 1941), 23, 123–125, 141, 185–186.
[10] Edward Hoffman, *The Right to Be Human: A Biography of Abraham Maslow* (New York: McGraw Hill, 1999), 90–93.
[11] Abraham H. Maslow, "A Theory of Human Motivation," *Psychological Review* 50 (1943), 370, 383, 386; Abraham H. Maslow, "The Authoritarian Character Structure," *The Journal of Social Psychology*, S.P.S.S.I. Bulletin, 18 (1943), 402–403, 411.

Indebted as he was to his friends Fromm and Horney, Maslow borrowed the language of "need" not from his New York colleagues, but from the American psychologist Henry Murray, director of the Harvard Psychological Clinic. Murray also spent World War II investigating the psychological origins of totalitarianism, at the bequest of the OSS. The wartime intelligence agency tasked Murray with constructing a psychological profile of Hitler. There was little in Murray's classified reports that would have surprised his civilian colleagues in New York. The basic idea of Murray's profile of Hitler, delivered in its final form in October of 1943, was that Hitler's pathological projection of strength was an attempt to compensate for the profound weakness, dependence, and "femininity" at the heart of his personality. "As a child he was frail and sickly, emotionally dependent on his mother," Murray wrote. He "never engaged in athletics, was turned down as forever unfit for conscription in the Austrian Army. Afraid of his father, his behavior was outwardly submissive." Hitler was unproductive: "He never did any manual work." Indeed, Murray concluded that despite his projection of dominance, Hitler secretly wanted to be overthrown. Murray suggested that the Allies publicly announce that all the Nazi leadership would be executed upon victory except for Hitler, who would instead be sent to Saint Helena, the island to which Napoleon was exiled. The opportunity to depict himself as following in Napoleon's tragic footsteps would give Hitler psychological cover to give into his innermost masochistic urges and surrender himself to the Allies.[12]

Murray was not the only scholar that the OSS enlisted to psychoanalyze the enemy. OSS brass demonstrated a particular interest in the so-called culture-and-personality school in American anthropology, led by Margaret Mead and Ruth Benedict. Benedict and Mead began from the premise, as Mead put it in her foreword to Benedict's 1934 *Patterns of Culture*, that culture itself could be understood as "personality writ large." The OSS hired Mead and Benedict in the early 1940s to produce studies of the cultural personality of the Axis nations, beginning a relationship between each scholar and the U.S. intelligence establishment that would continue into the Cold War. In the early years of the

---

[12] Henry A. Murray, Analysis of the Personality of Adolph Hitler: With Predictions of His Future Behavior and Suggestions for Dealing with Him Now and after Germany's Surrender, OSS Confidential Memo, October 1943, 4, 19, 35ff, http://s3.amazonaws.com/cul-hydra/nur/nur01134/pdfs/nur01134.pdf; Merve Emre, *The Personality Brokers* (New York: Doubleday, 2018), 107–115. Here I echo Ellen Herman's reminder of the extent to which the intellectual foundations for the Cold War period were laid during World War II, in *The Romance of American Psychology: Political Culture in the Age of Experts* (Berkeley: University of California Press, 1996).

postwar occupation of Japan. Benedict warned U.S. policymakers that it would take significant time for Japanese civilians to become psychologically capable of accepting American values such as "the imperative demand to be independent, the passion each individual has to choose his own mate, his own job, the house he will live in and the obligations he will assume." The "shame culture" of Japan made the Japanese character unproductive, dependent on the approval of others and incapable of acting in and on the world with a fully developed sense of one's individual self.[13]

The theorizing of the New York emigre community and the empirical social psychology of OSS-supported American scholars came together in the early Cold War period in the most enduringly influential statement of the psychological theory of totalitarianism, *The Authoritarian Personality* (1950). The treatise was the product of a seven-year research project helmed by the Frankfurt School member Theodor Adorno and a team of Berkeley psychologists, including Henry Murray's former doctoral student Nevitt Sanford. The most famous contribution of the book was what the authors called the "F-scale," a survey instrument that could be used to estimate an individual's proto-fascist proclivities quantitatively (a high F-score was worse). The F-scale was designed to pose questions that had the potential to reveal an authoritarian character structure without tipping off respondents that the survey was "actually" about prejudice and other more direct proxies of fascist attitudes. The F-scale depended, then, on a preestablished theory of the authoritarian character that was heavily indebted to Fromm, Maslow, and others – cited explicitly in the text. Like those scholars, the authors of *The Authoritarian Personality* perceived a weak ego festering within individuals who were susceptible to totalitarian movements. In high-F-score individuals, "a certain lack of personal identity is compensated for by a wish to 'belong,'" while in contrast, "low-scoring subjects tend to see themselves as *different, individualized, or unconventional.*" High scorers constantly seemed "to need external support." They spoke in clichés. There seemed "to be more actual or potential heterosexuality

---

[13] Margaret Mead, preface to Ruth Benedict, *Patterns of Culture* (Boston: Houghton Mifflin Harcourt, 2005), xiii; Ruth Benedict, *The Chrysanthemum and the Sword* (Boston: Houghton Mifflin, 1946), 314–315. On the involvement of American anthropologists, including Benedict and Mead, with the U.S. intelligence establishment, see David Price, *Anthropological Intelligence: The Deployment and Neglect of American Anthropology in the Second World War* (Durham, NC: Duke University Press, 2008) and *Cold War Anthropology: The CIA, The Pentagon and the Growth of Dual Use Anthropology* (Durham, NC: Duke University Press, 2016). See also Peter Mandler, *Return from the Natives: How Margaret Mead Won the Second World War and Lost the Cold War* (Yale University Press, 2013).

in low scorers," since insecure high scorers were plagued by "hidden aggression toward the opposite sex."[14]

In a word, the low scorers were productive where the high scorers were not. The egos of the fascists-in-waiting were too fragile for them to really put themselves into their work, even if they occasionally exhibited a compensatory idolization of manual labor. On the whole, low scorers were "oriented toward work" and toward *"real achievement,"* while authoritarians exhibited "a narrowly opportunistic, externalized attitude toward work and the persons connected with it." "This is a nine-to-five job and when I am through I am through," one allegedly protofascist interviewee said. The ultimate low-scoring type – the "Genuine Liberal" filled with "a strong sense of personal autonomy and independence" – had an innate distaste for what the authors described as the "industrial standardization of innumerable phenomena of modern life," which left individuals without the ability to truly distinguish themselves through their work. It was not only corporate management that was to blame: One precocious anti-fascist college sophomore sensed "the danger that cumbersome, mammoth unions might become undemocratic." According to the authors, he was "anti-monopoly in the sense that he hopes to stop social trends by breaking down highly centralized units into smaller ones." In his own words: "I don't like large organizations."[15]

As its portrait of the Genuine Liberal suggested, at the same time that *The Authoritarian Personality* represented the culmination of the social-psychological approach to the study of totalitarianism, it also signaled the commencement of a Cold War–era initiative to reformulate political liberalism on sounder psychological footing – a register of the precipitous rise of the authority of the social sciences in contemporary American culture writ large, and especially the prestige that accrued to psychologists for their contributions to the war effort.[16] If the psychologists who helped America beat Hitler believed that totalitarianism was a kind of social psychopathology, then it made sense for liberals

---

[14] T. W. Adorno, Else Frenkel-Brunswik, Daniel J. Levinson, R. Nevitt Sanford et al., *The Authoritarian Personality* (New York: W.W. Norton & Company, 1950), 430–431, 476, 405, 441. See also Wheatland, *Frankfurt School*, chapter 6; Emre, *Personality Brokers*, 156–158; Jamie Cohen-Cole, *The Open Mind: Cold War Politics and the Sciences of Human Nature* (Chicago: University of Chicago Press, 2014), chapters 1–2.

[15] Adorno et al., *Authoritarian Personality*, 431, 416, 665, 781.

[16] See Herman, *Romance of American Psychology*, chapters 1–4; Mark Solovey and Hamilton Cravens, eds., *Cold War Social Science: Knowledge Production, Liberal Democracy, and Human Nature* (London: Palgrave Macmillan, 2012); Daniel Bessner and Nicolas Guilhot, eds., *The Decisionist Imagination: Sovereignty, Social Science and Democracy in the 20th Century* (New York: Berghahn Books, 2018).

to infer that their politics ought to seek to promote a kind of social-psychological health. (Indeed, as Daniel Smith and Anton Jäger argue later in this volume, Cold War liberals increasingly came to view their conservative domestic political opponents as similarly driven by psychopathology.) But where did the productive character come from, and how could it be developed more systematically?

Social Therapeutics

With widespread agreement that the authoritarian personality emerged from a chronic sense of insecurity, one obvious therapeutic approach was to ensure that what Maslow called the "security needs" were universally provided for. One standard bearer for this sort of psychological social democracy was David Riesman, a well-known professor of sociology at the University of Chicago (and Erich Fromm's former analysand). In his surprise bestseller *The Lonely Crowd* (1950), Riesman argued that the United States' twentieth-century economic development had outdated nineteenth-century Puritan asceticism, which derived from the material compulsion to work to survive. The immediate consequence, in Riesman's view, was an "other-directed" consumer culture. Nonetheless, he held out hope that freedom from precarity would enable the proliferation of the individualist posture he called "autonomy," a "personally productive orientation based on the human need for active participation in a creative task."[17] If individuals did not need to work in order to survive, they could work in order to develop their psychological capacity for independence and creativity.

Following *The Lonely Crowd*, Riesman used its theoretical framework to anchor a characteristically Cold War reframing of the meaning of "socialism." For Riesman, as for other American leftists eager to distinguish their political vision from the regnant ideology of the USSR under Stalin, "socialism" meant a program to secure the economic preconditions of individual autonomy rather than the political expression of working-class struggle. For a time, Riesman even toyed with the idea of founding a new anti-communist socialist party, to be led by Erich Fromm, Norman Thomas, and Riesman's friend George F. Kennan. In the 1950s, Riesman's social-democratic convictions positioned him as a critic of the more overtly authoritarian anti-communism emblematized by Joseph McCarthy. By the late 1960s, however, Riesman found himself denouncing the New Left and the student movement. In his

---

[17] David Riesman with Nathan Glazer and Reuel Denney, *The Lonely Crowd: A Study of the Changing American Character* (New Haven, CT: Yale University Press, 1962), 263.

view, they were extremists, uninterested in truly thinking for themselves, happy to be manipulated by ideologues such as Herbert Marcuse ("a really corrupt and cynical person who knows better and has a good racket going"). A "socialism" that aspired above all to enhance individuals' psychological capacity for self-sufficiency would always look askance on mass movement politics.[18]

For liberals of a more overtly Freudian persuasion, child-rearing rather than economic policy held the key to developing productive individuals. Riesman's friend Erik H. Erikson, a Danish-German emigre psychoanalyst, set the tone in *Childhood and Society* (1950). Erikson warned that Western society was wracked with "identity crisis," with "hundreds of thousands of 'psychoneurotics.'" In Erikson's narrative, as industrialization accelerated, fathers left the small proprietor's homestead to work for bosses in distant corporations, leaving to mothers the task of educating the child in moral and cultural values. Women were thus forced "to be mothers *and* fathers," dooming children to maternal overinvolvement. At the same time, the spread of the industrial "supermachine" encouraged mothers to train their children to be "machine-like and clocklike." Once they entered the workforce, the victims of "Momism and bossism" would simply discharge instructions rather than exercising productive initiative. This picture, of course, was exactly how the standard Cold War–era account of the USSR imagined the typical Soviet citizen. Erikson's jeremiad, in other words, was a characteristically liberal argument that Soviet-style totalitarianism could not be conquered merely by American military muscle – as more conservative hawks would have it – but would also require a quite literally domestic cultural *retournement*.[19]

In the early Cold War period, an entire industry emerged to cater to parents interested in raising creative, independent children. Toymakers, architects, children's authors, and the founders of new private schools and children's museums promised that their products would help prepare children for freedom from an early age. Millions of American parents in the 1950s and 1960s found an antidote to the pathologies Erikson described in Benjamin Spock's *Common Sense Book of Baby*

---

[18] On Riesman's ultimately abortive socialist party, see Folder "Erich Fromm [4 of 4]," Box 11, HUG(FP) 99.12, Papers of David Riesman, 1929–1988, Harvard University Archives, Pusey Library, Cambridge, MA (DRP). On Marcuse, see David Riesman to Nathan Glazer, July 8, 1968, Folder "Glazer, Nathan, 2 of 2," Box 13, HUG(FP) 99.12, DRP. See also Daniel Geary, "Children of the Lonely Crowd: David Riesman, the Young Radicals, and the Splitting of Liberalism in the 1960s," *Modern Intellectual History* 10, no. 3 (November 2013), 603–633.

[19] Erik H. Erikson, *Childhood and Society* (New York: W.W. Norton, 1963), 288, 295, 323–325.

and Child Care (1946). As the title suggested, Spock encouraged mothers, who were assigned the primary responsibility for child-rearing, to stop overthinking parenting and adopt a more permissive and intuitive approach that sought to nurture the child's capacity for independent action. Cold War mothers could not, however, simply raise their children on a laissez-faire basis. In controversial research funded by the Ford Foundation in the 1950s and 1960s, the emigre psychoanalyst Bruno Bettelheim contended that an epidemic of maternal coldness – embodied by what he called the "refrigerator mother" – was producing a generation of autistic children with a stunted emotional capacity comparable to that of concentration camp victims. Smothering and neglect were the mirror images of the totalitarian temptation in American child-rearing, leaving children bereft of the interior strength of self that was required for truly productive endeavors. To raise productive children, mothers would have to embody a particular feminine form of productivity in their own domestic work: endlessly giving but not too forceful about it; generative but not demanding; loving but not possessive.[20]

Much of the Cold War children's industry channeled a broader set of assumptions about the therapeutic benefits of exposure to the principles and methods of modern science. "Intrinsic to the nature of the trailblazing theorist or researcher," Abraham Maslow argued in 1966, were quintessential psychological traits of the healthy liberal such as "faith, connoisseurship, courage, self-confidence, and boldness." What Maslow called "the creative scientist" was the quintessential example of the productive character.[21] Institutions such as the San Francisco Exploratorium, founded in 1969 by physicist Frank Oppenheimer, sought to provide young people with a hands-on, participatory experience of the scientific process. The social studies curriculum "Man: A Course of Study," developed by the National Science Foundation and the Ford Foundation and taught to 400,000 pupils annually at its peak, also encouraged students to view themselves as social scientists in training, tasked with developing their own conclusions from social-scientific "raw materials" such as unnarrated ethnographic films. "MACOS" was

---

[20] Benjamin Spock, *The Common Sense Book of Baby and Child Care* (New York: Duell, Sloan, and Pearce, 1946); Amy F. Ogata, *Designing the Creative Child: Playthings and Places in Midcentury America* (Minneapolis: University of Minnesota Press, 2013); Bruno Bettelheim, *Love Is Not Enough: The Treatment of Emotionally Disturbed Children* (New York: Free Press, 1950); Bruno Bettelheim, *The Empty Fortress: Infantile Autism and the Birth of the Self* (New York: Free Press, 1967); Anne Harrington, "Mother Love and Mental Illness: An Emotional History," *Osiris* 31 (2016), 94–115.

[21] Abraham Maslow, *The Psychology of Science: A Reconnaissance* (New York: Harper & Row, 1966), 132–134.

productivity as pedagogy: Students would not simply take in knowledge from their teachers but learn how to produce their own.[22]

The idea that authentic science was anti-totalitarian also served to mollify Cold War concerns about the metastasized place of science in postwar society, what liberals such as Karl Popper and Michael Polanyi decried as "scientism." Scientism, in the liberal imagination, denoted the manipulation of scientific methods for the ends of control and regimentation, replacing the productive initiative of individuals with the mechanistic plans of experts.[23] Liberal psychologists were particularly concerned that the West's enemies might exploit the very psychological vulnerabilities they had identified to render populations more rather than less susceptible to the seductions of totalitarianism. There was a troublingly thin line between praiseworthy campaigns of propaganda or "psychological warfare" on behalf of Western freedom and disturbing Communist bloc "brainwashing" programs. John Frankenheimer's 1962 smash hit *The Manchurian Candidate* suggested that even an American war hero could succumb to the weapons made available by the development of psychological science. The creative-scientist ideal, however, suggested that the problem with scientism was not *too much* science but *not enough* science, conceived properly. For Maslow, scientism was not really hyperintellectual but intellectually inferior, the domain of those behaviorist colleagues that Maslow derisively termed "technicians." In order to serve as public models of psychologically healthy individualism, scientists needed to be willing to theorize more boldly and embrace self-styled heterodoxy – even as that "heterodoxy" was becoming embedded in the U.S. cultural mainstream.[24]

Many Cold War liberals held that spirituality as well as science provided a pathway to psychological renewal. In its founding manifesto, the Congress of Cultural Freedom – a transatlantic constellation of interlinked anti-communist foundations, conferences, and magazines

---

[22] Ogata, *Creative Child*, chapter 5; Jamie Cohen-Cole, *Open Mind*, especially chapter 7.

[23] Karl Popper, *The Poverty of Historicism* (London: Routledge, 1957); Michael Polanyi, *The Logic of Liberty: Reflections and Rejoinders* (London: Routledge, 1951); F. A. Hayek, "The Use of Knowledge in Society," *The American Economic Review* 35, no. 4 (September 1945), 519–530; Elena Aronova, "The Congress for Cultural Freedom, Minerva, and the Quest for Instituting 'Science Studies' in the Cold War," *Minerva* 50, no. 3 (2012), 307–337.

[24] Abraham Maslow, *Motivation and Personality* (New York: Harper & Row, 1954), 351; Rebecca Lemov, *World as Laboratory Experiments with Mice, Mazes, and Men* (New York: Farrar, Straus and Giroux, 2006), part three; Christopher Simpson, *Science of Coercion: Communication Research and Psychological Warfare, 1945–1960* (New York: Oxford University Press, 1994); Matthew Frye Jacobson and Gaspar González, *What Have They Built You to Do?: The Manchurian Candidate and Cold War America* (Minneapolis: University of Minnesota Press, 2006).

secretly bankrolled by the American CIA – proclaimed its intention to unleash "a new spiritual awareness, born of anguish and suffering, of the full meaning of freedom."[25] The manifesto's author, Arthur Koestler, traveled the world in a restless search for spiritual enlightenment and the sources of individual "creativity." (Perhaps the only constant in Koestler's chameleonic life was his sustained cruelty toward women.) He took LSD and psilocybin with the notorious Harvard psychologist Timothy Leary, whom Henry Murray had mentored. He met with parapsychology experts in North Carolina and in London to participate in experiments on clairvoyance and levitation. He also immersed himself in the work of neovitalist authors such as the theoretical biologist Ludwig von Bertalanffy. Koestler's popular book *The Act of Creation* (1964) built on Bertalanffy to argue that the essence of creativity, whether artistic, scientific, or entrepreneurial, consisted in what he called "the Eureka act," where the individual mind integrated ideas or domains of experience that had previously been kept separate – producing a "new synthesis" all at once in a "single, explosive contact." A sense of the "mystical" was the passageway to true creative work.[26]

The Swiss "analytic psychologist" Carl Gustav Jung, a central figure of Cold War intellectual life, also emphasized the relationship between mysticism and creative work. Jung was admired by scientists such as Abraham Maslow and Henry Murray, popular writers such as Joseph Campbell and Philip Wylie, and artists such as Mark Rothko and Jackson Pollock. In 1945, the wealthy philanthropist Paul Mellon founded the Bollingen Foundation, which translated and published Jung's collected works and provided financial support to a stable of Jungian intellectuals. Like Ludwig von Bertalanffy, Jung once harbored anti-Semitic and Aryanist convictions; after Hitler's rise to power, he became president of the General Medical Society of Psychotherapy, whose official journal published a pro-Nazi editorial under his name (allegedly authored by Hermann Göring's cousin Matthias Göring, leader of the society's German chapter). By the 1950s, however, many American intellectuals were willing to let bygones be bygones. Jung broke with the Nazis in the late 1930s and consulted the wartime

---

[25] Peter Coleman, "Arthur Koestler and the Congress for Cultural Freedom," *Polanyiana* no. 1–2 (2005), quotations 193–194; Frances Stonor Saunders, *The Cultural Cold War: The CIA and the World of Arts and Letters* (New York: New Press, 1999).

[26] David Cesarani, *Arthur Koestler: The Homeless Mind* (Portsmouth: William Heinemann, 1998); Michael Scammell, *Koestler: The Literary and Political Odyssey of a Twentieth-Century Skeptic* (New York: Random House, 2009). Arthur Koestler, *The Act of Creation* (London: Danube, 1969), 212, Appendix II; Manfred Drack et al., "On the Making of a System Theory of Life: Paul A. Weiss and Ludwig von Bertalanffy's Conceptual Connection," *The Quarterly Review of Biology* 82, no. 4 (December 2007), 349–373.

OSS on German "national character," embracing the consensus that Nazism and Communism were both symptomatic of a broader psychological propensity for individuals to submerge themselves in the currents of collective life. Jung's suggestion in *The Undiscovered Self* (1958) that religious and mystical practices could provide a counterbalance to "mass-mindedness" helped bestow an aura of intellectual seriousness on the spiritual searching of figures such as Arthur Koestler. No less a Cold War authority than Allen Dulles, the first civilian director of the CIA, was willing to testify to Jung's "deep antipathy to what Nazism and Fascism stood for."[27]

The goal of what Jung called "individuation," the ultimate fruit of Jungian analysis, was to consciously redirect instinctual energy into new "productive" channels, after its initial "canalization" by cultural norms had broken down. Art, spirituality, selfhood, and work were all bound up together in the practices of worldly engagement that analytic psychology recommended – the reason why expressionist artists such as Rothko and Pollock found Jungianism so generative. Jung himself was a prolific craftworker, constructing his stone house near Lake Zürich by hand. In the business world, the champions of the Jung-inspired Meyers–Briggs personality test hoped that employers could use Jungian principles to guide workers to jobs for which they felt uniquely well-suited.[28] For Cold War liberals, the psychological connection between individuality and productivity was as useful in generating practices of psychological development as it was in diagnosing the psychological roots of totalitarianism.

Preparing the World for Freedom

Children's science museums and Jungian mysticism were all well and good for safeguarding the liberal societies of the West from totalitarianism,

---

[27] C. G. Jung "Editorial," *Zentralblatt für Psychotherapie und ihre Grenzgebiete* VI, no. 3 (December 1933), 139–140, reprinted in C. G. Jung, *Civilization in Translation*, Collected Works, vol. 10, trans. R. F. C. Hull (Princeton: Bollingen Foundation, 1970); C. G. Jung, *The Undiscovered Self* (London: Routledge, 2002 [1958]); Richard Noll, *The Jung Cult: Origins of a Charismatic Movement* (New York: Free Press, 1994). On Jung and Dulles, see Allen Dulles to Paul Mellon, February 17, 1950, Folder 340.01, C. G. Jung, Box I:10, Bollingen Foundation Records, Library of Congress, Washington, DC. On Bollingen, see William McGuire, *Bollingen: An Adventure in Collecting the Past* (Princeton: Princeton University Press, 1989).

[28] C. G. Jung, "On Psychic Energy," in *Collected Works of C.G. Jung*, vol. 8, ed. and trans. Gerhard Adler and R. F. C. Hull (Princeton: Princeton University Press, 1972); Emre, *Personality Brokers*; C. G. Jung and Gordon Young, "The Art of Living," in *C.G. Jung Speaking: Interviews and Encounters*, ed. William McGuire and R. F. C. Hull (Princeton: Princeton University Press, 1987).

but what about those societies where modern liberalism had never developed in the first place? In the eyes of many elites in the United States, the Cold War would be won or lost in the postcolonial world rather than on American soil. As a brochure from a 1955 conference attended by *Time* publisher Henry Luce put it, the "word-wide revolution of many races and peoples is the environment which gives totalitarian tyranny its chance, and forces upon free nations the acceptance of the fact of political struggle." For the more psychologically inclined, the task of such political struggle was to instill the psychology of productive individuality where it did not flourish indigenously.[29]

The most influential psychologist working in the field of "development" was David McClelland, a Harvard colleague of Henry Murray. In his own spin on "needs" psychology, McClelland proposed that individuals were primarily motivated by one of three core needs, for "affiliation," "power," or "achievement." The needs for affiliation and power dominated "traditional" as well as totalitarian societies, but the need for achievement was the motor of progress and economic growth in the West. McClelland asserted that the psychological needs emphasized by a culture could be identified from an analysis of the culture's children's stories. In *The Achieving Society* (1961), McClelland presented statistics for various nations' achievement needs, as derived from their children's literature, and announced that his statistics showed a strong correlation with subsequent economic growth. Drawing on the work of his Harvard predecessor Joseph Schumpeter, McClelland concluded that the need for achievement was the basic characteristic of "entrepreneurial behavior." In fact, "entrepreneurship" *just meant* achievement motivation. It was not so much the formal position of business owner-operator that made someone entrepreneurial, but rather an individual's degree of "entrepreneurial role behavior," including "decisiveness," "energetic and/or novel instrumental activity," and "individual responsibility."[30]

McClelland argued that because contemporary modernization theorists too often downplayed the centrality of "psychological factors," United States development policy was inadequately oriented around the promotion of entrepreneurship in modernizing nations. With support from the Ford Foundation, McClelland designed a series of management training seminars that were attended by local executives in

---

[29] "Things you may want to remember from the Second National Conference on Spiritual Foundations," October 24–26 1955, Hotel Sheraton-Carlton, Washington, DC. (sponsored by FRASCO), Folder 1, Foundation for Religious Action in Social & Civil Order, 1954–1955, Box 37, Henry R. Luce Papers, Library of Congress, Washington, DC.

[30] David McClelland, *The Achieving Society* (Princeton: D. Van Nostrand Company, Inc., 1961), 15.

Mexico, India, and Japan during the 1960s. Participants would work with teachers to systematically revise their own impromptu storytelling to reflect greater "achievement thinking." McClelland hoped that the alums of his seminars would go on to model achievement thinking for other elites with whom they worked in business and government.[31]

McClelland's emphasis on the cultivation of entrepreneurial psychology quickly became common sense in Cold War development economics and sociology. The MIT modernization theorist Everett Hagen, in his influential book *On the Theory of Social Change: How Economic Growth Begins* (1962), echoed McClelland's juxtaposition of the "authoritarian personality" of "traditional societies" with the "entrepreneurial" or "creative" personality of "innovative" societies. In his contribution to the widely read collection *Elites in Latin America* (1967), the sociologist Seymour Martin Lipset contended that Latin American economic growth had been suppressed by the hostility of traditional Catholic culture to achievement-motivation psychology, leading to a dearth of "entrepreneurship." Abraham Maslow supplied perhaps the bluntest formulation, in a journal note on McClelland's work: "the most valuable 100 people to bring into a deteriorating society like, for instance, Peru, would be *not* 100 chemists, or politicians, or professors, or engineers, but rather 100 entrepreneurs."[32] Starting in the Kennedy and Johnson administrations, social scientists also adapted development psychology to analyze the "culture of poverty" supposedly endemic among Black city dwellers ("the representative of the poor races within the richest nation," as the management theorist Peter Drucker put it). War on Poverty programs such as the Jobs Corps, collaborating with psychologists including McClelland himself as well as his student Winthrop Adkins, sought to inculcate an achievement focus thought to be lacking in Black communities.[33]

---

[31] McClelland, *Achieving Society*, 67; Nils Gilman, *Mandarins of the Future: Modernization Theory in Cold War America* (Baltimore: Johns Hopkins University Press, 2004), 97ff. On McClelland's training programs, see Folders "Mexico," "India," "Ford Foundation," Box 105, Papers of David McClelland (HUGFP 145), Harvard University Archives, Pusey Library, Cambridge, MA.

[32] Everett E. Hagen, *On the Theory of Social Change: How Economic Growth Begins* (Homewood, IL: Dorsey Press, 1962); Seymour Martin Lipset, "Values, Education, and Entrepreneurship," in *Elites in Latin America*, ed. Seymour Martin Lipset and Aldo Solari (New York: Oxford University Press, 1967); Abraham Maslow, *Eupsychian Management: A Journal* (Homewood, IL: Richard D. Irwin, Inc., 1965), 202–204.

[33] Peter F. Drucker, *The Age of Discontinuity: Guidelines to Our Changing Society* (New York: Harper & Row, 1969), 103–104; Offner, *Sorting Out the Mixed Economy*, especially chapter 7; David C. McClelland, "Achievement Motivation Training for Potential High School Dropouts," Achievement Motivation Development Project Working Paper Number 4 (DHEW Office of Education, August 1968), ERIC #

Many Cold War liberals had little compunction about using ostensibly illiberal means to bolster U.S. hegemony. Such hegemony was supposedly necessary to introduce postcolonial managers and workers to productive patterns of thought without which such societies would be unprepared for liberalism. Many "underdeveloped countries," Maslow wrote in 1960, "would have to be administered & 'grown' by an elite from above for some time." While it was true that "the more they grew into mature countries, the more freedom & the less control they would need," in the meantime countries such as the Congo simply "have not yet developed enough persons to be democratic in the U.S. sense." In societies that were psychologically unprepared for freedom, it was easier to square liberal values with the use of coercive force to combat the spread of totalitarianism. A nation afflicted with the authoritarian personality had no legitimate right to self-determination. Maslow excoriated liberals who were "apt to be perfectionistic in demanding that the United States behave officially in a saintly fashion [while] being wholly willing to accept without a word of protest whatsoever horrible crimes and evils that the Communists are apt to perpetrate." If liberalism were to take the findings of social psychology seriously, it would have to acknowledge that American dominance was essential to provide the rest of the world with a model for the character traits that promoted development. "There is a lot of talk about 'American imperialism' nowadays," Maslow told a group of Saga Corporation middle managers in the late 1960s, "but the truth is that American workers simply are more efficient, desirable, and accomplished wherever they go." True illiberalism would be to deny the rest of the world access to the political and economic benefits of interaction with American personalities.[34]

Nils Gilman has argued that in the late twentieth century, free-market advocates exploited the decline of the Cold War liberal modernization paradigm to pour "neoliberal wine" into "the old bottle 'modernity.'" The liberal ideology of the turn of the millennium did differ from its Cold War predecessor in important ways. David Riesman's brand of social democracy, in particular, fell out of fashion. But attending to the psychological dimension of Cold War social thought suggests that

ED029067, 3; Barry Argento et al., *Alternative Education Models – Preliminary Findings of the Job Corps Educational Improvement Effort* (Employment and Training Administration, May 1980), 56.

[34] Richard J. Lowry, ed., *The Journals of A.H. Maslow*, vol. 1 (Monterey, CA: Brooks/Cole, 1979), 51 (August 13, 1960), 59 (September 10, 1960), 385 (August 3, 1964); Abraham Maslow, "Dynamics of American Management" (November 1969) in *Future Visions: The Unpublished Papers of Abraham Maslow*, ed. Edward Hoffman (Newbury Park, CA: Sage, 1996), 185–186.

neoliberals did not have to empty the old bottles entirely. Central concepts now associated with neoliberalism, such as entrepreneurship, were already present. Most significantly, Cold War social psychologists channeled the normative vision of liberalism into a language of individual health and development that persisted long after the fall of the Soviet Union. Today's liberal culture still demands that healthy individuals express their selfhood through productive work. As Margaret Thatcher put it: "Economics are the method; the object is to change the soul."[35]

---

[35] Gilman, *Mandarins of the Future*, 271; Ronald Butt, "Mrs. Thatcher: The First Two Years," *Sunday Times* (May 3, 1981).

7 Cold War Liberalism or Socialist Revisionism?
Transatlantic Sociology, "Industrial Society," and the Anti-totalitarian Style between France and America

David Sessions

When the American socialist Irving Howe, the editor of *Dissent*, spoke in 1965 of "a range of political views roughly between left liberalism and liberal leftism," the broader context of the Western European and American lefts made this all but a distinction without a difference.[1] Summing up the common sense of this "range" of views, Howe described three elements of the reaction of "leftist intellectuals" to the postwar era: first, "a feeling that the high drama ... of earlier Marxist or 'revolutionary' politics has been lost"; second, "a belief that the welfare state will, in effect, remain stable and basically unchanged into the indefinite future"; and third, "a belief that the welfare state is characteristic of all forms of advanced industrial society; that it offers bread and television, palliatives and opiates, to disarm all opposition."[2]

What Howe was summarizing was a transatlantic social-democratic consensus that had formed by the end of the 1950s around the idea of "industrial society." Industrial society was a macrosociological paradigm for postwar society that was born amid the vertigo of the European economic recovery in the 1950s and, in the 1960s, swung toward an optimistic outlook on the future. Capitalism and communism were different forms of "industrial society" which similarly deployed collective means to deliver productivity and growth and were similarly complex and technical. Industrial societies were no longer dominated by the hereditary ruling classes of the European past but were presided over by specialized experts who oversaw stable democratic processes. As a result, such societies were less and less "ideological." Revolution on the model of the old socialist and labor movements was increasingly

---

[1] Irving Howe, "Radical Criticism," 1965, 1, Box 97, Folder 8, Daniel Bell Personal Archive, Accession 18559, Harvard University Archives, Pusey Library, Cambridge, MA.
[2] Howe, "Radical Criticism," Daniel Bell Personal Archive, 13–14.

unthinkable, especially given the fact that the working classes were now being "integrated" by consumption and social bargaining; bitter and insurrectionary social conflicts now gave way to the more prosaic strains of alienation and lack of direct participation in political life.

If this was something like the consensus view of European social democrats in the mid-1960s, some of its principal architects in the 1950s were "Cold War liberals." This is perhaps not the paradox it might appear if, as Jan-Werner Müller writes, "Cold War liberals were effectively social democrats."[3] But was there a difference between socialists and Cold War liberals? Exploring differences between French and American sociologists who theorized "industrial society," this chapter argues that there was a difference, but not one that had much to do with sociological theory or policy beliefs. While all of these transatlantic sociologists came to agree on the broad outlines of what they called "industrial society," they exhibited markedly different styles of reacting to political challenges and conflicts. These differences were temperamental and conjunctural and came down to whether particular thinkers embraced what I will call the *anti-totalitarian style* that arose in the early Cold War: a pessimistic political disposition that, while often described as "liberal" and generally embracing "progressive" policies, sometimes drew on conservative arguments against political programs for social change.

After World War II, those who adopted the anti-totalitarian style deeply imbibed the new notion that "totalitarian" regimes – whether nominally left or right – were the result of a similarly combustible mixture of utopian ideology and mass political participation. This emphasis on democratic societies' susceptibility to emergency, especially the emergency of mass mobilization, was the core of their difference from other social democrats and democratic socialists who held a more positive view of democratic mobilization and maintained an optimistic outlook for international cooperation and a multipolar world order. Cold War liberals remained deeply anxious about grassroots mobilization, even in the context of stable democratic processes, and thus tended to prefer rule by apolitical experts under the umbrella of American military hegemony. This chapter proposes that what is commonly called "Cold War liberalism" among European and American intellectuals is perhaps best understood as an ideologically protean set of reactions at the core of which was the application of the lens of "totalitarianism" to domestic politics in Western Europe and the United

---

[3] Jan-Werner Müller, "Calming the Ideological Storms?: Reflections on Cold War Liberalism," in *Ideological Storms: Intellectuals, Dictators, and the Totalitarian Temptation*, ed. Vladimir Tismaneanu and Bogdan C. Iacob (Budapest: Central European University Press, 2019), 478.

States, and a fear of excessive – and excessively ideological – political mobilization of the demos. This core of the anti-totalitarian style would become crystal clear in the intellectual reaction to the political mobilizations of the 1960s, which anti-totalitarians often answered with anxious attacks – and which sometimes marked their transition from "Cold War liberalism" to identification with the political right.

But far from all sociologists and public intellectuals who theorized "industrial society" adopted the anti-totalitarian style or turned to the right, even if they were critical of communism or of what they considered the influence of outdated socialist ideology in their own nations' politics. As this chapter shows, there were marked differences between French and American sociologists, even if adoption of anti-totalitarianism did not break down cleanly along national or continental lines. Initial reactions to the Cold War shaped the different ways sociologists embraced the paradigm of "industrial society": whether as arguments for an optimistic, modernist socialism open to new movements for reform, or for a constrained social democracy more comfortable with technocratic governance and likely to recoil at any sign of a potentially disruptive social conflict. The differences between these reactions highlights the politics of emergency as a core feature of Cold War liberalism, one that distinguished it from democratic socialist thinking that otherwise shared its analysis of postwar "industrial society."

Sociology between France and America in the Early Cold War, 1945–1955

In the period from the late 1940s through the mid-1950s, numerous channels opened between France and the United States that brought social scientists from both sides of the Atlantic together. The "politics of productivity" that transferred technical and social-scientific knowledge from the U.S. to Europe was crucial, providing Europeans with new access to American interlocutors, ideas, and methods, supported financially both by European governments and American philanthropy.[4] While the fora for transnational exchange were all shaped by geopolitical conjuncture, they were not all infused with politics to the same degree. The new postwar school of French industrial sociology, led by the sociologist Georges Friedmann, was influenced most directly by academic

---

[4] Charles S. Maier, "The Politics of Productivity: Foundations of American International Economic Policy after World War II," *International Organization* 31, no. 4 (1977), 607–633; Richard F. Kuisel, "L'american way of life et les missions françaises de productivité," *Vingtième Siècle* 17, no. 1 (1988), 21–38.

relationships with American sociologists established on visits to the U.S., "productivity missions," and study-abroad exchanges. Sociologists from the Friedmann circle also participated in the International Sociological Association, founded by the Social Sciences Division of UNESCO, whose "world congresses" were diverse and relatively apolitical gatherings.[5] The Congress for Cultural Freedom (CCF) was a different story. Founded in 1950 to combat communist influence among the European intelligentsia, the CCF connected French and American intellectuals who embraced the Cold War as an existential struggle. Its militant posture and agenda of policing the intellectual sphere would make it anathema to most French intellectuals, including most sociologists, even if they came to share much of its analysis of the sociological evolution of postwar society. While the sociologist Raymond Aron would exemplify a French version of Cold War liberalism, Friedmann and some of his students represented more optimistic democratic socialism that looked toward deeper involvement of the demos in politics and a truly international way of organizing the world.

Despite his skepticism of the United States, Georges Friedmann saw relationships with American social scientists – particularly figures involved in "industrial relations" – as a potential continuation of his prewar search for a socialism to transform the alienated relationship between workers and machines. Under the auspices of the new Centre d'études sociologiques in Paris, Friedmann attracted a group of young researchers with varying leftist sympathies to study the condition of the working classes in France. The Friedmann circle saw sociology as a form of practical political engagement in the reconstruction of France on behalf of the working class.[6] Sociology was, as Henri Mendras put it, "for each one of us, a substitute for politics."[7] For Alain Touraine, they represented a position between the French Communist Party (Parti communiste français – PCF) and the French socialist party (SFIO – Section française de l'Internationale ouvrière): "We were crushed between the thinking of the PCF, which rejected any study of society, which imposed dogmas in flagrant contradiction with reality ... and a reactionary Atlanticist wave that carried away an SFIO that was in full degeneration."[8] Seeking a simultaneously intellectual and practical

---

[5] Jennifer Platt, *History of ISA, 1948–1997* (Paris: International Sociological Association, 1998).

[6] Jean-Michel Chapoulie, "La seconde fondation de la sociologie française, les États-Unis et la classe ouvrière," *Revue française de sociologie* 32, no. 3 (1991), 321–364.

[7] Henri Mendras, *Comment devenir sociologue: mémoires d'un vieux mandarin* (Paris: Actes Sud, 1995), 63.

[8] Alain Touraine, *Un désir d'histoire* (Paris: Stock, 1977), 68.

solution to the impasses of the French left, Friedmann and his students would embrace what Michel Crozier called an "open Marxism" – in practice, a vague desire to study the working class in action rather than merely theorize about class struggle.

The Friedmann circle's experiences of America were complex, marked by fascination with the "modernity," institutional organization, and resources of its social sciences along with a negative reaction to its political atmosphere during the McCarthy era. Friedmann made his first visit to the U.S. in 1948, sent by the French Ministry of Labor, and toured a wide range of sociology and industrial relations departments at American universities in the Northeast and Midwest, as well as several historically black universities in the South. Friedmann returned impressed with the omnidisciplinarity of American industrial relations research, criticized French Marxists for failing to recognize that the social problems of highly technological mass society were universal, and went beyond the differences in economic systems. "The organization, beyond capitalist disorder, of a rational system of production and distribution is a *necessary* condition for the future of civilization: but for those who hold to the observation of contemporary realities, and not a mystique, it appears in no way a *sufficient* condition."[9] But if Friedmann would work to import American-style industrial research to France, he remained ambivalent about the American "model," criticizing the manipulative features of Fordist productivism and America's persistent poverty and racial discrimination. Friedmann was anxious about America's "political psychosis" over communism and wondered if the problems with the American system perhaps belied its belief in the healing power of social science, problems that were "profoundly economic and social, closely linked to structures which the most ingenious expert recommendations are incapable of getting a grip on."[10]

That "political psychosis" would soon ensnare Friedmann himself. Applying for a visa to attend an industrial relations conference at Cornell in 1951, he was interrogated for two hours at the American consulate in Paris and asked if he "supported upsetting the government through violence."[11] The interventions of his American contacts with the State Department and Democratic senators were of no use in reversing the refusal of Friedmann's visa. His junior researchers, encouraged to

---

[9] Georges Friedmann, *Où va le travail humain?* (Paris: Gallimard, 1950), 11.
[10] Friedmann, *Où va le travail humain?*, 165, 200.
[11] "Memo concerning the refusal of a visa to M. Georges Friedmann by the Consulate General of the United States at Paris," May 1951, Everett C. Hughes Papers, Box 26, Folder 12, Hanna Holborn Gray Special Collections Research Center, University of Chicago, Chicago.

pursue sociological training in the U.S., found themselves at Harvard, Yale, Columbia, and Chicago at the height of McCarthyism in 1951–52, an experience that seemed to confirm Parisian intellectuals' dim view of America as a fanatical right-wing place. Alain Touraine, sent to study with Talcott Parsons at Harvard, formed a lasting association between American functionalism and the intellectual conformism of American elite academia. "I had a difficult time bearing this falsely liberal aristocratism," he later wrote, recalling how his Harvard colleagues deflected his questions about McCarthyism. "A very refined intellectual world, but which lacked courage in my eyes and did not dare to look society in the face, contenting itself to cover it over with the false splendors of reassuring theories."[12]

The Cold War, then, pushed members of the Friedmann school into a critical stance toward the United States despite their evident sympathy for its social sciences and even for aspects of its labor relations. While critical of French communist theories, hardline anti-communism was an unrealistic proposition when the PCF was the dominant left party in France, and, unlike Cold War liberals, they did not consider the Soviet Union an existential enemy. But at the same time, their experiences of the U.S. were confirming their suspicions about American paranoia and intolerance; other sociologists – in France, most notably Raymond Aron – were bringing American intellectual anti-communism to Paris through the CCF. Though sociologically they would entertain many of the same ideas during the 1950s, a fundamental gulf would divide the Friedmann school and the CCF's "Cold War liberals."

The intellectual politics of the CCF in the early 1950s were characterized by a militant, existential anti-communism based on the theory of "totalitarianism" and a pessimistic, anti-progressive view of politics. Müller is correct that Cold War liberals "were, above all, antitotalitarians."[13] The elaborate intellectual genealogies this tendency constructed for itself, often after the fact, should not distract from its conjunctural, instrumental characteristics. The concept of "totalitarianism" was itself instrumental, transposing the crimes of Nazism onto the Soviet state and thus facilitating a Manichean moral and conceptual demarcation between East and West.[14] Totalitarianism theory placed a central

---

[12] Touraine, *Un désir d'histoire*, 64–67.
[13] Müller, "Calming the Ideological Storms?," 467.
[14] Les K. Adler and Thomas G. Paterson, "Red Fascism: The Merger of Nazi Germany and Soviet Russia in the American Image of Totalitarianism, 1930's–1950's," *The American Historical Review* 75, no. 4 (April 1970), 1046–1064. For an excellent conceptual history of "totalitarianism," see Michael Scott Christofferson, *French Intellectuals*

emphasis on ideology as the core of "totalitarian" societies, and anti-totalitarians, too, analyzed politics as a battle between grand ideas and moral dispositions. Already in the late 1930s, Aron had theorized totalitarianism as an inherent feature of democracy; a number of postwar anti-totalitarians articulated the critique of democracy via a critique of Rousseau and the French Revolution as the origins of "chiliastic" or "monist" efforts to impose ideological blueprints on society.[15] All of these notions sounded old notes in the canon of conservative reaction to the rise of modern liberal and democratic politics. Aron's description of totalitarianism as "secular religion," with strong resonances of interwar Catholicism, also trained the focus directly on intellectuals: if "ideology" was a pursuit of an all-encompassing worldview for creating heaven on earth, it was uniquely attractive to the intellectuals who played the role of "clerics" in modern society – and thus meant sympathizers of communism could not be trusted with democracy.

That anti-totalitarianism placed such emphasis on ideas and on a back-of-the-napkin sociology of intellectuals was closely connected to the CCF's strategy of "defining the parameters of discourse" in Europe.[16] Anti-totalitarianism represented a set of polemical arguments designed to delegitimize divergence from American foreign policy, radical criticism of society, or any hint of dialogue with communists – all things that were attractive to European democratic socialists such as Friedmann and some of his younger protégés. It did so by furnishing a prefabricated explanation for intellectuals' attractions to dangerous illusions: whatever the abstract reflections of its participants on "value pluralism," the early years of the CCF in Europe gave lie to the notion that it represented a new form of a liberalism defined by an "ethos of dialogue."[17] If anti-totalitarians, as Müller argues, "understood that totalitarianism was not simply a political fantasy created by crazed and hateful minds," they gave little indication of how it might prove attractive to any *other* than

---

against the Left: The Antitotalitarian Moment of the 1970's (New York: Berghahn Books, 2004), 1–21.

[15] The purest distillation of this argument was J. L. Talmon, *The Origins of Totalitarian Democracy* (London: Secker & Warburg, 1952). Iain Stewart demonstrates that the same themes in Raymond Aron's thought were initially drawn from conservative and Catholic sources during the 1930s. Iain Stewart, *Raymond Aron and Liberal Thought in the Twentieth Century* (Cambridge: Cambridge University Press, 2019), 96–102. On Catholic anti-totalitarianism see James Chappel, "The Catholic Origins of Totalitarianism Theory in Interwar Europe," *Modern Intellectual History* 8, no. 9 (2011), 561–590.

[16] Giles Scott-Smith, "The Congress for Cultural Freedom, the End of Ideology and the 1955 Milan Conference: 'Defining the Parameters of Discourse,'" *Journal of Contemporary History* 37, no. 3 (2002), 437–455.

[17] Müller, "Calming the Ideological Storms?," 468.

crazed and hateful minds. As the French political scientist Maurice Duverger observed, the terms in which the anti-totalitarians framed the debate left no possibility that intellectuals might subscribe to Marxism or imagine working relationships with European communist parties for realistic reasons – or that they might genuinely be concerned about actual social injustice.[18] CCF journals such as *Preuves* in Paris and *Encounter* in London were attack organs deployed against intellectuals who criticized American policy or, worse in the eyes of Cold War liberals, rejected the Cold War binary entirely.[19] The centrality of the Cold War binary and the emergency of communism was reflected in Cold War liberals' hostility to European intellectuals who questioned it: *Preuves* and the Paris section of the CCF, for example, would prove particularly virulent against French intellectuals' skepticism of the proposed European Defense Community (EDC).

Transatlantic sociologists were central actors in spinning the anti-totalitarian style into grand theory. Aron's 1955 book *The Opium of the Intellectuals* was the ur-text, a brilliant polemic that – counter to the thrust of its explicit argument against ideological inflations of politics – transposed political debates in France onto a world-historical moral plane. Aron transfigured communism into a mutant, fanatical strain of the Enlightenment ideology of progress and – clearly against a significant swath of the historical liberal tradition – constructed liberal politics as a pessimistic, anti-progressive philosophy of human finitude. "The liberal regards men as basically imperfect and resigns himself to a system where the good will be the result of countless actions and never the object of a conscious choice. In the last resort, he subscribes to a pessimism which sees politics as the art of creating conditions in which the vices of men contribute to the good of the state."[20] Despite Aron's abstract philosophizing and digressions into intellectual history, the book's arguments were still closely linked to the CCF's strategic objectives in France: policing intellectual discourse by portraying Marxism as an "intellectuals' religion" and attacking French "neutralists" skeptical of American hegemony as provincial nationalists willfully blind to the self-evident benefits it offered Europe as a whole.[21]

---

[18] Maurice Duverger, "Opium des intellectuels ou trahison des clercs?," *Le Monde* (August 27, 1955).

[19] Anthony Arblaster, *The Rise and Decline of Western Liberalism* (Oxford and New York: Blackwell, 1984), 311; Pierre Grémion, "*Preuves* dans le Paris de guerre froide," *Vingtième Siècle* 13, no. 1 (1987), 63–82.

[20] Raymond Aron, *The Opium of the Intellectuals*, trans. Terence Kilmartin (New York: Doubleday & Company, 1957), 284.

[21] Grémion, "*Preuves* dans le Paris de guerre froide," 77.

Aron's version of anti-totalitarianism resonated with the American sociologists in the CCF and their postwar retreat from a radical critique in moment when, as Seymour Martin Lipset later put it, the threat of totalitarianism put "a heavy premium on intellectuals justifying the virtues of the societies in which they lived, and defined serious criticism as contributing to the enemy."[22] Daniel Bell adopted Aron's account of ideology as a "secular religion," an all-encompassing, "chiliastic" worldview driven by a "passion" to recreate heaven on earth.[23] He later connected his attraction to this idea to a "tragic" sense of the world that emerged in his thinking during the war and that he shared with other Jewish intellectuals such as Richard Hofstadter. "It involved the fear of anti-Semitism in the United States, the fear of mass politics, the fear of passionate politics, a fear of what happens when the world is so disordered there are no norms or rules."[24] Lipset, as well, evoked the tragic sense in CCF anti-totalitarianism, writing that Nazism and Stalinism alike demonstrated that "you can't change things simply because they're no good. ... When the mob takes over, even initially for good ends, it can become very totalitarian, very vicious."[25] Especially for American social scientists, the critique of intellectuals' "secular religion" would be closely related to a critique of the dangers of mass politics; if radical intellectuals were on the one hand dismissed as mere "rhetoricians," to borrow Bell's terms, on the other, their attraction to ideology raised the specter of impassioned masses that American anti-totalitarians came to believe were hard-wired for authoritarianism.[26]

As early Cold War anti-totalitarianism shifted to the background after the death of Stalin, the sociologists who had embraced it would become major contributors to the paradigm of "industrial society." But the anti-totalitarian style left tendencies that were absent from the thinking

---

[22] Seymour Martin Lipset, "The Possible Political Effects of Student Activism," *Social Science Information* 8, no. 2 (April 1, 1969), 17.

[23] Daniel Bell, *The End of Ideology: On the Exhaustion of Political Ideas in the Fifties* (New York and London: Free Press, 1960), 400–402.

[24] Quoted in Job L. Dittberner, *The End of Ideology and American Social Thought, 1930–1960* (Ann Arbor: UMI Research Press, 1979), 316.

[25] Quoted in Dittberner, *The End of Ideology and American Social Thought*, 339.

[26] Hofstadter's interpretation of the American populist tradition was the key influence on the American critique of mass politics and was generalized to both left and right in Lipset's theory of "working-class authoritarianism," originally composed for a CCF conference. Sidney M. Peck, "Ideology and 'Political Sociology': The Conservative Bias of Lipset's 'Political Man,'" *The American Catholic Sociological Review* 23, no. 2 (1962), 128–155. If its origins were different, during the Cold War it harmonized perfectly with critiques of mass politics by former German social democrats. Daniel Bessner, *Democracy in Exile: Hans Speier and the Rise of the Defense Intellectual* (Ithaca, NY: Cornell University Press, 2018), chapter one, 47.

of other industrial-society theorists: an antipathy to mass politics and a measured acceptance of post-ideological technocratic governance as a bulwark against the potential emergency of ideological mobilization. Both of these were a particular political spin – not the only possible one – placed on what they called the "end of ideology": that, though social conflict and debate would continue, politics were henceforth, as Bell put it, "resistant to the old terms of the ideological debate between 'left' and 'right'" and any future vision had to be "empirical."[27] For Aron, politics was best left to "skeptics" lest it fall into the hands of "fanatics."[28]

The Industrial Society Convergence: Redefining Socialism, 1955–1968

If anti-totalitarianism drove a wedge between American and French sociologists in the early 1950s, by the middle of the decade, relations had begun to thaw in parallel with the broader geopolitical situation. The death of Stalin in 1953 marked the beginning of the CCF's search for a path out of militant anti-totalitarianism, and the events in the communist world in 1956 – Khruschev's "secret speech" and the suppression of the Hungarian uprising – profoundly shifted the ideological atmosphere in Paris. Added to other major events in French politics – most notably the Algerian war and Charles de Gaulle's return to power on the threat of a military coup in 1958 – these shifts galvanized the noncommunist left and spurred an expansive search for a reformist left ideology. The Friedmann school, reaching maturity as sociologists and public intellectuals in the later 1950s, would find both a broader hearing in French public discourse and closer dialogue with CCF-affiliated sociologists such as Aron, Bell, and Lipset.

The 1955 CCF conference in Milan is typically identified as a turning point for the Congress from militant anti-totalitarianism to the analysis of industrial society – and one that involved a broader range of European socialists addressing the contemporary problems of social-democratic politics. The right wing of the British Labour Party was heavily represented, as were moderate figures from the French SFIO such as André Philip. Prominent topics of discussion included the role of economic growth in postwar society, the question of nationalization of enterprises, and the expansion of "industrial democracy" within the postwar mixed economy. The conference was defined by what Pierre Grémion calls "a new sociopolitical realism" that emphasized the

---

[27] Bell, *The End of Ideology*, 406, 405.
[28] Aron, *The Opium of the Intellectuals*, 324.

exhaustion of both the liberal and socialist ideologies of the nineteenth century and insisted that concrete social-scientific analysis of the contemporary conjuncture revealed, as Aron put it in one of the opening sessions, that "the economies of the Western world differ less in their action than in their rhetoric."[29]

This argument was central to Aron's lectures at the Sorbonne in the 1950s, which were among the first to at least purport to theorize "industrial society."[30] While the definition remained too vague to really amount to a theory, the lectures were based on a systematic comparison between capitalism and Soviet socialism as "ideal types," showing that they both confronted similar problems of growth, investment, and production. No actual society corresponded to the abstract doctrines of "liberalism" or "socialism," but in fact most actually existing societies were complex mixtures of different approaches to economic production and political management. While taking a detached, empirical tone different from his often fiery political commentary, Aron's argument was still directed against Marxism, made by showing that the problems of "industrial societies" were largely similar across societies that claimed different ideologies. Ostensibly "capitalist" societies could introduce elements of planning and economic control, while the Soviet Union still faced problems of labor discipline, social hierarchy, and inequality.

Friedmann had been excluded from the guest list of the Milan conference for political reasons – a residue of the ideological crusading that still marked the Congress despite its incipient shift away from antitotalitarianism.[31] In the meantime, however, sociology in France had become a haven for an academicization of Marxism that distanced it from the ideology of the Communist Party. The Russian-born sociologist Georges Gurvitch gave the first lectures on Marx in the history of the Sorbonne. Gurvitch was sympathetic to Marx but, like Aron, emphasized the incompleteness of Marxist class theory and the need to separate its sociological content from its "German mysticism."[32] With Gurvitch as their theoretical guide and Friedmann pushing them to adopt American-style fieldwork, Friedmann's students furnished new data on the "consciousness" of French workers. Their work pointed to reformist conclusions: Industrial automation was undermining the

---

[29] Pierre Grémion, *Intelligence de l'anticommunisme: le Congrès pour la liberté de la culture à Paris (1950–1975)* (Paris: Fayard, 1995), 175.
[30] Later published as *Dix-huit leçons sur la société industrielle* (Paris: Gallimard, 1962); *La lutte des classes : nouvelles leçons sur les sociétés industrielles* (Paris: Gallimard, 1964).
[31] Grémion, *Intelligence de l'anticommunisme*, 162–165.
[32] Georges Gurvitch, *Le concept de classe sociale de Marx à nos jours* (Paris: Centre de documentation universitaire, 1954), 9.

communitarian, producerist bases of proletarian class-consciousness, while new structures of promotion were making industrial workers less distinct from the rest of the diversifying workforce.[33] White-collar office workers were caught between their subordinated condition and their desire for "bourgeois" social mobility and tended to be more likely to complain about "bureaucratic alienation" than to exhibit anti-capitalist class consciousness.[34]

In terms that sometimes echoed those of the CCF intellectuals, and more than a few French socialists, Touraine, Crozier, and others of Friedmann's students increasingly criticized the outdated slogans of the institutional French left. Writing in reformist left journals, they argued that socialism was more plausible as a struggle for greater participation at work and enjoyment of the fruits of productivity than a revolutionary struggle against capitalism.[35] Without endorsing the tendentious anti-totalitarian critique of ideology, they attributed the weaknesses of the French noncommunist left to its attachment to obsolete "social doctrines" and emphasized the contributions social science could make to a modernized left politics. Bell's analysis of the American labor movement, which he first presented in Friedmann's seminar in 1957, was influential in the Friedmann circle.[36] Increasingly, its members borrowed Aron's concept of "industrial society" which, as Friedmann wrote, "is well elaborated for the comparison and comprehension of complex societies with progressive economies."[37] Touraine began to argue that capitalism had been a transitional phase in the development of a fully formed "industrial society." "The social doctrines that accompanied the processes of industrialization are important objects of study, but they contribute only very bad instruments of analysis," he wrote.[38]

---

[33] Alain Touraine, "L'évolution de la conscience ouvrière et l'idée socialiste," *Esprit* 24, no. 238 (May 1956), 692–705; Touraine, "Problèmes actuels du mouvement ouvrier," *Cahiers de la République* 4, no. 21 (October 1959), 22–38.

[34] Michel Crozier, "L'ambiguïté de la conscience de classe chez les employés et les petits fonctionnaires," *Cahiers Internationaux de Sociologie* 18 (1955), 78–97; Crozier, "Les tertiaires et le socialisme," *Esprit* 24, no. 238 (May 1956), 706–714.

[35] Alain Touraine, "Situation du mouvement ouvrier," *Arguments* 3, no. 12–13 (March 1959), 7–15; Michel Crozier, "L'ère du prolétariat s'achève," *Arguments* 3, no. 12–13 (March 1959), 31–33.

[36] Daniel Bell, "The Past and Future of American Unionism," 1957, Box 153, École des Hautes Études en Science Sociales Archives, Fonds CADIS, Paris, France; Georges Friedmann and Jean-Daniel Reynaud, "La société industrielle et son avenir," in *Histoire générale du travail: la civilisation industrielle (de 1914 à nos jours)*, ed. Alain Touraine, vol. 4, 4 vols. (Paris: Nouvelle Librairie de France, 1962), 342–253.

[37] Georges Friedmann, "La civilisation technicienne," *Arguments*, no. 27–28 (4th trimester 1962), 46–52.

[38] Alain Touraine, "Naissance des sociétés industrielles," *Arguments*, no. 27–28 (4th trimester 1962), 53–57.

By the early 1960s, the Cold War liberals of the CCF and a range of social-democratic sociologists had fully converged on the problematic of "industrial society." A wave of sociological texts theorizing industrial society, highly similar in fundamental arguments and each citing the work of most of the others, appeared at the end of the 1950s, summing up the debates of that decade.[39] Industrial society provided a name to what Norman Birnbaum called "loosely organized complexes of analysis, description, and prediction" – which had developed concurrently in sociology and social-democratic parties.[40] These "complexes" can be reduced to four basic hypotheses or centers of debate:

(1) the outlining of a *logic of industrialization*, or a long-durée process of social change associated with the evolution of technology or "rationalization," now seen as a more fundamental historical process than capitalism, because it was manifested equally in the communist world;
(2) the idea of a *managerial revolution*: that the unfolding of this evolutionary logic entailed a growing complexity of economic production and public administration, giving rise to new strata of expert "managers" and white-collar workers who complicated the traditional social structure and represented a new form of social authority;
(3) a future or actual *integration of class conflict*, the idea that the assertion of new forms of socialized "control" over production and administration, especially through state intervention, welfare provision, and collective bargaining, was "integrating" the working class into a social totality previously fractured by economic individualism and bitter social conflict;
(4) the notion of an *end of ideology* that to some extent inhered in the development of society itself, namely, the growing role of technical expertise and problem-solving at the expense of expansive, mobilizing moral and social visions whose plausibility and social bases were declining in the face of material transformations.[41]

---

[39] Ralf Dahrendorf, *Class and Class Conflict in Industrial Society* (Stanford: Stanford University Press, 1959); Seymour Martin Lipset, *Political Man: The Social Bases of Politics* (Garden City, NJ: Doubleday, 1960); Bell, *The End of Ideology*; Clark Kerr et al., *Industrialism and Industrial Man: The Problems of Labor Management in Economic Growth* (Oxford and New York: Oxford University Press, 1960); Georges Friedmann and Pierre Naville, eds., *Traité de sociologie du travail*, vol. 1 (Paris: Armand Colin, 1961); Aron, *Dix-huit leçons sur la société industrielle*; Michel Crozier, *Le phénomène bureaucratique* (Paris: Seuil, 1963); Alain Touraine, *Sociologie de l'action* (Paris: Seuil, 1965).
[40] Norman Birnbaum, "The Idea of Industrial Society," in *The Development of Industrial Societies*, ed. Paul Halmos (Keele: University of Keele, 1964), 6.
[41] Though I have somewhat modified his formulations here, I am indebted to Alexandre Chirat, "La société industrielle d'Aron et Galbraith: des regards croisés pour une vision convergente ?" *Cahiers d'économie politique* 76, no. 1 (July 10, 2019): 47–87.

Politically, the synthesis of these debates amounted to an update of social-democratic theory to account for postwar economic growth, welfare policies, and systems of social bargaining – a sociological assimilation of Cold War political economy.[42] "Industrial society" was understood as a break with laissez-faire capitalism – perhaps with capitalism itself – and the replacement of the domination of the *economy* with self-conscious coordination by *society*. Somewhat paradoxically, despite the centrality of economic growth to the theory of industrial society, economics tended to disappear from the analysis on the vague assumption that the nature of economic ownership and the power of private interests were no longer central to sociological analysis.[43] "In a politico-technological world," Daniel Bell wrote in an characteristic formulation, "property has increasingly lost its force as a determinant of power, and sometimes, even, of wealth."[44] All industrial-society theorists challenged property relations as a basis for social theory or class structure, which harmonized with European social democrats' battle against nationalizations as the basis of socialist policy.[45] Socialist abandonment of Marxism enabled them to embrace the state as the new center of "industrial society," but almost always without theorizing it; instead, they made superficial references to Robert Dahl and the pluralist school in American political science.[46] To the extent it was analyzed at all, the state became a neutral regulator of plural interests: in Touraine's words, it was "an ensemble of means for action," a "multilateral game of power."[47]

The popularity of the "industrial society" paradigm in the early 1960s testifies to its conceptual utility for a wide range of social scientists with different subjects of research as well as its proximity to the political-ideological debates of socialists and social democrats. But it had different political fortunes in different national contexts. In the United States, debate was centered on the problematic of the "end of ideology," and critics attacked industrial society ideas as a form of post-ideological, technocratic thinking. It was, as C. Wright Mills wrote, linking it explicitly to the CCF, the "weary discourse" of "smug conservatives, tired

---

[42] Donald Sassoon, *One Hundred Years of Socialism: The West European Left in the Twentieth Century* (New York: The New Press, 1996), 195–197.
[43] Howard Brick, *Transcending Capitalism: Visions of a New Society in Modern American Thought* (Ithaca, NY: Cornell University Press, 2006), chapter five.
[44] Bell, *The End of Ideology*, 398.
[45] For examples in British Labour and the French SFIO, see, respectively, C. A. R. Crosland, *The Future of Socialism* (New York: MacMillan, 1957); André Philip, *Le socialisme trahi* (Paris: Plon, 1957).
[46] On the absence of state theory in midcentury political science, see Rafael Khachaturian, "Discipline, Knowledge, and Critique: Marxist Theory and the Revival of the State in American Political Science, 1968–1989" (PhD diss., Indiana University, 2017).
[47] Touraine, *Sociologie de l'action*, 305–307.

liberals, and disillusioned radicals," in which "the sickness of complacency has prevailed, the bi-partisan banality flourished."[48] It was frequently charged that the true "end of ideology" was the end of any commitment to socialism – accurate enough given the way American thinkers such as Bell and Lipset interwove broader sociological themes with their personal path of deradicalization.[49]

In France, the "end of ideology" was only a minor theme of industrial-society thinking, and debate centered rather on the future of the working class. There, though the sociological arguments were the same, "industrial society" looked less like a post-ideological style of thinking than one position in an intra-left debate over political strategy. A wide range of left thinkers outside the PCF, including a number of self-identified Marxists, considered a "realistic" social-scientific picture of the contemporary social structure essential to escaping the political ghetto in the era of De Gaulle. Sociologists' analyses did not doom the working classes but suggested that different *categories* of workers might be drawn into the fight for socialism, fueling theories of the "new working class" in formations such as the Parti Socialiste Unifié.[50] If sociologists such as Alain Touraine argued that "industrial societies" were no longer capitalist, sociologists such as Serge Mallet adapted his ideas to a more traditionally Marxist analysis of capitalist exploitation.[51] Touraine himself had argued that technocracy was a deformation of the possibilities of industrial society and devoted much of his *Sociologie de l'action* to exploring how new "social movements" might play the old role of the working class.[52] In France, the industrial-society paradigm harbored a critique of technocracy that prefigured the arguments of student radicals in 1968.

The point of comparing the fate of the industrial-society paradigm is not only to underline differences between the American and European political contexts but also to show how virtually identical sociological arguments could be read differently depending on the wider reputation and political engagement of the figure advancing them. Aron, Bell, and Lipset were read as conservatives, centrists, or "Cold War liberals" because they manifested the anti-totalitarian style, while Friedmann, Touraine, and Dahrendorf were always clearly on the left despite their moderation and their skepticism of communism and Marxism. Critics sometimes overdrew these differences, exaggerating the conservatism of

---

[48] C. Wright Mills, "Letter to the New Left," *New Left Review*, no. 5 (1960), 18.
[49] Chaim I. Waxman, ed., *The End of Ideology Debate* (New York: Clarion, 1968).
[50] Frank Georgi, "La Nouvelle classe ouvrière: la construction politique d'une catégorie sociale dans la France des Trente Glorieuses," in *Sociologues et sociologies: La France des années 60*, ed. Jean-Michel Chapoulie et al. (Paris: L'Harmattan, 2005), 227–238.
[51] Serge Mallet, *La nouvelle classe ouvrière* (Paris: Seuil, 1963).
[52] Touraine, *Sociologie de l'action*, 483.

the former group and overstating the radicalism of the latter. But dispositions and conjunctural reactions mattered – all the more so in the era that opened in the 1960s.

Sociologists and 1968, or the Permanence of the Anti-totalitarian Style?

The explosion of student movements across the world in 1968 polarized academic sociology almost overnight.[53] A number of industrial-society theorists would have dramatic interactions with student protesters. The instigators of the French student movement, most notably Daniel Cohn-Bendit, were sociology students of Alain Touraine at Nanterre, and Touraine conducted an on-the-ground sociological study of the movement and served as a negotiator between students and the authorities. Ralf Dahrendorf famously debated the German student revolutionary Rudi Dutschke on the roof of a van in Freiburg, while the American New Left made Daniel Bell one of its ideological targets, precipitating his flight from Columbia to Harvard.[54] Student radicals lashed out against the ideas of their professors, often unaware of how much their own leftism drew on industrial society theory's critique of the old left. Among the countless examples, a group of Touraine's students denounced the French sociological professoriate for the "importation des doctrines made in U.S.A" and called for the "dissipation des mots d'ordre stalino-tourainiens" – despite the fact that Touraine had pioneered a similar critique of American sociology.[55] With more justification, different chapters of the Students for a Democratic Society in the U.S. published pamphlets rebutting Lipset's *Political Man* and Bell's *The End of Ideology*.[56]

In addition to the oedipal student–teacher dynamics of these confrontations, the explosion of social conflict bore directly on the sociological portrait of "industrial society" painted over the previous decade. Virtually all sociologists interpreted the student movements as an expression of the tensions of industrial society they already had analyzed and in some cases predicted. All ascribed the movements in part to an

---

[53] Pierre Grémion, "Les sociologues et 68: notes de recherche," *Le Débat* 149, no. 2 (2008): 20–36.
[54] Paul Berman, "Left Behind: Daniel Bell and the Class of '68," *Bookforum* (May 2005). www.bookforum.com/print/1201/daniel-bell-and-the-class-of-68-3051 (accessed November 22, 2020).
[55] Daniel Cohn-Bendit et al., "Pourquoi des sociologues ?," *Esprit*, no. 371 (1968), 877–882.
[56] Robert Alan Haber, *The End of Ideology as Ideology* (San Francisco: Students for a Democratic Society, 1960); Jim Jacobs, *S.M. Lipset: Social Scientist of the Smooth Society* (Ann Arbor, MI: Radical Education Project, 1969).

idealistic romanticism and could hardly avoid frustration in the face of what they saw as at adolescent calls to abolish what they had attributed to the forces of modern industrialization and considered foundational features of all advanced societies. But not all were dismissive, and the differences echoed earlier reactions to the Cold War. Cold War liberals tended to moralize the stakes of the student movement and focus on threats to established institutions, orders, and values as they lambasted the irresponsible intellectuals who legitimized them. In other words, they reformulated the specter of *emergency*. Others welcomed the student movements, whatever their limitations, as exactly the sort of social movements they had hoped would arise in "industrial society." While these reactions can only be evoked fleetingly, they provide a fitting conclusion that underscores the durability of the temperamental reaction and the politics of emergency that underlay "Cold War liberalism."

Much as they had been persuaded of the fragility of the "free world" during the early Cold War, anti-totalitarians saw student protesters as a threat to the hard-earned legitimacy of postwar institutions: from the "autonomous" university to economic growth itself. They soon responded by defending moralized concepts of "authority," "reason," and "pluralism" against "irrationality" and "populism." By his own account, Raymond Aron reacted to the May 1968 events in France with genuine panic before being reassured that the PCF would not launch an insurrection and shifting to his famous interpretation of the protests as a "psychodrama" and a "non-event." Aron fretted about the possibility of a turn to totalitarianism, and again attacked intellectuals for "weakening a fragile order." "The vague, emotional leftism of the intellectuals has overtaken the *bien-pensants* and their children," he wrote. "This bad conscience of those who hold authority was probably one of the causes of the decomposition of May."[57] Daniel Bell appears to have initially waffled between sympathy for and revulsion at the student movement, but by the late 1960s had concluded the threat to authority called for a *rappel à l'ordre*: the "language of democracy and populism," he wrote, "usually masks, simply, a desire to disestablish and render illegitimate all existing authority."[58] Among the sociological causes of the student movement, Lipset included the "intellectual *poujadisme*" of humanist professors and their students against the necessary hierarchy and managerialism of a complex society. "Many intellectuals react to the emphasis

---

[57] Raymond Aron, *La révolution introuvable: réflexions sur la révolution de mai* (Paris: Fayard, 1968), 172–173.
[58] Daniel Bell and Irving Kristol, "Introduction," in *Confrontation: The Student Rebellion and the Universities*, ed. Daniel Bell and Irving Kristol (New York and London: Basic Books, 1969), xi.

on social science and the concomitant belief in gradualism, expertise, and planning with a populist stress on the virtues of direct action against evil institutions and practices."[59] In a telling recollection, Bell attributed his reaction to the student movement, and those of his fellow "New York intellectuals," to the same one that had driven his turn to the Cold War, namely, a fear of "what happens when a mass gets out of hand and becomes a mob … a great suspicion and fear of mass action of a particular kind, and fear of those situations which in a sense tear down the very fragile bonds of society." In that sense, he concluded, "we all became somewhat conservative."[60]

Other industrial-society theorists, especially in France, did not see the mass mobilizations of the late 1960s as a threat to fragile democratic societies. Rather, they interpreted the student movements as confirmations of their own theories that industrial societies would produce new kinds of social conflict, and even welcomed them as rebellions against the technocratic deformations they themselves had warned against. "Each one of us should measure the immense possibility implied for French society by the unwinding [*défoulement*] within so many institutions, enterprises, meetings, and workplaces," Georges Friedmann wrote in a column for *Le Monde*. Though aware of its "irritating aspects," meaning its youthful excesses and rigidities, he asked: "is it not true, as we have so often heard said over the course of these weeks, that 'the French need to be awoken'?"[61] "The May movement," Touraine wrote in his sociology of the protests, "is not a refusal of industrial society and its culture, but the revelation of its contradictions and the new conflicts that are at the heart of that society." It was "a conflict between those who confuse social progress and their private power and those who, against them, call for the democratic management of economic and social change."[62] Ralf Dahrendorf, who, like Touraine, had intended his own theory of industrial society as an account of how societies produce new conflicts, excoriated fellow sociologists for explaining the student revolt in terms of values and psychology. Instead, he insisted that it be treated as part of a legitimate social struggle for expanded rights and participation.[63]

[59] Lipset, "The Possible Political Effects of Student Activism," 16.
[60] Interview quoted in Neil Jumonville, *Critical Crossings: The New York Intellectuals in Postwar America* (Berkeley: University of California Press, 1990), 222.
[61] Georges Friedmann, "Fin d'une étape," *Le Monde* (June 21, 1968).
[62] Alain Touraine, *Le mouvement de Mai ou le communisme utopique*, 4th ed. (Paris: Le Seuil, 2018), 9–10.
[63] On Dahrendorf's reaction to the student movements and critiques of "Cold War liberal" sociologists, see Marius Strubenhoff, "Ideas, Interests, and Institutions in Ralf Dahrendorf's Materialist Liberalism" (PhD diss., University of Cambridge, 2019), chapter five.

Dahrendorf was particularly scathing toward German social democrats who turned into reactionary critics of the student movement, accusing them of pulling up the drawbridge after having reached the "saving shore of social privileges."[64]

Though these divergent reactions to 1968 are only roughly sketched here, they highlight an enduring difference in temperament the social-democratic sociologists and Cold War anti-totalitarians. The anti-totalitarian temperament was characterized by a tendency toward political pessimism that fixated on the threatening possibilities of social conflict and remained skeptical of any but the most moderate calls for social reform. Consequences of this tendency included an emphasis on stability and legitimacy, a resolute anti-populism, and a marked preference that politics – and political debate – take place under authoritative elite guidance. If the sociological vision of industrial society that anti-totalitarians endorsed has mostly been consigned to history, the anti-totalitarian style has remained as a transpartisan feature of Atlantic intellectual and political life, especially as many "Cold War liberals" shifted toward neoconservatism in the 1970s.[65] Even as this article was being composed, the right-wing attorney general of the United States evoked the idea of "secular religion" to describe the "utopianism" of contemporary left politics, while a prominent liberal editor announced plans for a new publication that would revive liberalism as "a worldview ... an anti-ideological ideology."[66]

The French and American sociologists who constructed the industrial-society paradigm shared a theoretical framework for interpreting postwar society, but their differences underscore the centrality of the politics of emergency to Cold War liberalism as a distinct variant of liberalism. While democratic socialists remained committed to deepening democratic participation and hoped for cooperative forms of international organization beyond the Cold War binary, Cold War liberals' fear of the *demos* at home pushed them instead toward a darker vision in which some forms of domination and constraint were essential to guard against the permanent threat of too much democracy.

---

[64] Strubenhoff, "Ideas, Interests, and Institutions in Ralf Dahrendorf's Materialist Liberalism," 239.
[65] See the chapter by Michael Brenes and Michael Franczak in this volume.
[66] Charles Creitz, "Barr Blasts Far Left for Making Politics a 'Secular Religion,'" *FoxNews.com* (August 9, 2020), www.foxnews.com/politics/barr-far-left-politics-religion-democrats-cowards (accessed November 22, 2020); Ash Carter, "Taking – and Making – Liberties," *Air Mail* (August 15, 2020), https://airmail.news/issues/2020-8-15/taking-and-making-liberties (accessed November 22, 2020).

8 "Slavery Old and New"
Cold War Liberals in the Global Forced Labor Debate, 1947–1953

Emma Kuby

"Rally to the cause of free labor! Rally to stem the tide of slave labor! ... The struggle for free labor is the struggle for the future of all mankind!" These exhortations, which might at first glance appear to be slogans from a nineteenth-century abolitionist pamphlet, were the closing words of a 1947 "Manifesto" against "the new slavery" in the USSR by the American Federation of Labor (AFL).[1] The document heralded a long, fiercely waged international propaganda operation targeting the plight of Soviet labor camp inmates. With the eventual support of the United States government, the AFL succeeded by 1949 in bringing the issue before the United Nations' Economic and Social Council as a matter of global concern. That body subsequently voted to create a joint UN–International Labor Organization (ILO) investigatory committee dedicated to compiling testimony and documentation on forced labor systems worldwide. At the same time, labor leaders, writers, statesmen, and scholars from the United States and its Western European allies, particularly Great Britain and France, were drawn into the campaign against "twentieth-century slavery" in the communist bloc.[2] Members of this loose coalition all shared common goals: to shore up support for anti-Soviet Cold War mobilization and to dampen the appeal of communism in the West, especially among organized labor. But, over time, the means with which they sought to achieve their ends diverged.

With its emphasis on faceless masses condemned to toil and its reliance on a dry bureaucratic framework of international legal conventions, the anti-forced labor campaign of the late 1940s and early

---

[1] "Manifesto" of the Free Trade Union Committee of the American Federation of Labor, *International Free Trade Union News*, March 1947, reproduced in *Slave Labor in Russia: The Case Presented by the American Federation of Labor to the United Nations* (Washington DC: 1949), 10. (I hereafter refer to this collection as *SLR*.)
[2] Ibid., 9.

1950s has been overshadowed in the historical literature by more colorful elements of the cultural Cold War, like the Congress for Cultural Freedom (CCF) and Radio Free Europe. To date, the Western effort to stigmatize "totalitarian slavery" has chiefly aroused the attention of human rights scholars who focus on labor regulations, historians of propaganda bureaus, or specialists in the history of the ILO.[3] But the campaign deserves the attention of historians of Cold War liberalism as well, for three reasons. First, it demonstrates the importance of not only liberal labor leaders but also liberal ideas and rhetoric *about* labor – forced and otherwise – to the construction of a Cold War consensus in foreign policy. Second, it offers an opportunity to position Cold War–era actors within liberalism's long tradition of engagement with the problem of slavery versus "free" wage work – an issue that cuts to the core of how liberals have historically delimited the individual liberties that they claim to champion, especially freedom of contract. Third, though it is indeed true, as this volume's introduction claims, that liberalism achieved hegemonic status among post–World War II American elites, ideological alternatives to Cold War liberalism continued to flourish elsewhere in the Western anti-communist camp. The slave labor campaign compelled Cold War liberals to join forces with a diverse array of non-liberal European and émigré actors, from ex-Mensheviks and Trotskyists to Christian democrats and traditional conservatives; thus it allows historians to situate self-consciously "liberal" opposition to Soviet practices within a broader field of Cold War anti-communist discourse and to examine what set it apart.

Cold War liberalism, like liberalism *tout court*, is a protean term.[4] Its adherents were indeed, as Jan-Werner Müller writes, "above all anti-totalitarians" – but after all, so were many non-liberal or even

---

[3] Editorial, "Free Labor versus Slave Labor: Irrepressible Conflict," *International Free Trade Union News*, January 1947, reproduced in *SLR*, 5. For examples of these three approaches see, respectively, Sandrine Kott, "The Forced Labor Issue between Human and Social Rights, 1947–1957," trans. Joel Golb, *Humanity* 3, no. 3 (Winter 2012): 321–335; John Jenks, *British Propaganda and News Media in the Cold War* (Edinburgh: Edinburgh University Press, 2006); and Quenby Olmsted Hughes, "The American Federation of Labor's Cold War Campaign against 'Slave Labor' at the United Nations," in *American Labor's Global Ambassadors: The International History of the AFL-CIO during the Cold War*, ed. Robert Anthony Waters, Jr. and Geert van Goethem (New York: Palgrave MacMillan, 2013), 23–38, as well as Daniel Maul, "The International Labour Organization and the Struggle against Forced Labour from 1919 to the Present," *Labor History* 48, no. 4 (November 2007): 477–500. On the rise of American "gulag consciousness" more generally, see Susan L. Carruthers, *Cold War Captives: Imprisonment, Escape, and Brainwashing* (Berkeley: University of California Press, 2009), 98–135.

[4] Gary Gerstle, "The Protean Character of American Liberalism," *The American Historical Review* 99, no. 4 (1994): 1043–1073.

illiberal thinkers.[5] Hence the problem of identifying what (if anything) was specifically *liberal* about Cold War liberals' commitment to anti-totalitarianism remains.[6] Müller contends that a set of "actual political principles" and "underlying philosophical positions" placed liberal Cold War activism within a coherent intellectual framework.[7] He also suggests, following Judith Shklar, that "the imperative to avoid cruelty and atrocity" was the ethical core of the Cold War liberal project.[8] The history of the anti-forced labor campaign calls both elements of this interpretation into question. When it came to denouncing Soviet "slavery," it was non-liberal anti-totalitarians – notably French Buchenwald survivor and idiosyncratic leftist David Rousset – who more heavily emphasized the extreme bodily suffering imposed upon Stalin's actual victims. Self-identified liberals, in contrast, offered an abstract, legalistic, putatively universal defense of negative liberties, drawing on a selected canon of classical economic arguments for free labor and a set of civil libertarian principles concerning freedom of opinion.

What is more, after 1951 they seamlessly shifted into other ideological registers as these themes became politically inconvenient. Operating within an existential logic of emergency according to which all tactics were equally vindicated by Cold War necessity, the U.S. liberals at the forefront of the anti-forced labor crusade – now increasingly dominated by State Department actors – proved happy to abandon liberal talking points as strategy dictated and, instead, to embrace non-liberal lines of attack on the gulag system. Thus, the story of the AFL-led campaign against "totalitarian slavery" suggests that the liberalism of these American Cold Warriors may be best understood neither as a cry of moral revulsion against cruelty nor as a clearly defined set of political and philosophical principles but rather as a rich rhetorical resource. Liberalism's legalistic language of individual negative freedoms offered

---

[5] Jan-Werner Müller, "Calming the Ideological Storms?: Reflections on Cold War Liberalism," in *Ideological Storms: Intellectuals, Dictators, and the Totalitarian Temptation*, ed. Vladimir Tismaneanu and Bogdan C. Iacob (Budapest: Central European University Press, 2019), 465–485, here 467.

[6] For the argument that "the emergency defense of freedom against the Soviets in Cold War liberalism transformed [liberalism itself] almost beyond recognition," see Samuel Moyn, *Liberalism against Itself: Cold War Intellectuals and the Making of Our Times* (New Haven, CT: Yale University Press, 2023), 18.

[7] Müller, "Calming the Ideological Storms?," 467.

[8] Jan-Werner Müller, "Fear and Freedom: On Cold War Liberalism," *European Journal of Political Theory* 7, no.1 (2008), 45–64; see also Judith Shklar, "The Liberalism of Fear," in *Liberalism and the Moral Life*, ed. Nancy L. Rosenblum (Cambridge, MA: Harvard University Press, 1989), 21–38. Moyn, meanwhile, views Cold War liberals' orientation toward "harm reduction" as a catastrophic "retreat" from more robustly emancipatory pursuits: see *Liberalism against Itself*, 37 and 129.

one tool – among others, which eventually proved more effective – for elite actors to attempt to articulate to the Western public what was so uniquely objectionable about the internal practices of a distant state.[9]

To sketch out the historically shifting and substantively shallow nature of Cold War liberals' critique of Soviet forced labor, this essay proceeds chronologically in three movements. First, it surveys the initial attack of the AFL on Soviet "chattel slavery" in the late 1940s, highlighting its rhetorical reliance on a selectively reimagined liberal tradition that prized formal individual rights above all else and condemned enslavement not as racist subjugation but as the binary negation of workers' freedom to contract their labor. Second, the article considers what happened when the anti-slave labor campaign expanded to include Western European participants beginning in 1949. As in David Sessions's contribution to this volume, it is the French comparison that proves particularly revelatory. Bringing French anti-totalitarians such as Rousset into the picture demonstrates that American liberals were far less interested in stressing cruelty than were non-liberal continental counterparts. Finally, the essay explains why historical references to chattel slavery and pious invocations of civil liberties lost their practical utility to American Cold Warriors after the 1951 institutionalization of a UN-ILO Ad Hoc Committee on Forced Labor with a wide-ranging global mandate: Now the former could just as easily be wielded to attack Western colonial labor abuses, while the latter were rendered strategically irrelevant by the Committee's focus on the scope, not the purpose, of different forced labor schemes. In books and pamphlets on Soviet "slavery" produced in the early 1950s, old liberal talking points gave way to new, varied arguments, some economistic and some moral. Major liberal figures – among them ACLU founder Roger Nash Baldwin – remained at the helm of the crusade against forced labor. But, in the end, it was a lasting commitment to anti-Soviet mobilization rather than any specific or coherent set of liberal principles that gave meaning to these Cold Warriors' participation in "the struggle for the future of all mankind."

U.S. Labor Liberals against Soviet Slavery, 1947–1949

The AFL's anti-forced labor campaign was launched in 1947 by members of its international policy branch, the Free Trade Union Committee (FTUC).[10] The FTUC had been founded in 1944 for the more or less

---

[9] Müller, "Calming the Ideological Storms?," 467.
[10] For a comprehensive account of the FTUC, including its relationship with the CIA, see Anthony Carew, *American Labour's Cold War Abroad: From Deep Freeze to Détente, 1945–1970* (Edmonton: AU Press, 2018).

explicit purpose of helping foreign unions resist communist influence, especially in vulnerable Western Europe; its priorities and its audiences were consistently international and thus distinct from those of the larger Federation. Leaders included AFL Vice President Matthew Woll and the head of the International Ladies Garment Workers' Union (ILGWU), David Dubinsky, who was also a founder of Americans for Democratic Action and the Liberal Party of New York.[11] These men were longtime stalwarts of anti-communist labor organizing. But a January 1947 editorial in the *International Free Trade Union News*, "Free Labor versus Slave Labor: Irrepressible Conflict," marked a dramatic intensification of their assault on Soviet "slavery." With both its title and its themes borrowed from William Henry Seward's famous 1858 speech warning that "the slave system" and "the free labor system" could no longer coexist in the United States, the editorial opined that the "reappearance of slavery under a different name" was today occurring in the Eastern bloc – and thereby threatening the status of free workers worldwide.[12] "Free labor," the authors wrote, "has always opposed slave labor in any form or under any pretext. Slave labor anywhere in the world adversely affects the standards of free labor everywhere."[13] Two months later, an FTUC manifesto titled "Fight for Free Labor is Fight for World's Future" reiterated the narrative of a "return to chattel slavery … as unashamed and brutalizing as the worst slavery of old" and which threatened progress toward universal free labor "which it has taken centuries and colossal sacrifices to attain."[14] At the AFL's October 1947 convention in San Francisco, Dubinsky's ILGWU submitted a successful resolution for the Federation to petition the UN regarding "reversions to servitude" that, though localized, posed a "dangerous threat" to "free workers of all nations" and their access to "decent conditions of employment as free men."[15]

Dubinsky and other FTUC organizers were not the first Americans to pen broadsides against Soviet forced labor camps: The genre had

---

[11] On Dubinsky as a "Cold War liberal," see Robert Parmet, *The Master of Seventh Avenue: David Dubinsky and the American Labor Movement* (New York: NYU Press, 2005), 206–242. On his role in Americans for Democratic Action, see Steven M. Gillon, *Politics and Vision: The ADA and American Liberalism, 1947–1985* (New York: Oxford University Press, 1987).

[12] William Henry Seward, "On the Irrepressible Conflict," speech delivered at Rochester, October 25, 1858; "Free Labor versus Slave Labor," 4 and 5.

[13] Ibid.

[14] "Manifesto," 9.

[15] David Dubinsky, et al., "Resolution One," from the Report of the International Labor Relations Committee of the 66th Convention of the AFL, San Francisco, October 6–16, 1947, reproduced in *SLR*, 11–12.

been thriving since the early 1930s. Nor were they isolated voices in 1947, the same year that exiled Mensheviks David Dallin and Boris I. Nicolaevsky published their landmark study *Forced Labor in Soviet Russia*. Dallin and Nicolaevsky accused the USSR of creating a "huge class of forced laborers ... which constitutes the lower level of the social structure" in the Soviet world, thereby betraying Marx's vision of a classless society of emancipated workers.[16] The book offered a structural analysis of the disasters that forced labor economics had wreaked upon Dallin and Nicolaevsky's beloved Russia; by contrast, the FTUC focused on the ways in which the USSR was violating universal moral norms and posing an affront to "the ideals and ways of life" of "freedom-loving people of all nations." The FTUC's organizers, unlike Dallin and Nicolaevsky, were also careful to cite noncommunist offenders against free labor principles: For instance, they condemned the French and British for their continued extraction of compulsory toil from German prisoners-of-war and "wealthy Australian plantation owners" for their quasi-enslavement of indigenous agricultural workers. "Servitude," the group proclaimed, "is prejudicial ... to human liberty in general."[17] Of course, Dallin and Nicolaevsky drew implicitly on general moral codes in their denunciation of Soviet practices, too. But their language was that of civilization versus barbarism. The originality of the FTUC's approach was to frame the attack as a universalist defense of human liberty, identified with "free" wage labor.

In late 1948, with the FTUC's encouragement and Matthew Woll's direct participation, the New York-based Workers' Defense League (WDL) founded a Commission of Inquiry into Forced Labor. The WDL was closely affiliated with the socialist politician Norman Thomas and normally focused on domestic labor rights (including those of nonwhite workers). Now, however, the group asserted that it was high time to "bring to light the extent to which chattel slavery, peonage, and forced labor still exist in the world" beyond America's shores.[18] The new Commission, chaired by labor reporter Albert K. Herling and populated by iconic Cold War liberals such as Arthur Schlesinger, Jr., and George S. Counts, cast its work as a demand for the "freedom of the enslaved" offered in "the voice of the free world." Why? Because slavery anywhere was a "growing menace to free peoples everywhere."[19]

---

[16] David J. Dallin and Boris I. Nicolaevsky, *Forced Labor in Soviet Russia* (New Haven, CT: Yale University Press, 1947), 11. On their politics, see Andre Liebich, "Mensheviks Wage the Cold War," *Journal of Contemporary History* 30, no. 2 (1995): 247–264.
[17] "Manifesto," 7, 8, 10.
[18] Albert Konrad Herling, *The Soviet Slave Empire* (New York: Wilfred Funk, 1951), vii.
[19] Ibid., 207.

To dramatize parallels with antebellum chattel slavery in the U.S., Herling's 1951 account of the Commission's findings, *The Soviet Slave Empire*, was organized under chapter headings such as "The Auction Block in Action"; its epigraph came from abolitionist James Russell Lowell's poem "The Present Crisis," authored in 1844 during the clash between proslavery and antislavery forces over the annexation of Texas.[20] The solution to *today's* crisis, Herling asserted, was a vast and coordinated new "international abolitionist movement."[21]

With such rhetoric, American liberal crusaders against Soviet forced labor situated their efforts as a modern-day continuation of nineteenth-century liberals' efforts to eradicate chattel slavery in the Atlantic world. The real relationship between liberalism and slavery in the 1800s was complicated: Many liberals were proslavery, while many of the fiercest opponents of human bondage were Christian radicals, former slaves, and free Blacks, not "humanitarian" white liberals. But the FTUC's and WDL's campaigners ignored this, placing themselves within a carefully reconstructed liberal tradition of condemnation for slavery as the negative foil to freely contracted wage labor. Both Woll and FTUC executive secretary Jay Lovestone enjoyed regularly citing the "masterly" 1863 study *The Slave Power* by Irish classical economist John E. Cairnes, an antislavery tract that condemned the Confederacy via a ringing defense of the productive abilities and manly dignity of "free laborers."[22] Cairnes' book was prophetic in its denunciation of slavery's threat to waged work, wrote Woll: "What an accurate evaluation of Russia's system of planned economy!"[23] The AFL's 1947 proposal to place forced labor on the ECOSOC agenda, meanwhile, asserted that "free people" had opposed slavery "at all times" in history, citing as evidence the 1815 Congress of Vienna and the Brussels Anti-Slavery Act of 1890.[24] Two years later, when the ECOSOC did at last debate the issue, the Americans peppered their opening remarks with reminders that Westerners had produced history's most important rights-based affirmations of liberty and condemnations of enslavement: the French "Declaration of the Rights of Man and of the Citizen," for example, as well as the abolition of serfdom in the

---

[20] Ibid., 13 and xiii.
[21] Ibid., 207.
[22] Ibid., 17; John Elliott Cairnes, *The Slave Power: Its Character, Career, and Probable Designs* (New York: F. Foster & Co., 1863), 80. *The Slave Power* was dedicated to Cairnes's close friend and fellow abolitionist John Stuart Mill.
[23] Matthew Woll, "Slavery Old and New," *The Federationist*, April 1949, reproduced in *SLR*, 17.
[24] American Federation of Labor, "Proposed Survey on Forced Labor and Measures for its Abolition," November 24, 1947, reproduced in *SLR*, 21.

Austro-Hungarian Empire following the liberal revolutions of 1848 and Abraham Lincoln's "House Divided" speech.[25]

The FTUC and its supporters married their critique of Soviet "slavery" as an affront to economic liberalism's principles regarding free labor with a critique of it as a denial of the freedom of expression. For Dallin and Nicolaevsky, the chief motivating factor behind the Soviet gulag was the provision of a cheap and easily disciplined army of drudges.[26] This was not the case for the FTUC, despite its interest in casting slave labor as an existential threat to "free" workers. Instead, the organization insisted that the Soviets were driven primarily by a desire to censure and intimidate "political dissidents."[27] The "new slave system," charged Dubinsky's ILGWU, was at bottom "a means of punishing political opponents."[28] This accusation was repeated in the AFL proposal to the UN. In "wide areas belonging to members of the United Nations," the document added, "Political differences have been made a crime punishable without trial."[29] The WDL, too, stressed this theme. "In the totalitarian setup," Herling explained, "lack of economic or political orthodoxy, as well as real opposition to the regime, became a crime. A class of political prisoners was thus guaranteed."[30] Matthew Woll went still further in 1949, claiming that "Slave labor, with its huge system of political police, has become *the very foundation of the political power of the Stalin regime.*"[31]

The Soviet Union *did*, of course, brutally repress opposition – but the majority of forced labor camp inmates were not "politicals," a fact that Woll and other U.S. labor leaders had understood perfectly well in the 1930s.[32] Indeed, in an effort to underline the USSR's dangers for ordinary workers, they had emphasized it.[33] The post-1945 U.S. domestic context is therefore important for understanding why the FTUC now

---

[25] Toni Sender, speech in the ECOSOC, February 15, 1949, reproduced in *SLR*, 31-32; Willard Thorp, speech in the ECOSOC, February 14, 1949, reproduced in *SLR*, 27.
[26] See Dallin and Nicolaevsky, *Forced Labor in Soviet Russia*, 191-192.
[27] Woll, "Slavery Old and New," 14.
[28] David Dubinsky, et al., "Resolution One," 11.
[29] AFL, "Proposed Survey," 23.
[30] Herling, *Soviet Slave Empire*, 7.
[31] Woll, "Slavery Old and New," 19, emphasis in original.
[32] On the gulag's demography, see Steven A. Barnes, *Between Death and Redemption: The Gulag and the Shaping of Soviet Society* (Princeton, NJ: Princeton University Press, 2011).
[33] See "Woll Pledges War on Soviet 'Slavery,'" *New York Times*, April 1, 1931. Woll here offered a convoluted attack on "four major forms of slavery" in the USSR: political prisoners; "economic prisoners"; ordinary citizens "conscripted and mobilized ... for various special kinds of labor"; and "the entire industrial wage-earning class and that half of the hundred million peasants which is now collectivized."

chose to focus exclusively on politically motivated "slavery." In 1947, American organized labor was at war with the Republican-controlled Congress against the passage of the Taft–Hartley Act, a law curtailing the power of unions and limiting workers' ability to strike. AFL members energetically echoed the Truman administration's denunciation of Taft–Hartley as a "slave labor bill"; in May, in fact, Dubinsky and other FTUC stalwarts gave speeches at Madison Square Garden under an enormous banner to that effect. Therefore, when Taft–Hartley passed, it begged the question of why the U.S., too, should not be condemned in the same terms as the USSR.

Some American labor leaders did not hesitate to do just that. But such a choice was not viable for the FTUC, which always prioritized Cold War concerns above domestic ones and which crafted its propaganda materials primarily for international audiences. Instead, the group attempted to shift its critique of Soviet forced labor to safer ground, focusing on violations of citizens' political liberties rather than abrogations of workers' labor rights. Thus in the ECOSOC in February 1949, when a Russian delegate charged the U.S. with violating "the first prerequisite for the freedom of labor" by limiting workers' ability to unionize, AFL consultant Toni Sender blithely argued that the law had in fact "recently furnished the most magnificent example of the working of democracy in the United States" that she had ever seen: Voters had shown their displeasure with it at the ballot box by "freely elect[ing]" a Democratic president and Congress.[34] Sender thus cast the binary between "free" and "unfree" labor in terms that did not demand scrutiny of actual labor conditions, only of the formal political systems under which workers lived. Communist countries' delegates were predictably infuriated by this approach, observing that where workers were compelled to "battle for their subsistence," their work could not be categorized as uncoerced.[35]

American Liberals and French Non-liberals in the Anti-totalitarian Movement, 1949–1951

It is hardly surprising that American liberal constructions of "forced labor" were rejected by Communist UN representatives. What is more interesting – and more significant for an analysis of "liberal" versus other varieties of postwar anticommunism – is that the American angle of attack also provoked discomfort among delegates from an allied

---

[34] Debate in the ECOSOC, February 15, 1949, reproduced in *SLR*, 102 and 113. Sender, a Jewish SPD member and Reichstag representative, had migrated to the United States in 1935 after fleeing Germany in 1933.

[35] Debate in the ECOSOC, March 7, 1949, reproduced in *SLR*, 150.

Western capitalist democracy: France. Setting aside the lonely figure of philosopher Raymond Aron, liberalism as a philosophy of economic and political freedom held little appeal in France after 1945.[35] The French, moreover, did not possess a domestic history of conflict that pitted slavery against the toil of "free" workers, and their legal apparatus tended to deal with labor in the language of mutual obligations between state and citizen rather than individuals' purely negative liberties in the marketplace. France's Constitution of 1946, for example, declared that "Everyone has an obligation to work and the right to obtain a job."[37] French anti-communists were also sensitive to charges that their country's own colonial work-tax schemes amounted to a form of forced labor. It is little wonder, then, that in the February 1949 ECOSOC debates, French delegate Georges Boris, a Keynesian socialist, declared general support for the American position but also expressed strong reservations. "From the moral point of view," he declared, "the condemnation of forced labor must not be interpreted as approval of the principle of idleness." He and his countrymen, explained Boris, were "shocked not so much by forced labor as by the inhuman conditions and treatment which accompany it."[38]

Boris's emphasis on inhumanity throws into contrast the striking absence of this theme on the American side. Maltreatment appeared infrequently in U.S. propaganda against Soviet forced labor. Despite occasional rhetorical flourishes about "brutal and killing exploitation" in Soviet camps, FTUC leaders much preferred to cast abstractions such as "liberty" and "dissent" as the gulag's chief victims rather than dwelling on the physical sufferings of flesh-and-blood prisoners.[39] This "would be too harrowing for our readers," Woll piously claimed.[40] In reality, it is unlikely that he or other FTUC figures were motivated by such scruples; rather, they understood that highlighting "cruel and harsh treatment" was "incidental to the need for clearly establishing legally" that communist states were in violation of the ILO's 1930 Forced Labor Convention, which did not reference bodily abuses.[41]

---

[36] See Stephen W. Sawyer and Iain Stewart, eds., *In Search of the Liberal Moment: Democracy, Anti-Totalitarianism, and Intellectual Politics in France since 1950* (Basingstoke, Hampshire: Palgrave Macmillan, 2016); Iain Stewart, *Raymond Aron and Liberal Thought in the Twentieth Century* (Cambridge: Cambridge University Press, 2020).
[37] Constitution de 1946, IVe République, October 27, 1946, www.conseil-constitutionnel.fr/les-constitutions-dans-l-histoire/constitution-de-1946-ive-republique.
[38] Debate in the ECOSOC, March 4, 1949, reproduced in *SLR*, 130.
[39] Woll, "Slavery Old and New," 15.
[40] Ibid.
[41] Memorandum of Conversation, UN Mission to the United Nations, RG 84 Box 50, National Archives and Records Administration, Silver Spring, MD (hereafter NARA).

When the British joined the propaganda campaign in 1949 (over the howling protests of the Colonial Office, which feared exposure of forced labor in overseas territories controlled by Britain and its allies), they adopted the same avoidance of reference to cruelty. In the ECOSOC, British Labour politician Christopher Mayhew supported the inquiry in the name of Britain's "long and fine tradition of struggle against all forms of slavery" and in order to defend "workers' rights and workers' standards in the non-Communist world"; he said nearly nothing about the experience of gulag inmates themselves.[42] Staff of the Information Research Department (IRD), a propaganda wing of the Foreign Office founded by Mayhew in 1948, concurred that "blood-curdling 'building the Siberian pyramids out of human bones' stuff" was out of place in the anti-forced labor campaign: "Keep the knout out of it."[43]

Casting about for French counterparts who might also be drawn into the effort of producing "calm" propaganda about communist forced labor for the benefit of continental audiences, IRD officers predictably felt that Raymond Aron would be "the best choice on the whole."[44] Yet when the French did finally join the effort in the final weeks of 1949, it was not Aron the liberal philosopher who led the charge but a writer named David Rousset. A survivor of Neuengamme and Buchenwald and a personal friend of Jean-Paul Sartre, Rousset was France's "principal Marxist witness" to the atrocities committed in the Nazi concentration camps thanks to his celebrated postwar works of literary testimony.[45] Rousset had broken off his prewar affiliation with the Trotskyist Parti communiste internationaliste in 1946, but he was emphatically not a liberal: He recoiled at the "putrefactions of capitalist democracy," and his political role models remained Trotsky and Lenin.[46] On November 12, 1949, in the weekly culture journal *Le Figaro Littéraire*, he published a front-page indictment of the Soviet gulag titled "Help the Deportees in the Soviet Camps: An Appeal from David Rousset to the Former Deportees of the Nazi Camps."[47] The piece was illustrated with an AFL-produced map of Russian labor sites, but its tone could not have

---

[42] Christopher Mayhew, speech in the ECOSOC, February 15, 1949, reproduced in *SLR*, 107 and 110. See also Christopher Mayhew and Lyn Smith, *A War of Words: A Cold War Witness* (London: I.B. Tauris, 1998). Mayhew left Labour for the Liberal Party in 1974.
[43] IRD, "Suggestions for Production of a Basic Document," August 12, 1949, FO 1110/176, British National Archives, Kew (hereafter BNA).
[44] Ibid., E. A. Runacres, circular note, May 25, 1949, FO/1110/172, BNA.
[45] Albert Béguin, "Le choix des victimes," *Esprit* 139 (November 1947): 696–705, here 698.
[46] David Rousset, "Notre programme," *La Gauche* 1 (May 15–30, 1948).
[47] David Rousset, "Au secours des déportés dans les camps soviétiques. Un appel de David Rousset aux anciens déportés des camps nazis," *Le Figaro littéraire*, November 12, 1949.

been further from that of the FTUC.[48] Rousset did not discuss civil liberties – or, indeed, any liberties at all. The piece contained no references to political freedom, freedom of conscience, individual autonomy, democracy, or human rights. Nor did it treat the Soviet camp system as an affront to "free labor" and a fresh instantiation of chattel slavery; in fact, it only used the word "*esclave*" once, in passing. Instead, in excruciatingly sensory language – the feeling of feet slowly freezing, the "stink of men dying in their own excrement" – Rousset insisted that Soviet forced laborers were undergoing identical bodily suffering to that which Nazi camp inmates had once experienced.[49]

By equating the Nazi and Soviet camp systems, thereby tapping into a deep vein of sentiment about Western Europeans' own painful past, Rousset's "Appeal" caused a sensation across France and the broader continent. So, too, did the high-profile libel trial that followed on its heels after the communist press accused the author of inventing crude falsehoods. Rousset approached an array of Cold War liberal intellectuals and labor leaders in the U.S. and the UK in early 1950, seeking their support for his project (and, especially, their help paying his trial expenses). Ecstatic over the propaganda value of the initiative in French labor and intellectual milieux, which they viewed as uniquely vulnerable to communist influence, these figures nevertheless recognized that it was being waged on different terms than their own campaign. Naturally, FTUC members and British Foreign Officers drew parallels between the Nazi and Soviet camp systems, too, under the rubric of "totalitarian slavery."[50] But Rousset, writing for an audience whose memories of World War II's horrors were different from those of the Anglo-Americans, placed the comparison at the core of his message. Moreover, he condemned the gulag in the name of his own anguished memories and as an act of solidarity among atrocity survivors, avoiding any reference to liberal principle.

Two observations can be made about Anglo-American liberals' response to what one bemused IRD officer labelled Rousset's "rather original line."[51] First, they found his terms of engagement alien and sought to reframe all his invocations of limit-case bodily anguish with references to threatened universal freedoms. An American attempt to repackage Rousset's *Figaro Littéraire* piece as an "Appeal to Humanity" is telling in this regard. This "abridged" essay was published as a full-page

---

[48] On this map's dissemination, see Timothy Barney, "'Gulag' – Slavery, Inc.: The Power of Place and the Rhetorical Life of a Cold War Map," *Rhetoric and Public Affairs* 16, no. 2 (Summer 2013): 317–354.
[49] Rousset, "Au secours des déportés "
[50] "Free Labor versus Slave Labor," 5.
[51] E. A. Runacres, Minutes, November 24, 1949, FO/1110/179, BNA.

display advertisement in the *New York Times* on February 28, 1950, by the Iron Curtain Refugee Campaign, a project of the CIA-funded International Rescue Committee. Signatures of support from figures such as Roger Nash Baldwin, John Dewey, Reinhold Niebuhr, Hubert Humphrey, Arthur Schlesinger, Jr., Adlai Stevenson, Earl Warren, and AFL President William Green took up a quarter of the page. The ad faithfully translated much of Rousset's original prose but altered his opening words to address "the conscience of all free men." Despite the fact that Rousset plainly had nothing whatsoever to say about freedom, only about suffering, the Iron Curtain Refugee Campaign's organizers informed readers that "the cause of human freedom and decency" was at stake in his efforts and that "our allies in the struggle for freedom are being systematically exterminated."[52]

Second, despite this rhetorical disjuncture, American liberals recognized Rousset as a brother-in-arms in the broader anti-Soviet cause. His idiosyncratic approach to condemning the gulag proved no impediment to their support for him. In fact, they understood immediately that Rousset had hit upon a better rhetoric for arousing anti-Soviet sentiment in continental Europe than their own – and were happy to exploit this fact. The FTUC not only donated to Rousset's coffers itself but eventually facilitated his receipt of regular direct funding from the CIA.[53] The IRD likewise offered him years' worth of aid. Intellectuals embraced him as well: Baldwin, Niebuhr, Counts, and Schlesinger joined Arthur Koestler, Norman Thomas, and Sidney Hook in publishing a letter to the *New York Times* in 1951 on Rousset's "full-dress indictment of the entire system of slave labor," which they categorized as "a tremendous event comparable in moral significance and surpassing in human scope the Dreyfus trial of a half-century ago."[54] Rousset was brought on board as a keynote speaker at the 1951 Congress of the Liberal International and as a founding executive committee member of the CCF. The CCF also opened the pages of its French-language journal, *Preuves*, to his followers (who included fellow ex-Trotskyists along with unaffiliated leftists, Christian Democrats, and Gaullists) to rail against the Soviets' continued deployment of the same tortures that "the deportees of Nazi Germany experienced in their flesh."[55] To some degree, certainly,

---

[52] Display advertisement, *New York Times*, February 28, 1950. This text was also published as David Rousset, "An Appeal to the Conscience of the World," *New Leader* 33, no. 10 (March 1950).

[53] See Emma Kuby, *Political Survivors: The Resistance, the Cold War, and the Fight against Concentration Camps after 1945* (Ithaca, NY: Cornell University Press, 2019).

[54] Arthur Koestler et al., letter to the editor, *New York Times*, February 15, 1951.

[55] Théo Bernard, "Le travail forcé devant l'ONU," *Preuves* 34 (December 1953): 67–70.

common principles united Rousset with his American supporters. But their coalition cannot be described as a liberal one in intellectual terms. The liberal discourse of "freedom" was just one language in which anti-totalitarianism could be expressed – other languages were possible, too.

Forced Labor at the UN: Changed Circumstances and New Rhetoric, 1951–1953

On March 7, 1949, overriding the votes of Eastern bloc delegates, ECOSOC passed an American resolution to take preliminary steps toward conducting a joint UN-ILO survey of forced labor practices around the world. After much further maneuvering, this act resulted in the 1951 formation of the Ad Hoc Committee on Forced Labor, chaired by Indian diplomat and jurist A. Ramaswami Mudaliar. The committee's purview was theoretically universal, but as one IRD officer observed, from the Western perspective "the object of this exercise is at least 99% propaganda" intended to serve "an operation of the Cold War."[56] The ECOSOC thus formulated the Committee's mandate with great care to include only forced labor systems "which are employed as a means of political coercion or punishment for holding or expressing political views."[57] Fatefully, Mudaliar and his colleagues – Mexican Félix Fulgencio Palavicini and Norwegian Paal Berg – rebelled against these terms of engagement. After intense internal debate, they announced that they would equally consider "non-political" labor extracted "for economic or other reasons."[58] They also stressed their interest in receiving hard, factual evidence of the scale, scope, and systemic nature of the problem in any given locale, in particular via either "the text of laws and regulations" or documentation of the breadth of their application.[59]

In response to the unwelcome news of the Ad Hoc Committee's independent-mindedness, the AFL shifted its rhetorical strategy – and began to partner more and more closely with U.S. state actors to carry it out. Despite beginning to fund FTUC operations covertly in the late 1940s, the U.S. government had been, in Jay Lovestone's words, "cold" to "the entire slave labor business."[60] This shifted dramatically in the early 1950s, as the division of international organizational affairs at the State

---

[56] C.M. Le Quesne, memorandum, July 17, 1950, FO 371/88871, BNA.
[57] United Nations – International Labour Office, *Report of the Ad Hoc Committee on Forced Labour* (Geneva: 1953), 4.
[58] Ibid., 5. Palavicini died after the Committee's early sessions and was replaced by a Peruvian, Enrique García Sayán.
[59] Ibid., 6.
[60] Jay Lovestone, letter to Norris Chipman, March 20, 1950, Box 35, Folder 11, Jay Lovestone Papers, Meany Memorial Archives, University of Maryland, Silver Spring.

Department under Austrian-born Walter Kotschnig, a Truman appointee, came alive to the propaganda possibilities offered by the UN-ILO forced labor hearings. Kotschnig's division took over the anti-slave labor campaign, churning out materials that non-state actors could present to the Ad Hoc Committee as their own. Lovestone's friend Bertram Wolfe labeled the 1951 propaganda booklet *Slave Labor in the Soviet World*, officially authored by the FTUC, "the best propaganda pamphlet our Government ever got out."[61] The text was in fact a product of the International Press and Publications Division, and it broke radically with the tone of earlier FTUC slave labor materials. Primarily a collection of "Soviet laws and decrees" in translation as well as other "hitherto confidential documents," the text was intended to demonstrate through facts and figures that "the Soviet economy rests heavily on the institution of slave labor."[62] It drew no historical parallels to chattel slavery, did not invoke any threat posed to "free workers" by communist practices, and only referred to "so-called 'political' prisoners" on the twenty-eighth of its thirty pages.[63] Shortly after this pamphlet was published, Toni Sender joined Herling, Dallin, Wolfe, and others in a joint governmental/non-governmental "Working Group on Forced Labor" under Kotschnig. This ideologically diverse committee dwelt not on how to develop the AFL and WDL's earlier themes regarding political and economic liberties but how (in Herling's words) to "correlate the evidence on forced labor with the economic development of the particular country concerned."[64] In 1952, Kotschnig's officers personally drafted Matthew Woll's testimony to the Ad Hoc Committee within this dry framework.[65]

By the time the Ad Hoc Committee completed its work, then, the FTUC had shelved the overtly liberal language with which it had initially launched the campaign against Soviet slavery. Gone were references to both free labor and freedom of political expression. The new rhetoric about forced labor's "important role in the planned economy of the U.S.S.R." due to the creation of a "self-renewing" new "concentration-camp class" was indistinguishable from that of non-liberal anti-communists such as Dallin.[66] This was an unsurprising development, given the new institutional exigencies introduced by the Ad Hoc Committee mandate. The

---

[61] Bertram Wolfe, note to Walter Kotschnig, November 29, 1951, RG 84 Box 50, NARA.
[62] Free Trade Union Committee, *Slave Labor in the Soviet World* (New York: 1951), 4 and 5.
[63] Ibid., 28.
[64] Albert Herling, in Forrest D. Murden Jr., Memorandum of Conversation, "NGO and United States Government Cooperation on Collection and Presentation of Forced Labor Materials," November 14, 1951, RG 84 Box 50, NARA.
[65] Walter Kotschnig, memorandum of conversation, April 10, 1952, RG 84 Box 50, NARA.
[66] Free Trade Union Committee, *Slave Labor in the Soviet World*, 6 and 29.

total disappearance of references to antebellum chattel slavery is particularly understandable: With anti-Black racialized forced labor regimes such as that of South Africa now squarely within the Committee's purview, comparative invocations of the antebellum U.S. south were likely to miss their Soviet mark. As for the AFL's abandonment of charges that forced labor served as punishment for political speech in the USSR, here domestic politics played a role as well: It became less feasible to attack the communist world for its treatment of "political dissidents" at the height of the McCarthy years. FTUC organizers had never been terribly bothered by the idea that the anti-forced labor campaign might occasion a certain amount of blowback since, as Lovestone insisted in 1950, the goal was not to portray the capitalist West as "perfect."[67] Nonetheless, he and other FTUC leaders did hope to draw a bright line between the "free" and "unfree" worlds – and as the U.S. witch hunts of the 1950s progressed, it made little sense to do so by harping on the Soviet Union's intolerance for dissent rather than simply highlighting the massive scale and considerable economic role of its gulag system. The FTUC's "liberal" attack on Soviet slave labor in the 1940s had been opportunistic; its discarding of liberal rhetoric in the 1950s was, as well.

It is worth noting, as a kind of exception that proves the rule, that one committed American liberal did make a final effort in 1953 – just before the Ad Hoc Committee published its results – to again articulate an explicitly liberal case against the USSR's "new slavery." This was Roger Nash Baldwin, founder of the American Civil Liberties Union. Like many Cold War liberals, Baldwin had once admired the USSR: In his favorable 1928 treatise *Liberty under the Soviets*, he admitted that "no civil liberty as we understand it in the West exists in Russia" but nonetheless insisted that because "economic liberty underlies all others ... the society the Communists seek to create will be freed ... of repression."[68] With the signing of the Nazi–Soviet Pact, however, "like so many liberals," he became "disillusioned" with the USSR – and with Marxist ideology.[69] From here on, Baldwin embraced liberalism as a "freedom from any 'isms.'"[70] For those who scorned "Utopian dogmas," he now wrote, "the fight for civil liberties takes first place."[71]

---

[67] Lovestone, letter to Chipman.
[68] Roger N. Baldwin, *Liberty under the Soviets* (New York: Vanguard Press, 1928), 3–4.
[69] Roger N. Baldwin, ed., *A New Slavery. Forced Labor: The Communist Betrayal of Human Rights* (New York: Oceana, 1953), 18.
[70] Roger Baldwin, "Liberalism and the United Front," in *Whose Revolution? A Study of the Future Course of Liberalism in the United States*, ed. Irving DeWitt Talmadge (New York: Howell, Soskin, 1941), 166–184, here 168.
[71] Ibid., 168 and 170.

By this Baldwin meant "those liberties by which men freely express their needs and desires, create their cultures, and associate together for their common interests."[72] His edited book on Soviet forced labor, titled *A New Slavery. Forced Labor: The Communist Betrayal of Human Rights*, attacked the USSR in terms of its denial of these ideals.

Baldwin's chief contributions to *A New Slavery* were an introduction and an epilogue, both of which directly echoed FTUC and WDL propaganda of the late 1940s in terms of their emphasis on political freedoms. "Our preoccupation with forced labor in communist states," Baldwin wrote, "may appear to ignore the same evil elsewhere." But other countries, even those guided by belief in "white racial supremacy," only sought "cheap labor." Thus their wrongs did "not compare with the systematic liquidation of dissent to perpetuate the tyranny of a communist dictatorship."[73] Baldwin acknowledged that "economic motives" shaped communist actions, too, but he maintained that "political motives of control are always present": The Soviet forced labor regime was best understood as a "new political weapon" for suppressing dissent and opposition, not a brute mode of exploiting workers.[74] Like FTUC writers before him, Baldwin also had very little to say about cruelty. Yet his framing was incongruous with the material actually contained in the body of *A New Slavery*, which comprised research compiled by scholars (including Dallin) for the CIA-funded National Committee for a Free Europe. The bulk of the book was focused on providing evidence for "the economic importance of forced labor in Soviet economic plans" as well as the "bestial," "deplorable," and "almost incredible" conditions of "human hardship" – especially hunger – that prevailed for workers in camps throughout the Eastern bloc.[75] The book was thus a strangely hybrid text in both structural and ideological terms: The language of thwarted civil liberties dominated the first and last pages of an account that primarily highlighted quite different anti-totalitarian talking points. And, uncomfortably, the primary role that Baldwin's liberal rhetoric played in the text was not to articulate an alternative political vision to the one that had produced the gulag but, instead, to justify disregard for forced labor imposed on indigenous, colonial, or minority populations in the noncommunist world since, after all, it was not primarily intended to suppress dissent.

This same logic – one of distinguishing communist states' deeds from the "lesser" sins of mere "economic" slave labor purveyors – also characterized a few American responses when the Ad Hoc Committee's report

---

[72] Ibid., 183.
[73] Baldwin, *A New Slavery*, 22.
[74] Ibid., 43–44 and 45; 34.
[75] Ibid., 59, 66, 54.

was finally released in June 1953. In it, Mudaliar and his colleagues were most critical of the Soviet-dominated bloc but also censured Belgian forced labor policies in Congo and Portuguese activities in Angola; moreover, they condemned the South African government for its treatment of the Black laboring population "almost as thoroughly" as they denounced the USSR. This produced a "formidable dilemma" for the American government: "We may lose Western European votes if we do not proceed carefully on the South African question," wrote Eisenhower's ambassador to the UN, Henry Cabot Lodge, Jr., but "we will not get the Afro-Asian votes if we defend only persecuted white people."[76] Some liberal voices dealt with the sticky situation by falling back on Baldwin's distinction between mere economic coercion and the more serious offense of repressing dissent (while, for obvious reasons, assiduously continuing to avoid reviving any invocations of African chattel slavery in U.S. history). A long *New York Times* editorial on the Ad Hoc Committee's report, for example, did not mention any noncommunist states, stressing that the report "focuse[d]" on how the USSR, alone, was "destroying all right to independent thought, opinion, and conviction."[77]

Most intellectuals and labor leaders, however, did not bother to resuscitate this old critique. David Dubinsky's ILGWU, petitioning the AFL about the Soviets once again in 1953, failed this time to mention their punishment of "political opponents" as it had done in 1947. Instead, it simply asserted that the Ad Hoc Committee's findings had "[borne] out the indictment made by the AF of L" regarding "slave labor as an organic part of the economic system behind the Iron Curtain."[78] In the end, the AFL's campaign against Soviet "slavery" had outlasted the utility of its own original premises. Liberal framings of the objectionability of forced labor – both on economic grounds, as an attack on "free labor," and on political ones, as a denial of the right to dissent – were disposable; they possessed no intrinsic centrality to the effort to discredit the gulag. Antipathy to the Soviet regime rather than a consistently articulated set of beliefs about the nature and value of workers' liberty was the common thread running through "the fight for free labor." The "liberalism" of the Cold War liberals involved in this struggle was variable; the constant was the Cold War, and the imperative to wage it with whatever weapons were to hand.

---

[76] Ambassador Lodge and Gilbert W. Stuart, "Forced Labor" memorandum, August 25, 1953, RG 84 Box 50, NARA.
[77] Editorial, "Report on Forced Labor," *New York Times*, June 24, 1953.
[78] Resolution no. 145, 1953 AFL Convention, reproduced in American Federation of Labor, *For Peace and Freedom* (Washington, DC: 1953), 70.

9 The City That Could Have Been
Planning Los Angeles for the Postwar Era

Courtney Rawlings

In the mid twentieth century, Los Angeles architects built low-cost housing projects whose formal organization and modernist idiom reflected the still-live possibility of a more progressive – even socialist – future.[1] In 1941, Rockwell D. Hunt, the eminent California historian and University of Southern California Professor of Economics, noted that "to insure the largest measure of success in the metropolitan area [of Los Angeles], the self-interest principle and the incentive of private gain must be consciously geared to the social welfare idea and made progressively subsidiary to the common weal." According to Hunt and others writing and working in Los Angeles at the time, housing, the organization of neighborhoods, and community amenities needed to be carefully planned by government-appointed architects, economists, sociologists, and designers dedicated to assuring mutual social welfare.[2] By providing everyone with the minimum amenities and resources required to participate in local and national politics – housing, food, transportation, recreation, and public forums – architects argued that they would bring about a more progressive, wholly democratic society.[3]

---

[1] "Progressive" here refers to the politics of the generation of social democratic- and liberal-aligned thinkers who came of age in the 1920s and 1930s. What makes the architects, designers, and others working on housing and city planning at this time "progressive" is their operating within a broadly left-liberal, New Deal Order, which assumes that the government ought to minimize the disparity between the rich and poor by investing in subsidized, low-cost housing, free childcare, the protection and development of public parks, schools, and countless other public infrastructures developed and organized by experts. As Doug Rossinow notes, "left, liberal, and progressive are terms whose meanings shift and float" and, moreover, both leftists and liberals are equally able to be described as "progressive." Doug Rossinow, *Visions of Progress: The Left-Liberal Tradition in America* (Philadelphia: University of Pennsylvania Press, 2008), 1, 3.

[2] Rockwell D. Hunt, "The Social Significance of Planning," in *Preface to a Master Plan* (Los Angeles: The Pacific Southwest Academy, 1941), 296.

[3] Like many at the time, architects embraced Deweyan models of thinking about human agency. Namely, they believed that experts could use design, planning, and architecture to influence the behaviors of citizens and redirect any individual's self-interest toward serving the common good. See Mel Scott, *Cities Are for People: The Los Angeles Region Plans for Living* (Los Angeles: Pacific Southwest Academy Publication XXI, 1942).

"Wise planning," Hunt wrote, demanded "the services of the ablest, most highly trained leaders, representing all the legitimate interests in the community, co-ordinated into a harmonious unity."[4]

The New Deal made large-scale planning a central tenet of American liberalism. Throughout the 1930s, United States experts allied with the growing U.S. state to promote a novel form of scientifically informed governance. As heirs to this project, architects building low-cost public housing projects in 1940s Los Angeles – including Lloyd Wright, Jr. (1890–1978), Richard Neutra (1892–1970) and Paul R. Williams (1894–1980) – believed themselves indispensable to buoying the liberal, New Deal state and ameliorating the failures of the free market. Moreover, as more monies were poured into public projects during World War II, Los Angeles architects and designers – who were working in the country's second largest war economy – considered their expertise essential to ensuring the success of the large-scale planning efforts being undertaken to win the war.[5]

It was during this period that left-wing and liberal Los Angeles architects developed a singular modernist form *cum* style known as California Modernism, which is today referred to as "Midcentury Modernism." California Modernist architects proffered a viable alternative to the single-family home by constructing low-rise, superblock communities organized for cooperative use as they retained familial privacy. According to progressive architects, "integrated communal projects" were necessary for a democratic society.[6] The architects and planners who first intervened on behalf of the United States Housing Authority to clear slums, house the poor, and eventually, house war workers, saw their projects as foreshadowing a postwar future where all citizens, regardless of class, would reside in new, specially planned, socially (and often-times racially) integrated housing communities.

The architects who belonged to the California Modern movement hailed from distinctive backgrounds and embraced a diversity of ideas.[7] Nonetheless, they were united by their commitment to developing flexible, cost-effective housing projects intended to serve as models for how housing ought to develop. Every progressive architect advocated

---

[4] Hunt, "The Social Significance of Planning," 295.
[5] Los Angeles Board of Harbor Commissioners, *Annual Report of the Board of Harbor Commissioners of the City of Los Angeles, California, Fiscal Year July 1, 1946 to June 30, 1947* (Los Angeles: Board of Harbor Commissioners, 1947), 18–20.
[6] Richard Neutra, "Homes and Housing," in *Preface to a Master Plan* (Los Angeles: The Pacific Southwest Academy, 1941), 195.
[7] See Ehrhard Bahr, *Weimar on the Pacific: German Exile Culture in Los Angeles and the Crisis of Modernism* (Berkeley: University of California Press, 2007), 143–171.

Figure 9.1 Maynard Parker, photographer, "Projects by Paul R. Williams: Photomontage: Hacienda and Pueblo del Rio Housing Projects, Airport, Zangston Terrace, Arrowhead Springs Hotel," 1940. Courtesy of The Huntington Library, San Marino, California.

for the integration of "employment, community, and family life" so as to create a more balanced life for all.[8] In an *Arts and Architecture* article from January 1943, for example, Neutra explained how the new city, as

[8] Greg Hise, *Magnetic Los Angeles* (Baltimore: Johns Hopkins University Press, 1997), 51.

reflected in the development of Los Angeles, would "advance housing projects" that "excel in an *extension and continuity of communal areas, uninterrupted by rolling traffic,* safely enjoyed by children *and endowed with community buildings, day nurseries, kindergartens, and recreational facilities* for all ages."[9] For California modernists such as Neutra, the future of the city – and the nation itself – depended on reimagining the very nature of housing by centering the community.

This essay focuses on the construction of Pueblo del Rio – a paradigmatic low-cost public housing project – to explore how architects such as Neutra and Williams envisioned their future as Cold War liberal elites. The architects and their designs initially centered quintessential liberal ideas, such as the notions that large-scale planning would ensure a sound economy or that state welfarism would help individuals thrive. Their conviction was simple: *If* architects' affordable housing communities could provide their residents the ability to walk to work, spend more time with their families, and actively participate in their communities, *then* these projects would become the template for city building in the postwar period. However, this centralized, communal vision of architecture never became part of Cold War liberal practice. Put simply, McCarthyism, both as public opinion and government policy, defunded and defanged housing authorities by associating left-liberal architects, designers, and other advocates of communal housing with the Communist Party. By the mid-1950s, the very concept of mass housing had become linked with totalitarian regimes.[10]

"Housing," it turned out, was antithetical to the specific form of Cold War liberalism that became the United States' de facto ideology. As a result, many of these same California Modern architects turned from communalism to individualism, from centralization to decentralization, from statism to the free market in their unabashed embrace of the single-family home. Focusing on the rise of architects as local elites allows me to track and explain how city planning became imperative to, and then antithetical to, the postwar imaginary. In so doing, this essay demonstrates the veracity of Ellen Schrecker's suggestion "that McCarthyism's main impact may well have been in what did not happen rather than in what did."[11]

---

[9] Richard Neutra, "Housing: A Definition," in *Arts and Architecture* (January 1943), 27. Folder 1, Channel Heights Management Conference Pamphlet 1942, Box 1460, Correspondence, Collection 1179, Richard Neutra Papers, University of California, Los Angeles, Department of Special Collections, Los Angeles, California.

[10] See Don Parson, "The Decline of Public Housing and the Politics of the Red Scare: The Significance of the Los Angeles Public Housing War," *Journal of Urban History* 33, no. 3 (March 2007), 400–417.

[11] Ellen Schrecker, *The Age of McCarthyism: A Brief History with Documents* (Boston: Bedford Books of St. Martin's Press, 1994), 92.

Los Angeles at midcentury is a story of the Cold War liberal city that could have been but never was.

★★★

Emboldened by the Wagner–Steagall Act of 1937, which secured funds for slum clearance and the construction of low-cost housing, and the Lanham Act of 1940, which allocated money to construct defense industry housing, Los Angeles consciously invested in its postwar future more than most U.S. cities. Its architects considered themselves "social scientists," if not clinicians, who would use housing as "education campaigns" aimed at ameliorating the slum dweller's "warped habits and modes of living" so that she might be included in the educated, "broadened base" of the coming postwar democracy.[12] While experts would make decisions for the time being, once the new housing projects and city plans were in place and the populous properly educated, the people themselves would become their own leaders and educators.[13]

Between 1941 and 1942, the Housing Authority for the City of Los Angeles (HACLA) financed the construction of 9 superblock communities that comprised 3,468 apartment units that housed tens of thousands of low-income residents.[14] Each of these nine projects – and the myriad others to follow – were intended to be synecdochal of the larger city to come. For example, a photomontage from 1940 displaying three of Paul R. Williams's low-cost housing projects, one of his airport designs, and an image of an unfinished hotel shows that the five complexes were brought together like patchwork to create a model metropolis, in which the urban swatch is at once a single entity and a collection of individual sites whose contours remain legible despite their cohesive interlock (Figure 9.1).

At the center of the photomontage Williams presents a scale model of Pueblo del Rio, a Los Angeles housing project begun on November 2, 1941, and designed by Williams, Neutra, Gordon B. Kauffman, Adrian Wilson, Welton Becket, and Walter Wurderman, who were collectively known as Southeast Housing Architects Associated.[15] The project is sandwiched between two other of Williams's housing projects: Langston Terrace (Washington, DC, 1935–38) and Hacienda Village

---

[12] Of course, this assumes that decisions must be limited to the elite class until people have been properly educated. Richard Neutra, *Architecture of Social Concern in Regions of Mild Climate* (Los Angeles: Gerth Todtmann, 1948), 194–203.

[13] Hunt, "The Social Significance of Planning," 295.

[14] Don Parson, "Houses for the Rich," in *Public Los Angles: A Private City's Activist Future*, ed. Donald Craig Parson (Athens: University of Georgia Press, 2019), 70.

[15] "Housing Project Starts Today," *Los Angeles Times* (June 20, 1941).

(Los Angeles, 1942). The former, which Williams designed with fellow African–American architect Hilyard Robinson, was his first attempt at low-cost housing. It was also the first public housing project in the District of Columbia and, crucially, was formally distinctive from the housing projects he designed for Los Angeles. In the photomontage, Langston Terrace stands out on the page, disrupting the predictable pattern of housing rows at Pueblo del Rio and Hacienda Village. The entry, center, and endpoint of Langston Terrace are each easily identifiable. The entryway, for instance, is marked by two low-rise buildings that come together to form a narrow space that separates the project from the street. These low-rise buildings are flanked by a J-shaped string of four-story apartment buildings that form a large semicircle of two-, four-, and five-story apartment buildings that surround a central greenspace. The break between inside Langston Terrace and outside is made salient by the dramatic entryway. This decisive break that helps produce the project's felt monumentality is precisely what Williams *would not* emphasize in his later, Los Angeles-based housing projects.

Williams refused this kind of monumentality in producing housing projects in Los Angeles. As the repeatable formulations of both Pueblo del Rio and Hacienda Village suggest, by the early 1940s Williams had begun to concern himself with creating projects that could be expanded without undermining their overall sense of the structure. The simplified program and housing rows at Pueblo del Rio emphasized the projects' flexibility; it could easily be expanded ad infinitum. Therefore, placing the Langston project at Pueblo del Rio's borders creates a definite break between the repeating low-rise buildings at Pueblo del Rio and the rest of the photomontage. Without Langston Terrace acting as a border for Pueblo del Rio, it would be unclear if the artist were including the entirety of Pueblo del Rio, if it had been included only in part, or if it had been arbitrarily cut off and could continue into the page's far-reaching distance in perpetuity.

★★★

Williams designed each of the housing projects reproduced in the photomontage in response to the affordable housing crisis that plagued the United States after the Great Depression. The crisis was especially severe in Williams's hometown of Los Angeles. In 1937, 20 percent of housing in Los Angeles was unfit for human habitation; 30 percent of domiciles had no indoor toilet; and 50 percent had no indoor bathtub.[16]

---

[16] "Housing Survey Covering Portions of the City of Los Angeles California. Constructed under the Supervision of the Housing Authority of the City of Los Angeles, California

Conditions worsened over the course of World War II, during which hundreds of thousands of workers migrated to Los Angeles to take jobs in the thriving defense industry. In fact, between 1940 and 1946, the city's population more than doubled. This strained an already burdened housing market; by war's end, 165,000 families were living on the streets or in temporary housing, which included tents, boats, and buses.

Restricted to a mere 5 percent of the city in the 1940s, African-American neighborhoods grew at an exaggerated rate. As a result, black Los Angelenos faced especially dire housing conditions. In an article written for *The Nation* in 1945, Dorothy Baruch described life in the Los Angeles slums:

> In place after place children lived in windowless rooms, amid peeling plaster, rats and the flies that gathered thick around food that stood on open shelves or kitchen-bedroom tables. Ordinarily there was no bathtub; never more than a single washbowl or lavatory. Sometimes as many as forty people shared one toilet. Families were separated only by sheets strung up between beds. Many of the beds were "hot," with people taking turns sleeping in them.[17]

The housing crisis hit all Los Angelenos hard, especially those in the working class. A 1940 survey commissioned by the HACLA revealed that 23.5 percent of the city's housing units were substandard, suffering from deterioration, insufficient amenities, or overcrowding.[18] In a letter to President Franklin D. Roosevelt, Mayor Fletcher Bowron succinctly summarized the housing problem: "There is simply no place for them to live."[19]

Projects such as Pueblo del Rio and Hacienda Village resulted from attempts by the U.S. Congress to address the national housing crisis with the passage of the Wagner–Steagall Act (1937). This act established the U.S. Housing Authority, which in turn propelled municipalities to set up their own local housing authorities. As a result, Los Angeles officials founded HACLA which, aided by the Federal Housing Administration's (FHA) low-cost mortgage insurances, inaugurated an era of experimental housing projects and city planning designed

---

and Published by Them as a Report of Work Projects Administration Project No. 65-1-07-70. Vol. 1. April 1940. With statement dated 6 June 1939 from Housing Authority on goals of survey 1939–1940," Folder 1, Box 1, Collection of Southern California Housing Reports and Photographs, Collection 0436, California Social Welfare Archives, Special Collections, University of Southern California Libraries, Los Angeles, California.

[17] Dorothy W. Baruch, "Sleep Comes Hard," *The Nation* (January 27, 1945), 95–96.
[18] U.S. Works Progress Administration, *Housing Survey, City of Los Angeles, California* (Los Angeles: Housing Authority of the City of Los Angeles, 1940).
[19] Fletcher Bowron to Franklin D. Roosevelt, March 5, 1945, cited in Parson, *Making a Better World*, 230.

to redress the housing shortage and, due to the progressive architects' ideology, build a more equitable city rid of "urban blight."[20]

A huge influx of African–American migration to Los Angeles for war-time jobs further underlined the urgency of housing construction. Between 1940 and 1944, Los Angeles's Black population more than doubled, exploding from 55,114 to 111,888.[21] Unsurprisingly, this population boom worsened an already dreadful housing crisis. In a partial attempt to rectify this shortage, the National Office of Production Management granted Pueblo del Rio priority status, even as it shut down most other housing projects to save needed materials for the war effort.[22] HACLA did not intend for Pueblo del Rio to house war workers. In fact, they promised the residents whose dwellings had been cleared for the project priority consideration for residency. Nonetheless, once the United States entered the war after the Japanese attack on

Figure 9.2 Julius Shulman, photographer, "Job 6464: Pueblo del Rio (Los Angeles, California)," 1940–1941. Gelatin Silver Print. Folder 8, Box 89, Julius Shulman Photography Archive, 1936–1997. © J. Paul Getty Trust. Getty Research Institute, Los Angeles (2004.R.10).

---

[20] In a *Los Angeles Times* article entitled "Doom for Urban Blight: City Launches Drive on Slums" (October 24, 1948), the author uses "blight" and "slum" interchangeably.
[21] Marques Augusta Vestal, "Black Housing Politics in 1940s South Los Angeles" (Master's Thesis, University of California, Los Angeles, 2014), 24.
[22] "Public Housing Here Unchanged: Federal Ban Won't Half Program as Priorities Have Been Approved," *Los Angeles Times* (October 11, 1941), 2.

Pearl Harbor in December 1941, HACLA snubbed the slum-cleared residents in favor of people who had migrated to the city to work in the defense industry. Still, the demographics of the migration to Los Angeles meant that Pueblo del Rio remained a majority black project.

The first publicly funded housing projects in the United States, which had begun in 1935, relied heavily on English and Dutch precedent: They were usually one- and two-story apartment-like projects built in a modest, traditional style with few flourishes. In fact, countless housing advocates, including Harriet Shadd Butcher – a Black woman, friend of W. E. B. Du Bois, and advocate for all-black housing projects in Atlanta – visited Europe to take housing tours and explore "controlled housing" projects such as Asterdorp in Amsterdam (1927). Butcher evangelized Asterdorp, which she believed instilled "habits of regularity" and a "sense of responsibility" in its dwellers that acted as "direct forces [in] lifting these tenants to higher standards of conduct."[23] The project's robust managerial taskforce intervened in the lives of its occupants, instructing tenants on when to bathe; providing classes on budgeting one's finances; watching children for free while the adults went to work; and teaching valuable skills, such as shoe repair.

Williams was inspired by Butcher and other black housing theorists, and he similarly argued that low-cost dwellings could become the base from which black Americans would reach "higher cultural and economic level[s]," and in which they could develop more gainful habits to "solve [their] own problems, [to] raise [their] own standards, [and to] *earn* [their] right to self-respect."[24] According to Williams, black Americans could overcome race prejudice only through "individual effort,"[25] and he endorsed the Hooverite ideal that the black community would thrive when individuals "pull[ed] themselves up from their bootstraps."[26]

In his autobiographic essay "I Am a Negro" (1937), Williams recounted his biography in order to emphasize that it was his individual will that enabled him to become an architect. He noted, for instance, that he became interested in architecture even though one of his teachers thought the idea of a "Negro architect" absurd.[27] Williams, in other words, believed that he had personally overcome the "habit of being defeated" that defined black life in the United States. He thus dedicated

---

[23] From Harriet Shadd Butcher's outlining her trip visiting housing projects in Europe (1935). Atlanta University Center Archives, Robert W. Woodruff Library, Atlanta, Georgia. Box and folder number unknown.
[24] Paul R. Williams, "I am a Negro," *The American Magazine* (July 1937), 163.
[25] "Designer for a Living," *Ebony* (February 1946), 27.
[26] Paul R. Williams, "I am a Negro," 161.
[27] Ibid.

himself to transcending the "defeatism" that he found amongst black Americans.[28] As he stated, "I owe it to myself and to my people to accept this challenge. [...] White Americans have a reasonable basis for their prejudice against the Negro race, ... if that prejudice is ever to be overcome it must be through the efforts of Negroes to rise above the average cultural level of their kind."[29] One way to do so was through architecture, which could promote good habits by providing for tenants' immediate needs and encouraging new everyday practices. To take one prominent example, Williams's Pueblo del Rio was located within walking distance of tenants' workplaces, which he believed would make regularly arriving on time at a job quick and simple. As this suggests, habit formation was central to Williams's goal of cultivating a robust black middle class.

Williams's psychological understanding of the African–American condition – that is, that African–American poverty was ultimately caused by the "habit of being defeated" – precluded an analysis of capitalist exploitation. In Williams's telling, indigence was the result of "defeatism" that could not be solved through economic redistribution. By framing black poverty in this way, Williams simultaneously reinforced dominant stereotypes of African–American cultural inferiority and justified the capitalist system that played a crucial role in generating what he considered unfavorable behaviors. Because he rejected material analysis, Williams's solution to race-based poverty was to find a way to bring more black people into the middle and upper classes. In this way, Williams combined a conservative social politics with a progressive faith in government-funded housing projects. In near every respect, Williams's and his colleagues' program anticipated the Cold War liberal agenda and could have easily been amalgamated into the Cold War state.

Figure 9.3 Baldwin Hills Village (or The Village Green), Clarence Stein, Reginald Johnson, Robert Alexander, Fred Barlow, Jr., Lewis E. Wilson, architects, 1942. GoogleMaps (2025).

[28] Ibid.
[29] Ibid.

Williams's "uplift" ideology is evident in the architectural designs of Pueblo del Rio. The project, which was intended for a community of majority-black laborers and for which Williams was the primary architect (alongside Neutra and others), was defined by a series of two-story, flat-roofed apartments organized around a central greenspace and community center (Figure 9.2). This organization recalled the Garden City model introduced to Los Angeles by Clarence Stein (1882–1975) at Baldwin Hills Village (Figure 9.3), which emphasized community cooperation by stressing the importance of a shared lawn and collective amenities.[30] Like Stein's Baldwin Hills Village (1941), Williams designed Pueblo del Rio in a uniquely California-modernist lexicon. California modernism offered several benefits for mass-housing. Most importantly, it was economical: It was minimally detailed with simple massing; its materials, such as exposed concrete, were cheap; and its multifunctional design features, including flat roofs with overhanding eaves, large windows, and open-plan apartment layouts, kept costs down. As one author wrote in an article about Pueblo del Rio, "public housing projects are designed to be operated economically, above all with a minimum of upkeep and repair work."[31] This allowed occupants to focus on their personal and professional lives – and thus, their uplift – rather than on maintaining their dwelling.

While details were kept to a minimum, design features such as exposed wooden beams and large, picture windows beautified the apartments, imbuing them with an especially modern character (Figure 9.4). These sizable windows also expanded the tenants' felt or perceived living space. Neutra, who strongly advocated for these kinds of features, referred to perceptually expansive fenestration as "space auxiliaries," which kept costs per square foot down as they dissolved rigid distinctions between interior and exterior space.[32] Indeed, the architects placed large windows at both ends of each apartment and on both stories to bring air and sunlight into the dwellings' interiors.

A major reason for doing so was to improve tenants' health. Because many Americans associated traditional poor peoples' housing with overcrowding, fetor, and disease, public housing designers – in line

---

[30] Clarence Stein, "Baldwin Hills Village, Los Angeles," in *Toward New Towns for America* (Cambridge, MA: MIT Press, 1966), 188–216. For more on the sources of Stein's Garden City designs, see Ebenezer Howard, *Garden Cities of To-morrow: A Peaceful Path to Real Reform* (Cambridge: Cambridge University Press, 2010 [1898]).

[31] Fred'K W. Jones, "Pueblo del Rio: Los Angeles' Most Recent Housing Project," *Architect and Engineer* (September 1942), 11.

[32] Richard Neutra, *Architecture of Social Concern in Regions of Mild Climate* (São Paulo, Brazil: Gerth Todtann, 1948), 194.

Figure 9.4 Leonard Nadel, photographer, "Children Playing on Front Lawn," 1942. Pueblo del Rio (Los Angeles, California), Paul R. Williams, main architect. Housing Authority Photo Collection, Los Angeles Public Library.

Figure 9.5 "Exterior of Finished Buildings at Project's 'Point #3,'" 1942. Pueblo del Rio (Los Angeles, California), Paul R. Williams, main architect. Housing Authority Photo Collection, Los Angeles Public Library.

with the Cold War liberal state's desire to manage citizens' daily lives – focused on providing tenants with sunlight and air, which in the popular mind were associated with personal and mutual health. To assure an abundance of airflow and light, Williams situated each apartment building between fifty and sixty feet apart from one another (Figure 9.5). This had two benefits, one practical and one theoretical. First, it prevented overcrowding. Second, because each apartment building was capable of housing upwards of six families, it demonstrated to interested observers that superblock constructions could house many people without minimizing open space around the apartments or building high rises that would distance the buildings from California's low-rise tradition and aesthetic.

The Garden City superblock at Pueblo del Rio reveals Williams's conviction that modern architecture and modern amenities must be the basis of housing in postwar Los Angeles – and, indeed, the postwar United States. For the architects, housing projects were places where a person's basic and cultural needs could be satisfied. With plentiful greenspace, the verdant Pueblo del Rio afforded its residents a walkable superblock replete with multitudinous cultural and community services, including a free nursery school and countless classes and community organizations such as dance classes, children's pottery classes, a library, athletic clubs, and a handful of other neighborhood organizations (Figure 9.6).[33] The project showed that even with a tight budget, working-class people in Los Angeles could live comfortably in economical communities.[34]

For Williams, Pueblo del Rio was a site for cultural, and therefore racial, advancement. Following the young Du Bois and other Progressive Era reformers, at midcentury numerous black progressives argued that racial problems would be solved through cultural transformation.[35] Housing became one of the most important sites for intervention and thus cultural, and more dramatically, *biological*, change. For example, Williams's colleague at HACLA and Executive Director of the Urban League, Floyd C. Covington, insisted that changing one's habits through "human engineering" could change one's biology.[36] Put another way, Covington believed that if black Americans lived in a healthy, stimulating, and community-oriented environment, their biology would evolve and they would be able to participate in politics as active democratic citizens. According to Covington and fellow travelers like Williams, housing was not simply an experiment in bettering black American's everyday lives, but in making them literally new people.

---

[33] Folder 7057 11.5, Housing Authority of the City of Los Angeles – Directory of Commissioners, Undated, Box 11, Floyd C. Covington Papers, University of Southern California Special Collections/University Archives Library, Los Angeles, California.

[34] The PRW Project, "Pueblo del Rio Housing Project, Los Angeles, CA," Paul Revere Williams: American Architect, accessed 2018, www.paulrwilliamsproject.org/index.html.1.123.html.

[35] Touré F. Reed, *Not Alms but Opportunity: The Urban League and the Politics of Racial Uplift, 1910–1950* (Chapel Hill: University of North Carolina Press, 2008), 3.

[36] Featured in *The Human Culture Digest* 51, no. 8 (August 1943), Folder 7057 1.11, The Human Culture Digest [Two Articles Feature Floyd Covington] 1943, August; 1944 February, Box 1, Floyd C. Covington Papers, University of Southern California Special Collections/University Archives Library, Los Angeles, California.

Figure 9.6 Julius Shulman, photographer, "Job 056: Pueblo del Rio (Los Angeles, California)," 1942. Gelatin Silver Print. Folder 8, Box 89, Julius Shulman Photography Archive, 1936–1997. © J. Paul Getty Trust. Getty Research Institute, Los Angeles (2004.R.10).

Architectural critics considered Pueblo del Rio latent with transformative potential, portraying it as an augur for Los Angeles's prosperous future in which even the poor live good lives. In an article from the September 1942 issue of *Architect and Engineer*, innocuously titled "Pueblo del Rio: Los Angeles's Most Recent Housing Project," Fred K. Jones highlights that the project replaced cleared, majority black slums.[37] Two full-page photographs of the site and project are titled "Before" and "After" (Figures 9.7 and 9.8). The "Before" image depicts the site prior to its being cleared for construction. The image anticipates its own future: The debris in the photograph's foreground forestalls the still-standing slum dwellings in the middle and foreground. The completely obliterated structure that once stood at the foreground is reduced to rubble, leaving specter-like marks in the dirt. Only one of the "slum houses"

[37] Jones, "Pueblo del Rio," 12–13.

Figure 9.7 "Before and After" of Pueblo del Rio, Los Angeles, California, Paul R. Williams, main architect, 1942. From: Fred'K W. Jones, "Pueblo del Rio: Los Angeles' Most Recent Housing Project," Architect and Engineer, September 1942.

is shown in full: a small, flat roofed structure at left. The structure is not in poor condition. In fact, like another premonition, it looks remarkably like the modern apartments about to replace it. The photograph thus communicates that Pueblo del Rio represents not a total break with the past, but an improvement on it: a model that will build upon the fulfilled promises of the Western frontier.

The "After" picture is not actually a photograph of the site, but a mislabeled image of the site's model.[38] The Pueblo del Rio model highlights the apartments' lush setting. The fifty-seven apartment buildings, which contain six to eight units with three to six bedrooms each, are surrounded by grass, trees, and other greenery. While the greenspaces are divided in a way that implies they could be private lawns, this implication is quickly shattered when one notices that the plots do not conform to any predictable pattern; instead, they spread out from the apartments in asymmetric blocks. Indeed, some plots are not connected to any single apartment. The uneven distribution of the plots mimics those typical of

[38] Ibid.

single-family homes that use front yards to distinguish one private lot from the next. At Pueblo del Rio, however, the plots are parceled but not individually distributed; each belongs to the entire project and equally to all the project's tenants. By reproducing traditional front yards in form, the design both provided tenants a familiar and desirable arrangement while simultaneously undermining notions of private property. It would be features like these, as well as the communal nurseries and shared laundries that when imbued with the simple, modernist idiom would pose too live a threat to capitalist hegemony and exclude people like Williams's from designing the Cold War liberal project.

Williams's desire to distinguish Pueblo del Rio from the surrounding area by creating a cohesively designed superblock was aided by landscape architect Ralph D. Cornell (1890–1972). Specifically, Cornell surrounded the complex with trees that created "a skyline enclosure of planting" that broke up what could have been a monotonous space.[39] Trees also fostered community: practically, they offered shade from the Los Angeles sun (which provided people places to gather), while their fruit served as a shared food source. By the time the project was completed in 1942, Cornell had planted about 200 fruit trees, which meant there was a fruit tree for every two households. Furthermore, Cornell allotted each family a garden plot, which encouraged households to individually partake in the cooperative upkeep of the landscape while also lending the project agricultural and visual diversity. In short, the gardens individuated the apartments without undermining their communal character.

Cornell's garden plots heightened the distinction between private and public that remained irrevocably in flux. Indeed, Williams and his colleagues intentionally designed Pueblo del Rio so that its residents could easily transition between private and public greenspaces. This was partially for ideological reasons. Williams designed the connection between the private apartment and the public garden as a metaphor for the individual African–American's relationship to their group identity as "Negros." Greenspace only remained green if everyone took care of both their own plot and the space they shared with one another. In other words, the plots provided Williams with the opportunity to encourage the occupants to become productive members of their community – both their specific community at Pueblo del Rio and the larger community of black Americans.

A photograph of a young woman watering her plants at the project explores this phenomenon (Figure 9.8). Smiling at the camera while watering the plants outside her front door, a tall tangle of dense foliage

---

[39] Ralph D. Cornell, "Pueblo del Rio," *Architect and Engineer* (September 1942): 21.

Figure 9.8 Louis Clyde Stoumen, photographer, "Project's 'Garden of the Month' Contest Winner," c. 1942. Housing Authority Photo Collection, Los Angeles Public Library.

bisects the shared greenspace, separating her semiprivate green area from her neighbors'. However, just as the plant divider separates, it also connects the two apartments. For the plant divider to survive and thrive, both tenants must tend to it. At Pueblo del Rio, it was the *mutual* work of "individual Negros" that would raise "the average cultural level" of the race, eventually leading to the formation of a thriving black community.[40]

A crucial and ongoing concern for Williams was how the transition from slum to modern housing would affect an inhabitant's behavior. He was especially anxious that the shock resulting from a working person's sudden introduction to new ways of living would be so disorienting that the individual would be unable to function as a political person. His intermix of the private apartment and public space may therefore be read as an attempt to ease the transition from the single-family slum home to multifamily public housing. In this, Williams was inspired by his close colleague Neutra. As Neutra argued in his *Architecture of Social Concern in Regions of Mild Climate* (1948), the shock of the new must be combined with the expected comforts of the past: "like the transplanting and repotting of plants [rehousing] must be a gently supervised training venture; otherwise, people will not easily take root."[41] Having a private garden alongside public greenspace functioned as a "carefully designed education campaign" intended to imbue residents with community-oriented habits.[42] William's interventions and concerns about transitioning people into modern, cooperative housing,

---

[40] Williams, "I am a Negro," 161.
[41] Neutra, *Architecture of Social Concern*, 193–194.
[42] Ibid., 19.

foreshadowed later, Cold War liberal concerns about America's own transition into a new, postwar modernity, wherein Communism proffered an all-too appealing alternative to liberalism writ large. Like the Cold War liberals who succeeded them, California Modernists argued for the importance of foregrounding educative campaigns before turning democracy – eventually – over to the populous.

***

Between 1941 and 1955, the city funded approximately thirty-three large-scale superblock projects intended for defense and low-income workers. Private developers followed suit, building an additional twenty-seven middle-income Garden City projects during the same period.[43] For fourteen years, architects, academics, planners, and governmental officials alike shared a vision of Los Angeles as a city that would deploy superblock configurations in order to establish walkable, coherent communities. Moreover, the fact that so many of these projects were designed for working-class people suggested that there was a viable, mass, urban alternative to speculative home building and suburbanization.

Pueblo del Rio and other low-cost housing projects built by Williams represented a progressive trend in midcentury architecture that, when centered, transforms our understanding of American modernism. Williams's ideology, in fact, seemed to perfectly complement that of the Cold War liberals: He believed in expertise; considered planning essential to a healthy society; wanted to obliterate traditional social distinctions; hoped to provide housing to the workers building the "arsenal of democracy"; and intended to uplift Black Americans toward securing racial parity. But why, then, did Williams's form of housing not become part of Cold War liberal practice? There were two main reasons: McCarthyism and mass housings' challenge to private property. In the early 1950s, Williams's and other California Modernists' public housing experiments came to a definitive end with the rise of McCarthyism.

Anticommunist and anti-socialist fervor quickly swept through Los Angeles: In 1952, Proposition B, which would have legislated the construction of 10,000 new low-cost housing units, failed; that same year, the pro-housing Fletcher Bowron lost his bid for a fifth term as mayor; and in 1953, the head of HACLA, Frank Wilkinson, was forced out of the agency following accusations of Communist affiliations. Meanwhile, the Red Scare-era FBI investigated countless other

---

[43] Architectural Resources Group, Inc.: Architects, Planners, & Conservators, *Garden Apartments of Los Angeles: Historical Context Statement* (Los Angeles: Los Angeles Conservancy, 2012), 79–85.

architects, academics, and government officials for "anti-American" sympathies. This combined assault decisively ended Los Angeles's public housing program. Indeed, in 1955, Williams completed Nickerson Gardens, the city's last housing project, which in 1965 became one of the major sites of the Watts Uprising.

Perhaps the most important lesson contemporary intellectuals could learn from the failure of progressive modernists' public housing experiment is that, in the United States, social democratic policy has often been linked to American militarism. Throughout the twentieth century, U.S. policymakers at the local, state, and national levels have usually willingly pursued social democratic policies under the shadow of war. In the 1940s, they built public projects to house defense workers; in the 1960s, they pursued civil rights legislation to defang Soviet criticisms of the United States and to win the "hearts and minds" of the emergent Third World; and in the 1970s and after, they built a comprehensive welfare state, but, in the end, only for those who served in the military.[44] The question then, is whether it is possible in this country to have social democracy absent war and empire; this is a question, unfortunately, that remains very much open to debate. And of course, militarism can oftentimes be a conservative, Janus-faced force; McCarthyism, after all, was very much a Cold War project.

By the mid-1950s, the mass-housing project imagined by California Modernist architects ended as the once well-funded housing division faced mounting austerity. Indeed, the contemporary image of the "midcentury modern" aesthetic, which is today most associated with modish furniture designs and lavish single-family homes, reflects the fact that during the postwar boom modernist architects agreed to work within the limits of a Cold War liberal project that stressed individuality over communality. According to Cold War liberals, a disenfranchised underclass was inevitable and mass public housing was too socialist – too *Soviet* – for the United States. Modernist architects who began their careers devoted to housing for all thus ended them building homes for the wealthy and well-to-do.

---

[44] See Mary Dudziak, *Cold War Civil Rights: Race and the Image of American Democracy* (Princeton: Princeton University Press, 2001) and Jennifer Mittelstadt, *The Rise of the Military Welfare State* (Cambridge, MA: Harvard University Press, 2015).

10 Richard Hofstadter and the Demonology of the Cold War Right

Daniel Smith and Anton Jäger

Of the many prolific American intellectuals who could conceivably be associated with centrist Cold War liberalism in the postwar United States, few have the continued name recognition of Richard Hofstadter. The surprising political success of Donald Trump and the concomitant radical right-wing turn of the Republican Party in the mid-2010s has brought about a Hofstadter renaissance, with scholars and commentators turning to the work of an historian who had died nearly fifty years ago to explain seemingly new trends in American politics. Hofstadter's concept of the "paranoid style," originally developed to explain the appeal of right-wing anti-communism during the 1950s and 1960s, proved newly relevant in the wake of a widely unexpected populist zeitgeist. Dozens of op-eds cited Hofstadter and his ideas to explain the success of Trump, Brexit, and the broader emergence of a right-wing populist political culture in the early twenty-first century, attributing the success of the New Right to a psychosocial status anxiety unconsciously driving the political beliefs of conservative Americans. Renewed interest in Hofstadter culminated in the publication of a 1,000-page volume including 2 of Hofstadter's books, *Anti-intellectualism in American Life* and *The Paranoid Style in American Politics*, edited by Sean Wilentz.[1]

Wilentz has said that what "Hofstadter came to discover in the 1950s and early 1960s were challenges to American liberalism, mainly but not only from the right, challenges deeply rooted in our history, that threatened the foundations not just of liberal politics but democracy itself."[2] Hofstadter's personal move away from Marx – and the historian Charles Beard – in his later life was asymmetrically matched by a theoretical framework he constructed to explain the then-new phenomenon of

---

[1] Sean Wilentz, *Richard Hofstadter: Anti-Intellectualism in American Life, The Paranoid Style in American Politics, Uncollected Essays 1956–1965* (New York: Penguin Random House, 2020).

[2] Library of America, "Sean Wilentz: Richard Hofstadter and the 'Paranoid Style' as an American Phenomenon." September 15, 2020, www.loa.org/news-and-views/1735-sean-wilentz-richard-hofstadter-and-the-paranoid-style-as-an-american-phenomenon.

mass radical right-wing politics in the postwar United States. As Samuel Moyn has said, "Cold War liberalism was not just about legitimating the west against its global enemies, whether they were communist or global South liberationists. Cold War liberalism was also about proscribing a certain politics within the west itself." For Moyn, a resurgence of Cold War liberal thinking in the early twenty-first century has brought "a return of the democracy vs. authoritarianism frame[.]"[3] If Cold War liberalism was – and is – focused around a centrist rejection of radical left- and right-wing politics on the grounds that they are illiberal and, ultimately, undemocratic, Hofstadter surely belongs in the Cold War liberal camp. This chapter places Hofstadter firmly in the context of mid twentieth-century Cold War liberalism and argues that the association of Hofstadter's "paranoid style" phrase with concepts such as populism and status anxiety have contributed to analytical blind spots in the analysis of far-right politics in postwar America. By attributing the success of right-wing movements, leaders, and ideologies primarily to a "status anxiety" unconsciously experienced by right-wing voters and activists, the novel organizational forms and media strategies embraced by political entrepreneurs of the American radical right have been ignored by analysts and public commentators alike.

Hofstadter's Intellectual Origins

Like many of his fellow Cold War liberals, Hofstadter trod a well-worn path from youthful political radicalism to a self-styled enlightened centrism. A short-lived tenure in the Communist Party of the United States of America as a doctoral student in the late 1930s was followed, just over five years later, with a decisive theoretical break from the class-centric historiographical approach espoused by the historian Charles Beard. The break was not an easy one; Hofstadter's first scholarly work had engaged closely with Beard's arguments, and he even acknowledged that his own interest in history was inspired by Beard's *The Rise of American Civilization*.[4] Rejecting the Beardian notion that American history was driven by a series of class conflicts, the Hofstadter of the late 1940s turned to insights from sociology and psychology to flesh out his historiographical project. In his canonical 1964 work, *The Paranoid*

---

[3] Daniel McAteer, "A Conversation with Samuel Moyn: The Cold War and the Canon of Liberalism," April 1, 2022, Centre for Intellectual History at the University of Oxford, https://intellectualhistory.web.ox.ac.uk/article/a-conversation-with-samuel-moyn-the-cold-war-and-the-canon-of-liberalism.

[4] Christopher Lasch, "On Richard Hofstadter," *The New York Review of Books* (March 8, 1973), www.nybooks.com/articles/1973/03/08/on-richard-hofstadter/.

Style in American Politics, Hofstadter explained that the application of psychological theories to the study of politics had "made us acutely aware that politics can be a projective arena for feelings and impulses that are only marginally related to the manifest issues."[5]

Hofstadter's preoccupation with the populists and Progressives of the late twentieth century culminated in the publication of his Pulitzer Prize–winning *Age of Reform* in 1955. His attempts to reconcile these movements with broader trends in American history would go on to shape his scholarly interest in what was, in the immediate postwar years, the newest and most visible faction in American politics: the anti-communist American Right. Hofstadter wrote over a dozen essays and books touching on the American Right from the early 1950s onward, connecting that movement's "paranoid style" to a broader populist tradition in American history. Drawing on his earlier work on the populist tradition of the late nineteenth century, Hofstadter argued that the postwar right-wing backlash against Communism, liberalism, and internationalism was similarly animated primarily by an "unconscious" status anxiety. In one of his earliest pieces on the topic, a 1954 essay entitled "The Pseudo-Conservative Revolt," Hofstadter offered an Adorno-inspired account of pseudo-conservatism in which (unconscious) status anxiety motivated the militant and hysterical attitudes and views espoused by American rightists. Hofstadter rejected the notion that "the new pseudo-conservatism is simply the old ultra-conservatism and the old isolationism heightened by the extraordinary pressures of the contemporary world." Instead, he set out the "speculative hypothesis" that "*pseudo-conservatism is in good part a product of the rootlessness and heterogeneity of American life, and above all, of its peculiar scramble for status and its peculiar search for secure identity.*"[6] He then argued that postwar America had transitioned from a period in which interest politics reigned to one of an emergent "status politics," which he defined as "the clash of various projective rationalizations arising from status aspirations and other personal motives."[7]

Starting with this essay and continuing with later works such as 1963s *Anti-Intellectualism in American Life* and 1964s *Paranoid Style*, Hofstadter constructed a crucial ideological pillar of Cold War liberalism and bequeathed the tradition some of its most hallowed tropes – "status anxiety," "paranoid style," and "populism." The most lasting and politically

---

[5] Richard Hofstadter, *The Paranoid Style in American Politics* (New York: Random House, 2008 [1964]), xxxiii.
[6] Richard Hofstadter, "The Pseudo-Conservative Revolt," *The American Scholar* 24, no. 1 (Winter 1944–1945), 9–27.
[7] Ibid., 18.

significant element of Hofstadter's legacy was his contribution to a specific postwar "demonology" of the far right. Two arguments proved crucial to this demonology: first, Hofstadter's tracing of the postwar far right to the late nineteenth-century populist movement and second, his psychosocial analysis of the same postwar right as being driven fundamentally by an ideological revolt against status decline. Both ideas also underwent a sustained attack during the 1950s and 1960s, when a so-called Hofstadter controversy took the American academe by storm. Though Hofstadter was a historian, his thesis was paralleled in social science by authors such as Seymour Martin Lipset, Daniel Bell, Peter Viereck, Talcott Parsons, and Edward Shils.[8] This tradition faced significant criticism in the 1960s and 1970s, which was mounted by "counter-revisionist" writers such as C. Vann Woodward, Norman Pollack, Michael Paul Rogin, Christopher Lasch, Walter Nugent, and Lawrence Goodwyn. By 1991, the success of this counteroffensive led Goodwyn to conclude that "the world of populism constructed by Hofstadter now languishes in ruin," including its Cold War encasing.[9]

While the counter-revisionists had won their campaign in the discipline of history, the fate of Hofstadter's motifs outside of that field was less clear-cut. Goodwin himself acknowledged that the Hofstadter thesis survived intact as both a "research strategy" and "untested cultural hypothesis."[10] In the social sciences, Hofstadter's theses seemed to enjoy a spectral afterlife, consolidated in works on postmodern status politics and the populist right that emerged in the 1980s and 1990s. These studies assured the entry of the term "populism" into mainstream discourse and continue to inform scholarship on the far right.[11] Even though Hofstadter himself by the late 1960s ultimately rejected the more extreme versions of his own theory of populism, the durability of his ideas – and the far-right demonology they spawned – assured the reproduction of some of Cold War liberalism's most powerful ideologemes, especially its anti-radicalism and anti-populism.

---

[8] See Robert Collins, "The Originality Trap: Hofstadter on Populism," *The Journal of American History* 76, no. 1 (June 1989), 150–167; David Greenberg, "Richard Hofstadter Reconsidered," *Reviews in American History* 35, no. 3 (September 2007), 144–179; Daniel Walker Howe and Peter Elliott Finn, "Richard Hofstadter: The Ironies of an American Historian," *Pacific Historical Review* 43, no. 1 (February 1974), 1–23.

[9] Lawrence Goodwyn, "Rethinking 'Populism': Paradoxes of Historiography and Democracy," *Telos* 88 (1991), 37–56.

[10] Ibid., 42.

[11] See Cas Mudde and Cristóbal Rovira Kaltwasser, *Populism: A Very Short Introduction* (London: Oxford University Press, 2017); Nadia Urbinati, "Political Theory of Populism," *Annual Review of Political Science* 22, no. 1 (2019), 111–127; Yves Mény and Yves Surel, eds. *Democracies and the Populist Challenge* (London: Palgrave Macmillan, 2002); Margaret Canovan, *Populism* (New York: Harcourt Brace Jovanovich, 1981).

Despite its afterlives, Hofstadter's approach remains controversial. In late 2018 historian Leo Ribuffo, whose work documenting the twentieth-century Christian Right has attracted renewed attention in recent years, wrote that Hofstadter's "paranoid style" catchphrase:

should be buried with a stake in its heart. As someone who has tried to hammer in the stake for several decades, I cannot help noticing that the term has risen again from the grave as in a horror movie populated, not by vampires, zombies, and terrified teenagers, but by Donald Trump, superficial pundits, and terrified liberals and radicals. The application of the "paranoid style" to Trump and his followers began in 2015 and has continued unabated.[12]

More recently, David Art argued that social scientists have overemphasized populism in their analyses of Trump and other rightists, obscuring the real ideological core of their movement: right-wing nativism.[13] And, as the final section of this chapter will show, a new generation of American historians have improved on Hofstadter's analysis of the postwar American Right by focusing on the novel political strategies – notably the mass media entrepreneurship – successfully employed by the postwar rightist leaders.

The following section will trace Hofstadter's intellectual development and engagement with contemporary debates on both the role of populism in American history and its analytical utility for understanding political phenomena. The subsequent section will consider the way that Hofstadter's work shaped subsequent scholarship and analyses of the postwar American Right and the right-wing populist movements that appeared in the late twentieth and early twenty-first centuries. The final section will consider how the implicit anti-populism of the Hofstadterian project continues to be a key component of Cold War liberal ideology in the present day.

Populism in Hofstadter's History and Politics

On May 11, 1962, the American historian C. Vann Woodward drafted a letter to his friend Richard Hofstadter. He wrote:

Dick, you just can't do this. No amount of Adorno, Stouffer, Hartley, etc. will sustain it. If you mean by fundamentalists those addicted to "literal scanning of Scripture" you take in a hell of a proportion of the population from the

---

[12] Leo Ribuffo, "Donald Trump and the 'Paranoid Style' in American (Intellectual) Politics," in *Chaos in the Liberal Order*, ed. Robert Jervis et al. (New York: Columbia University Press, 2018), 343.

[13] David Art, "The Myth of Global Populism," *Perspectives on Politics* 20, no. 3 (November 2020), 999–1011.

seventeenth down through the nineteenth centuries – including a hell of a lot of intellectuals, even some leading ones way down into the nineteenth century. I see several dangers here.[14]

The book under discussion – Hofstadter's *Anti-Intellectualism in American Life*, eventually published in early 1963 – might have had some "circumspect and cautious" moments, but Woodward thought its overall tenor looked like Hofstadter "let go with both barrels" and overstepped his bounds as a scholar.[15] Above all, Woodward felt that Hofstadter's criticisms of the original populist movement, a group of radical farmers' associations that arose in the 1880s and 1890s in the Midwest and the South that later consolidated into one of the most significant third parties in American history, were unduly strong. Hofstadter saw them as assailants of academic freedom and critical consciousness. But as Woodward noted in an earlier assessment of his friend's work, "uncritical repetition and occasional exaggeration" threatened "to result in establishing a new maxim in American political thought: *Radix malorum est Populismus*."[16] Hofstadter had already launched a full-scale revision of the populist movement with his 1955 book, *The Age of Reform*, followed by a critical essay in an edited volume with Daniel Bell and Seymour Martin Lipset. Earlier that year, his "Pseudo-Conservative Revolt" essay outlined the early contours of the piece that would be forever identified with him: "The Paranoid Style in American Politics." Initially published as the cover essay in *Harper's Magazine*, Hofstadter released a 315-page book with the same title a year later. Together with prior work by Irwin Unger, Oscar Handlin, and Daniel Bell, these publications steadily coagulated into a literature steadily identified, by historians still under the influence of Marx and Beard, as "revisionist."[17]

It was not the first time that Woodward found himself in disagreement with his colleague over populist questions. Hofstadter's 1955 assessment of the populists was a self-conscious break with previous scholarship. In the 1920s and 1930s, American historians still looked back on the original populist episode with fondness, granting it a prime place in their histories. To Charles Beard, doyen of the Progressive School, for instance, populism represented the final revolt of the small

---

[14] John Herbert Roper, *C. Vann Woodward: A Southern Historian and His Critics* (Athens: University of Georgia Press, 2012), 121.
[15] Ibid.
[16] C. Vann Woodward, *The Burden of Southern History* (Baton Rouge: LSU Press, 1960), 147; Gene Wise, *American Historical Explanations: A Strategy for Grounded Inquiry* (Ann Arbor: University of Michigan, 1973).
[17] John Higham, "Beyond Consensus: The Historian as a Moral Critic," *The American Historical Review* 67, no. 3 (April 1962), 609–625.

freeholding class before its crushing by industrial society; the farmer's last stand against the new corporate order.[18] Other writers in this tradition, including Vernon Parrington, Solon Buck, and John Hicks, shared Beard's sentiment. Parrington's last volume of his tripartite 1930 *Main Currents in American Thought* cast populism as a revolt of small property holders wielding the Jeffersonian settler ideal and claiming a pedigree which went back to the Founders' Age and the era of Jacksonian mass democracy.[19] As Gary Marotta notes, these scholars considered the populist movement "evidence of a salutary and democratic agrarian resistance to capitalist exploitation."[20] John D. Hicks's 1931 classic *The Populist Revolt* tracked a similar genealogy, showing how the aims of the original populists were transposed into Progressivism and the radicalism of the incipient New Deal.[21] "Thanks to the triumph of populist principles," Hicks declared in 1931, "one may almost say that ... the people now rule."[22] The common theme underlying all these treatments was thus an abiding sense of populist rationality: populist farmers were right to rebel against overweening corporations and merchants, even when they voiced these discontents in an overheated register.

Hofstadter's thesis rejected this perspective. To him, the agrarian rebels were not benevolent reformists or crypto-socialists; rather, they were the unwitting forebears of a "paranoid style in American politics." In his *Age of Reform*, which Alan Brinkley later called "the most influential book ever published on the history of twentieth-century America," Hofstadter drew a sharp contrast between the populist "Agrarian Myth" and the "Commercial Realities" of the late nineteenth century.[23] In Hofstadter's view, farmers sought the benefits of a newly commercialized economy but still postured as pastoral victims of a "conspiracy hatched in the distance."[24] The rise of the corporation not only destabilized prior notions of citizenship, but also uprooted older Jeffersonian ideals of small property holders who previously exercised direct influence on the

---

[18] Clyde Barrow, *More than a Historian: The Political and Economic Thought of Charles A. Beard* (New York: Routledge, 2000), 120–133.
[19] Vernon Parrington, *Main Currents in American Thought, Vol. 3: The Beginnings of Critical Realism in America, 1860–1920* (Norman: University of Oklahoma Press, 1930), 264–270.
[20] Gary Marotta, "Richard Hofstadter's Populist Problem and His Identity as a Jewish Intellectual," in *Transformations of Populism in Europe and the Americas*, ed. Paul Taggart and John Abromeit (London: Bloomsbury, 2016), 105–115.
[21] John Hicks, *The Populist Revolt* (Minneapolis: University of Minnesota Press, 1931).
[22] Ibid., 421.
[23] Alan Brinkley, "Review of Richard Hofstadter's the Age of Reform: A Reconsideration," *Reviews in American History* 13, no. 3 (September 1985), 462–480.
[24] Richard Hofstadter, *The Age of Reform* (New York: Penguin Random House, 1960 [1955]), 33.

state. Large Atlantic trading routes meant that farmers became subject to impersonal market forces and dependent on new financial mediators. Rather than bucolic victims of economic distress, in Hofstadter's view, populists were the product of America's inherited rural ideals crashing into financial reality. As he put it:

> Rank in society! That was close to the heart of the matter, for the farmer was beginning to realize acutely not merely that the best of the world's goods were to be had in the cities and that the urban middle and upper classes had much more of them than he did but also that he was losing in status and respect as compared with them.[25]

Hofstadter's combination of social-scientific and historical registers was also at one with the history discipline's mood in the 1950s. This decade was characterized by a flurry of new methodologies, in which classical genres of literary history were being enriched by new sociological methods – a fusion that tended to produce, as Dorothy Ross put it, "social theories rather than political narratives" and led to a decline in explanations centered on "interest" or "class."[26] Oscar Handlin, David Potter, Edmund Morgan, Louis Hartz, and Hofstadter stood as prime representatives of this trend; in an introduction to a 1968 collection on *Sociology and History*, for instance, Hofstadter looked back on the 1950s as an era defined by a new "analytical history" that had greater "sociological awareness" and a more "complex conceptual task" than previous historiography.[27] Symptomatically, *The Age of Reform*, rather than sticking to the catchall of "interest" or "class," carefully imported into American history new psychoanalytic and sociological categories such as "status," "ressentiment," and "frustration."

Hofstadter's turn to the concept of "status" to help explain populism had both political and intellectual roots. Academically, it was the outgrowth of an engagement with Max Weber that began in the 1930s, later taken up by Columbia's "Seminar on the State" and the New York–based "Stern Group" – a complex to which Bell later gave the name

---

[25] Ibid., 33.
[26] Dorothy Ross, "The New and Newer Histories: Social Theory and Historiography in an American Key," in *Imagined Histories: American Historians Interpret the Past*, ed. Gordon S. Wood and Anthony Molho (Princeton: Princeton University Press, 2018), 85; Alan Brinkley, *Liberalism and Its Discontents* (Cambridge, MA: Harvard University Press, 1998), 137–140; Andrew Abbott, "History and Sociology: The Lost Synthesis," *Social Science History* 15, no. 2 (Summer 1991), 201–238; Dorothy Ross, "Grand Narrative in American Historical Writing: From Romance to Uncertainty," *The American Historical Review* 100, no. 3 (June 1995), 661–662.
[27] Richard Hofstadter, "History and Sociology in the United States," in *Sociology and History: Methods*, ed. Seymour Martin Lipset and Richard Hofstadter (New York: Basic Books, 1968), 15.

"Upper West Side Kibbutz."[28] Contributors to the seminar included Bell, Seymour Martin Lipset, Karl Wittfogel, and Franz Neumann.[29] To these intellectuals, Weber offered a potent critique of economistic theories of social action prevalent since the 1920s, which stipulated a narrow notion of "class" or "interest" as its organizing principle.[30]

The American Weber renaissance was a prominent point of entry for post-economistic thinkers such as Hofstadter. Hofstadter first encountered Weber's work at the State University of New York at Buffalo in the 1930s, mediated by translators such as Talcott Parsons and Frank Knight and later imported by Columbia affiliates such as Karl Wittfogel and Franz Neumann.[31] As Bell recalled, by the 1940s "Weber had become rather important ... for us" and further claimed that "it was basically Weber's influence on Marty [Seymour Martin Lipset]" that led Hofstadter to engage seriously with the German thinker.[32] In addition to his reputation as an "intellectual desperado," Weber also seemed to offer a value-neutral model of social inquiry that chimed well with the prudent politics of the 1950s and the continuing impasse of Marxist approaches. In initial American translations, Weber's notion of *Stand* or *Stände* had been rendered into English as "status," here denoting the symbolic – rather than economic – power social actors enjoyed over their peers.[33] Weber's social theory, in turn, weakened the link between class position and ideology that had been prevalent in both the Marxian and Beardian tradition, offering a refuge from perceived economic reductionism.

A similar sentiment drove Hofstadter's interest in Theodor Adorno's work on the "authoritarian personality" and "pseudo-conservatism," which had identified a gulf between the classical aristocratic culture of Wilhelmine Germany and the plebeian populism of the Nazi period.[34]

---

[28] Oliver Neun, *Daniel Bell und der Kreis der "New York Intellectuals": Frühe amerikanische öffentliche Soziologie* (Berlin: Springer, 2014), 374–380.

[29] Other contributors included Nathan Glazer, William Leuchtenburg, Harold Laswell, William T. R. Fox, David Truman, Franz Neumann, and Otto Kirchheimer.

[30] William Leuchtenburg, "The Uses and Abuses of History," *History and Politics Newsletter* 2 (Fall 1991), 6–7.

[31] Lawrence Scaff, "Max Weber in the United States," *Societa Mutamento Politica* 5 (2014), 16.

[32] David Brown, *Richard Hofstadter: An Intellectual Biography* (Chicago: University of Chicago Press, 2008), 13.

[33] This translation was identified as controversial by many later commentators. See Keith Tribe, "Translating Weber," in *Why Concepts Matter: Translating Social and Political Thought*, ed. Martin Burke and Melvin Richter (London: Brill, 2012), 216; Keith Tribe, "Talcott Parsons as Translator of Max Weber's Basic Sociological Categories," *History of European Ideas* 33, no. 2 (June 2007), 212–233.

[34] Richard Hofstadter, *Anti-Intellectualism in American Life* (New York: Vintage, 1963), 64. As Hofstadter noted, he "borrow[ed] the term from the study of *The Authoritarian Personality* published five years ago by Theodore (sic) W. Adorno and his associates"

Moreover, Hofstadter's turn to "symbolism" was strengthened by his encounter with Karl Mannheim's writings. Mannheim's social theory, especially his canonical 1929 *Ideology and Utopia*, ushered in the final uncoupling of class position and ideology that had previously tied together the Beardian thesis by showing how the ideological position of "free floating intellectuals" could expand beyond their social location, allow for useful abstraction, and enable an intellectual to view society in its totality. And as Bell noted, when it came to moving past economism, "Dick very quickly took the lead."[35]

The theoretical utility of the Weberian approach became even more clear to Hofstadter and his colleagues during the 1950s. A primary question then facing Hofstadter's generation was the rise of McCarthyism. Why did this movement, only vaguely situated on class lines, arise in the "affluent society" of the midcentury United States? The question was even more puzzling in light of this generation's previous political experience. The Beardian tradition decreed that politics itself was to be seen as the institutional translation of economic strife, while the residual Trotskyism of some members of the Stern Group implied that they should be looking for class motives in their historical analyses. "My generation," Hofstadter recalled in the early 1960s, "was raised in the conviction that the basic motive power in political behaviour is the economic interest of groups."[36] McCarthyism and the emergence of a postwar New Right, however, proved that this schema was "wanting as an account of much [of] the vital political behavior of our own time."[37] McCarythites' frantic calls for disclosure, their insistence on the essentially moral nature of their revolt, and their endless perorations on the need for a religious "war against communism" were not comprehensible in terms of ruling class interest. The rise of Joseph McCarthy, Hofstadter later noted, revealed the existence of a "wide range of behavior for which the economic interpretation of politics" seemed to "be inadequate."[38] And in the opinion of Hofstadter and his colleagues, McCarthy did not arise ex nihilo. Rather, his desire for

---

and had drawn "heavily upon this enlightening study," although he had "some reservations about its methods and conclusions." Hofstadter, *Anti-Intellectualism in American Life*, 79. Norbert Guterman and Leo Lowenthal's 1949 book, *Prophets of Deceit*, which already used the "populism" label for some American agitators, was of equal importance to Hofstadter. See Leo Lowenthal and Norbert Guterman, *Prophets of Deceit* (New York: Harper, 1949); Theodor W. Adorno et al., *The Authoritarian Personality* (New York: Harper, 1950).

[35] Brown, *Richard* Hofstadter, 91.
[36] Christopher Lasch, *The True and Only Heaven: Progress and Its Critics* (New York: W.W. Norton, 1991), 456.
[37] Hofstadter, *Anti-Intellectualism in American Life*, 83.
[38] Ibid., 82.

publicity and conspiratorial tendencies could be traced back to the late nineteenth-century populists, who underwent a similar status revolution. It was this "dark side" of populism that for Hofstadter "foreshadow[ed] some aspects of the cranky pseudoconservatism of our time."[39]

In 1956, one year after *The Age of Reform* was published, Hofstadter and other "pluralists" – those who considered both the Communist left and the anti-Communist right as part of a longer tradition of irrational populism in American history – gathered their criticisms of economism in a collection of essays named *The New American Right*. Edited by Daniel Bell, the volume was indebted to prior meetings of Columbia's "Seminar on the State" and became a classic in far-right studies. As Bell noted in an introduction to the 1964 edition, the "idea for the original edition of this volume" arose in 1954 in "a faculty seminar on political behavior, at Columbia University," where participants there agreed that "standard explanations of American political behavior in terms of economic-interest-group conflict or the role of the electoral structure were inadequate to the task."[40] Instead, the Weberian devices deployed by Hofstadter, conceived from a "historian's vantage point," seemed more useful. In a strict sense, only two contributions to the book explicitly drew a connection between late nineteenth-century American populism and McCarthyism – the chapters written by Richard Hofstadter and Peter Viereck on "pseudo-conservatism" and "unadjusted men."[41] "When real economic-interest-group issues were lacking," Hofstadter claimed, "a psychological or status dimension" informed calls for direct participation and anti-bureaucratic sensibilities and a "peculiar scramble for status" and "peculiar search for secure identity."[42] "This outburst of direct democracy," Viereck noted, "comes straight from the leftist rhetoric of the old populists." That these anxieties flared up in an "age of affluence" was also no surprise. As Hofstadter put it in his essay, in a United States "where physical needs have on the whole been met," "the luxury of questing after status has assumed an unusually prominent place in our civic consciousness." Both McCarthyism and populism obeyed this status logic, albeit in separate epochs and with different demands. This status mentality also informed a particular

---

[39] Hofstadter, "The Pseudo-Conservative Revolt," 19.
[40] Daniel Bell, ed. *The Radical Right: The New American Right: Expanded and Updated*, ed. Daniel Bell (New York: Anchor, 1963), xi.
[41] Peter Viereck, "The Revolt against the Elite," in *The New American Right*, ed. Daniel Bell (New York: Anchor, 1955), 91–116.
[42] Richard Hofstadter, "The Pseudo-Conservative Revolt – 1955," in *The Radical Right: The New American Right: Expanded and Updated*, ed. Daniel Bell (New York: Anchor, 1963), 69.

ideology, in which impediments to direct expressions of the people's will would be swept away for the plebiscitary process. Executives and legislatures were thus considered as more authentic expressions of popular power than the parties or associations that made possible rotation into an administrative apparatus.

Hofstadter's theory of populism was only a pitched version of a far more general theme in the 1950s.[43] In political science and political sociology, writers such as David Merton and Robert Dahl had applied the "populist" label to Jefferson and Paine, emphasizing their plebiscitary sympathies.[44] Political scientist Victor Ferkiss, in turn, claimed to have found a direct link between American populism and the fascism of the 1930s.[45] In their "hatred of social democracy and socialism, the belief that representative democracy is a mask for rule by a predatory economic plutocracy" and their "peculiar interpretation of history which sees in events a working-out of a dialectic which opposes the financier and the producer," Ferkiss claimed, fascists and populists neatly joined hands.[46] The most sophisticated version of this thesis, however, came from University of Chicago sociologist Edward Shils. Shils had been a colleague of Bell's at Chicago before the latter moved to Columbia in the early 1950s. He had also been close to the New York Intellectuals in the 1930s, variously described as both at "a distance" from and a "cousin" by Bell.[47] Their intellectual affinity was clear, however, and they shared a suspicion of populism. Shils first presented his argument about populism at a University of Chicago conference on "Populism and the Rule of Law," which was attended by Dahl and Lipset.[48] The architecture for Shils's argument, however, was set in the 1930s, when he explored Weber's "views about charismatic authority over and over again," though he only saw "their potentials for extension ... about twenty-five years later."[49]

---

[43] Richard Pells, *The Liberal Mind in a Conservative Age: American Intellectuals in the 1940s and 1950s* (New York: Wesleyan University Press, 1989), 151–154.

[44] See Robert W. Dahl, *Who Governs? Democracy and Power in an American City* (New Haven, CT: Yale University Press, 1966).

[45] See Victor Ferkiss, "Populist Influences on American Fascism," *The Western Political Quarterly* 10, no. 2 (June 1957), 367; Victor Ferkiss, "Ezra Pound and American Fascism," *The Journal of Politics* 17, no. 2 (May 1955), 174–195; William P. Tucker, "Ezra Pound, Fascism, and Populism," *The Journal of Politics* 18, no. 1 (February 1956), 105–107; Paul Holbo, "Wheat or What? Populism and American Fascism," *The Western Political Quarterly* 14, no. 3 (September 1961), 727–735.

[46] Ferkiss, "Populist Influences," 367.

[47] Nei l Jumonville, *Critical Crossings: The New York Intellectuals in Postwar America* (Oakland: University of California Press, 1991), 267.

[48] Edward Shils, "Populism and the Rule of Law," *University of Chicago Law School Conference on Jurisprudence and Politics*, April 1954, 97–107.

[49] Edward Shils, *The Constitution of Society* (Chicago: University of Chicago Press, 1982), xviii.

The Demonology of the Cold War Right 215

Shils's notion of populism was both more conceptually specific and empirically flexible than Hofstadter and Bell's. In his 1956 *The Torment of Secrecy*, he detected traces of a "populist" mentality in both communism and fascism. But Shils's populists also shared a specifically anti-bureaucratic philosophy. They emphasized the importance of direct plebiscites for popular power and were hostile to mediators placed between individuals and the state. Populism, Shils claimed, "inclines towards a conception of the legislative branch which may be designated as 'identity' in contrast with 'representation.'"[50] In this view, legislators were expected to be "identical" with the popular will rather than "representatives" who would interpret that will and enact it in modified form.[51] Populists thus were "impatient [with] institutional procedures" and hostile to "checks and balances." Crucially, the historical reaches of this attitude were not always clear, with Shils affirming that his was a populism "not just ... in the specific historical meaning, although that was an instance of the species."[52]

Shils thereby enlarged the scope of Hofstadter's concept while finessing its outlines. He retained the emphasis on "status" and the diffuse class bases of populism but offered a larger argument about populism's hostility to intermediary bodies. In 1959, Hofstadter integrated these theses in a memo for the Ford Foundation on the dangers of the contemporary extreme right. Shils, he claimed, had "pointed out how much the recent concern with secrecy and the opposition to secret covenants ... has in common with the old populistic suspicion of everything that was not immediately accessible to the public eye."[53] He connected this attitude to the "pseudo-conservatism" of the New Right, which had traded its veneration of tradition for a facile plebeian ethos. Lipset followed up on this judgement in the 1960 edition of *Political Man*, updating the status analysis offered in *The New Radical Right*. Lipset now cast populism as "antiparliamentary," suspicious of parties, and again inimical to checks and balances – populists, he claimed, showed a "strong distrust of parliamentary or constitutional democracy," were "particularly antagonistic to the concept of party," and tried to "create as much direct democracy as possible."[54] Bell then

---

[50] Edward Shils, *The Torment of Secrecy: The Background and Consequences of American Security Policies* (Chicago: University of Chicago Press, 1956), 102.
[51] Ibid., 102.
[52] Ibid., 103.
[53] See Richard Hofstadter, "*The Contemporary Extreme Right Wing in the United States*," 81, Box 24, Richard Hofstadter Papers, Rare Book and Manuscript Library, Columbia University Library, New York, New York.
[54] Seymour Martin Lipset, *Political Man: The Social Bases of Politics* (New York: Doubleday and Company, 1960), 136.

inserted a paragraph on the effects of populism on American statecraft in his 1960 *The End of Ideology*, claiming that populism "vehemently denied" that "some are more qualified than others" and that the state should invade private opinion.[55] Both Lipset and Bell also spoke of populist politics as a phenomenon that existed outside of the United States, with figures such as Poujade, Hitler, and Mussolini now all qualifying for the label. By 1963, books such as Kornhauser's *The Politics of Mass Society*, Lipset's *Political Man*, Shils's *The Torment of Secrecy*, and of course Hofstadter's *Anti-Intellectualism* expressed the contours of a revisionist thesis that steadily pushed into public commentary.

Opposition to Hofstadter's thesis almost immediately took off within the field of American history. Although John Hicks had initially celebrated Hofstadter's achievements, he later castigated his performance as a caricature and claimed Hofstadter's base in New York made him unfit as a commentator; "his background," Hicks wrote to a student, was "quite inadequate for any reasonable understanding of Populism."[56] The most elaborate response, though, came from Hofstadter's confidants, such as C. Vann Woodward, who pushed back against his reading in a series of personal essays and letters. Woodward's acquaintance with the populist question went back decades. His first book, which was based on his dissertation, was released in 1938 and was a biography of the Georgia populist Thomas E. Watson, while his 1951 book on the New South emphasized the key role taken up by populism in the years from 1880 to 1910.[57] Both books also spoke about the "hopeful contingency" of the populist cause.[58] In the case of Watson, it centered on the biracial "marriage of convenience" initiated by Southern populists in the early 1890s, in which agrarian radicals rallied black sharecroppers and white yeomen to fight an incipient Jim Crow. In the case of the New South, Woodward emphasized the "forgotten alternatives" offered by Populism in the transitional atmosphere of the 1880s, a judgment he strengthened in his 1955 classic, *The Strange Career of Jim Crow*.

---

[55] Daniel Bell, *The End of Ideology: On the Exhaustion of Political Ideas in the Fifties* (Cambridge, MA: Harvard University Press, 1988 [1960]), 144.

[56] John Hicks, "Politics in Pattern," *Saturday Review* (October 22, 1955), 12; Jon Lauck, *The Lost Region: Toward a Revival of Midwestern History* (Des Moines: University of Iowa Press, 2013), 57.

[57] See C. Vann Woodward, *Origins of the New South, 1877–1913* (Baton Rouge: LSU Press, 1951); C. Vann Woodward, *Tom Watson: Agrarian Rebel* (New York: Martino Fine Books, 1938); J. Morgan Kousser et al., *Region, Race, and Reconstruction: Essays in Honor of C. Vann Woodward* (London: Oxford University Press, 1982), 455–456.

[58] Robert C. McMath, "C. Vann Woodward and the Burden of Southern Populism," *The Journal of Southern History* 67, no. 4 (November 2001), 741–768.

In his scholarship, Woodward had drawn on sociological tools similar to those later employed by Hofstadter in his work on the New Right. For instance, Woodward deployed the "status" concept to explain the changing coalitions that the South's lower classes entered in the 1890s, finessing the psychological arguments first made in his biography of Watson.[59] Woodward's disagreements with Hofstadter were thus not prima facie methodological. Rather, he parted ways with Hofstadter's mobilization of psychohistorical concepts to explain the populist episode, insisting that these strained the evidence. Woodward was especially concerned with the roots of populist protest and how these expressed themselves on the level of ideology. "I wonder," Woodward contended in a 1959 letter to Hofstadter discussing his earlier work and the theses of *The Radical Right*

> about the usefulness of retaining either "Populism" or "populism" as the designation of what we are talking about. ... Isn't what we are talking about in the case of "small-p" populism the ancient fallacies of the democratic dogma, its tendency to glorify the masses, to bow before the majority, to minimize the importance of liberty, to give short shrift to minorities, to undervalue excellence, to override dissent, to sacrifice everything (including reality) for the sake of unanimity. What you call aptly called "the utopian diffusion of social decision."[60]

Two facets of the revisionist thesis proved particularly vulnerable to attack. The first concerned McCarthy's status as an heir to a nominal "populist" tradition as well as McCarthyism's relationship to a rural support base. Counter-revisionists responded to this charge by pushing back against the Southern focus of the pluralists and contesting McCarthy's presumed status as a "grass roots" militant. The second concerned the ideology of the original populists. As the 1960s progressed, a growing body of scholarship began to show that Populism's economic grievances were not merely rhetorical. Finally, counter-revisionists rejected the opposition to intermediary bodies that Shils had posited in 1956.[61]

Crucially, there was an ethnic inflection to the controversy over populism. Except for Shils, writers such as Bell, Lipset, and Hofstadter had all passed through a youthful Trotskyism in the 1930s; furthermore, all were Jewish and hailed from urban settings. As this suggests, most

---

[59] Woodward, *Tom Watson*, 101–105.
[60] C. Vann Woodward, "125: Letter to Hofstadter," in *The Letters of C. Vann Woodward*, ed. Michael O'Brien (New Haven, CT: Yale University Press, 2012), 197–198.
[61] Christopher Lasch's own 1967 *The New Radicalism* already diagnoses this predicament in Hofstadter's generation. Christopher Lasch, *The New Radicalism in America, 1889–1963: The Intellectual as a Social Type* (New York: Vintage, 1965).

revisionists shared a background in a Jewish-inflected urban radicalism, with memories of the show trials and enmity between socialists and communists fresh in their minds. Although none of them comfortably fit within the category of "Cold War liberalism" and most were skeptics of modernization theory, their political sympathies were acutely antipopulist. The Great Depression, the rise of Nazism, and the horrors of World War II left Hofstadter's generation with an acute sense of the limits of reform.[62] By contrast, most of the counter-revisionists – save for Norman Pollack, who was Jewish – shared Southern and Midwestern backgrounds.

As Bell put it, the pluralists had a "particularly Jewish fear" of "mass action" and "passions let loose."[63] While this urban–rural divide never totally defined the debate, it clearly articulated two different political traditions: the insurgent, petty bourgeois radicalism of the Midwest and South faced a liberal and urban "organized capitalism" that accepted the reality of corporate rule and large-scale industry. For their part, counter-revisionists did little to dispel this frame. Hicks mentioned Hofstadter's New York background, while Merle Curti – a former teacher of Hofstadter's – considered *The Age of Reform* "biased by [Hofstadter's] urban background," much like the "rural background and traditional agrarian sympathies" of a previous generation of historians had clouded judgment.[64]

Despite its success, over time Hofstadter came to doubt his thesis and even made a public retraction at a 1967 conference at the London School of Economics. Organized by Ernest Gellner and Ghiță Ionescu, the conference featured a number of prominent thinkers, with Isaiah Berlin, Leonard Schapiro, and Hofstadter all adorning the list of speakers.[65] Papers on the topic of "populism" were distributed beforehand. Chairman Schapiro presented the conference's task as "a work of instant research."[66] After having delegated tasks to all attendants, Schapiro proposed three questions that were to serve as guidelines for discussions:

---

[62] See Daniel Bessner and Nicolas Guilhot, "Introduction: Who Decides?" in *The Decisionist Imagination: Sovereignty, Social Science, and Democracy in the Twentieth Century*, ed. Daniel Bessner and Nicolas Guilhot (New York: Berghahn, 2019), 1–25.

[63] Howard Brick, *Daniel Bell and the Decline of Intellectual Radicalism: Social Theory and Political Reconciliation in the 1940s* (Madison: University of Wisconsin Press, 1986).

[64] Jon Lauck, *The Lost Region: Toward a Revival of Midwestern History* (Des Moines: University of Iowa Press, 2013), 57.

[65] Peter Worsley, "The Concept of Populism," in *Populism: Its Meaning and National Characteristics*, ed. Ernest Gellner and Ghiţa Ionescu (New York: Macmillan, 1969), 212–250; London School of Economics: Conference on Populism, May 20–21, 1967: Verbatim Report, http://eprints.lse.ac.uk/102463/1/Conference_on_Populism_1967_Report_0001.pdf.

[66] Ibid., 3.

"What is and what is not populist ideology?"; "Why is populism a political movement and yet does it not usually crystallize in political parties?; and, finally, "What are the differences between the populism of before the World War I and after the World War II?".[67]

The conference's proceedings were fraught. From the outset, participants were divided into two camps that centered on how each understood the terms "populism" and "populist." One side, termed "localists" by one of the conveners, the social scientist Peter Worsley, adhered to a particularistic reading that insisted populism was an ideology that pertained to specific movements that could not be grouped under one coherent rubric.[68] Localists stood in opposition to a group Worsley named "universalists."[69] Heavily influenced by recent studies in modernization theory, the universalists cast populism as the ideology of regimes in transition that, first, did not live up to classical patterns of social change and, second, had "failed" to integrate their masses into civil society.

Hofstadter himself was slightly dazzled by the wide range of movements currently discussed under the rubric of "populism." He opened his plenary remarks by stating that he expected a conference discussing only two types, either a Russian populism or an American populism. Responding to earlier critiques of his work on McCarthyism, he now conceded that the "genetic affiliation" of McCarthyism to "earlier agrarian movements" was "doubtless miscarried."[70] Even if McCarthy and other embodiments of the "paranoid style" did "twang these populist strings," they no longer qualified as substantial "populists," sharing only an ancillary connection to the original populism.[71] This was a remarkable retreat from the position Hofstadter had espoused in 1955. Still, Hofstadter insisted on the persistence of "small-p populist" themes in U.S. history, claiming that certain "populist" leaders within the Civil Rights Movement drew on the "serious trauma about identity" experienced by the African American population, something he personally had seen at work when marching on Selma two years prior.[72] Beyond this, Hofstader also urged a more local focus on other participants, who all seemed on the lookout for more general frames.

Gellner and Ionescu's conference was met with responses from Americans. One of these came from Theodore Saloutos, who had collaborated with John Hicks in the 1950s and launched some of the first

[67] Ibid., 3–4.
[68] Ibid., 28.
[69] Ibid.
[70] Ibid., 60.
[71] Ibid., 60–61.
[72] Ibid., 61.

counter-revisionist attacks in the 1960s. In a 1970 review of the conference, Saloutos deemed its results wholly unsuitable for academic inquiry. "Why two editors," he wondered, "should attempt anything as sweeping and premature as this study defies explanation."[73] He decried "[t]he inability of the writers to come up with any acceptable definition of populism," which "simply confounds the reader." What remained, according to Saloutos, was a "maze of phraseologies" that emerged from an unwillingness to do "the necessary empirical digging."[74] Although the idea behind the book "had merit," Saloutos determined that:

> [the] limited and superficial treatment given to sweeping topics hardly does justice to them, the collaborators, and the publishers. The term "populism" is misused and abused, in the opinion of the reviewer; setting up a qualified definition of it would have given the volume a sense of cohesion. But as it now stands it lacks focus, it is amorphous and cluttered with a mass of undigested data that prompt one to label it a serious mistake. And even this is a charitable evaluation.[75]

This sense of confusion was only amplified, Saloutos noted, by Hofstadter's own contribution to the volume. Instead of defending his erstwhile position on populism, he had reverted to a more classical, Hicksian reading of the populists as hard-nosed reformists. "Those who know his analysis of populism in *The Age of Reform*," Saloutos stated, "probably will be baffled by his presentation, for it is a reversion to a more traditional approach." "Why such a shift," he finished, "is not clear. Certainly it was not one of convenience."[76]

The Problem with Hofstadter

Though Hofstadter retracted most of his theses on populism near the end of his life, the impact of his theorization of the American Right was significant. Hofstadter wrote over a dozen pieces on the postwar far right from the early 1950s onward, focusing more on the historical roots of the "paranoid style" than on the particular tactics of postwar conservatism's leading lights, the novelty of its discourse, its organizational forms, or its propaganda strategy. In retrospect, Hofstadter's psychosocial analysis of the New Right neglected the novelty of the New Right's political entrepreneurs, who combined old-school oratory

---

[73] Theodore Saloutos, review of *Populism: Its Meaning and National Characteristics*, by Ghita Ionescu and Ernest Gellner, *Technology and Culture* 11, no. 2 (April 1970), 326–328.
[74] Ibid., 328.
[75] Ibid, 329.
[76] Ibid.

and mass media wizardry to construct a new type of political movement. By focusing excessively on the inscrutable psychological motivations animating support for New Right organizations and leaders like the Birch Society and Senator Joseph McCarthy during the 1950s and 1960s, Hofstadter failed to account for the top-down, elite-driven processes by which New Right ideologues spread their message and mobilized the right-wing revolt against New Deal liberalism.

A recent generation of historians has analyzed the variety of right-wing broadcasters, book publishers, and political entrepreneurs who propagated their anti-communist brand of "Americanism" to the masses, throwing the psychosocial limits of Hofstadter's analytical approach to the study of the Right into sharp relief.[77] The right-wing ideology that Hofstadter called "pseudo-conservatism" did not appear spontaneously as a mechanistic response to the Cold War and the rumblings of progressive social change among white Americans in the 1950s and 1960s. Instead, that "paranoid" worldview was fashioned and marketed by men and women who spent their lives acting on their fervent belief that the United States was urgently threatened by Communism, internationalism, socialism, and liberalism. The postwar decades witnessed the emergence and consolidation of right-wing activist networks, whose membership spent its time and money subscribing to rightist publications, attending conservative conferences, supporting political groups, and voting for conservative candidates and third parties. Groups such as the John Birch Society and the Liberty Lobby were formed by people such as Robert Welch and Willis Carto, who operated within these networks and leveraged their connections with other activists to raise funds, pay writers for contributions, and build sizable audiences for conservative publications. These and dozens of other rightist groups, though frequently divided by intra-ideological battles, formed part of an unconsciously coherent ideological campaign to publish and propagate right-wing media purporting to reveal the nature of a leftist-liberal conspiracy to destroy America.

Thus, contrary to popular assumptions about manipulative demagogues preying on the downwardly mobile, the radical right's leaders

---

[77] Paul Matzko, *The Radio Right: How a Band of Broadcasters Took on The Federal Government and Built The Modern Conservative Movement* (Oxford: Oxford University Press, 2020); Heather Hendershot, *What's Fair on the Air: Cold War Right-Wing Broadcasting and the Public Interest* (Chicago: University of Chicago Press, 2011); Nicole Hemmer, *Messengers of the Right: Conservative Media and the Transformation of American Politics* (Philadelphia: University of Pennsylvania Press, 2016); Geoffrey Kabaservice, *Rule and Ruin: The Downfall of Moderation and the Destruction of the Republican Party, from Eisenhower to the Tea Party* (Oxford: Oxford University Press, 2012).

were sophisticated operators who built complex political institutions committed to the elaboration and propagation of a distinctly American version of conservatism. *Contra* Hofstadter, then, the postwar conservative movement was more than a reactionary backlash against modernization; it was a complex social and political formation whose supporters were solidly middle-class, educated, and well-integrated into activist communities. Indeed, right-wing movement leaders embodied a new type of political elite composed of people who simultaneously set ideological frames, spread these into people's homes and mailboxes, and served as social movement leaders for dispersed followers.

The fundamental flaw of Hofstadter's approach to the right was that he sought to understand "why do people believe these things?" instead of "how did they come to believe them?" While Hofstadter was correct to observe that elements of the "Pseudo-Conservative Revolt" reflected long-standing American political traditions of nativism, religious fundamentalism, and a conspiratorial fear of foreign ideologies and ideologisms, he was writing at a historical moment in which it was impossible to appreciate that the "pseudo-conservatives" he criticized were the first of multiple generations of "New Right" ideological entrepreneurs, each of which used mass media to mobilize, and radicalize, the millions of Americans who constituted the conservative movement. By focusing on the genealogy of the populist and conspiracist elements of right-wing rhetoric instead of the media in which it was imbued, Hofstadter missed a crucial point that was famously expressed by one of his contemporaries: the medium is the message.

In retrospect, Hofstadter's short-sighted commitment to developing a psychoanalytically inflected mode of historical explanation and political analysis is made painfully clear in his 1954 essay on pseudo-conservatism. Explicitly citing Adorno's *Authoritarian Personality*, Hofstadter argued that the "political reactions [of radical rightists] express ... a profound if largely unconscious hatred of our society and its ways – a hatred which one would hesitate to impute to them if one did not have suggestive clinical evidence."[78] More than seventy years later, it is clear that Hofstadter's commitment to psychoanalysis limited his ability to explain the rise of the radical right.

Nevertheless, these deficiencies did not limit the impact of Hofstadter's arguments because the historian's approach mapped onto a liberal self-image that lionized the controlled partisanship supposedly inherent to liberal capitalist democracy. According to Hofstadter and fellow travelers, the "organized capitalism" of the postwar years

---

[78] Hofstadter, "The Pseudo-Conservative Revolt," 10.

suggested that the New Deal order was robust and that its enemies were nostalgic and atavistic free marketeers who sought a return to an obsolete laissez-faire world. Ironically, such perspectives had the consequence of strengthening a sense of complacency in the face of the New Right of the 1960s and 1970s, which liberals too often cast as a rearguard resistance against modernization rather than as the assertive political force it actually was.

Hofstadter as Cold War Liberal

Richard Hofstadter's status as a leading Cold War liberal is hard to question. Few, if any, of the other New York intellectuals of the postwar era are still cited as frequently as he is. Unlike peers like Daniel Bell, who developed different interests and turned toward neoconservatism later in life, Hofstadter's early death in 1970 means that his prolific body of work as a scholar and public intellectual in the 1950s and 1960s is frozen in amber. In particular, his writings reflect the concerns of Cold War liberalism, especially the conviction that the two-party system is a stabilizing force in American politics, which implicitly rests on a substantive distinction between "legitimate" conservatism and "illegitimate" far-right populism and extremism. Hofstadter's significant influence on the study of the radical right, in fact, is clearly displayed in the continued salience – and assumed negative valence – of concepts such as "populism" and "extremism." For the past seventy years, Hofstadter's ideas have played a key role in constructing the notion of a vital center flanked on both sides by bigots, revolutionaries, populists, and cranks. It is only with the benefit of hindsight that historians can appreciate the problems with his approach and begin to move out of Hofstadter's long shadow.

11 Conservatives in a "Liberal Age"
Rethinking the Neoconservative Turn in the 1960s

Michael Brenes and Michael Franczak

In 1981, according to *The Boston Globe*, Eugene V. Rostow – former Yale Law School dean, Johnson Administration official, and brother to Walt, the "father of modernization theory" – was the leading face of a second Cold War. *The New Yorker* had just published a sweeping expose of the Committee on the Present Danger (CPD) and now the *Globe* wanted its turn. As both outlets reported, the CPD, consisting mostly of national security officials with deep ties to the Democratic Party, advocated nuclear rearmament to confront "the Soviet drive for dominance based upon unparalleled military buildup." What concerned *The New Yorker*, however, was that thirteen of the CPD's members had just been nominated to foreign policy posts in the Ronald Reagan administration. Just six years earlier, Rostow helped form and lead the Coalition of the Democratic Majority (CDM). Initially focused on the Democratic Party's domestic platform, the CDM retooled in the mid-1970s to highlight the "drift toward military vulnerability and political timidity in which the nation seems to be caught up" during the years of Gerald Ford and Jimmy Carter. By the end of the decade, old Cold War liberals like Rostow found a new home in the Republican Party of Ronald Reagan. Rostow was soon to be appointed Director of the Arms Control and Disarmament Agency – "the proverbial fox in the henhouse," according to the *Globe* – where he would be one of many self-identified Democrats (or "neoconservatives") shaping Reagan's aggressively anti-communist foreign policy.[1]

---

[1] "Their Mission is to Keep Strength on the Barricades," *Boston Globe* (April 28, 1981), Committee on the Present Danger Records, Box 198, Folder 5, Hoover Institution on War, Revolution, and Peace, Stanford, California; Richard J. Barnet, "The Search for National Security," *The New Yorker* (April 27, 1981), pp. 50–140; "For an Adequate Defense," The Second Statement by the Foreign Policy Task Force of the Coalition for a Democratic Majority, Box 8, folder "Coalition for a Democratic Majority – Defense Policy Statement," John Marsh Files, Gerald R. Ford Presidential Library, Ann Arbor, MI, www.fordlibrarymuseum.gov/library/document/0067/1562863.pdf.

Rostow's political shift is seen as part of a "neoconservative turn" that Cold War liberals underwent in the 1970s, one that contributed to the rightward shift in American politics. Neoconservatism – a self-adopted label embraced by Cold War liberals to distinguish their politics from "New Politics" liberals in the Democratic Party – is thus seen as a coherent movement and ideology born in the 1970s, and that triumphed in the 1980s. This conclusion, we argue, reaffirms neoconservatives' own teleological arc without critique – that neoconservatives floundered in the political wilderness during the 1970s, only to become architects of Reagan's foreign policy in the 1980s. Historians who promulgate this narrative have implicitly adopted the self-fulfilling and retrospective flatteries offered by neoconservatives about themselves: that they, and their ideas, were unfairly ostracized in the 1960s only to be vindicated by Ronald Reagan's election and proven correct by the conservative "backlash" of the 1980s. They see Cold War liberalism dying with the growth of the New Right, only to be reincarnated in the offices of Reagan's Pentagon.[2]

But Cold War liberals were never exiling in American politics. This essay argues that Cold War liberals remained influential in the 1970s because of the networks they created in the 1950s and 1960s when they were associated with the Democratic Party. Cold War liberals did not become neoconservatives; rather, changes to American politics in the 1970s led Cold War liberals to create institutions and intellectual outlets that transformed their influence in American politics when Cold War liberalism fell out of favor with the American public. This transformation led them to adopt "neoconservatism" as a label for their ideology, but without rejecting liberalism.

The institutions that enabled this transformation took two forms: Literary and political. Cold War liberals worked within groups like the Democratic National Committee and the Democratic Advisory Council (DAC) to amass a political coalition of Democrats disaffected by the antiwar, left-wing shift in the Party. In terms of literature, two journals were particularly important for translating neoconservative thought into power during this time: *Commentary* and *The Public Interest*. Both venues shared contributors who felt ostracized from the Democratic Party. While *The Public Interest* was concerned with domestic social policy, by the early 1970s *Commentary* had dedicated itself full-time to criticizing

---

[2] See Justin Vaïsse, *Neoconservatism: The Biography of a Movement* (Cambridge, MA: Harvard University Press, 2010); John Ehrman, *The Rise of Neoconservatism: Intellectuals and Foreign Affairs, 1945–1994* (New Haven, CT: Yale University Press, 1995); Peter Steinfels, *The Neoconservatives: The Origins of a Movement: From Dissident to Political Power* (New York: Simon and Schuster, 1979).

U.S. foreign policy, particularly toward the "Third World." These outlets, in their aggregate, became the foundation for the mobilization of peoples and ideas to reinvigorate Cold War liberalism after the Vietnam War, a project that led Cold War liberals to form lasting alliances with conservatives.[3]

Why did this happen? Why did liberals become neoconservatives – if in name only? Rather than asking why Cold War liberals shifted to the right, as scholars have done in the past, the better question (for us) is why Cold War liberals accommodated the rightward shift so well – and so quickly. Cold War liberals transitioned to neoconservatism because of the a priori, conservative attributes of Cold War liberalism. By the 1970s, Cold War liberals felt "left behind." But they did not eschew their ideology; they did not "become conservatives."[4]

Instead, the explanation for Cold War liberals' shift to neoconservatism lies in the definition of Cold War liberalism itself, one offered at the beginning of this volume.[5] From our perspective, Cold War liberalism was a set of ideas and beliefs premised on fear of enemies abroad and at home, one that combined with an overarching, systemic fear of disorder. These collective fears manifested in a campaign for political consensus to support the U. S. position of global hegemony, one erected on a trans-partisan faith in American military power and reinforced by unprecedented American wealth. Indeed, it wasn't the radicalism of the 1960s that made neoconservatives, but preexisting conservative ideas embedded in Cold War liberalism – above all a preoccupation with national security and national defense as the basis of a healthy nation.

Cold War liberalism, in our view, was a conservative political project. It was an effort to revive political order amidst global uncertainty, to maintain American military and economic predominance, and to promote a national purpose premised upon unrivaled U.S. power. We examine this thesis through the lives and careers of a few Cold War liberals turned neoconservatives: Irving Kristol (cofounder of *The Public Interest*), Charles Tyroler (the head of the Committee on Present

---

[3] Kim Phillips-Fein has argued that while conservatives have consistently seen "themselves as outsiders on the defensive, they were never the excluded figures they believed themselves to be." The same conclusion, we argue, applies to neoconservatives. See Kim Phillips-Fein, "Conservatism: A Round Table," *Journal of American History* 98, no. 3 (December 2011), 739.

[4] Our thesis contradicts the position by the "godfather" of neoconservatives, Irving Kristol, who argued that neoconservatives "modernized" the Republican Party and that the GOP rejected "isolationism" just as the Democrats embraced it – and that this was the reason that "dissident liberals" like himself switched to the Republican Party. Irving Kristol, *Neoconservatism: A Biography of an Idea* (Chicago: Ivan R. Dee, 1995), x–xi.

[5] Daniel Bessner, "Introduction," *Power in a Time of Emergency*.

Danger), Norman Podhoretz (the editor of *Commentary*), and Daniel Patrick Moynihan (adviser to presidents Lyndon Johnson and Richard Nixon). These men believed in the promise of American military power to further freedom and prosperity in the world. They feared a thaw in the Cold War, combined with a more left-leaning Democratic Party, imperiled American national security and the future of democratic principles. In responding to these fears, both real and imagined, they relied upon organizations and publications that propelled them to power and notoriety in the 1960s, institutions within and beyond the Democratic Party that conservatives effectively employed to further their power in the 1970s and beyond.

Unmaking the Cold War Consensus, 1956–1968

While (some) Cold War liberals became Republicans in the 1970s, up until 1968, Cold War liberals held a comfortable space within the Democratic Party. Many – like Arthur Schlesinger, Jr., Senator Henry Jackson, and Zbigniew Brzezinski – were registered Democrats since the 1930s. They were longstanding supporters of Franklin D. Roosevelt and the New Deal order and backed his wartime policies as well. Indeed, World War II enhanced liberal internationalism, a cornerstone of Cold War liberal thought. FDR created a wartime economy to eradicate unemployment, provide social mobility, and enhance economic and civil rights for disenfranchised Americans. When World War II virtually eradicated unemployment, liberals adopted a faith in wartime capitalism – in a "warfare state" – to further prosperity in both economic and social terms.[6] These policies and beliefs lay at the core of Cold War liberals' politics.

Until the late 1960s, the Democratic Party was therefore the best, and only, vehicle for Cold War liberals' political agenda. Democrats supported a welfare state organized around equal opportunity for all that was simultaneously premised on American military might be able to secure, and if necessary, vanquish, enemies abroad.[7] World War II enhanced the power and politics of Cold War liberals in the Democratic Party. The war furthered their racial liberalism and support for civil rights, causing the first fissures between Cold War liberals and Southern Democrats. At the Democratic National Convention in 1948, a young

---

[6] James Sparrow, *Warfare State: Americans in the Age of Big Government* (New York: Oxford University Press, 2011), Chapter 1.
[7] Jonathan Bell, *The Liberal State on Trial: The Cold War and American Politics in the Truman Years* (New York: Columbia University Press, 2004).

Hubert Humphrey pleaded "for the Democratic Party to get out of the shadow of states' rights and to walk forthrightly into the bright sunshine of human rights." Humphrey's speech represented the growing schisms within its ranks, with Cold War liberals prevailing on civil rights in the 1960s.[8] Prioritizing racial liberalism helped Cold War liberals purge the class-based politics of Popular Front, as it created a moral vision that united new coalitions of "civic officials, politicians, labor leaders, religious leaders, and industrialists" that marginalized the power of the left in a time of growing anti-communism.[9]

Cold War liberals' influence in the Democratic Party waned in the late 1960s due to the Vietnam War. Some Cold War liberals opposed the war, including Arthur Schlesinger, Jr., but could not escape the fact that their support for military primacy, for American dominance over communism, contributed to the war's origins. Liberals' faith in containment spurred an illegal war in Vietnam, claimed the antiwar left. The New Left thus posed the first sizeable threat to America's Cold War order, to the "fighting faith" of Cold War liberals.[10] Antiwar demonstrations and police violence at the 1968 Democratic National Convention in Chicago revealed the extent to which the "politics of consensus," that had its roots in New Deal liberalism, had come undone.[11] According to Cold War liberals like Humphrey, who witnessed the mass beatings and arrests in the Windy City as he awaited the Democratic nomination, the protests were the work of petulant demonstrators plagued with an immaturity of thought and an inchoate, visceral distrust of authority. "There are certain people in the United States who feel that all you have to do is riot and you can get your way. I have no time for that," said Humphrey.[12]

---

[8] Hubert H. Humphrey, 1948 Democratic National Convention Address, July 14, 1948, www.americanrhetoric.com/speeches/huberthumphey1948dnc.html. Cold War liberals rejected the Southern contours of the New Deal state but lauded the New Deal era because they felt that, however, imperfect the outcomes from government intervention on the social life of Americans, federal power provided protections to the most vulnerable against the most unfair, rapacious elements of American capitalism, and also ensured the civil rights of Black Americans. Only the Democrats could achieve these ends. Indeed, Cold War liberals who later became neoconservatives – like Jackson or Irving Kristol – were active contributors to the presidential campaigns of John Kennedy in 1960, Lyndon Johnson in 1964, and Hubert Humphrey in 1968. See Eric Schickler, *Racial Realignment: The Transformation of American Liberalism, 1932–1968* (Princeton: Princeton University Press, 2016), 224–236.

[9] Jennifer A. Delton, *Making Minnesota Liberal: Civil Rights and the Transformation of the Democratic Party* (Minneapolis: University of Minnesota Press, 2002), xxii and Chapter 8.

[10] Kevin Mattson, *When America Was Great: The Fighting Faith of Liberalism in Postwar America* (New York: Routledge, 2006), 108.

[11] Wendy Wall, *Inventing the "American Way": The Politics of Consensus from the New Deal to the Civil Rights Movement* (New York: Oxford University Press, 2008), 5–6.

[12] David Farber, *Chicago '68* (Chicago: University of Chicago Press, 1994), 206.

Cold War liberals saw the New Left as a threat to the body politic in 1968, but also felt that the antiwar, activist left represented a minority of voters, that it could be contained and defeated. Writing in *The New Republic* in defense of Hubert Humphrey, Irving Kristol castigated left-wing activists as ancillary and irrelevant to progress and contrary to the liberal ethos of most Americans. "Both Negro militants and student militants unquestionably voice real grievances in their constituencies," Kristol acceded. "On the other hand, the evidence is quite convincing that they do not really represent, in their ideological posture, the majority of even these constituencies." Giving the left further undue attention would only lend it false legitimacy when "the fact that the overwhelming majority of the American electorate is non-black, non-young, and non-poor," and held an animus toward the activists. The antiwar Left was sure to generate "a massive 'backlash'" that would undo their movement.[13]

Humphrey's defeat at the hands of Richard Nixon shook Cold War liberals like Kristol. But Nixon's win in 1968 caused less of a concern to Cold War liberals than a left-wing takeover of the Democratic Party. Dejected by Humphrey's loss, Cold War liberals feared for the fate of their party and their country – and began to organize. To do so, they relied upon institutions and structures erected by the Democratic Party since the 1950s. Many of these institutions were created by reform-minded liberals after World War II. Liberal Democrats like Humphrey, who sought to escape the Democrats' racist path by mobilizing the Party's base out of the South in the 1950s (and push it toward civil rights reform), formed organizations in the 1960s to ensure that Cold War liberalism found a place in the party's vanguard after 1968. Organizations that liberals founded in the 1950s to push the party leftward were remade in the 1960s in ways that sought to move the Party to the right, particularly on foreign policy.

Among the most prominent of these organizations was the DAC. Headed by Paul Butler, a pro-civil rights reformist liberal from Indiana, the DAC operated with an ethos like that by embraced groups like the Americans for Democratic Action (ADA), which pushed for issues-based transformation of the party that would make it a national force rather than an appendage of Southern politics and Jim Crow backwardness. But in contrast to the ADA, which remained small and "was really just a whipping boy" during the Eisenhower years, the DAC had numbers. Indeed, it proved able to gather voices from the Northern

---

[13] Irving Kristol, "Why I am for Humphrey," *The New Republic* (June 8, 1968), https://newrepublic.com/article/69463/why-i-am-humphrey

and mid-Western wings of the party, which provided a powerful bloc against the party's Southern base. The DAC was an outgrowth of the "Finletter Group," an ad hoc organization formed by Cold War liberals, which included Kenneth Galbraith, Leon Keyserling, Arthur Schlesinger, Jr., and Paul Nitze, that sought to advise presidential candidate Adlai Stevenson in his renewed bid for the presidency in 1956. The Finletter group pressured Eisenhower to adopt a hard-line foreign policy, but also domestic policies that made social democrats envious: Full employment, universal health care, and civil rights for Black Americans. In the words of historian Sam Rosenfeld, the Finletter group conveyed "a coherent articulation of Cold War liberal orthodoxy – hawkish and internationalist, aggressively Keynesian, and committed to enhancing New Deal vintage activism in labor relations, health care, social insurance, and agriculture." By the time the Finletter group was disbanded in 1956, Butler was appointed chairman of the DAC, only a year after he became the head of the Democratic National Committee (DNC). The DNC at that time held little sway over the party's nominating process and policy platforms, but Butler thought it was able to help organize Cold War liberals after Stevenson lost to Eisenhower again in 1956.[14]

Enter Charles Tyroler II, a lesser-known Democratic operative and former campaign manager for 1956 vice presidential candidate Estes Kefauver (D-TN), who became the DAC's executive director that year. Like Butler, Tyroler viewed the DAC as a vehicle for the "liberal, national oriented wing of the party." Under Tyroler and Butler, the DAC became an unofficial think tank operating adjacent to the DNC. The DAC collected a rolodex of sympathetic names that would help in "issuing policy statements," its main function during its lifespan. Their mission worked. The DAC garnered attention from leading Democrats throughout the 1950s, including senator-turned presidential candidate John F. Kennedy. DAC sent Kennedy the twenty-page policy reports that made the DAC infamous in 1958. Less than two years later, the DAC could count Kennedy as a member. DAC leaders held repeated meetings with the soon-to-be presidential candidate, offering Kennedy policy advice during the 1960 primary.[15]

---

[14] On the DAC, see Sam Rosenfeld, *The Polarizers: Postwar Architects of Our Partisan Era* (Chicago: University of Chicago Press, 2018), 31–34; Schickler, *Racial Realignment*, 226–229; Tim Barker, "Arms against Austerity: Cold War Liberals and the Unbalanced Budget," unpublished paper in author's possession.

[15] Rosenfeld, *Polarizers*, 38; "The Democratic Advisory Council as Military Experts," *Congressional Record, United States Senate* (Washington, DC: Government Printing Office, 1959), 11027; "2 JOIN DEMOCRATIC UNIT: Party Advisory Council

Kennedy was most interested in U.S. foreign policy, an issue area well within the DAC's purview. Kennedy wanted policy ideas on how the United States could win the Cold War through military primacy but also find a way out of a nuclear stalemate with the Soviet Union. DAC circulated proposals to Kennedy for a "peace agency" that would find ways to escape from the Cold War in the long term. "Why didn't we devote money for peace when we were devoting so much for war," Tyroler said, recounting the genesis for the agency. "Simple idea." That idea took off, attracting support from the press and international community, and earning greater attention for the DAC. At the next meeting Tyroler held with Kennedy, the Senator wanted to make sure "his name was listed as a signer on the peace agency statement." It seemed that Tyroler and his ideas made a mark on Kennedy, who then toured the country on the campaign trail, making statements in support of a peace agency in states like New Hampshire. "But he [Kennedy] wanted to change the name of it," Tyroler remembered. "He thought the peace agency, it was too public relations-oriented type of thing." Kennedy floated the idea of naming "it arms control and disarmament," which eerily sounded like its eventual name: the Arms Control and Disarmament Agency.[16]

Tyroler's actions influenced the future president, but also offered a precedent for how liberal advisory groups could shape American politics while working independently from the White House. Before the DAC disbanded in 1961, Tyroler led an operation that provided a model for inter-party organizing and coalition building within the Democratic Party. Tyroler soon formed partnerships with the liberal-minded Democratic Study Group (DSG) and even partly financing, at times, the Democratic National Committee. Tyroler would go on to work for Kennedy's campaign, his administrative skills put to work on behalf of issues such as agriculture and civil rights.[17]

Throughout the 1960s, Tyroler would go on to serve several roles – party apparatchik, fundraiser, and networker – in Astroturf, innocuous sounding yet ambitiously named organizations such as the Citizens Committee for Peace with Freedom in Vietnam. Tyroler detested Lyndon Johnson in the 1950s; Tyroler became an advocate for the Vietnam War

Adds Kennedy and Symington," *New York Times* (November 12, 1959); Oral History of Charles Tyroler (1 of 2), John F. Kennedy Library, Boston, MA, www.jfklibrary.org/sites/default/files/archives/JFKOH/Tyroler%2C%20Charles%2C%20II/JFKOH-COT-01/JFKOH-COT-01-TR.pdf, pp. 1–3 and 13.

[16] Oral History of Charles Tyroler (1 of 2), pp. 1 and 4.
[17] Oral History of Charles Tyroler (2 of 2), John F. Kennedy Library, Boston, www.jfklibrary.org/sites/default/files/archives/JFKOH/Tyroler%2C%20Charles%2C%20II/JFKOH-COT-02/JFKOH-COT-02-TR.pdf, p. 33.

in the 1960s. As a figure behind the scenes, manipulating the machinations of Democratic Party electioneering, Tyroler gained valuable skills and impressive allies on behalf of America's mission in Vietnam. It was in 1967, as head of the Citizens Committee for Peace with Freedom in Vietnam, that Tyroler learned how efforts to revive Cold War adventurism could unite disaffected Democrats and Cold War liberals, who comprised the members of his organization.[18]

Tyroler would then go on to campaign for Humphrey in 1968. But in the wake of Humphrey's loss, groups founded with similar purposes, such as the DAC were born, taking similar three-word names. Like the Finletter group and the DAC, these organizations sought to diagnose the reasons for the Democrats' loss and offer an affirmative strategy for taking back the White House. Among the more well-known was the Democratic Policy Council (DPC). Created in September 1969 and led by Humphrey, many of the over seventy members of the DPC resisted the "New Politics" wing of the Party that aimed to reform the Party's nomination process and make the Party more inclusive of Blacks, women, and minorities left out of the delegation process. The New Politics constituency opposed the war in Vietnam and looked to move the Party away from establishment figures like Chicago Mayor Richard Daley and AFL-CIO leader George Meany – the Party bosses and labor leaders that controlled the Democratic machine.[19]

And like the DAC, the DPC sought to be an organization within a broader bureaucracy controlled by the DNC. The DPC aimed to be, like the DAC, a vehicle that could "determine the issues on which a [Democratic] candidate could run" for president.[20] But unlike the DAC, the DPC hoped to be ensconced in Democratic networks, aiming "to avoid the role of the DAC of the Eisenhower years, which spent most of its time proclaiming liberal doctrine and feuding with Democratic congressional leaders." Indeed, DNC chair Fred Harris authorized the creation of the DPC, after Humphrey convinced him to do so.[21] But the DPC soon descended into intraorganizational disputes, mainly over Vietnam. Humphrey looked to disassociate Cold War liberalism from Vietnam. Humphrey used the DPC to request a "firm

---

[18] "Private Group Lauds Vietnamization," *New York Times* (May 8, 1970); Jerry Wayne Sanders, *Peddlers of Crisis: The Committee on the Present Danger and the Politics of Containment* (Cambridge, MA: South End Press, 1983), 153.

[19] Bruce Miroff, *The Liberals' Moment: The McGovern Insurgency and the Identity Crisis of the Democratic Party* (Lawrence: University Press of Kansas, 2009), 23–24.

[20] Carl Solberg, *Hubert Humphrey: A Biography* (New York: W.W. Norton, 1984), 422.

[21] Richard Lowitt, *Fred Harris: His Journey from Liberalism to Populism* (Lanham, MD: Rowan and Littlefield, 2002), 94.

and unequivocal commitment to withdrawal" of remaining troops in Vietnam in 18 months." Humphrey wanted the economy, rather than Vietnam, to be the major issue for Democrats. The appeal fell flat. The DPC represented the split between the Cold War liberals of old and new, as some Cold War liberals, such as Arthur Schlesinger and John Kenneth Galbraith denounced the group's formation, claiming it was nothing less than an attempt to "harmonize the political elements of defeated establishment." Other Democrats said that Humphrey had "lost his clout" and was simply "out of touch"[22]

The DPC carried on in the 1970s, despite Humphrey's reputation. In 1971, it advocated to cut off U.S. funds to South Vietnam and to ensure the "complete federalization of the nation's welfare program over the next three years ... and the immediate enactment of a family assistance program that would provide for a minimum family income averaging about $4,000 a year."[23] But Humphrey's DPC also defended Nixon's emphasis on "law and order." Humphrey told his fellow liberals that they must let "the hard-hats, Mr. and Mrs. Middle America," know that they too condemn crime and riots and violence and extreme social turbulence, and that they scorn extremists of the left as well as the extremists of the right."[24] Humphrey remained at the helm of the DPC after getting reelected to the Senate in 1971, where he called for an end to the antiballistic missile program, and a quicker withdrawal from Vietnam, while not "urging cuts in the defense budget" anytime soon.[25]

The formation of groups like the DPC saved Cold War liberalism, keeping it alive for the 1970s. It helped Cold War liberals move on from Vietnam but retain support for American military predominance. Moreover, organizations such as the DAC, DPC, and ADA represented the institutional power of Cold War liberalism in the Democratic Party and became the locus for organizing elite liberals in the 1970s. The reformers of the Democratic Party in the 1950s became the conservatives of the 1960s; the revolutionaries who sought remake the Democratic Party now controlled an *ancien régime*. Such was the twisted fate that the liberal organizations which made the Democratic Party a vehicle for progressive reforms in the 1950s – on civil rights, full employment, and

---

[22] Solberg, *Hubert Humphrey*, 417; "Democrats Set Up Policy Unit; Humphrey Named Chairman," *New York Times* (September 17, 1969); "Liberals Attack Democratic Unit," *New York Times* (September 21, 1969); R. W. Apple, Jr., "Dilemma of Hubert Humphrey," *New York Times* (March 7, 1970)
[23] R. W. Apple, Jr., "Democratic Policy Council Asks Total Federalization of Welfare," *New York Times* (May 14, 1971).
[24] Solberg, *Hubert Humphrey*, 418.
[25] "Humphrey Urges Limit on Arms," *New York Times* (March 26, 1971).

health care – became agents of conservatism in the 1970s. Or maybe it was no twist of fate; maybe it was the natural course of events given that such social progress was always ancillary to a project of Cold War expansionism and military spending. For these were never on opposing terms; the DAC's success proved that foreign policy became the means to ensure a social democratic domestic policy. And so, it made sense that foreign policy became the operative issue to move Cold War liberals closer to power. Foreign policy issues became the basis for trans-party alliances between Cold War liberals and conservative Republicans as the United States headed into the 1970s.

The Intellectuals' Interest, 1965–1972

As liberals like Tyroler ensured the DAC provided the institutional and bureaucratic means for Cold War liberals to remain influential in the Democratic Party (and American politics overall), others turned their attention to the realm of ideas, creating the intellectual spaces where Cold War liberals' ideas gained traction in policymaking circles. When Irving Kristol and Daniel Bell launched *The Public Interest* in Fall 1965, the idea was to refine Cold War liberalism. Not yet the distinctly pro-business neoconservative he would evolve into, Kristol was at the time a self-described "skeptical liberal,"[26] who chastened at the "liberal ideas behind [the Great Society] and of the programs they spawned." Great Society liberalism, in Kristol's view, rejected the universalist reforms of the New Deal in favor of programs that addressed racial inequality, but that ultimately produced a reactionary backlash.[27] Bell, a fellow "New York Intellectual" and City College alumnus, was a professor at Columbia University and avowed "democratic socialist." "The aim of *The Public Interest* is at once modest and presumptuous," the two declared in its inaugural issue. "It is to help all of us, when we discuss issues of public policy, to know a little better what we are talking about- and preferably in time to make such knowledge effective."[28]

By the end of the essay, Bell and Kristol had exhausted their modesty, though not their presumption. The "public interest," the two approvingly quoted Walter Lippmann, was "what men would choose

---

[26] Irving Kristol, "Forty Good Years," American Enterprise Institute, May 25, 2005, www.aei.org/articles/forty-good-years/.
[27] Irving Kristol, *Neoconservatism*, 28, 204.
[28] Daniel Bell and Irving Kristol, "What Is the Public Interest?" *The Public Interest* no. 1 (Fall 1965), 3, www.nationalaffairs.com/storage/app/uploads/public/58e/1a4/9ee/58e1a49eea60e937247032.pdf.

if they saw clearly, thought rationally, acted disinterestedly and benevolently." Along with postwar prosperity came questions over distribution, both economic and political. The success of the early 1960s Civil Rights movement coincided with the "discovery" of vast pockets of urban and rural poverty. Like most other Cold War liberals, Bell and Kristol initially welcomed the former and supported Lyndon Johnson's call in 1964 for a "War on Poverty" that would extend the benefits of the New Deal. Yet here domestic Cold War liberalism showed its conservative instincts: "Disinterested" and "benevolent" social scientists had to make sure the scale did not tip too far toward the people, for the masses could not be trusted to determine social policy. The masses were too self-interested, and not aware of how to care for the common good. "A democratic society, with its particular encouragement to individual ambition, private appetite, and personal concerns has a greater need than any other to keep the idea of the public interest before it," Bell and Kristol explained. Now more than ever, they believed, America needed its Cold War intellectuals to guard the gates of social policy, preventing both liberal overreach and conservative counterreaction. "Democracy, after all, is government by public opinion," the pair concluded. "It is such a public opinion that *The Public Interest* seeks to serve."[29]

Kristol and Bell's assumption of authority over public policy, and to an extent democracy, requires context. Contrary to Bell's Columbia colleague (and *Public Interest* contributor) Richard Hofstadter, whose 1963 *Anti-Intellectualism in American Life* asserted that Americans had a deep and historical prejudice against "intellectuals," by the mid-1960s American intellectuals had never been more influential.[30] As historian David Halberstam showed in his 1972 bestseller *The Best and the Brightest*, academics on loan from America's top universities and think tanks provided "brilliant policies that defied common sense" for Kennedy and Johnson's senseless war in Vietnam. Some, like Harvard historian Arthur Schlesinger, Jr. and economist John Kenneth Galbraith, became bestselling authors and household names through their ties to glamorous Camelot. None would match Henry Kissinger, another Harvard academic (albeit an untenured one) with government

---

[29] Ibid., 5.

[30] "A member of *The Public Interest* circle before his death in 1970," Moynihan greatly admired Hofstadter. For the magazine's 20th anniversary, in 1985, Moynihan selected "The Paranoid Style in American Politics Revisited" for his topic. A decade later, he remained certain that Hofstadter's essay was prophetic, an "eerie evocation of things to come, some of it on the left ... but more importantly the movements of the right." Daniel Patrick Moynihan, *Miles to Go: A Personal History of Social Policy* (Cambridge, MA: Harvard University Press, 1996), 67.

ties and ambitions. After angling for White House jobs under Kennedy and Johnson, Kissinger finally found an unlikely ally in Richard Nixon, under whom he served as National Security Advisor and Secretary of State (from 1973 to 1974, he was both). In other words, *The Public Interest*'s presumption – that the same intellectuals who created a mess should decide how to clean it up – was by no means unique.

The Public Interest would go on to publish dozens of essays on issues relating to American domestic policy from a largely rotating cast of liberal social scientists. In addition to Bell and Kristol, regular contributors included sociologists Nathan Glazer, who in 1964 coauthored *The Melting Pot*, an important book on New York ethnic politics, with Kennedy Administration aide Daniel Patrick Moynihan; Seymour Matin Lipset, whose assertion that economic development was a handmaiden to liberal democracy was incorporated into 1960s "modernization theory"; and James Q. Wilson, author of the influential "broken windows" theory of policing adopted in nearly every large American city in the 1980s and 90s.

Most contributors to *The Public Interest* were former members of the anti-Stalinist left and all considered themselves progressive liberals. As Wilson later recalled, "We felt the Community Action Program particularly, urban renewal programs, Medicare – these were all signs to us [social scientists] of government being heavy-handed about achieving objectives that most of us didn't quarrel with."[31] *The Public Interest*'s second issue, for instance, carried an article by Adam Yarmolinsky, a young Johnson Administration official who opposed the president's war in Vietnam as he crafted the War on Poverty.[32] Yarmolinsky's conclusion – as summarized by Bell – reflected these Cold War liberals' essentially conservative commitment to gradual, small scale change: "It's very easy to have ideas. It's harder to translate ideas into programs. It's harder to translate the programs into policy. It's even harder to translate policy into legislation. It's hard to translate legislation into institutions. And it's harder to get the institutions going toward the objectives you had in the first place."[33]

The major contributors to *Public Interest* rejected Richard Nixon as a presidential candidate in 1968, yet it was in the Nixon Administration where *The Public Interest* achieved its first great influence. And this

---

[31] Joseph Dorman, *Arguing the World: The New York Intellectuals in Their Own Words* (Chicago: University of Chicago Press, 2001), 159–160.
[32] Adam Yarmolinsky, "Ideas into Programs," *The Public Interest* no. 2 (Winter 1966), 70–79, www.nationalaffairs.com/storage/app/uploads/public/58e/1a4/a00/58e1a4a003d30707313026.pdf
[33] Bell quoted in Dorman, *Arguing the World*, 159.

was largely through the efforts of frequent contributor Daniel Patrick Moynihan, the famous New Deal liberal who became the embodiment of neoconservatism in the 1970s. "Moynihan fit easily into the liberal postwar consensus," explains historian John Ehrman.[34] The Irish-Catholic former longshoreman was, as one early biography put it, "a strong supporter of Harry Truman" in 1948 and "equally strong opponent of Henry Wallace," whom he believed to be a tool of the U.S. Communist Party.[35] An ADA charter member, in the 1950s Moynihan first worked for New York Governor and Democratic presidential candidate W. Averell Harriman and, while a young Harvard professor, campaigned for John F. Kennedy.

Eager to grow his government career, in March 1965, Moynihan (then Johnson's Assistant Secretary of Labor) was thrust into the national spotlight for a controversial study on race and welfare. "The Negro Family: The Case for National Action," quickly dubbed the Moynihan report, became a lightning-rod for its argument that, despite the legal successes of the Civil Rights movement, the "deterioration of the Negro family" was preventing African Americans' economic advancement. (Indeed, William Ryan, a sociologist and civil rights activist, coined the term "blaming the victim" in response.[36]) Less remembered is the article Moynihan wrote for the *Public Interest's* first issue, later that fall.

In "The Professionalization of Reform," Moynihan sounded a much more optimistic note about the power of government in general and its ability to ameliorate poverty. Since 1945, "the industrial democracies of the world have been able to operate their economies on a high and steadily expanding level of production and employment. Nothing like it has ever happened before in history. It is perhaps the central fact of world politics today." The result, according to Moynihan, was both the acceleration of various redistributive economic programs and the "professionalization" of the "reform" process through social workers, community activists, and lawyers. Rule by these new middle-class Mandarins was not unwelcome; on the contrary, it held great promise: "It is a technique that will not appeal to everyone, and in which many will perceive the not altogether imaginary danger of a too-powerful

---

[34] John Ehrman, *The Rise of Neoconservatism: Intellectuals and Foreign Affairs, 1945–1994* (New Haven, CT: Yale University Press, 1995), 66.
[35] Douglas Schoen, *Pat: A Biography of Daniel Patrick Moynihan* (New York: Harper & Row, 1979), 34.
[36] Ryan expanded on what he called the "lies we tell ourselves about race, poverty, and the poor" in an influential book of the same title. See William Ryan, *Blaming the Victim* (New York: Random House, 1970).

government. But it is also a technique that offers a profound promise of social sanity and stability in time to come."[37]

Three years later, on the eve of the 1968 elections, Moynihan had soured on the new "professional reformers." In *The Public Interest*'s fall 1968 issue, just months after the "Moynihan Report" fiasco, he published an article on "The Crises of Welfare" warning of a right-wing backlash if liberals did not acknowledge that welfare "dependence" (a) existed and (b) was undesirable. In order to avoid right-wing dismantling of welfare outright, Moynihan argued, liberals had to face the facts and develop reforms that would rein in short-term costs. In the long-term, they needed to eliminate "dependence" on the ever-growing Aid to Families of Dependent Children, which, he noted, cost the country more than its social security commitments. The political and economic solution to this debacle was a guaranteed annual "family allowance." Which would head off more difficult demands from the left for structural economic change or full-employment policies. This would, he proclaimed, benefit liberals, as it "may prove easier to redistribute money than power."[38]

In December 1969, Richard Nixon appointed Moynihan his assistant for urban affairs. Later, the latter became the executive director of the Urban Affairs Council. Moynihan described this time in his 1973 book, *The Politics of a Guaranteed Income*. The book's heroes were Moynihan and his fellow "liberal social scientists" who were willing to give Nixon a shot, but also the politically shrewd Nixon, who in January 1969 reached out to *them* for help putting together an "urban policy" able to "satisfy a conservative or moderate majority of the public and a liberal or left majority of a profession [i.e., social scientists]." Nixon's appeal to Cold War liberalism's commitment to political compromise and governance by social scientists was music to Moynihan's ears.[39]

Eight months after President Nixon proposed the idea of a Family Assistance Program in August 1969, the U.S. House of Representatives passed it by a margin of two-to-one. After another eight months of deliberation, the U.S. Senate narrowly voted it down. Nixon's "negative" campaign didn't help, but in the end it was Democrats – who

---

[37] Daniel Patrick Moynihan, "The Professionalization of Reform," *The Public Interest* no. 1 (Fall 1965), 10, 8, www.nationalaffairs.com/storage/app/uploads/public/58e/1a4/9e9/58e1a49e939a5835456873.pdf.

[38] Daniel Patrick Moynihan, "The Crises in Welfare," *The Public Interest* no. 10 (Winter 1968), 4, 24, www.nationalaffairs.com/storage/app/uploads/public/58e/1a4/a6a/58e1a4a6aedf8647273327.pdf.

[39] Daniel Patrick Moynihan, *The Politics of a Guaranteed Income: The Nixon Administration and the Family Assistance Plan* (New York: Random House, 1973), 70.

controlled both houses of Congress – who had vetoed "one of the half-dozen or dozen most important pieces of social legislation in American history," one that "all three national news magazines" – that is, *Newsweek* ("WELFARE: There Must be a Better Way"), *Time* ("The Welfare Maze"), and *U.S. News and World Report* ("Welfare out of Control") – then endorsed.[40] In the end, only Moynihan and his fellow intellectuals come out clean, showing just how deeply committed he remained to *The Public Interest*'s technocratic (and self-interested) vision of liberal governance:

> But to a marked degree the crisis [in welfare] had been foreseen – and foretold – and had been the subject of fairly powerful analysis.[41] A number of social scientists had seen what was coming, and had put forth a range of proposals as to what might be done. None were adopted, but when the time came, as it did, that a general clamor arose to do *something*, government was not at a total loss.

In other words, the American government was simply not competent enough to implement the best-laid plans of America's liberal intellectuals. "This is a perhaps underappreciated role of the academic disciplines," Moynihan opined further. "Society need not always be blind, need not constantly lurch from obliviousness to panic and back … . The development of FAP is an instance of such forehandedness."[42]

Moynihan and *Commentary*: "In Opposition," 1970–1976

The FAP's failure was just the beginning of Moynihan's involvement in the Nixon Administration, and of Republican presidents' nurturing of Cold War liberals and their ideas. Moynihan and other Cold War liberals turned neoconservatives would make an even greater mark on public policy through their involvement with another high-brow/low-circulation magazine, *Commentary*.

In contrast to *The Public Interest*, *Commentary* was a broad but provocative magazine covering everything from philosophy to film to foreign affairs. Founded in 1945 by the American Jewish Committee (though editorially independent), *Commentary* quickly emerged as a serious outlet for the postwar literary and cultural left. Through the 1950s and 1960s, it was not uncommon to see new American Jewish writers such as Saul Bellow and Philip Roth writing next to old left figures Dwight Macdonald and Mary McCarthy or European philosophers such as

---

[40] Moynihan, *The Politics of a Guaranteed Income*, 3–6.
[41] As evidence, Moynihan cites the work of *Public Interest* contributors and political scientists Bill Cavala and Aaron Wildavsky.
[42] Moynihan, *The Politics of a Guaranteed Income*, 6–7.

Hannah Arendt and Herbert Marcuse. That its contributors believed in the necessity of a welfare state was a given – nearly all were located somewhere on the socialist or social democratic left. They were also all anti-totalitarians. In the 1930s and 1940s, the totalitarian was Hitler, then Stalin; in the 1950s and early 1960s, it was Stalin's successor Khrushchev and puppet-dictators across the Eastern Bloc.

Starting in the late 1960s, however, *Commentary* refocused its critique on the United States itself. The problem was not so much the direction of American social policy, which is what *The Public Interest* had decided, but rather anti-liberal critics on the New Left. Still, as late as 1969, *Commentary* published Noam Chomsky, which would have been impossible a year later when Podhoretz declared "full-scale war" on the New Left.[43] Yet *Commentary* was about to make an equally significant turn, one that would define it long after the New Left had dissipated: Namely, it declared support for an interventionist and unilateralist foreign policy and defended inequality within an American-led world order.

On May 1, 1974 – International Labor Day – the UN General Assembly adopted the "Group of 77" (G-77) developing countries' call for a "New International Economic Order" (NIEO).[44] Acting just months after Arab members of the Organization of Petroleum Exporting Countries (OPEC) quadrupled the price of oil, the NIEO's Third World supporters hoped to negotiate a redistribution of money and power from the global North to the Global South. Their weapon was control over the price of major commodities, especially oil, that had made North Atlantic prosperity possible after World War II. "What we aim," explained Venezuela's president and OPEC leader Carlos Andrés Pérez, "is to take advantage of this opportunity when raw materials, and energy materials primarily, are worth just as much as capital and technology, in order to reach agreements that will ensure fair and lasting balances."[45]

In January 1974, three months into the oil crisis, *Commentary* published an influential essay by U.S. political scientist Robert W. Tucker. Titled "Oil: The Issue of American Intervention," the article argued that

---

[43] Vaisse, *Neoconservatism*, 70.
[44] UN General Assembly, Resolution 3201, "Declaration on the Establishment of a New International Economic Order," May 1, 1974, www.un-documents.net/s6r3201.htm. For a background of the NIEO's philosophy and terms, see Daniel J. Whelan, "'Under the Aegis of Man': The Right to Development and the Origins of the New International Economic Order," *Humanity* 6, no. 1 (Spring 2015), 93–108.
[45] "A Letter from the President of Venezuela to the Chairman of the World Food Conference Meeting in Rome," Caracas, November 5, 1974 (Caracas: Oficina Central de Información). See also Michael Franczak, *Global Inequality and American Foreign Policy in the 1970s* (Ithaca, NY: Cornell University Press, 2022).

the Nixon administration should consider the use of military force to resolve the oil crisis.[46] For Tucker, the oil crisis embodied a larger shift in global politics: "[A]n egalitarianism which, if permitted to run its logical course, is likely to result first in chaos and then in an international system far harsher than today's or yesterday's system."[47]

The oil crisis and NIEO led *Commentary* to turn its attention to attacking this "new egalitarianism." The magazine published two other essays by Tucker on the NIEO in 1975–76; the three were collected in a 1977 book, *The Inequality of Nations*. In addition to essays by Walter Laqueur, fresh from his 1973 opus *A History of Zionism*, *Commentary* would publish several more essays on the NIEO, including four from British neoliberal P. T. Bauer.[48] Moynihan was also a participant in this debate. In a May 1, 1974, essay titled "Was Woodrow Wilson Right?" Moynihan determined that U.S. elites were in the middle of a "crisis of faith ... demoralized, even victimized" by a combination of the radical left at home and the "poisonously anti-American" political elites of "most of the rest of the world."[49]

Subsequent events only reinforced Moynihan's suspicions. At the World Food Conference in November 1974, the U.S. delegation confronted sweeping demands for the implementation of the NIEO while OPEC leaders refused to discuss oil prices until the United States agreed to comprehensive global negotiations (which it eventually did). One month later, the U.S. delegation to the UN found itself outvoted and isolated when the General Assembly, including most of Western Europe, overwhelmingly approved the G-77's Charter of Economic Rights and Duties of States, essentially a legal blueprint for the NIEO. After resigning from his next post as ambassador to India in January 1975, Moynihan, at Podhoretz's urging, collected his views on the North–South crisis in a lengthy essay in *Commentary*'s March issue. That same month, U.S. Secretary of State Henry Kissinger invited

---

[46] Fouad Ajami, "The Global Logic of the Neoconservatives," *World Politics* 30, no. 3 (April 1978), 451.

[47] Robert W. Tucker, "Oil: The Issue of American Intervention," *Commentary* (January 1, 1974), 31.

[48] P.T. Bauer, "Western Guilt and Third World Poverty," *Commentary* 61, no. 1 (January 1, 1976), 31–38; Bauer and B. S. Yamey, "Against the New Economic Order," *Commentary* 63, no. 4 (April 1, 1977), 25–31; Bauer and John O'Sullivan, "Foreign Aid for What?" *Commentary* 66, no. 5 (December 1, 1978), 41–48; Bauer and B. S. Yamey, "East–West/North–South: Peace and Prosperity?" *Commentary* 70, no. 3 (September 1, 1980), 57–63. Bauer also wrote a lengthy response letter to Moynihan's February 1975 article "The U.S. in Opposition," which *Commentary* published (along with a counter-response from Moynihan) in its August 1975 issue.

[49] Daniel Patrick Moynihan, "Was Woodrow Wilson Right?" *Commentary* 57, no. 5 (May 1974), 25–31.

Moynihan to the White House to talk about his essay, "The U.S. in Opposition," in which he implored U.S. leaders to defend the validity of the American-led world order in moral, even Churchillian terms.[50]

In June 1975, Moynihan joined the Ford Administration as ambassador to the UN, where his aggressive posture left the United States isolated from the Third World and Europe alike and eventually cost him Kissinger's support. "Moynihan has enraged Third World delegates, discomfited his Western European colleagues, and brought cheer to the hearts of Americans," *Time* rhapsodized in a glowing January 1976 profile of "The Fighting Irishman at the UN."[51] The Ambassador's attacks on anti-liberalism and anti-Americanism at the UN, especially the infamous November 1975 "Zionism as Racism" resolution, brought him wide esteem from other "right wing liberals" alienated by the Democratic Party's apparent embrace of egalitarianism, multi-culturalism, and non-interventionism. Moynihan wasted little time in securing political support from party power brokers for a run for office. In early June 1976, just four months after stepping down from his position at the UN, Moynihan declared his candidacy for the Democratic nomination for senator from New York. After narrowly defeating outspoken liberal and party favorite Bella Abzug in the primary, he easily triumphed in the general election, making Moynihan "the first neoconservative intellectual to be elected to public office."[52]

Conclusion

Moynihan personified the extent to which the neoconservative label depended upon a faith in American military power that overrode a faith in a New Deal social welfare state – as opposed to the two complementing each other. Cold War liberals "became neoconservatives" by relying on the networks they established in the 1950s and 1960s as Democrats. The successors to these organizations gave them opportunities to shape foreign policy in the Nixon and Reagan administrations. These networks changed in the late 1970s, as men like Tyroler resurfaced in the Coalition for a Democratic Majority and the CPD. His allies were powerful, but fewer – as many of them had made themselves

---

[50] Daniel Patrick Moynihan, "The U.S. in Opposition," *Commentary* 59, no. 3 (March 1975), 31–44. For a detailed account of that article, the Kissinger meeting, and Moynihan's tenure at the UN, see Michael Franczak, "Losing the Battle, Winning the War: Neoconservatives versus the New International Economic Order, 1974–82," *Diplomatic History* 43, no. 5 (November 2019), 867–889.

[51] "Diplomacy: A Fighting Irishman at the U.N.," *Time*, 107, no. 4 (January 26, 1976), Files of the National Security Adviser, Gerald Ford Presidential Library.

[52] Ehrman, *The Rise of Neoconservatism*, 91–92.

persona non grata within the Democratic Party, at least in terms of any sizable influence in party leadership. Gone were the days when Cold War liberals could rely upon a coterie of New Deal democrats. Schlesinger Jr., Galbraith, and Scoop Jackson had moved on from arms buildups to supporting détente with the Soviet Union, or Galbraith's case, advocating for the nationalization of the defense industry. Others faded from politics due to age or illness. Humphrey would soon be diagnosed with bladder cancer and pass away from it in January 1978.[53]

This meant that Cold War liberals had to broaden their tent and attract new allies who still believed that the Cold War was worth fighting. Indeed, the turbulence of antiwar movement, fear of Black Power "militants," and George McGovern's loss in 1972 against Richard Nixon were all potential selling points for Cold War liberals looking to expand their coalition; but none proved as fruitful as foreign policy issues – détente and the arms race, to be specific. As it had in the 1950s and 1960s, foreign policy led to the recruitment of financial interests that backed CPD and CDM in the mid-1970s. When formed in 1972, the Coalition for a Democratic Majority had one purpose: to counter the McGovern–Fraser reforms of 1969 that democratized the Democratic Party and the nominating process for presidential candidates. But political reform was not an effective means to build coalitions, and thus the CDM quickly grew to encompass the issue that truly galvanized people: fighting the Cold War. The CDM's Team B report on détente, released in 1974, spurred the formation of the CPD in 1976, which was headed by Tyroler.

The DAC provided a model for CPD, though with one major difference. When he organized the CPD, Tyroler focused primarily on recruiting CEOs, corporate titans, and the scions of Republican officials because he could no longer rely upon the Democratic Party to fund his outfit. Happily, for Tyroler, foreign policy attracted a number of donors – of both parties, no less – to the CPD. In the coming years, the membership of the CPD would encompass a who's who of the industry and financial worlds, who would join erstwhile Cold War liberals who had for decades comprised Tyroler's circle in the 1950s.[54]

---

[53] Kenneth Galbraith, *How to Control the Military* (New York: Doubleday, 1969); Michael Brenes, *For Might and Right: Cold War Defense Spending and the Remaking of American Democracy* (Amherst: University of Massachusetts Press, 2020), 123.

[54] See the article "Listing the Rich: Richer-Richest 400 in the United States," *Washington Post* (August 28, 1982), Box 53, Folder 2, Committee on Present Danger Records. See the list of CPD members' names in this folder as well. Tyroler sought to recruit many Republicans, including Henry Cabot Lodge, Jr., Nixon's Secretary of State William Rogers, and Tom Killefer, president of U.S. Trust Corp., who served as executive director of the Inter-American Development Bank.

The CPD solidified connections between neoliberals and neoconservatives, between Cold War liberals and Republican hawks that grew out of the distrust of the dovish shift in the Democratic Party after 1968.[55]

The CPD's alliance between neoliberals and Cold War hawks helped shed Cold War liberalism of its last vestiges of social democracy. The CPD accentuated the political split between Cold War liberals still concerned with labor and civil rights and neoconservatives, who were foreign policy hawks, almost exclusively. The rise of neoconservatism of the 1970s was ultimately a revival of Cold War liberalism but without the emphasis on social welfare. This ultimately gave neoconservatism social currency – neoconservatism repackaged Cold War liberalism for a creeping age of austerity. The financial backers of Cold War liberals' projects (business and political elites who also sought common cause with the New Right), provided the connective tissue between neoliberalism and Cold War liberalism – the money and the influence. The CPD's focus on national defense and the arms race therefore united the common strands between American conservatism and Cold War liberalism, while downplaying many of its members' former connections to American liberalism and the domestic policies associated with the Democratic Party.[56]

The foreign policies of the Reagan Administration offered Cold War liberals the chance to become neoconservatives, to remake themselves as concerned citizens distressed about the state of national security – while granting them the opportunity to abandon, or set aside, their still liberal views on domestic policy. While Moynihan remained a pro-labor, New Deal–style Democrat in the U.S. Senate until his death in 2001, he was an outlier. More common was what historian Justin Vaisse calls the "hybrid": people such as Podhoretz, Midge Decter, Irving Kristol, and other "first generation" neoconservatives who joined in alliance with Reagan's conservative Republican supporters on issues such as the UN, the Third World, and the Soviet Union. Literally dozens joined the Reagan administration in top national security posts, with the CPD acting as a crucial pipeline. Indeed, Charles Tyroler would eventually be appointed to the President's Intelligence Oversight Board during the Reagan and George H. W. Bush administrations.[57]

---

[55] See Joseph Hamburger and Daniel Steinmetz-Jenkins, "Why Did Neoconservatives Join Forces with Neoliberals? Irving Kristol from Critic to Ally of Free-Market Economics," *Global Intellectual History* 6, no. 2 (2021), 215–230.

[56] On neoliberalism and neoconservatism, see ibid. and Melinda Cooper, *Family Values: Between Neoliberalism and the New Social Conservatism* (New York: Zone Books, 2017).

[57] Vaisse, *Neoconservatism*, 207.

Remarkably, a *Commentary* essay once again facilitated the ascension of the second neoconservative Democrat to the United States' top post at the UN. Jeanne Kirkpatrick's November 1979 article "Dictatorships and Double Standards" – written shortly after her own stint at AEI, at Kristol's invitation – accused Carter of holding U.S. allies in the Third World to a higher standard on human rights than its communist enemies and justified support for right-wing, authoritarian Third World governments on the basis that they could be "reformed," while Marxist or totalitarian ones could not. The self-proclaimed "AFL-CIO Democrat" soon received an enthusiastic phone call from candidate Reagan, who brought her on first as his chief foreign policy advisor and then as U.S. Ambassador to the UN (1981–85).

The disparate stories of such figures – from Charles Tyroler to Jeanne Kirkpatrick – illustrate how the characteristics of Cold War liberalism (its focus on ensuring American predominance in defense, above all) so easily aligned with the rightward shift in American politics in the 1970s, forever cementing its influence on the conservative policies that many of its members opposed in the 1950s, but ultimately came to endorse – implicitly or explicitly – as figures in the Reagan administration.

12 The Noncommunist Boom
The Transformation of Carlos Fuentes and the Democratic Left in Latin America, 1959–1990

Andrés Sánchez-Padilla

The 1966 Congress of the PEN Club took place in New York City – the first time it was held in the United States since 1924 – with a prominent representation of Latin American writers who hailed from the Left, including such luminaries as Mario Vargas Llosa, Pablo Neruda, Ernesto Sábato, and Carlos Fuentes in an effort to correct the prior marginalization of the continent. Fuentes himself chronicled the event in an article that concluded with the stunning declaration that "the XXXIV International Congress of the P.E.N. Club will be remembered as the burial of the Cold War in literature."[1] Fuentes proclaimed that Cold War era ideological divisions did not matter anymore in a brave new world that was superseding them.

Equally remarkable was the fact that Fuentes, a well-known supporter of the Cuban Revolution and contributor to the Cuban literary magazine *Casa de las Américas*, decided to publish his account of the event in the pages of *LIFE en Español*, the Spanish-language edition of *LIFE* magazine. For *LIFE en Español* was no mere translation: It had been devised to convey a more favorable image of American democracy in Latin America and was considered a tool of U.S. imperialism by the Cuban government and its allies.[2] The fact that Fuentes chose to publish

---

[1] Carlos Fuentes, "El P.E.N.: Entierro de la Guerra Fría en la Literatura," *LIFE en Español*, August 1, 1966, 57. Unless otherwise stated, all translations from Spanish citations are my own.

[2] Seçao Livre, "'Cartas de Norteamérica': *Life en Español* e a Guerra Fria cultural (1953–1957)," *Estudos Ibero-Americanos* 45, no. 3 (September–December 2019): 169–182, www.doi.org/10.15448/1980-864X.2019.3.33287. Indeed, another Mexican writer awarded twice by *Casa de las Américas*, Jorge Ibargüengoitia, became persona non grata on the island after publishing an article in the magazine, Maria Cristina Secci, "Guerra Fría cultural: la relación de Jorge Ibargüengoitia con Casa de las Américas a raíz del Simposio de Chichen Itzá y de *Life en Español*," *Cultura Latinoamericana. Revista de Estudios Interculturales* 39, no. 1 (2024): 60–81, www.doi.org/10.14718/CulturaLatinoam.2024.39.1.2. On the other hand, Julio Cortázar saw being interviewed by the magazine as a way to "subvert" it from within, Deborah Cohn, *The Latin American Literary Boom and U.S. Nationalism during the Cold War* (Nashville: Vanderbilt University Press, 2012), 205–206.

his chronicle in such a controversial magazine speaks to one of the defining tenets of Cold War liberalism in Latin America, or what was more frequently called the anti-communist or Democratic Left (Izquierda Democrática).³ Cold War liberalism did not have deep intellectual roots in Latin America and was dependent on official and unofficial U.S. sources of support. The Democratic Left was initially identified with a group of anti-communist social democratic parties striving to depose authoritarian regimes in Costa Rica, Venezuela, Cuba, and other Latin American countries after World War II. However, over time the label was attached to or appropriated by those individuals and organizations critical with the Cuban Revolution and favoring incremental change over social revolution.⁴

In 1990, many of the same Latin American intellectuals who went to the PEN Congress attended a very different gathering in Mexico City, this time organized by Mexican poet Octavio Paz to discuss the end of the Cold War. But in the collected volume *El siglo XX: La experiencia de la libertad* ("The Twentieth Century: The Experience of Freedom"), the participants extolled the virtues of (neo)liberalism over socialism. To be sure, this time Carlos Fuentes was not invited to the affair – but that had more to do with his longstanding personal feud with Octavio Paz, a casualty of Mexico's shifting intellectual alliances.⁵ For Fuentes wholeheartedly shared Paz's faith in the superiority of liberal democracy over Marxism. In

---

[3] Fuentes, along with Neruda, was viciously attacked in the Cuban press for attending the event and publishing in the U.S. magazine, Deborah Cohn, "PEN and the Sword: U.S.-Latin American Cultural Diplomacy and the 1966 PEN Club Congress," in *Hemispheric American Studies*, ed. Caroline F. Levander and Robert S. Levine (New Brunswick: Rutgers University Press, 2008), 206–222; Cohn, *The Latin American Literary Boom*, 65–93; Joel Whitney, *Finks: How the CIA Tricked the World's Best Writers* (New York: OR Books, 2016), Chapter 11. Fuentes deemed the criticism emanating from Cuba as showing that "sometimes, our Left seems (and is) the refuge of the schmucks," Carlos Fuentes to José Donoso, Paris, July 24, 1966, Box 381, Folder 6, Carlos Fuentes Papers, 1830s–2012, Manuscripts Division, Princeton University Library, One Washington Road, Princeton, NJ.

[4] Patrick J. Iber, "'Who Will Impose Democracy?': Sacha Volman and the Contradictions of CIA Support for the Anticommunist Left in Latin America," *Diplomatic History* 37, no. 5 (November 2013): 995–1028, www.doi.org/10.1093/dh/dht041; Jorge A. Nállim, "Integración cultural y guerra fría en América Latina en la década de 1950," in *Historia comparada de las Américas. Perspectivas de la integración cultural*, ed. Liliana Weinberg (México: Centro de Investigaciones sobre América Latina y el Caribe, 2016), 269–295.

[5] Octavio Paz and Enrique Krauze, ed., *La experiencia de la libertad* (México: Vuelta, 1991); Patrick J. Iber, *Neither Peace nor Freedom: The Cultural Cold War in Latin America* (Cambridge; London: Harvard University Press, 2015), 232–234; John King, *The Role of Mexico's Plural in Latin American Literary and Political Culture: From Tlatelolco to the "Philanthropic Ogre"* (Basingstoke: Palgrave Macmillan, 2007), 15. A recent work on the Fuentes-Paz relationship is Malva Flores, *Estrella de dos puntas. Octavio Paz y Carlos Fuentes: historia de una amistad* (Barcelona: Ariel, 2020).

his 1983 commencement speech at Harvard University, Fuentes referred to the Soviet regime as a "tyranny," criticized the "brutal diplomacy of the Soviet Union," bemoaned the "repressive government" of Communist Poland, and expressed Latin American solidarity with the anti-communist Polish trade union *Solidarity*, before concluding that "sooner or later, the rebellion of the outlying nations in the Soviet sphere will eat, more and more deeply, into the innards of what Lord Carrington recently called 'a decaying Byzantium'."[6] More importantly, Fuentes would go on to cheer the neoliberal policies carried out by Mexican President Carlos Salinas de Gortari (1988–94), including the passage of NAFTA, as much-welcomed steps to integrate Mexico in the global economy – all the while scolding the Left for its residual Marxist-Leninism. Even the collapse of the Mexican economy during the monetary crisis of 1994–95 did not shake his newfound faith in the righteousness of the neoliberal path.[7]

The present chapter seeks to advance two arguments about Cold War liberalism in Latin America. First, that the ideological trajectory of Mexican intellectual Carlos Fuentes between the Cuban Revolution and the end of the Cold War is representative of the larger changes experienced by Cold War liberalism in the region. Although initially identified with the ambiguous notion of "democratic socialism," over time Fuentes lost his faith in state power as the primary engine for social change and came to embrace the role of global markets in disciplining national governments.

But the second argument is that this ideological metamorphosis was, in turn, the result of two distinct features: the late arrival of Cold War liberalism to the region and the coincidence of the intellectual split over the Cuban Revolution with the "dirty wars" and the global crisis of the 1970s. Both factors contributed to the particular inflection of Cold War liberalism in the Western Hemisphere: Whereas elitism and expert-led rule came naturally to Latin American intellectuals from privileged upbringings such as Fuentes himself, emergency politics and liberal empire carried a bad reputation in the region; the first one was associated with the military dictatorships that had historically haunted Latin America and was never truly endorsed; whereas liberal empire was deeply questioned against the backdrop of U.S. imperialism in the region until the Latin American nationalist creed of development came crashing down in the 1970s.

---

[6] Carlos Fuentes, "A Harvard Commencement," in *Myself with Others: Selected Essays* (New York: Farrar, Straus and Giroux, 1988), 199, 202–203.
[7] Carlos Fuentes, "Una nueva izquierda latinoamericana," *El País*, December 27, 1993, www.elpais.com/diario/1993/12/27/opinion/756946810_850215.html; Maarten van Delden, *Carlos Fuentes, Mexico, and Modernity* (Nashville: Vanderbilt University Press, 1998), 197–199.

Cold War liberalism was introduced to the region by foreign-born intellectuals without local roots but strong ties to the United States. Only in the 1960s did Cold War liberalism find a stronger foothold by attracting moderate left-wingers like Carlos Fuentes to the cause of modernization and incremental change. This shaky platform did not last amidst the scandal of its association with the CIA, even though the Cuban cultural front also lost its charm after the "Padilla affair." However, as in the North Atlantic, in Latin America Cold War liberalism did not simply fade away: Instead, it was reborn in 1970s Mexico when the left-wing split over the Cuban Revolution finally created the conditions for a genuine form of Cold War liberalism devoid of its previous suspicious associations. However, the timing of the split with the crisis of capitalism over the long 1970s made it morph its previous modernization ethos into a gradual embrace of neoliberalism. During that pivotal decade, the economic failure of the nationalist model of development dominant since the 1940s produced a historic loss of faith in the state as the engine for progress.[8]

Drawing on the nonfiction writings of Carlos Fuentes and his personal correspondence, this chapter will map out the complicated path of Cold War liberalism in the Western Hemisphere. Carlos Fuentes (1928–2012) was one of the most important Mexican writers of the twentieth century and a prominent exponent of the Latin American "Boom," a literary movement that revolutionized Latin American letters by integrating its writers into the mainstream of international literature and turning them into international celebrities. Indeed, Fuentes had begun his career as part of a new generation of cosmopolitan Mexican writers striving to modernize Mexican literature – the generation of *Medio Siglo*. Under the mentorship of Octavio Paz, these writers came to dominate Mexican cultural production between the fifties and seventies, earning them the nickname *la mafia* – a label later applied to the "Boom" writers themselves.[9]

---

[8] Jeremy Adelman, "International Finance and Political Legitimacy: A Latin American View of the Global Shock," in *The Shock of the Global: The 1970s in Perspective*, eds. Niall Ferguson, Charles S. Maier, Erez Manela and Daniel J. Sargent (Cambridge: The Belknap Press of Harvard University Press, 2010), 113–127. On the global history of neoliberalism, Quinn Slobodian, *Globalists: The End of Empire and the Birth of Neoliberalism* (Cambridge/London Harvard University Press, 2018).

[9] Deborah Cohn, "The Mexican Intelligentsia, 1950–1968: Cosmopolitanism, National Identity, and the State," *Mexican Studies/Estudios Mexicanos* 21, no. 1 (2005): 141, www.doi.org/10.1525/msem.2005 21.1.141; Patrick J. Iber, "The Cold War Politics of Literature and the Centro Mexicano de Escritores," *Journal of Latin American Studies* 48, no. 2 (May 2016): 264, www.doi.org/10.1017/S0022216X15001492. Eventually, the term "mafia" or "mafia internacional" was appropriated by the "Boom" generation, see Gabriel García Márquez to Carlos Fuentes, January 26, n.d., Box 381, Folder 3, Carlos

But Fuentes was more than a novelist. In Latin America, writers enjoyed an unparalleled degree of political influence and literary magazines were vehicles to "determine the political vision and cultural values of generations of readers."[10] In a region of "'lettered cities' [...] surrounded by seas of illiteracy,"[11] in which academics were few in number and mistrusted as opinion makers, writers were by definition public intellectuals, and used literary magazines to shape public opinion.[12] Fuentes declared that in Latin America, the writer "is the spokesman for those who cannot make themselves heard, who feels that his exact function lies in denouncing injustice, defending the downtrodden and documenting the reality of his country."[13] Furthermore, unlike in the North Atlantic, the Latin American intellectual scene of the mid twentieth century was defined by the hegemony of the Left.[14]

But Fuentes was not only an engaged intellectual, he also had lifelong political aspirations, serving under several administrations of the one-party system ruling Mexico between 1929 and 2000 – the PRI (Partido Revolucionario Institucional).[15] He was successively assistant director of public relations of the Secretaría de Relaciones Exteriores (SRE, "Ministry of Foreign Affairs," 1954–57), director of the Dirección General de Relaciones Culturales ("Department of Cultural Affairs," 1957–60), occasional speechwriter for the SRE and, following in the footsteps of his father – a career diplomat himself – ambassador to France (1975–77).[16]

Apparently, Fuentes never saw any conflict between his official duties and his role as a public intellectual speaking truth to power.

Fuentes Papers, 1830s–2012, Manuscripts Division, Princeton University Library, One Washington Road, Princeton, NJ; Gabriel García Márquez to Carlos Fuentes, June 5, n.d., Box 381, Folder 8, Carlos Fuentes Papers, 1830s–2012, Manuscripts Division, Princeton University Library, One Washington Road, Princeton, NJ; Gabriel García Márquez to Carlos Fuentes, September 30, n.d., Box 381, Folder 8, Carlos Fuentes Papers, 1830s–2012, Manuscripts Division, Princeton University Library, One Washington Road, Princeton, NJ.

[10] Russell S. Cobb, "Our Men in Paris? Mundo Nuevo, the Cuban Revolution, and the Politics of Cultural Freedom" (PhD diss., University of Texas at Austin, 2007), 42.
[11] Iber, *Neither Peace nor Freedom*, 8.
[12] Iber, *Neither Peace nor Freedom*, 1. Carlos Fuentes would even assert that the "real historians in Latin America are the novelists," "Assertions of a Nation's Identity," *The Times*, June 9, 1986, 19.
[13] Carlos Fuentes, *La nueva novela hispanoamericana* (Mexico: Joaquín Mortiz, 1969), 12.
[14] "Beginning with the triumph and the example of the Cuban revolution, the intelligentsia of our countries is located, mostly, on the Left," Fuentes, *La nueva novela hispanoamericana*, 29.
[15] Indeed, his Chilean childhood friend and fellow "Boom" writer José Donoso characterized Fuentes as "extremely politicized," José Donoso to Carlos Fuentes, Calaceite, January 6, 1972, Box 381, Folder 5, Carlos Fuentes Papers, 1830s–2012, Manuscripts Division, Princeton University Library, One Washington Road, Princeton, NJ.
[16] Eric Zolov, *The Last Good Neighbor: Mexico in the Global Sixties* (Durham: Duke University Press, 2020), 165–166.

Indeed, the Mexican one-party system encouraged and even sponsored a certain degree of criticism from left-wing intellectuals as a way to harness progressive energies and thus boost its internal legitimacy.[17] But despite being initially taken with the Cuban Revolution, Fuentes always defined himself as a member of the Latin American Democratic Left. To be sure, he grew more skeptical of ideology with age, echoing Daniel Bell in a 1984 interview: "Ideologies are rigid. I am against ideologies. They are very neat, rationalized and stiff." He even denied ever having been a proper Marxist.[18]

Even though there is no shortage of critical studies on the politics of Carlos Fuentes, the focus has remained on the national rather than international context: He has been variously characterized as "always-progressive," a "radical democrat" of a "progressive and social democratic nature," or a member of the Mexican "heterodox Left."[19] But this misses the larger North Atlantic intellectual constellation which Fuentes was a part of: As one biographer aptly put it, his formative political experiences included "the Mexico of Lázaro Cárdenas, the United States of the New Deal, and Chile in the wake of the Popular Front."[20] Throughout his career, he alternated with ease between the intellectual settings of Mexico City, London, Paris, or the U.S. East Coast.[21] More than any other Cold War liberal in the Americas (Octavio Paz, Guillermo Cabrera Infante, Gabriel Zaid, etc.), both his influences and his audiences were of global reach, from C. Wright Mills to Daniel Bell,

---

[17] Vanessa Freije, *Citizens of Scandal: Journalism, Secrecy, and the Politics of Reckoning in Mexico* (Durham and London: Duke University Press, 2020), 8–10; Zolov, *The Last Good Neighbor*, 87. On paper, the 1917 Mexican Constitution had established a pluralist democracy with competitive elections and civil rights, but the PRI monopolized political power through electoral fraud and other mechanisms that always guaranteed its candidates landslide victories, while curtailing freedom of the press through the state paper monopoly, PIPSA. Fuentes himself described the system as "one party holding together opposing interests in the name of national unity," Carlos Fuentes to Norman Mailer, Mexico City, December 12, 1971, Box 381, Folder 10, Carlos Fuentes Papers, 1830s–2012, Manuscripts Division, Princeton University Library, One Washington Road, Princeton, NJ.

[18] Nicholas Shrady, "Carlos Fuentes: Life and Language," *New York Times*, August 19, 1984, 26–27. Despite American accusations to the contrary, there is no evidence that he was ever a member of the Mexican Communist Party, Zolov, *The Last Good Neighbor*, 342.

[19] Raymond Leslie Williams, *The Writings of Carlos Fuentes* (Austin: University of Texas Press, 1996), 17, 29; Delden, *Carlos Fuentes*, 193; Wendolin López Arriaga, "Carlos Fuentes y la Revolución Cubana: los dilemas del compromiso intelectual en las décadas de 1960 y 1970 en América Latina" (PhD diss., Universidad Nacional Autónoma de México, 2022), 57.

[20] Williams, *The Writings of Carlos Fuentes*, 30.

[21] As he put it to José Donoso, "It's true: I do not feel your vital and dramatic need to come back to the potato patch," Carlos Fuentes to José Donoso, Princeton, September 6, 1980, Box 381, Folder 5, Carlos Fuentes Papers, 1830s–2012, Manuscripts Division, Princeton University Library, One Washington Road, Princeton, NJ.

from J. William Fulbright to Valery Giscard d'Estaing. Indeed, Fuentes's Harvard address mentioned earlier was a carefully worded statement aimed at U.S. Secretary of Defense Caspar Weinberger, seated in the front row, at a deeply strained time in the U.S.–Mexican relationship due to American interference in the 1980s Central American civil wars.[22]

To be fair, the recent works of Deborah Cohn and Eric Zolov do situate Fuentes within the North Atlantic context as a "cultural ambassador" of Latin America and "left-wing interlocutor," respectively, but do not venture beyond the 1960s.[23] Thus, although not previously described as a Cold War liberal, the label provides a more comprehensive framework to encompass the whole span of Carlos Fuentes's political engagement with the intellectual battle lines of the Cold War.

The Discrete Charm of Cold War Liberalism, 1959–1963

As many scholars have pointed out, Carlos Fuentes's career started out on the Left of Mexican politics but intersected with the institutional evolution of the groups that provided the structure for promoting Cold War liberalism in Latin America. Initially, the high expectations generated by the Cuban Revolution set Fuentes and Cold War liberals apart, but the inability of the Cuban model to reform Mexican politics and its increasingly authoritarian nature laid the foundations for their future understanding.

Cold War liberalism came to the Americas through the hands of cultural diplomacy. Given the scarcity of homegrown liberal outlets, since the 1930s American would-be cultural Cold Warriors and philanthropists promoted groups and individuals in the region that could enhance the appeal of liberalism against its fascist and communist alternatives. Not surprisingly, Mexico was the main site for these efforts, as the Mexican Revolution had installed the first regime in the region that seriously threatened American liberal values: Not for nothing, in the 1930s and 1940s, Mexico City had become a "haven for left-wing exiles" and "a magnet for revolutionaries from other parts of the world," including such heterodox figures as Leon Trotsky.[24] Indeed, the most enthusiastic Cold War liberals to be found in the Western Hemisphere after World War II were the anti-communist Spanish exiles who fought

---

[22] "Walesa, in Smuggled Speech Text, Tells Harvard's Graduates of Hope," *New York Times*, June 10, 1983, 17. On U.S.–Mexican tensions in the 1980s, Jacqueline Mazza, "The U.S. and Democracy in Mexico: 1980–1995. Don't Disturb the Neighbors" (PhD diss., The Johns Hopkins University, 1998), 71–130.
[23] Cohn, *The Latin American Literary Boom*; Zolov, *The Last Good Neighbor*.
[24] Iber, *Neither Peace nor Freedom*, 22–23.

General Franco in the Spanish Civil War (1936–39) and fell out with their erstwhile communist allies. They eventually ended up running the Latin American department of the Congress for Cultural Freedom (CCF), the most prominent front organization deployed by the U.S. government as part of the cultural Cold War.[25]

But Mexico's significance went beyond its revolutionary legacy: Not only did it possess the leading publishing industry in Latin America alongside Argentina and nurture the careers of many members of the "Boom" generation but also lay dangerously close to the United States – sharing a 2,000-mile border. Indeed, the Mexican administration of Miguel Alemán (1946–52) mirrored its U.S. counterpart in going after local communists and undermining the radical labor movement after World War II.[26] Furthermore, American cultural efforts in Mexico were not limited to the CCF: They also included organizing institutions such as the Benjamin Franklin Library (1942) and the Centro Mexicano de Escritores (1951), as well as subsidizing major Mexican publishers such as the state-owned Fondo de Cultura Económica, to cover the costs of translating and publishing relevant American works.[27] Carlos Fuentes was one of the many beneficiaries of these initiatives, being awarded a grant by the Centro Mexicano de Escritores to complete his first novel, *La región más transparente* ("Where the Air Is Clear," 1958), a modernist narrative in the fashion of John Dos Passos released by Fondo de Cultura Económica – becoming an immediate sensation in Mexico and arguably launching the Latin American "Boom."[28]

---

[25] The CCF had been created in 1950 as a transatlantic venue for anti-totalitarian writers and opened its Latin American department in 1953, see among others Peter Coleman, *The Liberal Conspiracy: The Congress for Cultural Freedom and the Struggle for the Mind of Postwar Europe* (New York: The Free Press, 1989); Frances S. Saunders, *The Cultural Cold War: The CIA and the World of Arts and Letters* (New York: The New Press, 1999); Giles Scott-Smith, *The Politics of Apolitical Culture: The Congress for Cultural Freedom, the CIA and Post-War American Hegemony* (London: Routledge, 2002); Iber, *Neither Peace nor Freedom*, 83–115; Giles Scott-Smith and Charlotte A. Lerg, eds., *Campaigning Culture and the Global Cold War. The Journals of the Congress for Cultural Freedom* (London: Palgrave Macmillan, 2017); Hugh Wilford, *The Mighty Wurlitzer: How the CIA Played America* (Cambridge, MA: Harvard University Press, 2008), Chapter 5.

[26] William A. Booth, "Rethinking Latin America's Cold War," *The Historical Journal* 64, no. 4 (2021): 1134, 1148–1149. For the process in the U.S., see Daniel Bessner, "Introduction: Cold War Liberalism in Historical Perspective," this volume.

[27] José A. Montero, "El despliegue de la diplomacia pública de los Estados Unidos en México: de la Buena Vecindad a la Campaña de la Verdad," in *Guerra Fría y propaganda. Estados Unidos y su cruzada cultural en Europa y América Latina*, ed. Antonio Niño and José A. Montero (Madrid: Biblioteca Nueva, 2012), 311–341.

[28] Iber, "The Cold War Politics of Literature," 247–272. For Fuentes and his first novel as the launching pad for the Latin American "Boom," José Donoso to Carlos Fuentes, Calaceite, September 14, 1971, Box 381, Folder 5, Carlos Fuentes Papers, 1830s–2012, Manuscripts Division, Princeton University Library, One Washington Road, Princeton, NJ.

Although he had already founded a minor literary magazine (*Revista Mexicana de Literatura*, 1955–65) and collaborated with other prestigious literary outlets like *Revista de la Universidad de México*, the instant celebrity brought by his first novel allowed Fuentes to become an influential public intellectual. However, he refused to cooperate with the Latin American magazines promoted by the CCF, such as its flagship journal for the region, *Cuadernos del Congreso por la Libertad de la Cultura* (1953–65) or any of its purely Mexican offshoots (*Letras por la Libertad, Examen, Panoramas*, etc.) – even though he did consider publishing some of its literary criticism in the London-based *Encounter* – the most prestigious CCF magazine at the time.[29] But to discuss political events Fuentes would choose only homegrown left-wing magazines, especially *el espectador* (deliberately typed in lowercase, 1959–60) and *Política* (1961–64).[30]

Fuentes's reluctance had much to do with the poor reputation that the CCF enjoyed in Latin America. First of all, the prominent role played by Spanish exiles as editors and contributors meant that *Cuadernos* was widely panned and distrusted by Latin American intellectuals for its crude anti-communism and total disregard for the region's problems, making it even harder to integrate local collaborators.[31] In addition, the CCF was always tainted in locals' minds because the latter suspected that the CIA funded it (which turned out to be true), and the agency was widely resented in the region for its role in toppling democratic governments, like Jacobo Árbenz's in Guatemala (1954).

Another reason to reject collaboration with the Asociación Mexicana por la Libertad de la Cultura (the Mexican branch of the CCF) was the Cuban Revolution of 1959. Although the multiclass uprising enjoyed widespread support on the island and was initially hailed by the CCF itself (which even supported Castro before his triumph) as a democratic revolution, its rapid radicalization (mass shootings included) and transformation into a socialist regime after 1961 made its erstwhile liberal supporters aghast.[32] On the contrary, most Latin American intellectuals

---

[29] Carlos Fuentes to José Donoso, Mexico City, September 1, 1964, Box 381, Folder 6, Carlos Fuentes Papers, 1830s–2012, Manuscripts Division, Princeton University Library, One Washington Road, Princeton, NJ.

[30] On these two publications, Zolov, *The Last Good Neighbor*, 35–38, 86–91.

[31] Olga Glondys, *La Guerra Fría cultural y el exilio republicano español* (Madrid: CSIC, 2012). See also her "*Cuadernos del Congreso por la Libertad de la Cultura* (1953–1965) and the Failure of a Cold War Liberal Project for Latin America," in *Campaigning Culture and the Global Cold War: The Journals of the Congress for Cultural Freedom*, ed. Giles Scott-Smith and Charlotte A. Lerg (London: Palgrave Macmillan, 2017), 187–206.

[32] On the radicalization of the Cuban Revolution, Iber, *Neither Peace nor Freedom*, 140–144; Ada Ferrer, *Cuba: An American History* (New York: Scribner, 2021), 315–350.

welcomed the revolution with open arms, even after its socialist turn, as a much-needed reassertion of sovereignty against U.S. imperialism. Carlos Fuentes would go so far as to say that after 1959, "the intellectual from Latin America only sees the perspective of revolution."[33]

He became a fervent supporter of the Revolution early on, flying to Havana in January 1959 to meet Fidel Castro, publishing occasionally in the short-lived Cuban literary supplement *Lunes de Revolución* (edited by his close friend and fellow "Boom" writer Guillermo Cabrera Infante)[34] and praising the revolutionary regime enthusiastically in *el espectador* and *Política* against its growing number of enemies. During that period Fuentes probably wrote his most radical pieces.[35] In fact, his staunch defense of the Revolution and heavy criticism of American meddling in Cuba earned him the wrath of Washington. In particular, the failed Bay of Pigs invasion of April 1961, when an army of Cuban exiles trained by the CIA landed on the island to topple the Castro regime but was easily defeated, and the expulsion of Cuba from the Organization of American States the following year, were strongly criticized by Fuentes and other Latin American intellectuals. After that, the U.S. State Department deemed him a communist fellow traveler and denied him the visa to enter the country on several occasions between 1962 and 1969 under the McCarran–Walter Act – even though he had not had any trouble visiting the U.S. before since he lived in the country as a child.[36]

But Fuentes's support for the Revolution was more qualified than it might seem at first sight. First, he defended the Cuban Revolution as an example of democratic change and, even after it officially became

---

[33] Fuentes, *La nueva novela hispanoamericana*, 29.
[34] Guillermo Cabrera Infante to Carlos Fuentes, Havana, March 15, 1960, Box 381, Folder 1, Carlos Fuentes Papers, 1830s–2012, Manuscripts Division, Princeton University Library, One Washington Road, Princeton, NJ. The magazine was shut down by the Castro regime in 1961 after a falling-out over Cabrera Infante's involvement with a documentary on Havana's night life deemed counter-revolutionary, see Guillermo Cabrera Infante to Carlos Fuentes [1961], Box 381, Folder 1, Carlos Fuentes Papers, 1830s–2012, Manuscripts Division, Princeton University Library, One Washington Road, Princeton, NJ. See also Alejandro Herrero-Olaizola, *The Censorship Files: Latin American Writers and Franco's Spain* (Albany, NY: State University of New York Press, 2007), chapter 3.
[35] Williams, *The Writings of Carlos Fuentes*, 29.
[36] Section 212(a)(28) of the act provided for the denial of visas to foreigners associated in any way with communism, Cohn, *The Latin American Literary Boom*, 37–39, 49–63. Fuentes later described his childhood in the U.S. thus: "For me, as a child, the United States seemed a world where intelligence was equated with energy, zest, enthusiasm […] I had a primary impression of a nation of boundless energy, imagination, and the will to confront and solve the great social issues of the times without blinking or looking for scapegoats," Carlos Fuentes, "How I Started to Write," in *Myself with Others*, 5–6.

a Marxist–Leninist system, as an example of Latin American socialism compatible with freedom, for he hoped that the Cuban Revolution would chart its own course and not follow the discredited model of Soviet Communism – chiefly characterized in his mind by the absence of creative freedom and individual rights.[37] As early as 1954, Fuentes had identified with the anti-totalitarian politics championed by George Orwell, affirming "liberty as the primary condition of human integrity" against those that "kidnap it while paradise on earth is achieved" – inadvertently echoing Hans Speier's antinomy between terror/persecution and liberty/democracy.[38]

Furthermore, Fuentes did not think that the revolutionary example should be followed everywhere, least of all in Mexico. Above all, Fuentes interpreted the Cuban Revolution in a social democratic light, as "the avant-garde of the democratic Revolution in all countries on the continent," and even thought it initially compatible with U.S. hegemony in the Western Hemisphere. Indeed, in 1959 he was not afraid to emphasize his proximity to "the liberal wing of the Democratic Party."[39] In essence, what Fuentes was saying was that Cuba should be celebrated not so much as a model but as a catalyst to enact the long overdue social democratic reforms that the rest of Latin America needed, starting with Mexico:

> Electoral freedom, freedom of the press, freedom of unionization, fulfillment of the agrarian reform, reinforcement of state intervention, submission of the bourgeoisie to the national interests, removal of the *caciques*, defense of Mexico's natural resources, ensuing party life and independence of the legislative chambers. And, above all, economic measures that straighten the tragic course of the distribution, more unfair each day, of national income.[40]

In other words, for Fuentes the Cuban Revolution was most useful as a model to inspire social democratic reform elsewhere. This belief underpinned his only venture into mass politics between 1961 and 1964: the multiparty Movimiento de Liberación National ("National Liberation Movement," MLN). Strongly inspired by the Cuban Revolution, the MLN brought together several left-wing organizations under the leadership of former Mexican President Lázaro Cárdenas (an old hero of Fuentes's) to challenge the authoritarian one-party system and

---

[37] López Arriaga, "Carlos Fuentes y la Revolución Cubana," 72–103.
[38] Carlos Fuentes, "Algunas notas sobre George Orwell," *Revista de la Universidad de México*, September 1954, 12, 21. For Speier's quote, see Daniel Bessner, "Introduction: Cold War Liberalism in Historical Perspective," this volume.
[39] Carlos Fuentes, "América Latina y Estados Unidos. Notas para un panorama," *Revista de la Universidad de México*, March 1959, 15.
[40] Carlos Fuentes, "América Latina y Estados Unidos," 12, 15.

democratize Mexican politics, spousing the same causes prioritized by Fuentes: political rights, agrarian reform, economic nationalism, support for the Cuban Revolution, etc. Fuentes followed Cárdenas as he traveled around the country to exert pressure on the Mexican government on the basis of his mass appeal. However, the MLN was always tainted in the eyes of Cold War liberals by its connections in terms of support and personnel with the World Peace Congress (WPC), the main Soviet front organization on the cultural front, and the participation in it of several communist organizations. However, Cárdenas made sure that the MLN was never funded by the Soviets.[41]

Indeed, what attracted Fuentes to the MLN was precisely its independence from any communist control, as he told his American literary agent, Carl Brandt ("the Communists will no longer have the rhetorical ownership of certain issues"); in private, Fuentes did not fear to lash out against the tiny Mexican Communist Party (Partido Comunista Mexicano – PCM), but he did not dare to do so in public because anticommunism was tantamount to a cover for U.S. imperialism in the region, making noncommunist left-wing intellectuals extremely reluctant to take that step.[42] In the event, the MLN proved impotent to change government policies and disintegrated into factional struggling by 1962, not being able to even field a candidate for the 1964 presidential election. Afterwards, Carlos Fuentes resigned from *Política* due to what he deemed its increasingly Stalinist views and practices.[43]

The sectarian strife that brought down the MLN broke the faith of Fuentes in the ability of the masses to effectuate meaningful reform and initiated his gradual alienation from the Mexican Left, feeding a growing skepticism about the feasibility of radical change in Latin American politics. In addition to that, the increasingly open authoritarianism of the Cuban Revolution and the abandonment of its democratic promises also contributed to the gradual cooling off of his revolutionary fervor. Both factors sent Fuentes down the road in search of an ideological third way, equidistant of "the extreme left" and the "extreme right," which would coincide with the changes in orientation of the cultural organizations promoting Cold War liberalism in the region.

---

[41] On the MLN, Iber, *Neither Peace nor Freedom*, 145–173; Zolov, *The Last Good Neighbor*, 21–54.

[42] Carlos Fuentes to Carl Brandt, May 10, 1962, Box 89, Folder 34, Carlos Fuentes Papers, 1830s–2012, Manuscripts Division, Princeton University Library, One Washington Road, Princeton, NJ, cited in Zolov, *The Last Good Neighbor*, 164.

[43] López Arriaga, "Carlos Fuentes y la Revolución Cubana," 105–119. Indeed, the newsmagazine was partially funded by the Cuban news agency *Prensa Latina*, Zolov, *The Last Good Neighbor*, 88.

The Search for Democratic Socialism, 1964–1968

Between 1964 and 1968, Carlos Fuentes tried to find a way forward for "democratic socialism" that steered clear of both revolutionary turmoil and the rigid polarization of the Cold War. He parted ways with what he characterized as the "dogmatic Left" (*izquierda dogmática*) in Mexican politics, which he blamed for the collapse of the MLN, and grew more skeptical about the Cuban Revolution in private, although he still did not dare to criticize it in public – opting instead for an indirect censure of the course charted in Havana by lambasting Soviet Communism.

The shift coincided with the global rise of Fuentes's literary prestige, propelled by the ability of his U.S. literary agents to secure rapid translation into English of his main novels with Farrar, Straus and Giroux, including "Where the Air is Clear" (1960), "The Good Conscience" (1961), "The Death of Artemio Cruz" (1964), "Aura" (1965), and "A Change of Skin" (1968). Since the work of other celebrated Latin American novelists (García Márquez, Cortázar, Vargas Llosa, etc.) was still unavailable in English, Fuentes – who spoke English flawlessly – virtually became the only Latin American fiction writer widely known in the North Atlantic until the late sixties. This cultural currency opened the gates of the American college circuit to Fuentes, giving him the opportunity to modulate his ideas for a broader audience: In particular, he sought to go beyond Mexico and tried to reach U.S. elites.[44] As he later admitted, Fuentes found in the American (particularly New York) intellectual scene the kind of congenial, non-sectarian climate that he sorely missed in Mexico, "where everyone takes cover under the banner of the revolution, the Left, nationalism, etc."[45]

---

[44] He taught his first college course at Colorado State University in 1966–67 under the auspices of José Donoso – by then an experienced lecturer at the Iowa Writers' Workshop who remained a trusted guide on U.S. college life, José Donoso to Carlos Fuentes, Iowa City, April 6, 1966, Box 381, Folder 5, Carlos Fuentes Papers, 1830s–2012, Manuscripts Division, Princeton University Library, One Washington Road, Princeton, NJ; Carlos Fuentes to José Donoso, Paris, May 26, 1966, Box 381, Folder 6, Carlos Fuentes Papers, 1830s–2012, Manuscripts Division, Princeton University Library, One Washington Road, Princeton, NJ. On creative writing programs and the Cold War, see Eric Bennett, *Workshops of Empire: Stegner, Engle, and American Creative Writing during the Cold War* (Iowa City: University of Iowa Press, 2015).

[45] Carlos Fuentes, "El rapto del lenguaje," in "Mesa redonda del P.E.N. Club: papel del escritor en América Latina," *Mundo Nuevo* 5, November 1966, 29; Cohn, *The Latin American Literary Boom*, 52. In private he was even blunter, claiming that after comparing "the New York and European environment with what I left in Mexico, I won't have a change of scenery under any circumstances," Carlos Fuentes to José Donoso, Paris, July 24, 1966, Box 381, Folder 6, Carlos Fuentes Papers, 1830s–2012, Manuscripts Division, Princeton University Library, One Washington Road, Princeton, NJ.

Since his first collaborations in the United States ("Latinos vs. Gringos: Some Hard Truths We Should Know about the Mexicans," *Holiday*, October 1962; "The Argument of Latin America: Words for the North Americans," *Monthly Review*, January 1963), Fuentes advanced two main arguments about Latin America for U.S. readers: That revolutionary upheaval on the continent was the product of underdevelopment more than communist infiltration and that Washington's failures in Latin America stemmed above all from its ignorance of local realities.[46]

In the *New York Review of Books*, Fuentes went one step further, reassuring American readers that Mexico was not going to follow in Cuba's footsteps because the Mexican Revolution had already broken "the Spanish feudal inheritance that still shackles the rest of the Latin continent" via agrarian reform. However, Cuban-style guerrilla warfare was to be expected wherever these "feudal" structures remained in place. Thus, the motivating force behind the rise of Fidel Castro was not so much communist conspiracy as nationalist yearning.[47] As Fuentes summarized it years later, "Will the United States finally understand that the driving force behind all movements for change in Latin America is not Marxism but nationalism – a yearning for dignity and independence, a struggle for identity?"[48]

Therefore, Fuentes claimed that Castro had triumphed because he had given dignity back to the Cubans. More broadly, what Latin Americans like himself were searching for was some form of "democratic socialism": "Community, together with personal freedom," or the "belief that people can rule themselves without sacrificing either social welfare or personal freedom."[49] Sadly, Fuentes was implying, the Cuban Revolution had failed to deliver on those promises.

If, as Patrick Iber declares, the litmus test for a Latin American leftwing intellectual in the sixties was "his or her position vis-à-vis Fidel Castro's exercise of power in Cuba," disenchantment with Cuban-style socialism set in early for the Mexican writer. In 1964, Fuentes already

---

[46] Zolov, *The Last Good Neighbor*, 168–170. Money seemed to have been another powerful motive to publish in U.S. magazines, as Fuentes considered that there was "no more fruitful economic outcome for a Latin American writer than the collaboration with these magazines to supplement his income," Carlos Fuentes to José Donoso, Mexico City, September 1, 1964, Box 381, Folder 6, Carlos Fuentes Papers, 1830s–2012, Manuscripts Division, Princeton University Library, One Washington Road, Princeton, NJ

[47] Carlos Fuentes, "A Life," *New York Review of Books*, June 25, 1964, www.nybooks.com/articles/1964/06/25/a-life/; "Viva Zapata," *New York Review of Books*, March 13, 1969, www.nybooks.com/articles/1969/03/13/viva-zapata/.

[48] Carlos Fuentes, "Dominoes – Again?" *New York Times*, September 19, 1980, 27.

[49] Fuentes, "Viva Zapata."

admitted to Keith Botsford, a U.S. novelist and then CCF operative in Mexico, that the situation on the island "was far from ideal."[50] A year later State Department officials recorded Fuentes's disillusionment with the revolution: "He no longer believes in the efficacy of organized political action to bring about the New Jerusalem."[51] However, he was not ready to go on record condemning the Castro regime. Doing so could be equated with excusing imperialist aggression against the only successful socialist revolution in the Western Hemisphere. Thus, romanticization of the Cuban Revolution made "anti-anti-communism" the default position for Latin American intellectuals.[52] Indeed, Fuentes would not dare to pen a full-frontal attack on the Cuban regime until 2003: As he asked rhetorically then, "How to be against the Cuban Revolution?"[53]

Veiled criticism of Cuba via the Soviet example seemed a safer route to delineate what democratic socialism meant, as Soviet Communism elicited little enthusiasm among Latin American intellectuals.[54] For instance, the 1966 Sinyavsky–Daniel trial, the first show trial in the Soviet Union prosecuting offenses in works of fiction against authors Andrei Sinyavsky and Yuli Daniel, became an opportunity to advocate expert-led change for the masses. In his essay "Socialismo y cultura" ("Socialism and Culture"), Fuentes's description of what he called "our socialism" could be read against the backdrop of the failure of mass politics epitomized by the MLN, as his socialism had a strongly modernizing and technocratic flavor: It sought agrarian reform, agricultural mechanization, a larger internal market for consumers,

---

[50] Iber, *Neither Peace nor Freedom*, 188; for Botsford, 179–180. Interestingly, Fuentes seemed to be very hostile toward Botsford personally and considered him a spy, Carlos Fuentes to José Donoso, London, March 15, 1968, Box 381, Folder 5, Carlos Fuentes Papers, 1830s–2012, Manuscripts Division, Princeton University Library, One Washington Road, Princeton, NJ.

[51] Darwin Flakoll to Luis Mercier Vega, "Conversations with Fuentes," October 25, 1965, cited in Cobb, "Our Men in Paris," 139.

[52] On the other hand, López Arriaga, "Carlos Fuentes y la Revolución Cubana," 140–193, argues confusingly that the break up with Cuba did not really happen until the nineties, although her claims rely solely on Cuban sources and some Cuban propaganda works taken at face value.

[53] Carlos Fuentes, "Infidelidades," *Reforma*, April 16, 2003, www.cubaencuentro.com/opinion/articulos/infidelidades-276768. The article came out in the context of a huge government crackdown on Cuban dissidents.

[54] "Libre y América Latina," *Libre* 1, September–November 1971, 26, reprinted in *Libre. Revista de crítica literaria (1971–1972)*, ed. Plinio Apuleyo Mendoza (Madrid: Turner, 1990), 5. On the other hand, according to Tobias Rupprecht the Soviet model did find more support among certain anti-Western Latin Americans, "Latin American *Tercermundistas* in the Soviet Union: Paradise Lost and Found," in *Latin America and the Global Cold War*, eds. Thomas C. Field, Jr., Stella Krepp and Vanni Pettinà (Chapel Hill: The University of North Carolina Press, 2020), 221–240.

industrialization, economic autonomy for states, and, of course, cultural freedom and free speech. Hardly worth saying, these enlightened reforms were to be delivered by expert elites.[55]

But given the polarization unleashed by the Cuban Revolution, this moderate and elite-driven socialism only found venues available in the magazines sponsored by U.S. organizations, whose orientation shifted to the Left under the Kennedy and Johnson administrations. In the context of Kennedy's Alliance for Progress, designed to stave off revolutionary contagion in Latin America by promoting development, a cultural rapprochement of sorts with the Left took place. In particular, the CIA agents in charge of the CCF in Latin America – Michael Josselson and John Hunt, along with Belgian anarchist Luis Mercier Vega – launched a new strategy more in tune with left-wing sensibilities that came to be known as *Fidelismo sin Fidel* ("Fidelism without Fidel"), seeking to persuade prominent leftists to question the revolutionary path. This involved dismissing most of the Spanish exiles who had run the CCF since its founding.[56] Yet, despite all the changes, the program continued to be directed toward the elites, in true Cold War liberal fashion.

The CIA's overhaul culminated in 1966 with the replacement of the Latin American department of the CCF by an independent affiliate, the Instituto Latinoamericano de Relaciones Internacionales (ILARI), and the release of an entirely new literary magazine, *Mundo Nuevo*. This short-lived publication (1966–1971), edited by Uruguayan critic Emir Rodríguez Monegal, became the finest distillation of Cold War liberalism in Latin America. Alongside a small coterie of Spanish and Latin American publishers – each subsidized by Washington – the magazine played an instrumental role in promoting the Latin American literary "Boom" and succeeded in enticing prominent left-wing writers to contribute to its pages, from Gabriel García Márquez to Pablo Neruda.[57]

---

[55] Carlos Fuentes, "Socialismo y cultura," in *Casa con dos puertas* (México: Joaquín Mortiz, 1970), 129–130. On the Sinyavsky–Daniel show trial, David Caute, *Politics and the Novel during the Cold War* (London/New York: Routledge, 2017), 219–227.

[56] Olga Glondys, "Dismissals of the Congress for Cultural Freedom's Representatives in Latin America as part of the strategy of 'Opening to the Left'," *Culture and History Digital Journal* 7, no. 1 (2018): 1–11, www.doi.org/10.3989/chdj.2018.010; Marta Ruiz Galbete, "¿'Fidelismo sin Fidel'? El Congreso por la Libertad de la Cultura y la Revolución Cubana," *Historia Crítica*, 67 (2018): 111–137, www.doi.org/10.7440/histcrit67.2018.06; Patrick Iber, "The Cost of Freedom: The Congress for Cultural Freedom in Latin America," and Andrés Sánchez-Padilla, "Development by the Book: US Book Diplomacy and the Latin American Cultural Cold War," in *US Public Diplomacy Strategies in Latin America During the Sixties: Time for Persuasion*, eds. Francisco Rodríguez-Jiménez, Lorenzo Delgado Gómez-Escalonilla and Benedetta Calandra (New York; Abingdon: Routledge, 2024), 88–115, 116–138.

[57] Russell S. Cobb, "Our Men in Paris?". See also María Eugenia Mudrovcic, "*Mundo Nuevo*: Behind the Scenes of a Spanish *Encounter*," in *Campaigning Culture and the*

But *Mundo Nuevo*, like *Cuadernos* before it, also aspired to force the politics of Latin Americans away from the Cuban Revolution and toward what it called "a culture without borders, free of dogma and fanatical servitudes."[58] Put another way, it wanted to encourage Latin American intellectuals to travel a middle path between the extremes of Left and Right.[59] Fuentes expressed himself in the same terms when he symbolically buried the Cold War in literature in his piece on the 1966 PEN Club Congress which angered the Cuban intelligentsia so much.[60]

Although his contributions were not openly political, Carlos Fuentes relied on *Mundo Nuevo* to promote a cosmopolitan idea of literature detached from mass politics that was plainly at odds with the cultural agenda of revolutionary engagement emanating from Havana. In particular, he warned that excessive political commitment could be detrimental to critical thinking: "the left-leaning writer, all too frequently, also covers himself with an ideological umbrella that excuses him of thinking for himself, disguises himself with the decalogue of the coming apocalypse and stops writing."[61] Fuentes claimed to be fighting against the suffocating "naturalist and documentary tendency of the Spanish-American novel," but his artistic rebukes could also be easily read as thinly disguised charges against the oppressive intellectual climate of Cuba, and the Cubans certainly did so.[62]

Global Cold War: The Journals of the Congress for Cultural Freedom, ed. Giles Scott-Smith and Charlotte A. Lerg (London: Palgrave Macmillan, 2017), 207–225; Whitney, *Finks*, chapter 11.

[58] "Presentación," *Mundo Nuevo* 1, July 1966, 4. Gabriel García Márquez defined the publication as a "great magazine" but refused to be part of its editorial board due to suspected U.S. sponsorship, Gabriel García Márquez to Carlos Fuentes, September 30, n.d., Box 381, Folder 8, Carlos Fuentes Papers, 1830s–2012, Manuscripts Division, Princeton University Library, One Washington Road, Princeton, NJ.

[59] In addition to *Mundo Nuevo*, in Mexico the CIA also supported a literary journal along the same lines, *Diálogos* (1964–71), Willard C. Curtis, "Dispatch: Mexican Program," October 28, 1963, Record Number 104-10211-10045, CIA Files, The President John F. Kennedy Assassination Records, National Archives and Records Administration (NARA), College Park, MD; José María Espinasa, ed., *Revista Diálogos. Antología* (México: El Colegio de México, 2008); Guillermo Sheridan, "La CIA planea una revista cultural mexicana," *Letras Libres*, July 7, 2017, www.letraslibres.com/historia/la-cia-planea-una-revista-cultural-mexicana/; "La CIA apadrina una revista mexicana," *Letras Libres*, July 14, 2017, www.letraslibres.com/historia/la-cia-apadrina-una-revista-mexicana/; Iber, "The Cost of Freedom," 104.

[60] To be fair, Cuban overreaction over Fuentes angered even strong admirers of its revolution like García Márquez, Gabriel García Márquez to Carlos Fuentes, March 4 [1966], Box 381, Folder 8, Carlos Fuentes Papers, 1830s–2012, Manuscripts Division, Princeton University Library, One Washington Road, Princeton, NJ.

[61] Carlos Fuentes, "Situación del escritor en América Latina," *Mundo Nuevo* 1, July 1966, 21.

[62] Fuentes, *La nueva novela hispanoamericana*, 11; López Arriaga, "Carlos Fuentes y la Revolución Cubana," 167–193.

Fuentes's faith in elite expertise to carry out social reform was further expressed by his enthusiasm for the "culture of poverty" theory developed by American anthropologist Oscar Lewis, which posited that the personal experiences of the urban poor might engender a self-sustaining cycle of poverty extremely difficult to eradicate. Lewis's work proved deeply controversial in Mexico due to the fact that his research was based on real Mexican subjects. Fuentes, however, dismissed any such criticism as reflecting the very parochial nationalism he was fighting against in the literary realm.[53]

Nonetheless, the 1966–67 revelations by the *New York Times* and *Ramparts* that the CIA had been secretly funding noncommunist organizations through proxy foundations, including the CCF, dealt a mortal blow to the Cold War liberal dream of an apolitical culture in Latin America that might weaken the appeal of revolution among intellectuals. The revelations thoroughly discredited the International Association for Cultural Freedom (IACF), the successor to the CCF, as well as its Latin American offshoot ILARI – which irreversibly disintegrated over the following decade. For its part, the revelations lost *Mundo Nuevo* its charismatic editor Emir Rodríguez Monegal and, with him, its most distinguished left-wing contributors. The magazine disappeared in 1971, quickly followed by the rest of the ILARI magazines.[64]

In contrast to other left-wing intellectuals like Gabriel Garcia Márquez, who denounced *Mundo Nuevo* and vowed to never publish there again, Fuentes continued to publish and give interviews to the magazine until Rodríguez Monegal's exit, seemingly unruffled by the CIA revelations, since his heterodox views did not have much space in existing Mexican publications.[65] But the demise of *Mundo Nuevo* did not exactly spell the end of Cold War liberalism, as the political turmoil after 1968 motivated

---

[63] Carlos Fuentes, "Oscar Lewis," in *Casa con dos puertas*, 115–118. On Oscar Lewis and the "culture of poverty," Patrick J. Iber, "Social Science, Cultural Imperialism, and the Ford Foundation in Latin America in the 1960s," in *The Global 1960s: Convention, Contest and Counterculture*, ed. Tamara Chaplin and Jadwiga Pieper Mooney (London: Routledge, 2017), 96–114; Karin Alejandra Rosemblatt, "Other Americas: Transnationalism, Scholarship, and the Culture of Poverty in Mexico and the United States," *Hispanic American Historical Review* 89, no. 4 (2009): 603–641, www.doi.org/10.1215/00182168-2009-047; Sánchez-Padilla, "Development by the Book," 125–126. On the scandal surrounding the translation and release in 1960s Mexico of Lewis's book *The Children of Sánchez*, Freije, *Citizens of Scandal*, 37–46.

[64] Iber, *Neither Peace nor Freedom*, 215–221.

[65] Oscar Lewis, K. S. Karol and Carlos Fuentes, "Pobreza, burguesía y revolución," *Mundo Nuevo* 11, May 1967, 5–18, "'Cambio de piel' en Italia," *Mundo Nuevo* 21, March 1968, 20–22. To be sure, García Márquez had harbored such reservations about *Mundo Nuevo* from the start, but that did not deter his initial participation, Gabriel García Márquez to Carlos Fuentes, September 30, n.d., Box 381, Folder 8, Carlos Fuentes Papers, 1830s–2012, Manuscripts Division, Princeton University Library, One Washington Road, Princeton, NJ.

Fuentes to establish a new Latin American magazine free of parochialisms and untainted by suspicions of compromised funding.

The Long 1970s and the Neoliberal Turn

During the 1970s, the Mexican "dirty war" and the split on the Left managed to resuscitate Cold War liberalism in Mexico under a new form after U.S. cultural Cold Warriors left the field – and just when it was being increasingly replaced by neoconservatism in the U.S.[66] If elite-driven reform was already embraced by Fuentes and other members of the Mexican intelligentsia, by the end of the decade liberal empire also came to be seen as the answer to the economic dilemmas of the age. However, by then the new Latin American Cold War liberals had replaced social democracy with neoliberalism to tame the powers of the nation-state.

The Tlatelolco massacre (October 2, 1968), in which the Mexican army killed hundreds of students in Mexico City to crush the rising student movement, has been interpreted as the opening salvo of decades of "dirty war" and human rights abuses by the Mexican government against various left-wing guerrillas, students, peasants, trade unions, indigenous groups and sexual workers – even if considered relatively tame by comparison with the repression of right-wing dictatorships across the region. It also profoundly shook Carlos Fuentes and the rest of the Mexican intelligentsia, forcing a prolonged intellectual reckoning with the abuses of state power.[67] As Fuentes said a year later, "The Tlatelolco massacre left an open wound in all consciences and in many bodies."[68]

---

[66] See the chapter by Michael Brenes and Michael Franczak in this volume, "Conservatives in a 'Liberal Age': Rethinking the Neoconservative Turn in the 1960s."

[67] Claire Brewster, *Responding to Crisis in Contemporary Mexico: The Political Writings of Paz, Fuentes, Monsiváis and Poniatowska* (Tucson: The University of Arizona Press, 2005): 69–101; Iber, *Neither Peace nor Freedom*, 146; King, *The Role of Mexico's Plural*, 47; Zolov, *The Last Good Neighbor*, 287–289. The Truth Commission established by the Mexican government in 2021 to investigate human rights violations between 1965 and 1990 documented thousands of victims of different crimes and blamed local and federal authorities, but suggested the real numbers might be greater due to the destruction of information by Mexican military and intelligence agencies, AP, "Revelan nuevos datos de la represión entre 1965 y 1990, incluidos los 'vuelos de la muerte,'" *Proceso* (August 16, 2024), www.proceso.com.mx/nacional/2024/8/16/revelan-nuevos-datos-de-la-represion-entre-1965-1990-incluidos-los-vuelos-de-la-muerte-334987.html; due to internal differences regarding the scope of political violence, the Commission released two different reports with the broadest one identifying more than 8,500 victims, Mexico Project, "Fifty Years of Silence: Mexico Faces the Legacy of Its Dirty War," *National Security Archive* (December 20, 2024), https://nsarchive.gwu.edu/briefing-book/mexico/2024-12-20/fifty-years-silence-mexico-faces-legacy-its-dirty-war.

[68] Carlos Fuentes to José Donoso, Cuernavaca, August 27, 1969, Box 381, Folder 6, Carlos Fuentes Papers, 1830s–2012, Manuscripts Division, Princeton University Library, One

At first, Fuentes sought to create a new Latin American magazine with his old mentor Octavio Paz to promote the cause of "democratic socialism" as the answer to the dilemmas of the "dirty war." After the foundering of *Mundo Nuevo*, Fuentes abandoned *La cultura en México* (the last Mexican left-wing magazine where he still published and which he edited on occasion)[69] and joined forces with Spanish exile Juan Goytisolo to set up another literary enterprise that tried to reunite all strands of the Latin American Left not by being apolitical, but by openly promoting "democratic socialism": the magazine *Libre*. Edited from Paris by Goytisolo (like *Mundo Nuevo*), *Libre* relied on the wealthy scion of a Bolivian tin magnate for funding.

In the end, *Libre* only accelerated the intellectual polarization brought about by the Cuban Revolution. The allure of an apolitical culture that *Mundo Nuevo* had briefly held up by avoiding overt criticism of Cuba was no longer possible: After the "Padilla affair," *Libre* was forced to confront the only socialist regime in Latin America directly. In early 1971, Cuban poet Heberto Padilla had been detained, tortured, and subjected to a humiliating show trial with Stalinist self-criticism included for his increasingly critical poetry and the resulting scandal forced the Latin American intelligentsia to explicitly take sides for or against Cuba.

Fuentes publicly defended the Cuban writer and criticized (in private) what he called "cliché socialism."[70] Two open letters signed by other prominent intellectuals like Mario Vargas Llosa or Octavio Paz and a lengthy debate in the pages of *Libre* followed. Even though authors like Julio Cortázar and Gabriel García Márquez, after some equivocation, sided with Fidel Castro, the similarities with the Stalinist playbook were hard to deny.[71] To be sure, the critics hardly offered a stinging rebuke of the Cuban regime, but the whole controversy

Washington Road, Princeton, NJ. In the aftermath of the massacre, Fuentes remained in Europe after being labeled a traitor to the country and denounced before the prosecutor's office, describing the situation in Mexico as "hellish and shitty," Carlos Fuentes to José Donoso, Paris, November 1, 1968, Box 381, Folder 6, Carlos Fuentes Papers, 1830s–2012, Manuscripts Division, Princeton University Library, One Washington Road, Princeton, NJ; Gabriel García Márquez to Carlos Fuentes, November 2 [1968], Box 381, Folder 8, Carlos Fuentes Papers, 1830s–2012, Manuscripts Division, Princeton University Library, One Washington Road, Princeton, NJ.

[69] Carlos Fuentes to José Donoso, Mexico City, September 4, 1971, Box 381, Folder 6, Carlos Fuentes Papers, 1830s–2012, Manuscripts Division, Princeton University Library, One Washington Road, Princeton, NJ.

[70] Carlos Fuentes to Norman Mailer, Mexico City, December 12, 1971, Box 381, Folder 10, Carlos Fuentes Papers, 1830s–2012, Manuscripts Division, Princeton University Library, One Washington Road, Princeton, NJ.

[71] "An Open Letter to Fidel Castro," *New York Review of Books*, May 6, 1971, www.nybooks.com/articles/1971/05/06/an-open-letter-to-fidel-castro/. The Cuban response

signaled a turning point for the former defenders of "democratic socialism": If the sole Latin American socialist state that had held up so much promise had irreversibly turned into another Marxist–Leninist nightmare, it was only confirmation that the real problem was state power rather than U.S. imperialism. Thus, the "Padilla affair" revealed that the split on the Left regarding Cuba was also a disagreement about the role of the state in Latin American politics.[72]

After the collapse of *Libre* over Cuba, Fuentes supported Octavio Paz's new literary magazine. *Plural* (1971–76), run from Mexico City, would prioritize Mexican concerns. Paz had withdrawn from *Libre* when it became clear that the price to pay for the unity of the Left was the exclusion of valuable authors who dared to publicly criticize the Cuban Revolution, particularly Cuban exile Guillermo Cabrera Infante.[73] If *Plural* managed to avoid the intellectual storms over the "Padilla affair" by steering clear of Cuba, it also became a vehicle for those who wanted to transition from "democratic socialism" to neoliberalism on the basis of the censure of state power – taking advantage of greater freedom of the press under the presidency of Luis Echeverría (1970–76).[74]

---

in "The Padilla Case," *New York Review of Books*, July 22, 1971, www.nybooks.com/articles/1971/07/22/the-padilla-case-2/.

[72] On the "Padilla affair," "Caso Padilla," *Libre* 1, September–November 1971, 26, reprinted in *Libre. Revista de crítica literaria (1971–1972)*, ed. Plinio Apuleyo Mendoza (Madrid: Turner, 1990): 130–135; Cohn, "PEN and the Sword," 218–219; Iber, *Neither Peace nor Freedom*, 222–227.

[73] Cabrera Infante had been an enthusiastic supporter of the revolution in its early days, running the literary magazine *Lunes de Revolución* and even serving as cultural attaché in Brussels. But after several clashes with the Castro regime, Cabrera Infante went into exile and became a pariah for some time among Latin American intellectuals when he broke the taboo of criticizing Cuba in a 1968 interview for the Argentine magazine *Primera Plana*. Although Fuentes tried to enlist him for *Libre*, the opposition of Cortázar and García Márquez made it impossible, Guillermo Cabrera Infante to Carlos Fuentes, March 13, 1971, Box 381, Folder 1, Carlos Fuentes Papers, 1830s–2012, Manuscripts Division, Princeton University Library, One Washington Road, Princeton, NJ; Carlos Fuentes to Guillermo Cabrera Infante, December 16, 1971, Box 381, Folder 1, Carlos Fuentes Papers, 1830s–2012, Manuscripts Division, Princeton University Library, One Washington Road, Princeton, NJ. For his part, Cabrera Infante deemed Cortázar a Cuban agent, Guillermo Cabrera Infante to Carlos Fuentes, April 22, 1971, Box 381, Folder 1, Carlos Fuentes Papers, 1830s–2012, Manuscripts Division, Princeton University Library, One Washington Road, Princeton, NJ. See also Juan Goytisolo, *Forbidden Territory and Realms of Strife: The Memoirs of Juan Goytisolo* (London/New York: Verso, 2003): 299–328; King, *The Role of Mexico's* Plural, 53–57.

[74] King, *The Role of Mexico's* Plural, 75–108; Ignacio M. Sánchez Prado, "Claiming Liberalism: Enrique Krauze, *Vuelta*, *Letras Libres*, and the Reconfiguration of the Mexican Intellectual Class," *Mexican Studies/Estudios Mexicanos* 26, no. 1 (2010): 47–78, www.doi.org/10.1525/msem.2010.26.1.47.

If Fuentes traveled to the same destination, he followed a slightly slower route than his colleagues at *Plural* who had despaired of the Left after the "Padilla affair." Unlike them, Fuentes decided to throw in his lot with the Echeverría administration as the last, best hope of achieving "democratic socialism" in Mexico, eventually serving as ambassador to France.[75] Fuentes even excused Echeverría's involvement in the Mexican "dirty war," particularly the so-called Corpus Christi Massacre of June 10, 1971 – also known as *El Halconazo* because the state-sponsored militias that assaulted the students that day were called *los halcones* ("the falcons").

To be sure, Fuentes condemned the "dirty war" but thought that the Echeverría reforms known as democratic opening (*apertura democrática*) were the only realistic way to reform Mexican politics: Indeed, he saw Echeverría as the only one representing the reasonable center: "The extreme left hates Echeverría every bit as much as the extreme right."[76] Democratic socialism was still possible, but only if it abandoned its former association with Marxist dogmas: "The Democratic Left can only succeed in Mexico if it proposes itself modest but concrete and continuing objectives [...]. A badly digested Marxism keeps us, with all too much frequency, imprisoned in abstract schemes or in simple and apathetic expectation of the next catastrophe, fatal and spontaneous."[77] Furthermore, Fuentes put his faith in Echeverría because he saw the Mexican state, if properly led by enlightened elites,

---

[75] The Echeverría administration enlisted several big names among the Mexican intelligentsia – including Porfirio Muñoz Ledo – with a populist mixture of public spending at home and sponsorship of economic governance reform abroad despite Echeverría's own role in the Tlatelolco and Corpus Christi massacres and the fact that it expanded the "dirty war" started by its predecessor, see Christy Thornton, *Revolution in Development: Mexico and the Governance of the Global Economy* (Oakland: University of California Press, 2021): 166–170.

[76] Carlos Fuentes, "Mexico and Its Demons," *New York Review of Books* (September 20, 1973), www.nybooks.com/articles/1973/09/20/mexico-and-its-demons/. Fuentes was particularly enthusiastic about the lifting of restrictions to the press, Carlos Fuentes to Guillermo Cabrera Infante, January 6, 1971, Box 381, Folder 1, Carlos Fuentes Papers, 1830s–2012, Manuscripts Division, Princeton University Library, One Washington Road, Princeton, NJ; Carlos Fuentes to José Donoso, Paris, August 17, 1973, Box 381, Folder 6, Carlos Fuentes Papers, 1830s–2012, Manuscripts Division, Princeton University Library, One Washington Road, Princeton, NJ. In 2006, Echeverría was prosecuted for both massacres (Tlatelolco and Corpus Christi) by Mexican courts but eventually exonerated, "Mexican Court Restores Warrant for Ex-President," *Washington Post*, November 29, 2006, www.washingtonpost.com/archive/politics/2006/11/30/mexican-court-restores-warrant-for-ex-president/b7c32358-b963-4ea7-a72d-13cfadbdc386/.

[77] Carlos Fuentes, "La Disyuntiva Mexicana," *Libre* 2, December 1971–February 1972, 26, reprinted in *Libre. Revista de crítica literaria (1971–1972)*, ed. Plinio Apuleyo Mendoza (Madrid: Turner, 1990): 197–208.

as the only bulwark against the economic malaise of the seventies and the potential encroachment of U.S. imperialism: "The only, the minimal defensive card is constituted by certain states."[78]

However, these hopes were already in tension with Fuentes's visible unease about the merits of the nationalist model of development after thirty years of import-substitution industrialization (ISI), or *desarrollismo*[79]: the balance included "a limited internal market [...]; a drop in productivity [...]; a mounting dependence on onerous foreign loans and investments; a sky-rocketing foreign debt." Fuentes still thought that an enlightened state run by the right elites might be the answer in Mexico – even though he already concurred with the negative view of state centralization taken by Paz and others. In addition, he did not seem to concede much traction to contemporary Global South cooperation efforts like the New International Economic Order (NIEO) and the Charter of Economic Rights and Duties of States, wondering desperately: "Are the models offered by the dominant world systems the only ones available?"[80]

Alas, despite the best efforts of Echeverría, the Mexican state was unable to weather the economic storms of the seventies: Although his administration tried to diversify its traditional dependence on the U.S. economy, inflation and high prices led to an increase of the same foreign loans and debt that Fuentes had criticized, especially under the presidency of Echeverría's successor, José López Portillo (1976–82), making the Mexican economy more rather than less dependent on the United States and leading to the 1982 sovereign debt default sparked by the hike in U.S. interest rates carried out by the U.S. Federal Reserve.[81] It was this striking breakdown of state power that led to Fuentes's definitive loss of faith in the merits of state economic intervention to save Mexico.

During the same period, the U.S. political economy experienced a thorough reconfiguration that facilitated the advance of neoliberal globalization on the basis of the primacy of global markets over

---

[78] Carlos Fuentes, "Opciones críticas en el verano de nuestro descontento," *Plural* 11, August 1972, 6. Fuentes' finances were directly hit by the dollar devaluation that accompanied the collapse of the Bretton Woods system, Carlos Fuentes to José Donoso, Paris, August 17, 1973, Box 381, Folder 6, Carlos Fuentes Papers, 1830s–2012, Manuscripts Division, Princeton University Library, One Washington Road, Princeton, NJ.

[79] On Mexican import-substitution industrialization policies after World War II, Thornton, *Revolution in Development*, 145–148.

[80] Fuentes, "Mexico and Its Demons." On the Mexican role in these efforts, see Christy Thornton, "A Mexican New International Economic Order?" in *Latin America and the Global Cold War*, eds. Thomas C. Field, Jr., Stella Krepp and Vanni Pettinà (Chapel Hill: The University of North Carolina Press, 2020), 301–342.

[81] Thornton, *Revolution in Development*, 190–199; Zolov, *The Last Good Neighbor*, 290–295.

state power.[82] Fuentes became a privileged witness to that process after ending his political career for good when he resigned from his ambassadorship after the López Portillo administration appointed the "butcher of Tlatelolco," Gustavo Díaz Ordaz – the Mexican president during the 1968 massacre and a symbol of the abuses of state power – as ambassador to Spain.[83] Afterwards, he relocated to the United States (1978–86) as a regular lecturer on Latin American literature at some of the most elitist Ivy League universities – Columbia, UPenn, Princeton, Dartmouth, or Harvard, among others.[84] The resurgence of the U.S. economy at the helm of neoliberal globalization prompted in him a positive reconsideration of the advantages of the U.S. liberal empire. Fuentes came to the conclusion that the key behind American prosperity and Latin American underdevelopment lay in the primacy of civil society over the state: "The United States has a very developed civil society; therefore a writer can devote himself exclusively to writing because he knows that there is Congress, the unions, the press and a million other things that take care of the political issues."[85] Furthermore, whereas in the sixties he had extolled the moral commitment of writers, two decades later he sounded positively relieved by the social decline of public intellectuals: The time had passed when "a writer could send a boy to the death with an inflammatory sentence [...]. Writers only are socially important in societies without importance because he usurps [sic] functions, those of the society itself when is plural, intelligent, healthy."[86]

If Fuentes's criticism of U.S. foreign policy persisted, it was always counterbalanced by similar or stronger language for Soviet actions. For instance, in 1983, as he criticized American intervention in El Salvador and Guatemala, he declared that "we, the true friends of your nation in Latin America, we, the admirers of your extraordinary achievements in literature, science, and the arts and of your democratic institutions, of your Congress and your courts, your universities and publishing houses, and your free press, will not permit you to conduct yourselves in Latin American affairs as the Soviet Union conducts itself in East European and Central Asian affairs."

---

[82] Daniel J. Sargent, *A Superpower Transformed: The Remaking of U.S. Foreign Relations in the 1970s* (New York: Oxford University Press, 2014).
[83] Carlos Fuentes to José Donoso, Margency, October 11, 1977, Box 381, Folder 6, Carlos Fuentes Papers, 1830s–2012, Manuscripts Division, Princeton University Library, One Washington Road, Princeton, NJ. See also Delden, *Carlos Fuentes*, 119–120.
[84] Williams, *The Writings of Carlos Fuentes*, 40–44.
[85] Shrady, "Carlos Fuentes: Life and Language," 26–27.
[86] Carlos Fuentes to José Donoso, February 6, 1981, Box 381, Folder 6, Carlos Fuentes Papers, 1830s–2012, Manuscripts Division, Princeton University Library, One Washington Road, Princeton, NJ.

Fuentes's very public falling-out with Octavio Paz meant that his embrace of neoliberalism would not take place in the former's liberal magazine (*Vuelta*, 1976–98), but in the pages of the *New York Times* and *Harvard Review*, as well as in essays such as *Latin America at War with the Past* (1985) or *Myself with Others* (1988).[87] However, both *Vuelta* and, later on, its successor *Letras Libres* (1999–), were as enthusiastic about the virtues of free markets and U.S. global primacy as Fuentes.[88] Ultimately, all of them saw neoliberal policies, particularly the Washington Consensus, as the only way to discipline state power and bring prosperity to Latin America.[89]

Conclusions

The political trajectory of Carlos Fuentes as a public intellectual fleshes out the twisted road of Cold War liberalism in the Americas, which started out as a quest to bring a modicum of social democracy to the Western Hemisphere and ended up setting the stage for the dominance of neoliberalism by the late twentieth century. This ideological metamorphosis was, in turn, the result of two distinct features: the late arrival of Cold War liberalism to the region and the intersection of the split on the Left with the "dirty wars" and the 1970s global crisis of capitalism. Carlos Fuentes bore witness and took part in both developments.

Was Carlos Fuentes a Cold War liberal? Although he never used that label and claimed to be close to Marx at various points in his life, he did recognize himself as a member of the Democratic Left and eventually championed the neoliberal agenda of the United States for the region, based on the same extreme skepticism of mass politics of Cold War liberalism. Indeed, Fuentes remained a supporter of the Cuban Revolution only as long as it seemed to promise a social democratic outcome. "The turmoil of revolution, if permitted to run its course, promptly finds its institutional channels," he argued in an attempt to discourage interference

---

[87] Although the origins of the feud with Paz are disputed, Fuentes' continued support for Echeverría may have been a contributing factor, especially after Fuentes kept quiet about the *Excélsior* affair: In 1976, the editorial board of *Excélsior*, the newspaper that also edited *Plural*, was removed under government coercion for its increasingly critical reporting on the Echeverría presidency – leading to the exit of the team at the helm of *Plural* as well. Fuentes occasionally wrote for *Vuelta*, but stopped doing so after a savage 1988 piece assailing his entire body of work by Enrique Krauze, deputy director of the magazine, Freije, *Citizens of Scandal*, 82–86; King, *The Role of Mexico's* Plural, 5, 179–183.

[88] Maarten van Delden, "Mexico and the United States: The View from *Vuelta* (1976–1998)," *Discourse* 23, no. 2 (2001): 62–80, www.doi.org/10.1353/dis.2001.0019.

[89] Fuentes, "A Harvard Commencement," 202.

with the Sandinistas in the 1980s.[90] Although the "Padilla affair" is traditionally considered the turning point in the splintering of support for the Cuban Revolution, Fuentes's revolutionary disappointment predated the scandal.[91] Only the prevalence of "anti-anti-communism," the fear of favoring U.S. imperialism, delayed the public break up until 1971. But the rift legitimized criticism of the Cuban Revolution and thus turned the debate on the limits of state power rather than North-South inequality. However, Fuentes still saw a last chance to achieve "democratic socialism" in the presidency of Luis Echeverría – to the point of excusing his role in the widespread state violence of those years. After that attempt also failed, he joined the forces of the advocates of neoliberal globalization.

The trajectory of Carlos Fuentes thus shows how noncommunist social democracy was another route to neoliberalism. As it turned out, Cold War liberal ideas in Latin America paved the way for the eventual triumph of neoliberalism during the "Lost Decade" of the 1980s, when most Latin American countries experienced crushing debt crises after the Fed hiked interest rates in the U.S. The political agenda of the Democratic Left represented by Fuentes championed a platform of elitist modernization under U.S. global primacy, but after the disappointing reality of the Cuban Revolution and ISI policies in the region, it also set the terms for the neoliberal assault by storm in the 1980s. Therefore, the work of Fuentes contributed to the delegitimization of nationalist politics and the endorsement of U.S.-led neoliberal globalization, perhaps facilitating acceptance of the Washington Consensus agenda after the end of the Cold War. This ambivalent legacy of Cold War liberalism still remains with us today.

---

[90] Fuentes, "A Harvard Commencement," 204.
[91] Mario Vargas Llosa's ideological transformation does seem to have originated then, Patrick J. Iber, "The Metamorphosis: The Political Education of Mario Vargas Llosa," *The Nation*, April 29, 2019, 27–31, www.thenation.com/article/archive/mario-vargas-llosa-sabres-and-utopias-book-review/.

13 Afterword

Samuel Moyn

This collection takes the historical and political study of Cold War liberalism onto a new plane. Defining it as antidemocratic and imperialist, the introduction frames chapters making up a gallery of Cold War liberals and forms of Cold War liberalism, presented with unprecedented variety. In particular, this book transcends the existing historical writing on the topic by focusing on the 1960s and on Cold War liberalism in action in American policy around the globe. The Atlanticist geography and intellectualized bent of many presentations of Cold War liberalism make little sense, the editors imply, if what was at stake was an elitist ideology masking a project of world domination.

The few comments that follow offer a coda to the essays, without addressing their achievements individually. Rather, I reflect on how this volume reconceives the problem of Cold War liberalism as a category less in Atlantic intellectual history or political theory than in the history of the foreign relations of the American hegemon after World War II.

Of course, as the introduction to this book reports, almost all liberals, with few exceptions, have been antidemocratic or elitist. The founders of liberalism all rejected not just direct democracy but also many forms of representative democracy, especially after the French Revolution's experiments in universal suffrage. And it is certainly true that when it comes to the potential for tragedy that the Cold War liberals saw, they inherited a great deal from their liberal forebears. The French Revolution chastened as much as it inspired liberalism – which was founded on the dilemma of how to contain and institutionalize its emancipatory promise. In 1848, liberals turned on their own backing of freedom to join the side of repression. Long before the Cold War, there were threads of anxiety and pessimism at the heart of the liberal creed. Who could deny it?

This isn't the whole story, or the most interesting one, however. Far from being just a hypocritical lie, or even a permanent stance, liberals retreat to the lair of tragedy now and again – and never more thoroughly than in the early Cold War – even as they await the circumstances of ambitious world-domination. In a lasting pattern, they toggle between fear and hope, defense and offense, and what Cold War liberals debated as "containment" and "rollback" as circumstances allow and experience recommends.

This isn't to say, all the same, that there is nothing new under the liberal sun in the twentieth century, as if it were caught in exact repetition of the shifting options of liberalism again and again. The balance between hope and fear certainly did shift in the making of early Cold War liberalism relative to much liberal thinking of the past, which is hardly to deny – again, who could? – that American foreign policy evolved in an aggressive and indeed counter-emancipatory direction as the 1960s dawned.

Too reductive a set of conclusions about Cold War liberalism could miss its own historical dynamics, which were never set in stone. That is certainly obvious in Kyong-Min Son's brilliant exploration, which hardly means that the rise of managerial democracy is the same old hypocritical elitism of the capacitarian liberalism of the nineteenth century.[1] Nor are the forms and functions of American imperialism after World War II just a facsimile of those European powers developed before. The editors emphasize the continuity of Cold War liberalism with the liberal past, and fair enough. But there were novelties too. And the essays illustrate even more powerfully that there were changes afoot within the Cold War era of liberalism itself.

Easily the most important intervention in this book is that it honestly registers that "Cold War liberalism" is a category in the historiography of the United States, in general, and U.S. foreign relations in particular. Attempts to broaden it, including in this volume itself, sometimes mainly ratify how parochially American it still is. I have been struck by the reception of attempts to Europeanize the category and how dubious or even quizzical Europeans themselves sometimes are in seeing their countries and intellectuals characterized as having been marked by Cold War liberalism – even though France and Germany are often presumed to be the premier Cold War battleground. Even the political culture of the United Kingdom, admired by many an American Cold War liberal, has not welcomed the category. But then, this volume has not one chapter on that previously geopolitically leading country.

There are exceptions to any story of the supremacy of the United States in Cold War liberal historiography in this volume, but they prove the rule – much like the Cold War construct of the free world featured in this volume – that one country has pride of place. If the editors are right

---

[1] Kyong-Min Son, *The Eclipse of the Demos: The Cold War and the Crisis of Democracy before Neoliberalism* (Lawrence: University Press of Kansas, 2020).

and Cold War liberalism was little more than a smokescreen for empire, that is as it should be. Even accounts of other places in the era reflect this unholy American supremacy. Lisandro Claudio's *Liberalism and the Postcolony*, on Filipino history, has gone furthest in globalizing the story of Cold War liberalism in a way that to some extent provincializes the United States in our historiography – but if there is a future ahead of that project, it is still early days.[2]

In compensation, this volume does most of its work in advancing a new set of stories about the hegemonic ideology of the United States after World War II, and the more or less nefarious work that ideology did. As these chapters also show, this foreign policy could have a great deal of fallout in diverse political and cultural realms. The individuals and movements – and in one chapter, the planning of the city – that the volume redescribes with help from the category of Cold War liberalism are worthy topics and indicate how much more work there is to do for a comprehensive understanding of the period to be in view.

Chronologically, compared to other accounts of Cold War liberalism that dwell more specifically on a founding period in the more immediate aftermath of World War II, this volume pushes further into the 1960s and even 1970s. Insights abound about the earlier period here, but the durability and transformations of Cold War liberalism as it evolved in the later period are extraordinarily helpful for beginning to establish a full-fledged historiographical category. The chapters vindicate the proposition that no ideology is static. Cold War liberalism certainly did change – just what one would expect for an ideology apologetic for and hostage to imperial aims that themselves were never set in stone. There were conservative forms of Cold War liberalism; equally, there were ambitious and quasi-revolutionary ones, and the latter tended to prevail as time passed, and Cold War liberalism precipitated neoconservative thought in new circumstances.

The effect forces attention to how, beneath the fallen or tragic sensibility of Cold War liberal intellectuals that I and others have privileged, lurked a potential for grandiose confrontation with communism the world over. Taking the story forward through the 1960s certainly suggests as much. When, in a classic essay from the 2000s, Wendy Brown indicted the dispirited and minimalist ethics of Michael Ignatieff for masking imperialist designs that were quite ambitious and transformational, she made a criticism applicable to an older Cold War politics.[3]

---

[2] Lisandro E. Claudio, *Liberalism and the Postcolony: Thinking the State in 20th Century Philippines* (Singapore: NUS Press, 2017).

[3] Wendy Brown, "'The Most We Can Hope For ... ': Human Rights and the Politics of Fatalism," *South Atlantic Quarterly* 103, no. 2 (Spring 2004), 451–463.

Indeed, while no chapter in this volume pushes in this direction, all of them together help inspire the thought that the historiography might equally benefit from attention to the afterlives of Cold War liberalism – how it casts a long shadow, is constantly being rehabilitated, has its sages redeemed and revisited, and its basic posture everlasting no matter how destabilizing events are. Neoconservatism was one version of the legacy; arguably, neoliberalism was too, though it is an interesting fact that this volume privileges politics so valuably, even as it scants economics almost entirely.

There is a case to make, in fact, that Cold War liberalism outlasted the Cold War in diverse forms. If the days of Cold War liberalism are numbered, as with all historical phenomena, it is perhaps because the sun is setting on the American empire itself. Of course, that process is only beginning, though its symptoms are already flagrant. The 2020s have seen less powerful attempts to reinstate Cold War liberal perspectives. Donald Trump's first term and presidency and successful return to office were often analyzed in terms Cold War liberals would have found familiar – since even as Trump declared a Cold War against China, his enemies felt his deepest betrayal was of Cold War alliances protecting the world against Russia, or that he represented "autocracy" at home that the free world had always declared beyond the pale.

Its contemporary renaissance suggests that pondering how Cold War liberalism arose and dominated will continue to teach useful lessons about its senescent phase, which is likely to be drawn out and long. Someday geopolitical transformations will bring into being a world different enough from the Cold War liberal one that emerged in the middle of the twentieth century. Until then, the meanings and outcomes of Cold War liberalism will demand investigation, and this volume will likely play a pivotal role in an ongoing referendum on how contemporary politics came about, and on what should happen next.

Index

'Abd al-Karim, Qasim, 68, 80
Abraham Accords, 83
Abzug, Bella, 242
Acheson, Dean, 45, 49, 51
Achieving Society, The (McClelland), 143
Act of Creation, The (Koestler), 141
Addams, Jane, 70
Adenauer, Konrad, 48
Adkins, Winthrop, 144
Adorno, Theodor, 135, 205, 207, 211, 222
Afghanistan War (2001–2021), 87
'Aflaq, Michel, 77
Age of Reform, The (Hofstadter)
   Curti's critique of, 218
   methodological changes in study of history during 1950s and, 210
   populism and, 205, 208–209, 220
   Progressives and, 205
Aid to Families of Dependent Children, 238
Alemán, Miguel, 253
Alien Registration Act (1940), 12, 18
Alliance for Progress (Kennedy administration), 95, 261
American Catholic: The Sinners and Saints Who Built America's Most Powerful Church (Morris), 104
American Committee for Cultural Freedom, 6
American Federation of Labor (AFL)
   convention (1947) of, 170
   Free Trade Union Committee and, 169
   McCarthyism's impact on campaigns against Soviet forced labor and, 181
   Soviet Union's forced labor system and, 166, 168–170, 172, 183
   Taft–Hartley Act (1947) and, 174
American Jewish Committee, 239
Americans for Democratic Action (ADA)
   Cold War liberalism and, 6, 88, 101, 233
   Democratic Advisory Council and, 229
   Lippmann and, 89
Angola, 183

Anti-Intellectualism in American Life (Hofstadter), 203, 208, 216, 235
anti-totalitarianism. *See also* totalitarianism
   Catholicism and, 105
   Cold War liberalism and, 5
   fears of mass mobilization and, 30, 148–149, 155
   industrial society and, 148–149, 155
   neoconservatives and, 165
   politics of emergency and, 149
Applebaum, Anne, 28
Árbenz, Jacobo, 254
Architecture of Social Concern in Regions of Mild Climate (Neutra), 200
Arendt, Hannah, 3, 240
Armstrong, Hamilton Fish, 39
Aron, Raymond
   anti-communism and, 152, 154
   anti-totalitarianism and, 153–155, 161, 163
   Cold War liberalism and, 150
   Congress for Cultural Freedom and, 152
   economic liberalism and, 175
   forced labor in Soviet Union and, 176
   industrial society and, 157–158
   Sorbonne lectures (1950s) of, 157
   student movement of 1968 and, 163
Art, David, 207
Asociación Mexicana por la Libertad de la Cultura, 254
Asterdorp housing project (Amsterdam), 192
Aswan Dam (Egypt), 73
"Aura" (Fuentes), 258
Austro-Hungarian Empire, 173
Authoritarian Personality, The (Adorno et al.), 135–136, 222

Baghdad Pact, 67–68
Bahrain, 83
Baldwin, Roger Nash
   campaign against Soviet system of forced labor and, 169

276

Index

Iron Curtain Refugee Campaign and, 178
research and writing about Soviet forced labor system by, 182–183
Soviet Union supported before World War II by, 181
Baldwin Hills Village housing development (Los Angeles), 193–194
Balfour, Arthur, 75
Balibar, Étienne, 130
Barr, William, 165
Baruch, Dorothy, 190
basic national security policy (Rostow), 54–56
Ba'th Party (Iraq), 80
Ba'th Party (Syria), 77–78
Bauer, P. T., 241
Bay of Pigs invasion (Cuba, 1961), 255
Beard, Charles
class-based approach to historical study and, 204, 211–212
Hofstadter and, 203–204
populism and, 208
Becket, Welton, 188
Bell, Daniel
anti-totalitarianism and, 161
"end of ideology" and, 161
fears of mass mobilization and, 155, 164, 217–218
Frankfurt School and, 132
Friedmann and, 158
industrial society paradigm and, 160
neoconservatism and, 103, 223
New American Right and, 213
New Left's criticism of, 162
populism and, 206, 215
The Public Interest and, 234–235
Shils and, 214
small scale gradual change favored by, 236
student movement of 1968 and, 163–164
Weber and, 210–211
Bellow, Saul, 239
Benedict, Ruth, 134
Benjamin Franklin Library (Mexico City), 253
Berelson, Bernard, 3
Berg, Paal, 179
Berle, Adolf, 11
Berlin, Isaiah, 3, 6, 218
Berlin crisis (1961), 56
Bertalanffy, Ludwig von, 141
Bettelheim, Bruno, 139
Biden, Joe
"free world" and, 35, 58
Gaza War and, 82, 86–87

Israel-Saudi Arabia relations and, 83
Middle East and, 60
Birnbaum, Norman, 159
Black Americans
Black Power movement and, 102, 243
Cold War liberalism and, 19–20
development psychology and, 144
in Los Angeles, 190–191
Moynihan Report (1965) and, 237
Williams on cultural uplift of, 192–194
Blinken, Antony, 60, 82, 86
Bobbio, Norberto, 3
Bohlen, Chip, 43
Bollingen Foundation, 141
Boris, Georges, 175
Bowron, Fletcher, 190, 201
Brenes, Michael, 87
Brinkley, Alan, 209
Brown, Wendy, 274
Brown v. Board of Education, 17, 102
Brussels Anti-Slavery Act of 1890, 172
Bryan, William Jennings, 70, 97
Brzezinski, Zbigniew, 227
Buck, Solon, 209
Buckley, Jr., William F., 96–97
Bullet's Song, The (Pfaff), 125
Burgess, Anthony, 57
Burke, Edmund, 96, 100
Bush, George W., 35, 58, 123
Butcher, Harriet Shadd, 192
Butler, Paul, 229–230
Byrnes, James, 41

Cabrera Infante, Guillermo, 251
Cairnes, John E., 172
California Modernism
low construction costs as a benefit of, 194
McCarthyism and, 201
origins and ideals of, 31, 185–187, 201
public housing and, 202
Pueblo del Rio housing development and, 194
windows and, 194
Campbell, Joseph, 141
Cárdenas, Lázaro, 251, 256
Carrington, Lord, 248
Carter, Jimmy, 245
Carto, Willis, 221
Casey, William, 124
Castro, Fidel
Congress for Cultural Freedom and, 254
Cuban nationalism and, 259
Fuentes and, 255, 259
Lippmann on U.S. efforts to overthrow, 95
Padilla affair and, 265

278 Index

Catholicism
  American nationalism and, 110–111
  anti-communism and, 106
  anti-totalitarianism and, 105
  Catholic Worker movement and, 112
  internationalism and, 105, 127
  just war theory and, 112
  Lippmann and, 97–98
  McCarthy and, 104–105
  skepticism regarding democracy and, 105
  Spanish Civil War and, 111
  subsidiarity principle and, 127
  workers' rights and, 112
Central Intelligence Agency (CIA)
  American Committee for Cultural Freedom and, 6
  Congress for Cultural Freedom and, 6, 124–126, 141, 263
  Cuba and, 255, 261
  Free Europe Committee and, 106, 116
  Guatemala coup (1954) and, 254
  institutionalization of Cold War liberalism and, 3, 15–16
  Instituto Latinoamericano de Relaciones Internacionales and, 261
  Iran coup (1953) and, 69
  Iraq coup (February 1963) and, 80
  Pfaff's evaluation of Cold War record of, 124–126
  Syria and, 73, 77–78
Central Treaty Organization (CENTO), 68
Centre d'études sociologiques, 150
Centro Mexicano de Escritores, 253
Chamoun, Camille, 79–80
"Change of Skin, A" (Fuentes), 258
Chappel, James, 5, 106, 111
Chiang Kai-Shek, 50
Childhood and Society (Erikson), 138
Chile, 251
China
  Communist takeover (1949) of, 16, 23, 44, 113
  Nixon's visit (1972) to, 57
  Sino-Soviet split and, 35, 57
  Trump and, 275
  United Nations and, 45
Chomsky, Noam, 240
Citizens Committee for Peace with Freedom, 231
Civil Rights Act (1964), 17
Civil Rights Congress, 18
Clark, Thomas C., 18
Claudio, Lisandro, 274
Coalition for a Democratic Majority (CDM), 224, 242–243
Cogley, John, 115

Cohn, Deborah, 252
Cohn-Bendit, Daniel, 162
Commentary
  American Jewish Committee and, 239
  anti-totalitarianism and, 240
  Cold War liberals' alliances with conservatives and, 225
  Commonweal and, 112
  Kirkpatrick and, 245
  New International Economic Order and, 240–241
  New Left criticized by, 240
  U.S. unilateralist and interventionist foreign policy defended by, 240–242
Commission for a Just and Durable Peace, 71
Committee on the Present Danger (CPD)
  Democratic Advisory Council compared to, 243
  neoconservatives and, 244
  neoliberalism and, 244
  nuclear rearmament and, 224
  Reagan and, 224
  Tyroler and, 242–243
Common Sense Book of Baby and Child Care, The (Spock), 139
Commonweal
  anti-communism and, 104, 113–114
  "Catholic Modern" and, 106
  Catholic Worker movement and, 112
  Commentary and, 112
  Communist takeover of China and, 113
  Czechoslovakia's anticlerical campaign (1949) and, 114
  ecumenical initiatives of, 112
  internationalism of, 113–114
  Korean War and, 114–115
  lay leadership and identity of, 111
  McCarthy and, 104, 113
  New Deal and, 112
  Pfaff and, 104, 106–108, 115–116
  Spanish Civil War and, 111
  synthesis of Catholic internationalism and American nationalism in, 111
  workers' rights and, 112
  World War II and, 112
Communist Party (Syria), 77
Communist Party of the United States of America, 18
Condemned to Freedom (Pfaff), 122
Congo, 183
Congress for Cultural Freedom (CCF)
  anti-totalitarianism in European intellectual discourse and, 153–155
  Central Intelligence Agency funding for, 6, 124–126, 141, 263

Cold War liberalism and, 88, 101
Cuban Revolution and, 254
French intellectuals' rejection of, 150
industrial society and, 159
Latin America and, 253–254
Lippmann and, 89
Milan conference (1955) of, 156–157
Pfaff's retrospective evaluation of, 124–126
Preuves and, 154, 178
spirituality and, 140–141
Congress of Industrial Organizations, 19
Congress of Vienna (1815), 172
Connally, Tom, 46–47
Constant, Benjamin, 8
Cornell, Ralph D., 199
Corpus Christi Massacre (Mexico, 1971), 267
Cortázar, Julio, 258, 265
Coser, Lewis, 132
Costa Rica, 247
Counts, George S., 171, 178
Covington, Floyd C., 196
"Crises in Welfare, The" (Moynihan), 238
Crozier, Michel, 151, 158
Cuadernos, 254, 262
Cuba
 Bay of Pigs invasion (1961) in, 255
 Fidelismo sin Fidel program campaign by Central Intelligence Agency in, 261
 Lippmann on, 95
 missile crisis (1962) in, 56
 Padilla affair (1971) and, 249, 265–266, 271
 revolution (1959) in, 32, 248, 254–260, 262, 270
 Wilson and U.S. invasion (1917) of, 70
Curti, Merle, 218
Czechoslovakia, 114

Dahl, Robert, 160, 214
Dahrendorf, Ralf, 161–162, 164–165
Daley, Richard, 232
Dallin, David, 171, 173, 180, 182
Day, Dorothy, 112, 115
De Gaulle, Charles, 121, 156
de Staël, Germaine, 8
"Death of Artemio Cruz, The" (Fuentes), 258
"Declaration of the Rights of Man and of the Citizen" (French Revolution), 172
Decter, Midge, 27, 244
Defense Department, 15–16, 119
Democratic Advisory Council (DAC)
 Cold War foreign policy and, 231, 234

Committee on the Present Danger compared to, 243
Democratic Policy Council compared to, 232
Democratic Study Group and, 231
disbanding (1961) of, 231
institutionalization of Cold War liberalism and, 233–234
Kennedy and, 230–231
origins of, 230–231
Tyroler's leadership role in, 230
Democratic Left (Latin America), 247, 251
Democratic Party
 civil rights and racial equality promoted by, 17, 228
 Coalition for a Democratic Majority and, 224
 Democratic National Committee and, 225, 230
 Democratic National Convention (1948) and, 17, 227
 Democratic National Convention (1968) and, 228
 McGovern–Fraser reforms and, 243
 neoconservatives and, 224–225, 227
 New Left and, 28
 U.S. Senate primary in New York (1976) and, 242
 Vietnam War and, 228, 232–233
Democratic Policy Council (DPC), 232–233
Democratic Study Group (DSG), 231
Dewey, John, 26, 178
Dewey, Thomas, 44, 66
Díaz Ordaz, Gustavo, 269
"Dictatorships and Double Standards" (Kirkpatrick), 245
Diêm, Ngô Đình, 95
Đilas, Milovan, 117, 125
Dominican Republic, 65, 70
Drucker, Peter, 144
Du Bois, W. E. B., 52
Dubinsky, David, 170, 174
Dulles, Allen, 35, 62, 142
Dulles, John Foster
 Commission for a Just and Durable Peace and, 71
 covert operations and, 69–70
 death of, 61
 Egypt and, 72–73
 "free world" and, 45, 53
 imperialism and, 29, 63, 71–74
 Iran coup (1953) and, 76
 Japan and, 47
 Korean War and, 45
 Lebanon Crisis (1958) and, 79
 Lippmann and, 93

280   Index

Dulles, John Foster (cont.)
  Mandate system in the Middle East
    and, 71
  Middle East Defense Organization
    proposal and, 68
  Middle East prioritized by, 61–63
  national sovereignty in the world order
    and, 70, 76
  Paris Peace Conference (1919) and, 61
  Rockefeller Foundation and, 69
  Suez Crisis and, 94
  Syria and, 77–78
  United Nations and, 67
  Wilson and, 61
  World Council of Churches speech
    (1948) by, 66–67
  World War I reparations negotiations
    and, 64
Dutschke, Rudi, 162
Duverger, Maurice, 154

East Germany uprising (1953), 53
Echeverría, Luis, 266–268, 271
Egypt
  Aswan Dam in, 73
  British forces before 1956 in, 72–73
  coup (1953) in, 72
  Middle East Defense Organization
    proposal and, 68
  Suez Crisis (1956) and, 73–74, 94
Ehrman, John, 237
Eisenhower, Dwight D.
  Dulles and, 61
  Eisenhower Doctrine and, 78–79
  farewell address of, 100
  Finletter group and, 230
  "free world" and, 52–53
  Middle East Defense Organization
    proposal and, 68
  Suez Crisis and, 73, 78
el espectador, 254–255
El Salvador, 269
Ellsberg, Daniel, 120
Encounter, 154, 254
End of Ideology, The (Bell), 101, 216
Enlightenment philosophy, 7, 120, 154
Equal Rights Amendment, 102
Erikson, Erik H., 138
Espionage Act (1917), 10
European Defense Community (EDC), 154
Eveland, Wilbur, 62, 78–79
Exploratorium museum
  (San Francisco), 139

Fall, Bernard, 119
Family Assistance Program proposal,
  238–239

Farouk (King of Egypt), 72
Fawzi, Mahmoud, 72
Faysal I (King of Syria), 75
Faysal II (King of Iraq), 68
Federal Bureau of Investigation (FBI),
  12, 201
Federal Housing Administration
  (FHA), 190
Ferkiss, Victor, 214
"Fight for Free Labor is Fight for
  World's Future" (Free Trade Union
  Committee), 170
Finletter group, 230
Fitzgerald, F. Scott, 110
Fondo de Cultura Económica, 253
Forced Labor in Soviet Russia (Dallin and
  Nicolaevsky), 171
forced labor in Soviet Union
  abolitionist rhetoric in campaign against,
    170–173
  American Federation of Labor and, 166,
    168–170, 183
  Dallin and Nicolaevsky's criticism of, 171
  Iron Curtain Refugee Campaign and, 178
  physical brutality of, 175–177
  United Nations and, 166, 179–180,
    182–183
  Workers' Defense League criticism of,
    171–172
Foreign Assistance Act (1961,
  Leahy Amendments), 85
Foster, John (grandfather of John Foster
  Dulles), 63
Foster, William, 46–47
Foucault, Michel, 57
Fraenkel, Ernst, 3
France
  Algerian war (1954–1962) and, 156
  empire of, 21–22, 71, 175
  labor rights in, 175
  Mandate system in the Middle East
    and, 75
  Nazi conquest (1940) of, 13
  revolution of 1789 in, 7–8, 153, 272
  student movement of 1968 and,
    162–164
  Suez Crisis and, 73–74, 94
  Vietnam War and, 50
  West Germany and, 47–48
Frankenheimer, John, 140
Frankfurt School (Institute for Social
  Research), 132
Free Europe Committee (FEC)
  Central Intelligence Agency funding for,
    106, 116
  Pfaff's retrospective analysis of, 124–125
  Pfaff's work at, 116–117, 123–124

Index 281

Free Trade Union Committee (FTUC)
  comparisons of Soviet and Nazi systems by, 177
  economic liberalism cited in campaign against Soviet forced labor by, 173
  establishment (1944) of, 169
  "Fight for Free Labor is Fight for World's Future" manifesto and, 170
  McCarthyism's impact on campaigns against Soviet forced labor and, 181
  physical brutality of Soviet forced labor system and, 175
  Rousset and, 178
  Slave Labor in the Soviet World pamphlet by, 180
  Soviet forced labor system's violation of universal moral norms and, 171
  Taft–Hartley Act (1947) and, 174
"free world"
  anti-communism and, 23, 34, 41–49, 54, 93
  anti-racism and, 23
  containment doctrine and, 48–49
  countercultural critiques of, 57
  Japan and West Germany's incorporation into, 47–48
  Korean War and, 45–46, 57
  liberal internationalists of 1930s and, 39–40
  Mutual Security Act (1951) and, 46–47
  Non-Aligned Movement and, 34, 49–50, 56
  NSC-68 memorandum and, 44–45
  origins of concept of, 34–36
  rollback doctrine and, 52–53
  Sino-Soviet split and, 35, 57
  Soviet propaganda and, 50–51
  Third World and, 35
  Truman Doctrine and, 42–43
  United Nations and, 41
  U.S. leadership of, 23, 35, 48
  Vietnam War and, 50, 57
  War on Terror and, 35, 58
  World War I and, 38
  World War II and, 40–41
French Communist Party (Parti communiste français, PCF), 150, 152, 163
French Section of the Workers' International (Section française de l'Internationale ouvrière, SFIO), 150, 156
Friedmann, Georges
  Bell and, 158
  Centre d'études sociologiques and, 150
  Congress for Cultural Freedom and, 157
  democratic socialism and, 150, 153, 161
  Gurvitch and, 157
  industrial society research and, 150–151, 158
  International Sociological Association and, 149
  McCarthyism in United States and, 151
  "open Marxism" and, 151
  student movement of 1968 and, 164
Fromm, Erich
  anti-communist socialism and, 137
  Authoritarian Personality and, 135
  on individuals' inability to develop productive relationships under monopoly capitalism, 132–133
  Maslow and, 133
Fuentes, Carlos
  Bell and, 251
  Castro and, 255
  Cuban Revolution and, 32, 246, 251–252, 254–260, 270
  Democratic Left and, 251
  Echeverría and, 267–268, 271
  English-language skills of, 258
  faith in elite expertise and, 263
  Harvard University commencement speech (1983) by, 247, 252
  import-substitution industrialization policies and, 268
  Latin American Boom and, 249
  Mexican Communist Party and, 257
  Movimiento de Liberación National and, 256–257
  Mundo Nuevo and, 262–263
  neoliberalism and, 248, 269–270
  New International Economic Order and, 268
  Padilla affair and, 265
  Paz and, 247
  PEN Club Congress (1966) and, 246–247, 262
  Política and, 257
  political appointments of, 250–251
  Revista Mexicana de Literatura, 254
  revolutionary upheaval in Latin America and, 259
  skepticism regarding ideology and, 251
  Tlatelolco massacre (1968) and, 264
  U.S. civil society and foreign policy described by, 269
  U.S. professorial appointments of, 269
  U.S. visas denied during 1960s for, 255
Fulbright, J. William, 48, 252

Galbraith, John Kenneth, 3, 230, 233, 235, 243
Gallant, Yoav, 81–82
García Márquez, Gabriel, 258, 261, 265
Garden City housing model, 194, 201

282   Index

Gates, Robert, 124
Gaza War (2023–)
   Biden Administration and, 87
   extent of operations and damage in, 81
   human rights violations and, 81–82, 85
   Israel's blockade of humanitarian aid to Gaza during, 86
Gellner, Ernest, 218–219
General Agreement on Tariffs and Trade, 25
Genocide Convention (1948), 81–82
Gilman, Nils, 145
Giscard d'Estaing, Valery, 252
Glazer, Nathan, 132, 236
Goffman, Erving, 57
Goldwater, Barry, 96, 103
"Good Conscience, The" (Fuentes), 258
Good Society, The (Lippmann), 97, 99–100
Goodwyn, Lawrence, 206
Goytisolo, Juan, 265
Graham, Billy, 103
Great Britain
   aid to Greece and Turkey from, 42
   Baghdad Pact and, 68
   Brexit vote (2016) in, 203
   empire of, 21–22, 35, 71, 176
   Iran coup (1953) and, 69
   Malaya and, 50
   Mandate system in the Middle East and, 75
   military presence in Egypt before 1956 of, 72–73
   Suez Crisis and, 73–74, 94
   West Germany and, 47–48
   World War II and, 14
Great Depression
   authoritarianism and, 11, 218
   Cold War liberalism and, 9
   policy responses to, 10–11, 39
Great Society
   Kristol's criticisms of, 234
   Lippmann and, 95, 101–102
   War on Poverty programs and, 144, 235
Greece, 42–43, 93
Green, William, 178
Group of 77 (G-77), 240–241
Guam, 2, 13, 70
Guatemala, 254, 269
Gurian, Waldemar, 105, 108, 115
Gurvitch, Georges, 157

Hacienda Village housing project (Los Angeles), 189
Hacohen, Malachi, 8
Hagen, Everett, 144
Halberstam, David, 235
Hamas attack on Israel (2023), 80, 83
Handlin, Oscar, 208, 210
Harding, Warren, 38
Harriman, W. Averell, 237
Harrington, Michael, 3
Harris, Fred, 232
Hartz, Louis, 3, 210
Hayek, Friedrich von, 99
Heidegger, Martin, 66
"Help the Deportees in the Soviet Camps" (Rousset), 176–177
Herling, Albert K., 171–172
Herzog, Isaac, 81
Hezbollah, 83
Hicks, John, 209, 216, 218
Hitler, Adolf
   Murray's profile of, 134
   populism and, 216
   rise to power in 1930s of, 11, 128
Hofstadter, Richard
   Adorno and, 211, 222
   American Right and, 31, 205–206, 215, 220–223
   Beard and, 203–204
   Communist Party of the United States and, 204
   death of, 223
   Jewish fears of mass mobilization after the Holocaust and, 155, 217–218
   London School of Economics conference on populism (1967) and, 219–220
   Mannheim and, 212
   McCarthyism analyzed by, 212–213
   methodological changes in study of history during 1950s and, 210
   paranoid style in American politics and, 203–204, 207, 209
   populism and, 31, 204–220
   Progressivism and, 205
   Selma civil rights march (1965) and, 219
   Trump presidency and, 203
   Weber and, 211, 213
   Woodward and, 207–208
Hollywood Writers Mobilization for Defense, 18
Holocaust, 14
Hook, Sidney, 3, 178
Hoover, Herbert, 10, 39
Hopkins, Harry, 11
Horney, Karen, 131, 133
House, Edward, 75
Housing Authority for the City of Los Angeles (HACLA), 188, 190–191
Houthis, 83
Howe, Irving, 3, 147
Hughes, Thomas L., 56

Index 283

Humphrey, Hubert
  death of, 243
  Democratic National Convention (1948) and, 228
  Democratic Policy Council and, 232–233
  election (1968) and, 229, 232
  Iron Curtain Refugee Campaign and, 178
  law and order politics after 1968 and, 233
  Vietnam War and, 228, 232–233
Hungarian Revolution (1956), 53, 74, 156
Hunt, John, 261
Hunt, Rockwell D., 184
Hussein (King of Jordan), 68

"I Am a Negro" (Williams), 192–193
Iber, Patrick, 259
Ideology and Utopia (Mannheim), 212
Ignatieff, Michael, 274
Ilyan, Mikhail, 78
Immerman, Richard, 61
Immerwahr, Daniel, 22
Immigration Act (1918), 10
Immigration and Nationality Act (McCarran–Walter Act, 1952), 15, 255
India, 49
Indonesia, 24, 49
industrial society
  anti-totalitarianism and, 148–149, 155, 165
  Aron's analysis of, 157
  Congress for Cultural Freedom and, 159
  "end of ideology" and, 147, 156, 159–161
  French scholars' interest in research tradition of, 151
  integration of class conflict and, 159
  logic of industrialization and, 159
  managerial revolution and, 147, 159, 161
  property relations and, 160
  social movements and, 161, 163
  societal economic coordination favored over laissez-faire economics in, 148, 160
  student movement of 1968 and, 162–165
Inequality of Nations, The (Tucker), 241
Infante, Guillermo Cabrera, 255, 266
Instituto Latinoamericano de Relaciones Internacionales (ILARI), 261, 263
Internal Security Act of 1950, 18
International Association for Cultural Freedom (IACF), 263
International Court of Justice (ICJ), 81–82
International Criminal Court, 82
International Labor Organization (ILO), 166, 169, 175

International Ladies Garment Workers' Union (ILGWU), 170, 173, 183
International Monetary Fund, 25
International Sociological Association, 150
Ionescu, Ghiță, 218–219
Iran
  Baghdad Pact and, 68
  coup (1953) in, 64, 69, 76
  Non-Aligned Movement and, 50
  revolution (1979) in, 68
Iraq
  Baghdad Pact and, 68
  coup (February 1963) in, 80
  Mandate system in the Middle East and, 76
  U.S. war and occupation (2003–2011) of, 28, 84, 87
Iron Curtain Refugee Campaign, 178
Israel
  Abraham Accords and, 83
  Gaza War (2023–) and, 81–82, 85–86
  Hamas attack (2023) on, 80, 83
  International Court of Justice case against, 81–82
  Palestinian territories controlled by, 85
  Saudi Arabia and, 83
  Suez Crisis and, 73–74, 94

Jackson, Henry M. "Scoop," 28, 227–228, 243
James, William, 91, 98
Janken, Kenneth R., 19
Japan, 24, 47, 135
Jefferson, Thomas, 37, 214
John Birch Society, 221
Johnson, Chalmers, 22
Johnson, Lyndon B.
  Great Society and, 95, 101
  Lippmann and, 89, 95
  Vietnam War and, 95, 120, 235
  War on Poverty programs and, 235
Jones, Fred K., 197
Jordan, 68
Josselson, Michael, 261
Jung, Carl Gustav, 141–142

Kahn, Herman, 3, 117–118, 120, 122
Kauffman, Gordon B., 188
Kaysen, Carl, 55–56
Kennan, George
  containment doctrine and, 90
  Lippmann and, 91
  "Long Telegram" (1946) by, 41–42, 117
  Rostow's basic national security policy critiqued by, 55
  X Article (1947) by, 49, 90

284   Index

Kennedy, John F.
  Alliance for Progress and, 95, 261
  Democratic Advisory Council and, 230–231
  free world and, 54
  inaugural address (1961) of, 1–2
  Iraq coup (February 1963) and, 80
  Lippmann and, 95
  Pfaff and Stillman's foreign policy books and, 118
  Vietnam War and, 120, 235
Kennedy, Robert F., 120
Kesey, Ken, 57
Keynes, John Maynard, 4, 89, 99–100
Keyserling, Leon, 230
Khan, Karim, 82
Khrushchev, Nikita, 54, 94, 156, 240
King-Crane Commission, 74–75
Kirkpatrick, Jeanne, 245
Kissinger, Henry, 235, 241–242
Knight, Frank, 211
Knox, Frank, 40
Koestler, Arthur, 126, 141–142, 178
Kogon, Eugen, 3, 111
Korean War
  Commonweal and, 114–115
  "free world" and, 45–46, 57
  Lippmann on, 94–95
  military Keynesianism and, 17
  racialized views of, 23
  scope of destruction in, 24
  United Nations and, 45, 115
Kotschnig, Walter, 180
Kristol, Irving
  Great Society programs criticized by, 234
  neoconservatism and, 27, 226
  New Left criticized by, 229
  The Public Interest and, 234–235
  Reagan and, 244
Kushi, Sidita, 24

La cultura en México, 265
Labour Party (Great Britain), 156
Langston Terrace housing project (Washington, DC), 188–189
Lanham Act (1940), 188
Lansing, Robert, 61, 75
Laqueur, Walter, 241
Lasch, Christopher, 206
Lasky, Melvin, 3
Latin America at War with the Past (Fuentes), 270
"Lay Intellectual, The" (Pfaff), 108
League of Nations
  Article Ten collective security promises and, 66

  Covenant of, 65
  Mandate system in the Middle East and, 71, 75–76
  U.S. refusal to join, 38
League to Enforce Peace (LEP), 65
Leary, Timothy, 141
Lebanon, 64, 76, 79–80
Letras Libres, 270
Lewis, Oscar, 263
Liberalism and the Postcolony (Claudio), 274
Liberty Lobby, 221
Liberty under the Soviets (Baldwin), 181
Libre, 265–266
Libya, 83
LIFE en Español, 246
Lilla, Mark, 28
Lincoln, Abraham, 37–38, 40, 54, 173
Lippmann, Helen Byrne, 102
Lippmann, Walter
  anti-imperialism and, 91–92
  Atlantic Community and, 91–92, 94
  Black Power movement and, 102
  Brown v. Board of Education and, 102
  Buckley and, 96–97
  Burke and, 96, 100
  Catholicism and, 97–98
  containment doctrine and, 48, 90, 93
  Dulles and, 93
  isolationism and, 96
  "Jacobins" and, 96
  Johnson and, 95
  Kennan and, 91
  Kennedy and, 95
  Keynes and, 89, 99–100
  Korean War and, 94–95
  "Lippmann gap" on foreign policy commitments and, 92, 95
  Middle East and, 94
  modernization theory and, 92, 94
  Mont Pelerin Society and, 99
  New Deal and, 89, 98, 100
  Nixon and, 96, 103
  on public interest, 234
  Reagan and, 103
  regional security pacts and, 92
  Roosevelt and, 98
  Schlesinger and, 95, 97
  skepticism regarding mass electorates and, 97
  Suez Crisis and, 94
  Truman Doctrine and, 91–93
  U.S. military–industrial complex promoted by, 89, 100–101
  Vietnam War and, 95
  white supremacy opposed by, 102

Index

Wilsonianism critiqued by, 93
women's liberation and, 98, 102
Lipset, Seymour Martin
  anti-totalitarianism and, 155, 161
  Jewish fears of mass mobilization after the Holocaust and, 155, 217–218
  on Latin American economic growth and Catholic culture, 144
  on populism and antiparliamentarianism, 215
  Populism and the Rule of Law conference (1954) and, 214
  The Public Interest and, 236
  Stern Group and, 211
  student movement of 1968 and, 162–163
  Weber and, 211
Locke, John, 7
Lodge, Jr., Henry Cabot, 49, 183
Loewenstein, Karl, 3
Lonely Crowd, The (Riesman), 137
López Portillo, José, 268–269
Los Angeles (California)
  Black population in, 190–192
  Housing Authority for the City of Los Angeles and, 188, 190–191
  housing shortage during World War II in, 189–191
  Proposition B housing measure (1952) and, 201
  Watts Uprising (1965) in, 202
Lovestone, Jay, 172, 179, 181
Lowell, James Russell, 172
Luce, Henry, 143
Lunes de Revolución, 255

MacBride, Sean, 51
Macdonald, Dwight, 126, 132, 239
Main Currents in American Thought (Parrington), 209
Malik, Charles, 66–67, 79
Mallet, Serge, 161
"Man: A Course of Study" (social studies curriculum), 139
Manchurian Candidate, The (Frankenheimer), 140
Mann, Thomas, 39
Mannheim, Karl, 212
Marcuse, Herbert, 138, 240
Maritain, Jacques, 114
Marotta, Gary, 209
Marshall Plan, 43, 47, 93
Maslow, Abraham
  authoritarian personality concept and, 133, 135
  creative scientist ideal and, 139–140

Fromm and, 133
hierarchy of needs concept developed by, 133–134, 137
Horney and, 133
Jung and, 141
on rise of totalitarianism and World War II, 128
on underdeveloped societies, 144–145
Maurin, Peter, 112
Mayhew, Christopher, 176
McCarthy, Joseph
  Catholic supporters of, 104–105
  Cold War liberals as opponents of, 88
  Commonweal and, 104, 113
  French intellectuals affected by anti-communist campaign of, 151–152
  Hofstadter's analysis of, 212–213
  paranoid environment of 1950s national security state and, 16
  populism and, 212–214, 217, 219
  public housing programs attacked by, 187, 201–202
  Riesman's criticisms of, 137
  status anxiety and, 213–214
McCarthy, Mary, 239
McClelland, David, 143–144
McGovern, George, 96, 243
Mead, Margaret, 134
Meany, George, 232
Mellon, Paul, 141
Mendras, Henri, 150
Mercier Vega, Luis, 261
Merton, David, 214
Mexican Communist Party (Partido Comunista Mexicano, PCM), 257
Mexico
  Cold War liberalism and, 249, 252–253, 264
  constitution (1917) of, 250
  Corpus Christi Massacre (1971) in, 267
  "dirty war" (1970s) in, 264–265, 267
  election (1964) in, 257
  import-substitution industrialization policies in, 268
  monetary crisis (1994–1995) in, 248
  neoliberalism under Salinas de Gortari in, 248
  North American Free Trade Agreement and, 248
  Partido Revolucionario Institucional and, 250
  sovereign debt default (1982) in, 268
  Tlatelolco massacre (1968) in, 264
  Wilson and U.S. invasions (1914–1917) of, 65, 70
Mexico City (Mexico), 252–253

Midcentury Modernism. *See* California Modernism
Middle East Defense Organization proposal, 68
military Keynesianism, 13, 16, 18
Mills, C. Wright, 88, 160, 251
Monroe Doctrine, 36, 65
Mont Pelerin Society, 99
Montaigne, Michel de, 7
Moose, James, 77
Morgan, Edmund, 210
Morocco, 76, 83
Morris, Charles R., 104–105
Mosaddegh, Mohammad, 50, 69, 76
Mounk, Yascha, 28
Movimiento de Liberación National (MLN), 256–257, 260
Moyn, Samuel, 6, 204
Moynihan, Daniel Patrick
  Central Intelligence Agency and, 124
  election to U.S. Senate (1976) of, 242
  Family Assistance Program proposal and, 238–239
  Kissinger and, 241–242
  Moynihan Report (1965) by, 237
  neoconservatism and, 227, 237, 242
  New International Economic Order and, 241–242
  Nixon and, 238
  Pfaff and, 121, 124
  on "professional reformers," 237–238
  The Public Interest and, 237–238
  United Nations ambassadorship of, 242
  Urban Affairs Council and, 238
Mudaliar, A. Ramaswami, 179, 183
Müller, Jan-Werner, 128, 148, 152–153, 167
Mundo Nuevo, 261–265
Münzenberg, Willi, 126
Murray, Henry, 134, 141
Mussolini, Benito, 97
Mutual Security Act (1951), 46–47, 50
Myself with Others (Fuentes), 270

Naguib, Muhammad, 72
Napoleon Bonaparte, 21, 134
Nasser, Gamal Abdel, 73, 78–79, 94
National Association for the Advancement of Colored People, 19
National Committee for a Free Europe, 182
National Labor Relations Act (1935), 98
National Recovery Administration, 12, 98
National Security Agency (NSA), 15–16
National Security Council (NSC)
  institutionalization of Cold War liberalism and, 3, 15–16
  NSC-68 memorandum (1950) and, 44–46
  NSC 7 memorandum (1948) and, 49
Negro Family, The: The Case for Action (Moynihan Report), 237
Nehru, Jawaharlal, 49, 94
neoconservatives
  anti-totalitarianstyle and, 165
  Cold War liberals' transition into, 226, 264
  Committee on the Present Danger and, 244
  Democratic Party and, 224–225, 227
  emergence during 1970s of, 225, 244
  Iraq War (2003–2011) and, 28
  Reagan and, 225, 244
  U.S. global hegemony prioritized by, 27–28
neoliberalism
  Cold War liberalism and, 145–146
  Committee on the Present Danger and, 244
  emergence during 1970s of, 26
  Latin America and, 271
Neruda, Pablo, 246, 261
Netanyahu, Benjamin, 81–82
Neumann, Franz, 211
Neutra, Richard, 185–187, 194, 200
Neutrality Acts (1930s), 39
New American Right, The (Bell ed.), 213–214
New Deal
  Cold War liberalism and, 16, 227
  Commonweal and, 112
  Lippmann's critique of, 98, 100
  populism and, 209
  public housing and, 31, 185, 188, 190
  right-wing revolt against, 221
  unemployment assistance and, 10–11
New International Economic Order (NIEO), 240–241, 268
New Leader, The, 6, 104
New Left
  Cold War liberal critics of, 229
  Cold War liberalism rejected by, 26
  Commentary and criticism of, 240
  decline during 1970s of, 27
  decolonization supported by, 26
  Democratic Party and, 28
  Riesman's criticism of, 137
  student movement of 1968 and, 162–165
  Vietnam War and, 228
New School for Social Research, 131
New Slavery, A (Baldwin et al.), 182
Nickerson Gardens housing development (Los Angeles), 202
Nicolaevsky, Boris, 171, 173
Niebuhr, Reinhold, 97, 116, 178

Nitze, Paul, 230
Nixon, Richard M.
　China visit (1972) by, 57
　détente policies and, 96
　election (1968) and, 229
　election (1972) and, 243
　Family Assistance Program proposal
　　and, 238–239
　Keynesianism and, 103
　Lippmann and, 103
　Moynihan and, 238
　Watergate scandal and, 103
Non-Aligned Movement, 56
North American Free Trade Agreement
　(NAFTA), 248
North Atlantic Treaty Organization
　(NATO), 93
NSC-68 memorandum (1950), 46
Nugent, Walter, 206

Obama, Barack, 60
Office of Strategic Services (OSS), 134, 141
O'Malley, Francis
　"O'Malley Boys" and, 109
　Pfaff and, 108
　University of Notre Dame and, 103–110
On the Theory of Social Change (Hagen), 144
Opium of the Intellectuals, The (Aron), 154
Oppenheimer, Frank, 139
Organization of Petroleum Exporting
　Countries (OPEC), 240
Orwell, George, 256

Packer, George, 28
Padilla affair (Cuba, 1971), 249,
　265–266, 271
Pahlavi, Mohammad Reza
　(Shah of Iran), 68
Paine, Thomas, 214
Pakistan, 68
Palavicini, Félix Fulgencio, 179
Palestine
　Lippmann on, 94
　Mandate system in the Middle East
　　and, 76
　Palestinian National Authority and, 85
　Zionism and, 75
Pan-American Pact, 65
Paranoid Style in American Politics, The
　(Hofstadter), 203, 205, 208
Paris Peace Conference (1919), 61
Parrington, Vernon, 209
Parsons, Talcott, 152, 206, 211
Parti Socialiste Unifié, 161
Partido Revolucionario Institucional
　(PRI), 250

Partisan Review, 6
Paul (Saint), 7
Paz, Octavio
　Fuentes and, 247
　Latin American Boom and, 249
　Libre and, 265
　Mexican politics and, 268
　Padilla affair and, 265
　PEN Club Congress (1990) and, 247
　Plural and, 266
　Vuelta and, 270
Pearl Harbor attack (1941), 13–14, 192
PEN Club Congress (1966), 246–247, 262
PEN Club Congress (1990), 247
Pérez, Carlos Andrés, 240
Perle, Richard, 28
Pfaff, William
　anti-communism and, 117, 121
　Central Intelligence Agency's Cold War
　　record evaluated by, 124–126
　Commonweal and, 104, 106–108, 115–116
　Congress for Cultural Freedom and,
　　124–126
　foreign policy books coauthored with
　　Stillman and, 118
　Free Europe Committee and, 106,
　　116–117, 123–125
　Hudson Institute and, 106–107, 118,
　　120, 123
　International Herald Tribune and, 123
　internationalism and, 120–121
　Korean War and, 106, 115–116
　liberalism criticized by, 121–123
　Morris and, 104–105
　move to France by, 107, 122
　Moynihan and, 121, 124
　neoconservatism and, 107, 121
　New Left and, 107
　O'Malley and, 108
　Rome pilgrimage (1950) of, 117
　Schlesinger and, 122
　student movement of 1960s and, 122
　synthesis of Catholic internationalism
　　and American nationalism by,
　　110–111, 127
　thermonuclear war and, 117
　University of Notre Dame and, 106,
　　108–109
　Vietnam War and, 106, 119–120, 122
Phantom Public, The (Lippmann), 97
Philip, André, 156
Philippines
　independence (1945) of, 24
　James's opposition to U.S. annexation
　　of, 91
　NSC-68 memorandum and, 45

288   Index

Philippines (cont.)
  U.S. control (1898–1946) of, 2, 37, 70
  World War II and, 13
Phillips, William, 132
Plural, 266
Podhoretz, Norman, 28, 227, 240–241, 244
Point IV aid program, 69
Poland, 248
Polanyi, Michael, 3, 140
Política, 254–255, 257
Political Man (Lipset), 215
Politics of a Guaranteed Income, The
  (Moynihan), 238
Pollack, Norman, 206, 218
Pollock, Jackson, 141–142
Popper, Karl, 3, 5, 140
populism
  American Right and, 206
  antiparliamentarianism and
    anti-bureaucratism in, 215–216
  counter-revisionist interpretations of,
    206, 216–217
  fascism and, 214–215
  Hofstadter's study of, 31, 204–205,
    207–220
  Jeffersonianism and, 209
  London School of Economics
    conference (1967) on, 218–220
  McCarthyism and, 212–214, 217, 219
  New Deal and, 209
  paranoid style in American politics and,
    204, 209
  Progressives and, 209
  status anxiety and, 205, 213–214
Populism and the Rule of Law conference
  (1954), 214
Populist Revolt, The (Hicks), 209
Potter, David, 210
Preface to Morals, A (Lippmann), 97, 102
President's Committee on Civil Rights, 17
Preston, Andrew, 14
Preuves, 154, 178
"Professionalization of Reform, The"
  (Moynihan), 237
Progressives
  anti-imperialism and, 70
  Cold War liberals compared to, 90
  cultural transformation approach to
    racial problems favored by, 196
  Hofstadter's study of, 205
  meliorative social policies promoted by, 9
  populism and, 209
Proposition B (Los Angeles, 1952), 201
"Pseudo-Conservative Revolt, The"
  (Hofstadter), 205, 208, 222
Public Interest, The
  Cold War liberals' alliances with
    conservatives and, 225
  inaugural issue of, 234–235
  institutionalization of Cold War
    liberalism and, 234
  Moynihan and, 237–238
  small scale gradual change favored by
    authors in, 236
Public Opinion (Lippmann), 90, 97
Public Philosophy, The (Lippmann), 98
Pueblo del Rio housing development
  (Los Angeles)
  Black cultural uplift as a goal for,
    196–197, 199–200
  Black residents as majority
    population of, 192
  California Modern style and, 194
  classes and community
    organizations at, 196
  Garden City model and, 194
  green spaces in, 194, 196, 198–200
  health benefits of apartment spacing
    plan at, 194–196
  photographs of, 186, 188, 191, 195,
    197–198, 200
  priority status granted during World
    War II to construction of, 191
  proximity to workplaces of, 193
  slum clearance viewed as a goal of,
    197–198
  windows in, 194
Puerto Rico, 70
Putin, Vladimir, 28, 82

Quwatli, Shukri al-, 78

Radio Free Europe, 124, 167
Rahv, Phillip, 132
Reagan, Ronald
  Committee on the Present Danger
    and, 224
  Kirkpatrick and, 245
  neoconservatives and, 225, 244
Revista Mexicana de Literatura, 254
Rhee, Syngman, 50
Ribuffo, Leo, 207
Riesman, David, 137, 145
Rise of American Civilization, The
  (Beard), 204
Robinson, Hilyard, 189
Rockefeller, Nelson, 10
Rodríguez Monegal, Emir, 261, 263
Rogin, Michael Paul, 206
Roosevelt, Eleanor, 67
Roosevelt, Franklin D.
  Cold War liberals and, 227

Index

illiberal policies supported by, 12
Lippmann and, 98
National Recovery Administration and, 12
New Deal and, 10–11, 98
World War II and, 13
Roosevelt, Theodore, 37, 65, 92
Rosenfeld, Sam, 230
Rossiter, Clinton, 97
Rostow, Eugene V., 224–225
Rostow, Walt Whitman, 54–56, 94
Roth, Philip, 239
Rothko, Mark, 141–142
Rousseau, Jean-Jacques, 153
Rousset, David
   anti-totalitarianism and, 169
   comparisons of Soviet and Nazi systems by, 177
   concentration camp experiences of, 176
   Congress for Cultural Freedom and, 178
   Free Trade Union Committee and, 178
   Iron Curtain Refugee Campaign and, 178
   Le Figaro Littéraire polemic against Soviet forced labor (1949) by, 176–177
   libel trial against, 177
   physical cruelty of Soviet forced labor system condemned by, 168, 177
Rovere, Richard, 120
Russell, Richard, 48
Russian invasion of Ukraine War (2022–), 82
Russian Revolution, 10
Ryan, William, 237

Sábato, Ernesto, 246
Salinas de Gortari, Carlos, 248
Saloutos, Theodore, 219–220
Sanford, Nevitt, 135
Saudi Arabia, 83
Schapiro, Leonard, 218
Schlesinger, Jr., Arthur M.
   Commission of Inquiry into Forced Labor and, 171
   Democratic Party and, 227
   Democratic Party Council criticized by, 233
   Finletter group and, 230
   Iron Curtain Refugee Campaign and, 178
   Kennedy administration and, 235
   Lippmann and, 95, 97
   Pfaff and, 122
   Soviet forced labor system condemned by, 178
   student movement of 1960s and, 122
   Vietnam War and, 122, 228
   vital center and, 17, 88, 101
Schrecker, Ellen, 187

Schumpeter, Joseph, 143
scientism, 140
Sedition Act (1918), 10
Sender, Toni, 174, 180
September 11 terrorist attacks (2001), 58
Seward, William Henry, 170
Shils, Edward, 214–216
Shishakli, Adib, 69
Shklar, Judith N., 3, 5, 7, 168
Sinyavsky–Daniel trial (Soviet Union, 1966), 260
Slave Power, The (Cairnes), 172
Snyder, Timothy, 28
social psychology
   Authoritarian Personality, The and, 135–136
   child-rearing and, 138–140
   economic development and, 129, 142–146
   Frankfurt School and, 132
   liberalism analyzed via, 129
   New School for Social Research and, 131
   Office of Strategic Services and, 134
   productive character concept and, 132–133
   race and, 130
   scientism and, 140
   therapeutical approaches in, 137–142
   totalitarianism analyzed via, 30, 129–138, 141
"Socialismo y cultura" ("Socialism and Culture," Fuentes), 260
Son, Kyong-Min, 273
South Africa, 81, 181, 183
Southeast Housing Architects Associated, 188
Soviet Slave Empire, The (Herling), 172
Soviet Union
   collapse (1991) of, 33, 146
   Eastern Europe under dictatorial control of, 9
   forced labor in, 166–167, 169–183
   imperialism and, 72
   Korean War and, 45, 114
   Lebanon Crisis (1958) and, 79
   Middle East and, 76
   Nazi–Soviet Pact and, 181
   nuclear arsenal of, 2, 14, 16, 44
   propaganda campaigns by, 17, 50–51, 126
   Sino-Soviet split and, 35, 57
   Sinyavsky–Daniel trial and, 260
   United Nations and, 45
   World War II and, 14
   Yugoslavia and, 77
Spanish Civil War, 11, 253
Spanish-American War of 1898, 37

Speier, Hans, 3, 256
Spender, Stephen, 126
Sperber, Manès, 3
Spock, Benjamin, 138
Stakes of Diplomacy, The (Lippmann), 91
Stalin, Joseph
　death of, 54, 155–156
　forced labor regime under, 168, 173
　liberalism's failure to anticipate rise of, 128
　Tito's split with, 56
Steel, Ronald, 93
Stein, Clarence, 194
Steinmetz-Jenkins, Daniel, 87
Stern Group, 210, 212
Stevenson, Adlai, 178, 230
Stillman, Edmund
　foreign policy books coauthored with Pfaff and, 118
　Hudson Institute and, 118, 120, 122
　thermonuclear war and, 117
Stoddard, George D., 3
Stouffer, Samuel, 3, 207
Strange Career of Jim Crow, The (Woodward), 216
Strauss, Leo, 98
Students for a Democratic Society, 162
Sudan, 83
Suez Crisis (1956), 73–74, 94
Syria, 64, 73, 76–78

Taft, Robert, 115
Taft, William Howard, 65
Taft–Hartley Act (1947), 18, 174
Talmon, Jacob, 3, 6
Tatum, Dillon Stone, 21
Thatcher, Margaret, 146
Thomas, Norman, 137, 171, 178
Tito, Josip Broz, 56, 77
Tlatelolco massacre (Mexico, 1968), 264
Toft, Monica Duffy, 24
Torment of Secrecy, The (Shils), 215–216
totalitarianism. *See also* anti-totalitarianism
　Commentary and, 240
　in developing countries, 145
　French Revolution and, 153
　Nazi and Soviet crimes linked in theory of, 152
　public housing programs associated with, 187, 202
　social psychology as means of analyzing, 30, 129–138, 141
Touraine, Alain
　difference between French communist and socialist parties described by, 150
　French non-Communist left critiqued by, 158

　industrial society and, 158, 161
　McCarthyism in the United States and, 152
　skepticism toward communism of, 161
　the state and, 160
　student movement of 1968 and, 162, 164
Trilling, Lionel, 3, 6
Trotsky, Leon, 252
Truman, Harry S.
　communist propaganda described by, 50–51
　Executive Order 9835 and, 16, 18
　Executive Order 10290 and, 16
　"free world" and, 34, 45–46, 48, 51
　Korean War and, 46, 114
　Middle East Defense Organization proposal and, 68
　Mutual Security Act (1951) and, 46
　national security institutions established under, 15
　Point IV aid program and, 69
　Taft–Hartley Act (1947) and, 174
　Truman Doctrine and, 42–43, 57, 91–93
　U.S. global hegemony and, 20, 41
Trump, Donald
　Abraham Accords and, 83
　China and, 275
　Hofstadter and analysis of, 203
　isolationism and, 86
　Middle East and, 60
　populism and, 207
　Russia and, 275
Tucker, Robert W., 240–241
Tugwell, Rexford, 11
Turkey, 42–43, 68, 93
Tyroler II, Charles
　Coalition for a Democratic Majority and, 242
　Cold War foreign policy and, 231
　Committee on the Present Danger and, 242–243
　Democratic Advisory Council leadership role of, 230
　Humphrey and, 232
　neoconservatism and, 226
　Reagan and, 244
　Vietnam War and, 231–232

Undiscovered Self, The (Jung), 142
Unger, Irwin, 208
"Ungovernability of Man, The" (Lippmann), 103
United Arab Emirates, 83
United Arab Republic, 79

Index

United Nations
  Charter of, 41, 66
  Economic and Social Council of, 166, 172–174, 179–180
  establishment (1945) of, 25
  forced labor in Soviet Union and, 166, 169–170, 172–174, 179–180, 182–183
  "free world" and, 41
  Group of 77 (G-77) and, 240–241
  Korean War and, 45, 115
  lack of enforcement mechanisms and, 66
  Suez Crisis and, 73
  "Zionism as Racism" resolution (1975) at, 242
United Nations Educational, Scientific, and Cultural Organization (UNESCO), 150
United Nations Relief and Works Administration (UNRWA), 82
United States Housing Authority, 185
Universal Declaration of Human Rights (UDHR), 66
University of Notre Dame, 106, 108–110
U.S. Foreign Policy: Shield of the Republic (Lippmann), 92
"U.S. in Opposition, The" (Moynihan), 242
U.S. War Aims (Lippmann), 92

Vandenberg, Arthur, 43
Vargas Llosa, Mario, 246, 258, 265
Venezuela, 247
Viereck, Peter, 97, 206, 213
Vietnam War
  Cold War liberalism undermined by, 25–26
  Democratic Party and, 228, 232–233
  "free world" and, 50, 57
  Lippmann on, 95
  New Left and, 228
  Operation Rolling Thunder and, 95
  Pfaff and, 119–120
  racialized views of, 23
  scope of destruction in, 24
  Truman Doctrine and, 57
  Tyroler and, 231–232
Voting Rights Act (1965), 17
Vuelta, 270

Wagner–Steagall Act (1937), 188, 190
Wald, Lillian, 70
Wallace, Henry, 104
Wallas, Graham, 101
War on Terror (Bush administration), 35, 58

Warren, Earl, 178
"Was Woodrow Wilson Right?" (Moynihan), 241
Washington, George, 2, 36
Watson, Thomas E., 216–217
Watts Uprising (Los Angeles, 1965), 202
Weber, Max
  charismatic authority and, 214
  Hofstadter and, 211, 213
  on monopoly of the legitimate use of physical force, 85
  Stand (status) and, 211
  Stern Group and, 210
Wechsler, James, 3
Weinberger, Caspar, 252
Welch, Robert, 221
Wertheimer, Max, 131, 133
West Bank, 83, 86
West Germany (Federal Republic of Germany), 47–48
"Where the Air Is Clear" (Fuentes), 253, 258
Wilentz, Sean, 203
Wilkinson, Frank, 201
Williams, Paul R.
  Black cultural uplift and, 192–194, 196–197, 201
  Cold War liberalism and, 201
  Langston Terrace housing project and, 188–189
  New Deal ideals and, 185
  Pueblo del Rio housing development design elements and, 195–196
  Southeast Housing Architects Associated and, 188
Willkie, Wendell, 40
Wilson, Adrian, 188
Wilson, James Q., 235
Wilson, Woodrow
  Cuba invasion (1917) and, 70
  Dulles and, 61
  illiberal legislation promoted by, 10
  imperialism and, 63, 70–71, 74
  Jewish migration to Palestine and, 75
  King-Crane Commission and, 75
  League of Nations and, 38, 66
  Lippmann and, 89, 93
  Mexico invasion (1914–1917) and, 65, 70
  Middle East and, 62
  regional security alliances proposed by, 65–66
  World War I and, 10, 38–39, 70
Wittfogel, Karl, 211
Wolfe, Bertram, 180
Wolfowitz, Paul, 28

Woll, Matthew
  abolitionist rhetoric in campaign against Soviet forced labor and, 172
  forced labor as basis of power of Soviet regime described by, 173
  Free Trade Union Committee and, 170
  physical brutality of Soviet forced labor system described by, 175
  testimony to the United Nations Ad Hoc Committee on Forced Labor (1952) by, 180
  Workers' Defense League and, 171
Woodward, C. Vann
  Hofstadter and, 207–208
  populism and, 206, 216–217
Workers' Defense League (WDL), 171–173
World Bank, 25
World Food Conference (1974), 241
World Peace Congress (WPC), 257
World Peace Council, 52
World War I
  brutality and scale of, 64
  illiberal policies in United States during, 9
  imperialism and, 91
  internationalism following, 65
  outbreak of, 38
  Wilson's condemnation of Germany and, 70
World War II
  beginning (1939) of, 11
  crisis of liberalism and, 12–14
  "free world" and, 40–41
  Holocaust and, 14
  housing shortage in Los Angeles during, 189–191
  military Keynesianism and, 13
  Pearl Harbor attack (1941) and, 13–14, 192
Worsley, Peter, 219
Wright, Jr., Lloyd, 185
Wurderman, Walter, 188
Wylie, Philip, 141

Yarmolinsky, Adam, 236
Yemen, 83
Yugoslavia, 56, 77

Zaid, Gabriel, 251
Zolov, Eric, 252

For EU product safety concerns, contact us at Calle de José Abascal, 56–1º,
28003 Madrid, Spain or eugpsr@cambridge.org.

www.ingramcontent.com/pod-product-compliance
Ingram Content Group UK Ltd.
Pitfield, Milton Keynes, MK11 3LW, UK
UKHW042128180426
470083UK00012B/178